THE
NITPICKER'S
GUIDE

FOR

Next
Generation
Trekkers

THE NITPICKER'S GUIDE

FOR

Next Generation Trekkers

Phil Farrand

Published by
Dell Publishing
a division of
Bantam Doubleday Dell Publishing Group, Inc.
1540 Broadway
New York, NY 10036

This book has been designed by Michael Wolff & Company, Inc., New York. It has been wholly designed and produced by means of desktop-publishing technology.

Developed by Ettlinger Editorial Projects

ISBN: 0-440-50571-2

Printed in the United States of America

November 1993

TABLE OF CONTENTS

FIRST SEASON

Encounter at Farpoint 3
The Naked Now 7
Code of Honor...10
The Last Outpost..13
Where No One Has Gone Before...15
Lonely Among Us 18
Justice 21
The Battle...24
Hide and Q 27
Haven 29
The Big Good-bye..32
Datalore...35
The Nitpickers' Guild Entrance Exam 38
Angel One 42
11001001 44
Too Short a Season..47
When the Bough Breaks..49
Home Soil...51
Coming of Age 53
Heart of Glory 55
The Arsenal of Freedom..57
Symbiosis...59
Skin of Evil...61
We'll Always Have Paris...63
Conspiracy..66
The Neutral Zone 68
Damage Tote Board...70

SECOND SEASON

The Child 75
Where Silence Has Lease...78
Elementary, My Dear Data 81
The Outrageous Okona..85
Loud as a Whisper 87
The Schizoid Man..89
Unnatural Selection 92
A Matter of Honor 95
The Measure of a Man..97
The Dauphin...99

Contagion 103
Triathlon Trivia on Alien Life Forms 106
The Royale...108
Times Squared 110
The Icarus Factor 113
Pen Pals 114
Q Who 117
Samaritan Share..120
Up the Long Ladder..123
Manhunt 126
The Emissary...129
Peak Performance 132
Shades of Gray 134
My Personal Favorites 136

THIRD SEASON

Evolution..141
The Ensigns of Command 144
The Survivors...147
Who Watches the Watchers 149
The Bonding 151
Booby Trap...153
The Enemy...156
The Price 157
The Vengeance Factor..160
The Defector..162
The Hunted 164
The High Ground 167
Déjà Q...169
Romance Tote Board..171
A Matter of Perspective 173
Yesterday's Enterprise 175
The Offspring...177
Sins of the Father 179
Allegiance 181
Captain's Holiday...184
Tin Man 186
Hollow Pursuits 188
The Most Toys..191
Sarek 193
Ménage à Troi 195
Transfigurations...197
The Best of Both Worlds, Part 1 200

Triathlon Trivia for Planets...203

FOURTH SEASON

The Best of Both Worlds, Part 2 209
Family 212
Brothers...214
Suddenly Human 217
Remember Me 219
Legacy 221
Reunion..224
Future Imperfect 226
Final Mission..229
The Loss...231
Data's Day..233
The Wounded 235
Devil's Due 237
Trek Silliness: The Top Ten Oddities 240
Clues 242
First Contact 245
Galaxy's Child 247
Night Terrors..249
Identity Crisis 251
The Nth Degree 255
Qpid...257
The Drumhead 259
Half a Life...260
The Host...263
The Mind's Eye...266
In Theory 268
Redemption..271
Conundrum Tote Board 273

FIFTH SEASON

Redemption II 279
Darmok...283
Ensign Ro 285
Silicon Avatar...288
Disaster 291
The Game 294
Unification I 297
Unification II...299
A Matter of Time 302
New Ground 306

Hero Worship 309
Violations 312
The Masterpiece Society 315
Triathlon Trivia on Other Characters...317
Conundrum 320
Power Play 322
Ethics...325
The Outcast...327
Cause and Effect 329
The First Duty 332
Cost of Living 335
The Perfect Mate 337
Imaginary Friend...339
I Borg 341
The Next Phase...344
The Inner Light 346
Time's Arrow...348
The Creator Is Always Right...350

SIXTH SEASON

Time's Arrow, Part II 359
Realm of Fear 362
Man of the People...365
Relics...367
Schisms..369
True Q 371
Rascals 373
A Fistful of Datas 376
The Quality of Life...379
Chain of Command, Part 1..381
Chain of Command, Part 2..384
Ship in a Bottle 386
Aquiel...388
Face of the Enemy 390
Tapestry..392
Birthright, Part I 395
Birthright, Part II 397
Starship Mine...399
Lessons...402
The Chase 405
Frame of Mind..408
Suspicions...410
Rightful Heir...412

Second Chances 414
Timescape...417
Descent 420

★ ACKNOWLEDGMENTS

In the beginning there were just four of us—Cliff Cerce, Darrin Hull, Tim Strathdee, and myself. We would huddle before and after church discussing the latest episode, sharing what we had found. Thanks for your enthusiasm, guys. It helped me believe this project could work.

Then came Steve Ettlinger, book producer from New York City. At first, he wasn't sure. He didn't watch TV—had never seen *Star Trek: The Next Generation*. But he had enough business savvy to recognize potential. Thanks for taking on this project, Steve. I couldn't have done it without you.

Next came Jeanne Cavelos, senior editor with Dell Publishing. Not only was she skilled at her profession—she also was, and is, a Trekkie! I understand how fortunate I've been, Jeanne. Your clear direction and instructions made this a very enjoyable project. Thanks for keeping me balanced.

Through it all, my wife, Lynette, and my daughter, Elizabeth, shared their time and their strength. I am a privileged man to have you stand beside me, ladies.

And finally, I am forever grateful to you, Jesus Christ, for loving me. Without you, I am nothing.

I never meant to become a nit-picker. I've been an avid fan of *Star Trek: The Next Generation* from the first time I saw the *Enterprise* NCC 1701-D and Captain Jean-Luc Picard stepped out of the shadows at the very beginning of "Encounter at Farpoint." For the next several years, I watched the show each week with starry-eyed attention, enjoying not only the plots and characters but also the gadgetry. Being a programmer, I'm fascinated by computer technology.

Then came ... THE SCENE. The one that set me on my present course and made me what I am today. It happened during "The Offspring." In this episode, Data creates a daughter called "Lal." In the fateful scene, Wesley Crusher visits Data and Lal in Data's laboratory. They speak about the possibility of Lal attending school. Toward the end, Dr. Crusher's voice interrupts the conversation, "Dr. Crusher to Wesley Crusher: Aren't you supposed to be getting a haircut, Wesley?" Wesley begrudgingly responds, "I'm on my way." Then he shakes his head and says, "Parents!" before walking off.

That's when it happened. I thought, "Did Wesley's mother hear him say 'Parents!'?" I knew Wesley wouldn't make this kind of remark if his mom could hear him, but I couldn't find any indication that the communication channel had been closed. I sudden-

ly realized that either I didn't understand how the communicators worked, or somebody goofed on that scene. At the time, I thought Wesley should have touched his insignia to begin the conversation, spoken to his mom, and then touched it again to end the conversation before saying, "Parents!"

From then on, I kept a close eye on everything done with communications on the ship. I really wanted to understand how they worked. I wouldn't let myself believe that something this important hadn't been thought through. The episodes that followed only added to my confusion. Now I was sure I didn't understand how the communicators worked. I turned to my buddies Cliff Cerce, Darrin Hull, and Tim Strathdee for help. "How do these communicators work?" I asked. They offered lots of suggestions, and we came up with some great theories. Unfortunately, events from the episodes disproved them all. We finally decided that obviously even the directors and actors in *Star Trek: The Next Generation* weren't sure how the communicators worked! That's when we started chalking up "communicator discrepancies."

Of course, once we started tracking the communicator discrepancies, we quickly expanded our nitpicking to other areas as well. We made a game of spotting any inconsistency—technical or otherwise. Each week my friends and I would get together and try to outdo each other in finding things wrong with the latest episode. It was all in fun and came directly from our passion for the series, but then I started wondering, "Do other Trekkers do this? Would they be interested in a nitpicker's guide?" I had a feeling they would, so I set about to review every episode of *Star Trek: The Next Generation*—scene by scene, and often frame by frame. It's amazing what you can find when you look hard enough. Please understand, I'm still an avid fan. It's just that I've found a certain pleasure in being a nitpicker as well.

In this book you'll find reviews for the episodes of the six seasons of *Star Trek: The Next Generation*. For each I will list the title, star date, and a brief summary—in case you haven't seen the episode. Then I'll get to the good stuff! I've broken it down into four major categories: Plot Oversights, Changed Premises, Equipment Oddities, and Continuity and Production Problems.

Under Plot Oversights you'll find instances when the crew conveniently forgets some capability of the *Enterprise* so that a crisis will continue. Under Changed Premises you'll discover that sometimes information given in one show directly contradicts information in another. Under Equipment Oddities I'll point out the technical problems on the *Enterprise*. Lastly, the section on Continuity and Production Problems will expose errors in the actual filming of a show.

I've also included two *real* trivia questions per episode, an occasional rumination, and my picks for the great lines and great moments of the series.

If you happen to have any of the episodes on videotape, pull them out and grab the remote. You might find something I missed! If you do, write me at the address at the back of this book. You can join the Nitpickers' Guild.

Finally, I want you to understand that I've tried to be fair. All of the information presented comes directly from the television series. There are many sources I could have drawn from—*Star Trek* books, fan magazines, the original *Star Trek* series, *Star Trek* conventions, computer bulletin boards. For instance, during "Times Squared," Picard kills himself and then boards a turbolift on deck 6. However, Picard supposedly killed himself in Shuttle Bay 2 (which is on deck 11), so probably the door signage was wrong in that scene. But how do I prove that Shuttle Bay 2 is on deck 11? I have two ways. I *could* quote the *Star Trek: The Next Generation Technical Manual*. But instead of bringing in an outside source, I can simply point out that "Unnatural Selection" establishes that Shuttle Bay 3 is on deck 11. Since Shuttle Bay 2 and 3 share the same vertical position on the *Enterprise*, it's likely that Shuttle Bay 2 is also on deck 11. Granted, it's harder to prove using the second method, but I wanted anyone to be able to find the stuff I did, so I limited myself to only the information transmitted in the actual television series.

I felt so strongly about this that I made it my Nitpicker's Prime Directive. I want to assure you that this Nitpicker's Prime Directive is very important to me—so important that I would never violate it. Just to make sure you understand what my Nitpicker's Prime Directive is, let me restate it. The Nitpicker's Prime Direc-

tive: *The information in this book comes solely from the television series.* Probably the worst thing I could do as a nitpicker would be to violate this Prime Directive and use information from another source. That type of violation could get me kicked out of the Guild! (I think you've figured out where this is going.)

Have fun.

First Season

ENCOUNTER AT FARPOINT

Star Dates: 41153.7-41179.2

*T*he premiere episode of *Star Trek: The Next Generation* lasted two hours. However, all subsequent airings presented it as two one-hour episodes labeled "Part 1" and "Part 2."

PART 1

*A*s the episode begins, Picard takes the *Enterprise* to Deneb IV to look over the newly constructed Farpoint Station. Apparently the Bandi—the inhabitants of Deneb IV—built the station to demonstrate their desire to enter the United Federation of Planets. Yet, a mystery surrounds Farpoint Station. The Bandi do not possess the technological expertise to create such a station. Because of this, Picard's mission is twofold—negotiate the entrance of the Bandi to the Federation, and solve the mystery of Farpoint.

En route, a force field springs up like a giant net in front of the *Enterprise*. Q, of the Q Continuum, appears and demands that the human race cease its expansion into the galaxy. In the light of Q's obvious power, Picard orders a strategic re-

> **Trivia Questions**
>
> 1. What tune is Data trying to whistle in the holodeck?
>
> 2. When did Data graduate from Starfleet Academy?

treat—blasting the *Enterprise* into maximum warp. As soon as Q's force field recaptures the ship, he transports Picard, Data, Yar, and Troi to a midtwentyfirst–century postatomic horrors courtroom "to answer for multiple and grievous savagery of the species." After much wrangling, Picard finally admits that humans have been savage in the past. He then suggests that Q test the crew of the *Enterprise* to see that humanity has changed. Q accepts and cryptically states that Farpoint Station will provide the needed test. If Picard fails, Q will destroy him and the *Enterprise*. An instant later, Picard and the others reappear on the *Enterprise* and continue on to Farpoint.

PART 2

*T*rying to clarify the mystery of Farpoint Station, Picard orders Riker to form an away team and investigate. Below the station, the away team discovers unusual triangular-shaped passages made from an unknown material. Troi senses deep emotional distress but cannot locate its source.

A short while later, an alien ship

approaches the planet and begins firing on the Bandi city situated next to Farpoint Station. At the same time, Q appears on the *Enterprise* and mocks Picard for not understanding what's happening. Q then asserts that the alien ship holds the clues to solve the mystery. At this, Riker takes an away team to the alien ship.

They soon find that the passages of the alien ship are identical to the passages under Farpoint Station. Troi again senses an emotion, but this time it is anger. She suddenly realizes that her feelings are coming from the ship itself. Using this evidence, Captain Picard correctly deduces that Farpoint Station is actually a wounded alien life form that the Bandi managed to capture. They fed it only enough energy to force it to shape itself into whatever they desired. To test his theory, Picard orders Yar to beam energy toward Farpoint Station. As she does, the station mutates into an alien life form identical to the one in orbit. With satisfaction, the crew of the *Enterprise* watches the reunited aliens fly off. There are happy looks all around—except for Q. He leaves, disappointed.

RUMINATIONS

*T*he first time this episode played, it generated a lot of excitement around my house. Finally, Star Trek was coming back! All in all, the creators did a great job making it enough like the original series to pull in the Trekkers but different enough to avoid "rehash syndrome." One of the nice touches in the premiere was the cameo appearance of Dr. McCoy from the original series.

My fellow nitpicker Cliff Cerce suggested I treat this episode lightly. He said that the pilot is always different from the actual series. His point is well taken. A lot of time can elapse between the completion of the pilot and the production of the series. Things change. That's understandable. Just for the record, these are the obvious differences between the pilot and the rest of the shows of the first season:

Picard calls an additional log "supplementary" instead of "supplemental."

Troi wears a different outfit.

Troi is no longer referred to as "Commander."

The computer's voice changes. (Actually, it changes several times over the next few episodes.)

Riker and Troi no longer communicate telepathically.

PLOT OVERSIGHTS

• At the beginning of the episode, Picard calls Deneb IV a planet at the edge of "the great unexplored mass of the galaxy." In other words, Farpoint Station is "out in the sticks." Yet the *Enterprise* picks up several of its officers there. Additionally, the USS *Hood* brings an aging Admiral Mc-Coy—affectionately known as "Bones" in the original *Star Trek* series—to give the *Enterprise* a once-over. So Starfleet routinely ships its officers way out in the boonies to rendezvous with another starship? It's not like the officers are meeting the *Enterprise* at a midpoint somewhere. Farpoint Station isn't on the way *to* anywhere!

• Before Riker leads an away team down to Farpoint Station, he wanders into a holodeck to find Data. As they walk out together, Riker comments that he looked up Data's record. He then asks Data if his degree is honorary. Data responds that it is earned. If Riker looked up Data's record, wouldn't it include a notation that the android earned a degree at Starfleet?

• Toward the end of the episode, an alien ship rushes up to the planet and begins destroying the old Bandi city. Later the episode reveals that the alien ship does this because the Bandi captured its mate. Picard frees its mate by beaming energy to it.

Why didn't the alien ship beam energy down to its mate on the planet? It can fire energy pulses because that's what it used to attack the Bandi city. Supplying its mate with the needed energy would allow it to rise into orbit and preclude any possibility of a counterattack by the Bandi. The alien could then attack the old Bandi city with abandon.

CHANGED PREMISES

• During a trip to the holodeck, Wesley Crusher falls into a stream. When he walks out of the holodeck, he stays wet. This is consistent with the information in this episode. However, later in the series, the producers decided that matter created on the holodeck couldn't exist outside the holodeck. (See "The Big Good-bye" and "Elementary, My Dear Data.") If matter created on the holodeck can't

exist outside the holodeck, Wesley should be dry, shouldn't he?

EQUIPMENT ODDITIES

• At one point, the computer onboard the *Enterprise* gives Riker directions to a holodeck. As he walks down the last hall before the holodeck entrance, the computer tells him that the entrance is the next hatchway on his *right*. Riker spins around, goes *left*, and enters the holodeck.

CONTINUITY AND PRODUCTION PROBLEMS

• When Riker and Data are walking out of the holodeck, they pass behind a clump of ferns. Once the foliage hides both actors, the ferns "skew" sideways. Clearly, someone spliced two pieces of film together at this point. Either the creators couldn't get one good take of the scene or they were trying to illustrate how the holodeck continually adjusts the surrounding scenery.

• And speaking of bombarding the old Bandi city: Did anyone notice that there is only one destruction sequence with buildings blowing up? It's used three times, but it is the same shot every time. The second time, those clever creators use a reverse angle to mix things up a bit. (I know, I know ... they needed to save money.)

• When the creators broke the two-hour premiere into two one-hour episodes, they cut out two scenes. Soon after Riker joins the *Enterprise*, Yar sits him in front of a viewscreen and it rehashes the events en route to Farpoint. While the computer replays its logs for Riker, Picard goes to his ready room. At this point in the two-hour premiere, Riker continues watching the replay. When it finishes, he turns and comments on his disbelief that Picard would call the events only "a little adventure." These moments are missing from "Encounter at Farpoint," Part 1. The second scene that the creators cut occurs after the alien ship begins attacking the Bandi city. After Riker volunteers to lead an away team to the alien ship, Picard walks off the bridge. He goes to sick bay to have a heart-to-heart talk with Dr. Beverly Crusher. This whole conversation disappeared from "Encounter at Farpoint," Part 2. (I'm sure the scenes were cut to make space for the narration "Last time on *Star Trek: The Next Generation*" at the beginning of Part 2.)

Actually, the creators made very good choices in the scenes they cut. Originally, Riker's review of the events en route to Farpoint left out several important facts. By not showing Riker as he concludes the review, the creators leave an impression that it covered more than it did. Also, cutting out Picard's chat with Crusher removes a significant plot oversight. The *Enterprise* is, after all, in the middle of a crisis. Why would the captain suddenly walk off the bridge to have an apparently routine personnel meeting with his chief medical officer? The problem with cutting this scene, however, is that the viewer who hasn't seen the two-hour premiere has no idea where Picard goes. He just leaves and then comes back later!

TRIVIA ANSWERS

1. "Pop Goes the Weasel."
2. Class of '78.

THE NAKED NOW

The *Enterprise* responds to a series of strange messages from a science vessel called the USS *Tsiolkovsky*. For eight months, the *Tsiolkovsky* has been in close proximity to a star, monitoring its collapse from a red giant to a white dwarf. When an away team beams over, it finds that the entire crew is dead—apparently killed through their own bizarre behavior. Then, after returning, Lieutenant Commander Geordi La Forge begins acting strangely. Crusher tries to confine him to sick bay, but he escapes. As La Forge wanders around the ship, other crew members start behaving erratically as well.

Riker and Data search through the historical records and discover a reference to a similar situation. It states that intense gravitational fluctuations can cause water molecules to mutate into an alcohol-like substance. This substance then travels from person to person by touch, spreading the "intoxication" throughout the ship. Evidently, the gravitational fluctuations of the collapsing star have caused the same effect. Unfortunately, when Dr. Crusher tries the described cure, it doesn't work. The circumstances are only similar, not identical. Meanwhile, Wesley Crusher, drunk from the strange water, takes over Engineering and disables the bridge's control of the engines.

At the same time, the star collapses, hurling stellar matter toward the *Enterprise*. Riker finally breaks into engineering but not before a crew member removes all the chips that control the engines. Data works frantically to restore control, but he knows he doesn't have enough time to finish the job. In response, Wesley rigs a repulser beam and uses it to push the *Enterprise* away from the *Tsiolkovsky*. This action gives Data the time he needs. Moments later, the *Enterprise* warps away to safety as Crusher administers her newly discovered antidote to the crew.

Trivia Questions

1. How many people were on the *Tsiolkovsky*?

2. How old was Yar when she was abandoned?

GREAT LINES

"If you prick me, do I not bleek?"— Data trying to convince Picard that the intoxicating strange water affects him also by noting his similarities to humans.

RUMINATIONS

T *his episode continues the efforts of the creators to appeal to the fans of the original* Star Trek. *It parallels an episode called "The Naked Time" in the original series.*

PLOT OVERSIGHTS

• Even before La Forge begins to show signs of intoxication, Captain Picard records in his log that the *Enterprise* is downloading the research information the *Tsiolkovsky* gathered on the collapsing star. He also states that he is concerned "at being in such close orbit." Later, when Data states that the downloading will be complete in forty-one minutes, Picard shows slight irritation at the length of time. He asks Data how much danger there is from the star in the worst case. Data states that the *Enterprise* could outrun any stellar matter on half impulse power. At this point, the bridge still controls all the ship's functions. Given all his concern, why doesn't Picard just lock a tractor beam on the *Tsiolkovsky* and drag it to safety?

• This episode contains many other plot oversights, but it is, after all, only the second episode. It deserves gentle treatment. Here's a quick list:

• Dr. Crusher should recognize the effects of intoxication in Wesley, but she doesn't.

• The crew has the report from the old *Enterprise* and knows that the water is transmitted by contact, but no one avoids being touched.

• Wesley blocks the door to Engineering with a repulser beam. Riker spends his time trying to get the door open when he could just transport in.

• When Riker brings Troi to sick bay and touches Dr. Crusher, she tries to quarantine him. The intoxication is running rampant through the ship. Hundreds of crew members have it. La Forge is the only one confined to sick bay and Dr. Crusher's trying to quarantine Riker?

• Data gets drunk.

• Riker, although infected by the strange water, handles it surprisingly well considering what it's doing to the rest of the crew.

• Picard worries about the unstable star exploding through the entire show and then tells Worf to wait before giving him some strange readings from the star.

• Picard gets intoxicated very quickly after only breathing Dr. Crusher's breath.

• Dr. Crusher unzips her uniform. (See "The Price," Equipment Oddities.)

EQUIPMENT ODDITIES

• In one scene, Riker joins Data at the workstations that line the back of the bridge. As Riker talks, he sits down on the data entry section of the adjacent workstation. Wouldn't this be like sitting on a computer keyboard?

CONTINUITY PROBLEMS

• When Dr. Crusher gives La Forge his first shot, her hair is fixed beautifully. Moments later, Riker brings in Troi and then walks into Dr. Crusher's office. She looks up and her hair is flat. Evidently the humidity in sick bay is murder on 'dos!

TRIVIA ANSWERS

1. Eighty. (It's hard to tell if Picard says "eighty" or "eighteen." However, it can't be eighteen because Yar reports ten dead in Engineering, La Forge finds seven frozen, and at least two people died when the emergency hatch was blown on the *Tsiolkovsky*'s bridge. That makes at least nineteen.)

2. Five years old.

CODE OF HONOR

As the episode opens, the *Enterprise* arrives at Ligon II. The Ligonians possess a rare vaccine needed to combat a plague on the Federation planet Styris IV. After the *Enterprise* drops into standard orbit, a Ligonian delegation beams aboard to meet Picard and the crew of the *Enterprise*. Lutan, the head of the delegation, then surprises Picard by kidnapping Yar and beaming back down to the surface.

After reviewing Ligonian custom, the crew discovers that Lutan's act is considered heroic. The proper response calls for Picard politely to request Yar's return. Picard does so, and Lutan invites him to the surface. Shortly after Picard arrives, Lutan introduces him to Yareena, Lutan's "first one" (his primary wife). During the evening meal, Lutan makes a bold announcement. He states that he cannot part with Yar and wants her to be his "first one." Yareena protests and challenges Yar to a fight to the death. When Picard balks, Lutan says that if Yar refuses the challenge, he will not give the needed vaccine.

Trivia Questions

1. What is Yar's first name?

2. At this point in the series, how many jokes has Data told La Forge?

Picard concocts a plan, and Yar participates in the challenge. When Yar strikes Yareena with a death blow, she falls on top of Yareena and the *Enterprise* beams them both aboard. Thinking Yareena is dead, Lutan delivers the vaccine. Picard then kidnaps Lutan by transporting him to the ship. Moments later, in the observation lounge, Lutan meets Yareena—brought back to life by Dr. Crusher. According to Ligonian culture, a mating agreement dissolves at the moment of death. Because of this, the union between Lutan and Yareena no longer exists—and since Yareena holds the wealth of that union, Lutan loses everything.

PLOT OVERSIGHTS

• The first great crisis of this episode comes when Lutan kidnaps Yar. For several minutes afterward the crew scampers around, wondering what to do. Picard even fires a display blast of photon torpedoes into the atmosphere to get their attention.

Why don't they just lock on Yar's communicator and beam her back? Later in the show, they lock on the captain's communicator for the location to send La Forge and Data. They do eventually realize that they must work within the Ligonian code of honor to obtain the vaccine, but a considerable amount of time elapses while the crew thrashes around seeking for a solution while overlooking the obvious one.

• Just before the battle to the death between Yar and Yareena, a spokesman for Lutan says, "The rules are known. Let combat continue until there is a victory. It will not be interrupted." Yar and Yareena battle until Yareena's weapon flies off her hand. At this point, Lutan immediately stands and stops the fight until the weapon is returned to Yareena.

Why is he stopping the fight? I thought the other guy said the battle would not be interrupted. Isn't losing a weapon a fairly normal occurrence in hand-to-hand combat? Since Lutan hopes that Yar will kill his wife so he can inherit her wealth, wouldn't he be happy that Yareena lost her weapon?

CHANGED PREMISES

• While presenting Lutan with the statue of a horse at the beginning of the episode, Picard says that he is aware of the Ligonian culture's unique similarity to an ancient Earth culture that he *admires*. However, later in the show—after Data and La Forge beam down to examine the weapons Yar will use in battle—Picard states that the customs of the Ligonian culture are the "same kind of pompous strutting charades that endangered our own species a few centuries ago."

EQUIPMENT ODDITIES

• During "Encounter at Farpoint," Part 2, Picard states that the panel on the *right* side of his chair is for "log entries, library computer access retrieval, viewscreen control, and intercoms." However, when Lutan calls the *Enterprise*, Picard reaches for the *left* side of his chair to operate the intercom.

CONTINUITY AND PRODUCTION PROBLEMS

• Just before they beam down to the planet, Data visits La Forge in his quarters. As La Forge shaves, Data discusses the human condition with him. The director shot this scene from basically two camera angles— one over Data's shoulder showing La Forge's face, and the other over LaForge's shoulder showing Data's face. Unfortunately, La Forge's razor shows up in both shots. Since La Forge is swinging the razor back and forth across his face, every time the camera angle changes, the razor jumps to a different location!

• In preparation for the battle between Yar and Yareena, Ligonian guards bring in the weapons that will be used for the conflict. The men set the boxes down and leave. In the very next shot the boxes are suddenly closer.

• Both Yar and Yareena fight their battle with weapons on their left hands. At the end, when Yar falls on Yareena's lifeless body, the weapon is still on her left hand. As the two dematerialize in the transporter beam, the weapon is *still* on Yar's left hand. So why is it on her *right* hand when she materializes on the *Enterprise*?!?

to her as Tasha.)

2. Six hundred sixty-two.

TRIVIA ANSWERS

1. Natasha. (Though the crew refers

THE LAST OUTPOST

Star Dates: 41386.4-41386.5

As the episode begins, the *Enterprise* chases a "Ferengi" vessel. The Ferengi—a mysterious race that roams the Galaxy looking for business opportunities—took a T-9 energy converter from an unmanned monitoring post on Gamma Taouri IV. The *Enterprise* is trying to recover the converter and get a "first look" at the mysterious Ferengi. When the Ferengi vessel quickly drops out of warp and into orbit around a planet, the *Enterprise* does likewise. Suddenly energy begins to drain from the *Enterprise* as a powerful force field traps the ship. After some discussion, Picard decides to surrender. Obviously the Ferengi are much more powerful than believed. He contacts the Ferengi vessel and requests the terms of the Ferengi. After a few minutes, the Ferengi captain responds, refusing to surrender. Suddenly, Picard realizes the Ferengi are in the same predicament as the *Enterprise*. The crew then discovers that the force field actually comes from the planet.

Picard negotiates some cooperation from the Ferengi. They agree to send a joint away team to the planet. Once on the planet, however, the Ferengi attack the *Enterprise*'s away team. During the ensuing scuffle, a being appears. He is a "portal" for the Tkon Empire, an empire that became extinct long ago, while the portal slept. The portal challenges Riker to determine if humanity is worthy to enter the empire. After Riker passes the challenge, the portal frees the *Enterprise* from the force field. Riker also asks the portal to restore energy to the Ferengi ship. After he does so, the portal returns to sleep.

Trivia Questions

1. How long ago did the Tkon Empire become extinct?

2. Name a substance used in the outer casing of communicators.

CHANGED PREMISES

• After Picard and the captain of the Ferengi vessel agree to cooperate, Riker and Data indicate their distrust of the Ferengi. Troi then chimes in, stating that she senses the Ferengi captain is hiding something.

Did Troi really sense something, or is she just bootlicking? The episode "Ménage à Troi" indicates that Betazoids cannot read Ferengi minds. Data substantiates this when he claims that Ferengi minds are not empathically detectable in "The

13

Loss."

EQUIPMENT ODDITIES

• Just after the force field seizes the *Enterprise*, something begins reading information from the ship's computers. Data notices this because his workstation shows a rapid barrage of information as the information is read.

Is there some reason why Data's upper screen displays the information upside down? As the documents speed by, the workstation briefly shows both the Klingon and Federation symbols. Both are upside down.

• In Picard's first attempt to communicate with the Ferengi, he calls for open hailing frequencies, and Yar quickly responds. The "open hailing frequencies" sound tweeps in the background. Then Picard says, "At least we won't begin with weakness" before beginning his message. He doesn't say it very loudly, but later in the show Data whispers a phrase to La Forge, and the Ferengi captain hears it. We have to assume that the Ferengi captain can also hear Picard's comment about weakness. Why would Picard allow the Ferengi to hear his comment about weakness if he didn't want to begin with weakness?

Also, right after Picard says "Ferengi vessel, we await your response," Yar jumps in and adds, "Suggest first strike, sir." Did the Ferengi captain hear Yar contemplating an attack?

• When the team from the *Enterprise* beams down to the planet, Riker appears alone. He begins walking around and yelling for the others. Evidently he has forgotten about the communicator he wears. It is true that *Data* later discovers the communicators are out, but Riker never even makes the attempt.

CONTINUITY AND PRODUCTION PROBLEMS

• Just before the Ferengi captain communicates with the *Enterprise* for the first time, the front of the Ferengi vessel extends. Several scenes later, the ship is shown again, and the front is retracted. Just a few shots later, the ship is once again extended.

The Ferengi vessel is caught in the same energy-draining force field as the *Enterprise*. Why would the captain of that vessel waste energy moving the front of the ship in and out?

• The issue of gravity on board the *Enterprise* is never addressed. Presumably the *Enterprise* can generate its own gravity just as it generates its own life-support systems. Presumably generation of gravity requires energy, just as life support does. Yet in this episode, the *Enterprise* is completely drained of power. Shouldn't they lose the artificial gravity at the same time they lose life support? (I know ... too expensive to simulate.)

TRIVIA ANSWERS
1. Six hundred thousand years.
2. Gold.

WHERE NO ONE HAS GONE BEFORE

Star Dates: 41263.1-41263.4

For this episode, a propulsion expert named "Kozinski" and his assistant join the *Enterprise* amid skepticism from the crew. Prior to Kozinski's arrival, Data simulated the expert's warp drive alterations and found no improvement. However, due to Kozinski's success on two other ships, Picard allows him to proceed. When Kozinski arrives in Engineering, his assistant begins entering formulas on a workstation as Wesley Crusher watches. During Kozinski's first test run, the assistant looks to Wesley for a reaction. In that instant, a mistake occurs. The assistant tries to correct it by draping himself over the control station. Moments later, parts of him begin disappearing and reappearing. Immediately the *Enterprise*'s velocity blasts past warp 10. By the time the *Enterprise* comes to a stop, it has traveled 2.7 million light-years, too far to return within the crew's lifetimes using normal methods.

Although Kozinski immediately hails the experiment as a success, Picard is more concerned about getting back. He allows Kozinski to try to produce the speed explosion a second time. Unfortunately, the first test weakened Kozinski's assistant. Instead of returning to the Federation, the second test takes the *Enterprise* to a place where thought becomes reality. Picard realizes the *Enterprise* must leave this place quickly or they will lose their ability to distinguish between fantasy and reality.

Kozinski's assistant, called a "traveler," also understands the danger to the crew, and—though fatigued—agrees to try one more time. During the final test, Picard orders the crew to center their thoughts on the traveler's well-being. As the *Enterprise* returns to its original position, the traveler disappears.

Trivia Questions

1. How long would it take the *Enterprise* to travel 2.7 million light-years at maximum warp?

2. How much of the galaxy has the Federation charted during the past three hundred years?

PLOT OVERSIGHTS

• There are a limited number of ways to determine a ship's position in space. If you know your original location, your direction of travel, and your speed, you can estimate your new position with a few simple calculations. Likewise, if you can map the stars outside the ship to known constellations, you can figure your position respective to the stars. Finally, if your government has littered space with strategically placed beacons, you could triangulate your position using the signals from the beacons and calculating how long it took for each signal to reach you.

During the first test, the *Enterprise*'s sensors register an incredible increase in velocity. After the ship stops, Data and LaForge calculate the *Enterprise*'s new position. It is possible for them to use their speed and direction; both are known. It is also possible for them to use the stars, since they can see stars outside. It might even be possible for them to pick up Starfleet's navigational beacons. Data says that a subspace radio message will take fifty-one years to reach Starfleet. If Starfleet established the beacons more than fifty-one years ago, their signals might reach out this far.

After the second test, however, Data states that the sensors show they never exceeded warp 1.5. Given their location, that reading cannot be relied on. Therefore the *Enterprise* cannot establish its position using direction and speed. Neither are there any visible stars. And yet, in his log, Picard states that they are more than 1 billion light-years from their galaxy. How does he know that? Could they be using Starfleet's beacons? The answer is no. If it takes subspace radio fifty-one years to reach 2.7 million light-years, it would take almost nineteen thousand years for subspace transmissions to reach 1 bil-

lion light-years. Starfleet didn't exist that long ago. So how can Picard assert that they are more than 1 billion light-years from their galaxy? (I guess it just sounded good to put in the log. Later Picard finally admits that he doesn't know where they are!)

• After the first test, Data tells Picard that it will take a subspace signal "fifty-one years, ten months, *nine* weeks, sixteen days ..." to get back to the Federation. Fifty-one years, ten months, *nine* weeks? Why not fifty-two years, one week, and sixteen days? Maybe Data's home planet used a month with more than an average of four weeks in it. If that's true, though, all his estimates would be off, according to Earth standards. Then again, maybe in the future everyone uses the metric system.

CHANGED PREMISES

• At the very beginning of this episode, Picard discusses Kozinski's visit with the bridge crew. Picard states that Kozinski "will simply run tests on different ways of entering warp speed and different intermix formulas." "Intermix formula" always refers to the mixture of matter and antimatter in *Star Trek: The Next Generation*. Therefore, varying the intermix formula of matter and antimatter is one of the tests Kozinski will perform.

However, in "Coming of Age," Wesley's Starfleet entrance exam contains a question about intermix formulas. Wesley gets the right answer by deducing that it is a trick question. He and the other whiz kid at the test agree that there is only one intermix formula—one to one.

EQUIPMENT ODDITIES

• Are the blue "doughnut" lights on the engine chamber really connected to anything, or is there just a guy somewhere who fiddles with a control to make them go faster or slower? During the first test, the lights start out slowly and then speed up. That makes sense because the *Enterprise* is doing the same thing. In the second test, however, the lights speed up only a split second after the test begins and well before the traveler does anything. On the final test, one shot shows the lights ripping quickly through their sequence, but when Wesley stands up as the traveler disappears, the lights plod along in the background.

TRIVIA ANSWERS

1. More than three hundred years.
2. Eleven percent.

LONELY AMONG US

En route to the Federation diplomatic outpost "Parliament," the *Enterprise* sights an energy cloud traveling at warp velocity. Intrigued, Captain Picard changes course to investigate. As the *Enterprise* passes through the edge of the cloud, the sensor circuitry absorbs one of the sentient energy beings who live there. Seeking a way to communicate, the entity leaps from the circuitry into Worf. From Worf it travels to Dr. Crusher and then to the ship's main computer.

Finally it leaps into Picard. He suddenly turns the *Enterprise* around and heads back to the energy cloud. Once the *Enterprise* arrives at the energy cloud, Picard announces that he is going to beam out, energy only. The being has invited Picard to merge their energy patterns and explore the universe free from the constraints of matter. Riker and Crusher try to stop him, but Picard sends out bolts of electricity that paralyze the crew and allow the beam-out.

For the next hour, Riker and the crew search in vain for Picard. Suddenly Troi senses Picard's presence

in the energy cloud—the "merging" was unsuccessful, and Picard is dying. Riker moves the *Enterprise* forward into the cloud to allow Picard to enter the ship. Data uses Picard's physical pattern, still stored in the transporter's buffer, to reconstruct the captain, and the *Enterprise* continues to Parliament.

Trivia Questions

1. Whose theory on dilithium crystals is Wesley studying?

2. What is the name, rank, and title of the Starfleet officer who gets killed in this episode?

GREAT LINES

"I still don't remember having one"—Worf responding to Dr. Crusher's statement that she wants to discuss his memory block-out caused by the alien's presence.

CHANGED PREMISES

• At the beginning of the episode "Haven," Troi tries to explain why she failed to mention that she was genetically bonded for marriage to a man named Wyatt Miller. She says she thought those vows were far behind her, and she mentions her time serving in Starfleet as part of the reason. She refers to that time as "the years I spent on *this* mission." Presumably Troi is speaking about her time on the *Enterprise*. Evidently she isn't, though, because in "Lonely Among Us," Picard—frustrated at the systems failures on the *Enterprise*—makes a comment that the ship is "less than a year out of space dock."

• After the entity takes control of Picard, the captain orders a course change to take the *Enterprise* back to the energy cloud. Specifically he says, "Make our heading 9-2-5 mark 3-7." No wonder the crew is suspicious. The episode "Datalore" states that headings have a maximum of 360 for each number. Picard's first number is well above this limit.

• This episode establishes the orientation of Picard's ready-room window. Two facts assist in this deduction. First, while traveling at warp velocity the *Enterprise* can only fly forward. There is no reverse gear on the warp engines. Second, to give the viewers a visual clue for when the *Enterprise* flies at warp, the creators used "streaking stars." Supposedly, because the *Enterprise* exceeds the speed of light, the twinkle from the nearby stars gets smeared into a line. Using these two facts and examining the star streaks in Picard's ready-room window should establish which direction the window faces.

This episode contains a shot of the ready-room window while the *Enterprise* flies at warp. The camera shot actually catches the window at an angle, so some adjustment is needed. *The stars streak from left to right.* This means the window probably faces south—if north is toward the front of the ship. Looking directly out the window, the captain would see the stars racing away from the ship. However, if he sits down at his desk

and looks out the window toward the southeast, he could only see the stars to the east of the ship, and they would look like they were streaking from left to right.

On the other hand, the episode "Too Short a Season" contains a scene where the stars race by from *right to left*. This would mean the window would have to face west, since looking out the window at the same relative angle as before would mean the captain was looking southwest and seeing the stars to the west of the ship. In addition, after the first season of *Star Trek: The Next Generation* the window always faces southwest, since in "Where Silence Has Lease," "The Schizoid Man," and every other subsequent episode, the stars streak *away* from the window when viewed at the same relative angle.

Does Picard have some sort of crank he can turn to change the location of his ready room? This would be a nice perk for the captain, ensuring that he wouldn't become bored with the view from the only window in his office!

EQUIPMENT ODDITIES

• This episode raises an interesting point. When Picard beams out, the transporter retains his physical pattern in the transporter buffers. Data reconstructs Picard using that pattern. In essence, the transporter has duplicated Picard—duplicated the captain just as he was before beaming out.

This is a very convenient feature for the transporter to have. When someone dies on an away team, the crew could just use the transporter to duplicate the person. The formerly deceased would lose the memory of dying on the planet's surface, but that seems like a small price to pay. Given this capability, why is Riker so paranoid about Picard going on away team missions? Riker says that he is concerned for the captain's safety, but if the captain gets killed, they can just replicate him, right? Or does Riker just want to hog all the glory? (I realize that the *Technical Manual* says that the duplication of Picard as shown in this episode cannot be done. Evidently the manual is incorrect, because I saw it happen on TV, and I believe everything I see on TV. Wink, wink.)

CONTINUITY AND PRODUCTION PROBLEMS

• When Data first spots the energy cloud, he states that it is traveling at warp velocity. However, when the *Enterprise* makes its sensor pass, the stars aren't streaking in the background. Since streaking stars are the visual clue used to show the viewer that something is traveling at warp, somebody goofed.

TRIVIA ANSWERS

1. Dr. Channing.
2. Lieutenant Singh, assistant chief engineer.

JUSTICE

Star Dates: 41255.6-41255.9

After delivering a group of colonists to a planet in the Strnad system, the *Enterprise* discovers another M Class planet in the neighboring Rubicun system. An initial away team reports that the planet is beautiful and its inhabitants, the Edo, warm and friendly. Wanting to be certain that the planet is suitable for shore leave, Picard orders a second away team and invites Wesley to go along. Shortly after the team beams down, Wesley goes off to play with the other teenagers. In the process, he stumbles into a flowerbed. The other young people are shocked and then dismayed as they see "mediators" approach. Mediators are the Edo's policemen. They randomly choose the location of "punishment zones." Anyone breaking *any* law in a punishment zone faces the only recourse of Edo law: death. One of the mediators reaches into his pocket and pulls out a syringe. The rest of the away team arrives just in time to stop the execution.

Meanwhile, back on the *Enterprise*, a sensor "glitch" turns out to be a vessel that exists interdimensionally. The powerful beings aboard the vessel contact the *Enterprise*, temporarily rendering Data unconscious and exchanging information with him. When Picard beams down to deal with Wesley's situation, the Edo identify the interdimensional ship as God. An impossible conundrum faces Picard. If he does nothing, Wesley will die. If he saves Wesley, he violates Starfleet's Prime Directive and risks the wrath of the Edo's god. In the end, Picard decides to save Wesley. After a few tense moments, the Edo's god allows them to leave.

Trivia Questions

1. What is the name of the Edo's planet?

2. How many other planets could the Federation colonize in the star cluster?

RUMINATIONS

With all the skimpy outfits of the Edo, the costume designers had a heyday with the Theiss Titillation Theory in this episode. William Theiss was the costume designer for the original Star Trek *and designed the* Starfleet uniforms for The Next Generation. *His principle is simple: The titillation of any outfit is directly proportional to its perception of being "accident-prone." I read about Theiss's Titillation Theory in a book called* The Making of "Star Trek" *by*

Stephen E. Whitfield.

PLOT OVERSIGHTS

• When Yar returns from the initial away team she states that she has reviewed the Edo's laws and customs. Yet, later we find out that the Edo have only one punishment for any crime, and Yar didn't know about it. How can someone review laws and customs and never ask about the price for violating them?

• When Riker asks Picard to beam down to the planet, he is careful not to reveal that the problem concerns Wesley. Quite correctly, Riker realizes that Dr. Crusher might be listening in on their conversation. Later, after Picard beams down to the surface, Dr. Crusher calls him to report that Data has regained consciousness. At this point, Troi urges Picard to tell Crusher about Wesley but Picard refuses, saying that he wants to speak to Crusher personally about her son. Then, when Picard beams up to the *Enterprise*, Dr. Crusher flags him in the hall and demands to know what he is going to do about Wesley. She states that she read the away team report.

What away team report? The away team is still on the surface. Even if they made the report from the planet's surface, Picard just told the away team that he wanted to speak to Dr. Crusher in person about the problem with Wesley. Why would the away team mention Wesley in the report?

Then again, maybe Yar filed the report. It would be consistent with the type of day she is having. First she

forgets to ask about the punishment for breaking Edo law. Then she disregards Picard's wishes and files a report talking about the danger to Wesley knowing that Crusher will have access to it. How can a bridge officer on the *Enterprise* be capable of that level of incompetence? (You may recognize that I borrowed that phrase from Riker in "Future Imperfect.")

• With all the thrashing around about the Prime Directive, Picard overlooks the simple solution to the dilemma with Wesley. In fact, Picard has already used this solution to get the crew out of another dilemma concerning the Prime Directive. In "Code of Honor," Yar had to fight a woman named "Yareena" so that Picard could gain access to a desperately needed vaccine. Yet the fight was "to the death" with poisoned battle gloves, and Yar didn't want to kill Yareena. Picard instructed Yar to fight, strike Yareena with the weapon, allow her to die, and beam immediately to the *Enterprise*. Dr. Crusher then brought Yareena back to life.

Why not let the Edo inject Wesley, watch him die, beam him back to the ship, warp away, and resuscitate him? Riker took the syringe from the mediator. He could have passed it to Picard. Picard could have taken it to Dr. Crusher and rigged up an antidote. That way everybody would be happy. The Edo law would be fulfilled in that Wesley died. The Prime Directive would be intact (since—evidently—the captain didn't have any problem doing the same thing to Yareena in "Code of Honor"). And most importantly, Wesley would be alive and able to get them in trouble in later episodes. (I'm sorry, that was a bit petty.)

TRIVIA ANSWERS

1. Rubicun III.
2. Three thousand four.

THE BATTLE

Responding to a Ferengi invitation, the *Enterprise* flies to the Zendi Sabu star system. After rendezvousing with the *Enterprise*, a Ferengi vessel simply transmits "Stand by" and cuts off all communication for the next three days. During this time, Picard develops a headache—a rare occurrence in the twenty-fourth century. When the Ferengi finally reestablish contact, DaiMon Bok—the captain of the Ferengi vessel—presents Picard with an old derelict ship. It is the *Stargazer*, once captained by Picard. Nine years ago, Picard abandoned the badly damaged *Stargazer* after retaliating for a surprise attack by an unidentified vessel. Bok identifies the vessel that attacked the *Stargazer* as Ferengi and dismisses the incident as an accident.

As Picard takes possession of the *Stargazer*, however, Bok increases the intensity of his headaches. Using a thought-making device, he stirs up Picard's memories of the confrontation nine years ago. After this preparation, Bok takes mental control of Picard. He brings Picard to the *Stargazer* and plunges him back into the desperate struggle to save his ship. Bok hopes Picard will attack the *Enterprise* and be destroyed, just as Picard destroyed his son those many years ago. Leaving the thought-making device behind, Bok returns to his ship to watch the confrontation. However, Bok's plan fails because the bridge crew knows the tactic Picard used to destroy the Ferengi vessel after its surprise attack. This allows Riker to trap the *Stargazer* in a tractor beam, after which he convinces Picard to destroy the thought-making device. As Picard returns to normal, Bok's first officer relieves him of duty for engaging in the unprofitable adventure, and the Ferengi leave.

Trivia Questions

1. Where did the "Battle of Maxia" take place?

2. What is the class and registry of the *Stargazer*?

PLOT OVERSIGHTS

• After destroying the Ferengi vessel nine years ago, this episode claims that Picard abandoned the *Stargazer*. Why didn't Picard set the autodestruct sequence on the *Stargazer*? To allow a Starfleet craft to drift through space leaves it open to discovery by anyone. Would the Federation want the Romulans to get their hands on a Starfleet vessel? In the episode "11001001," Picard and Riker set the autodestruct sequence simply because the *Enterprise may* have fallen into enemy hands. Was the technology in the *Stargazer* so old that Starfleet didn't care if someone found it?

• After receiving the *Stargazer* from Bok, Picard tells the bridge crew about its final battle. After the *Stargazer* had been badly damaged during the surprise attack by the Ferengi, Picard executed a previously untried technique to catch his aggressor off guard. He took a sensor bearing on the other ship, blasted into high warp, stopped right off the Ferengi's bow, and fired all his weapons. Picard says that for an instant the *Stargazer* appeared to be in two places at once and the Ferengi fired at the wrong place. At the end of the episode, when Picard executes this maneuver again, the footage of the *Stargazer* supports this explanation. The *Stargazer* does appear to be in two places at the same time.

However, when Data calculates his defense against this maneuver he begins an explanation by saying, "... a vessel in the Picard Maneuver might seem to disappear ..." Vessels in the Picard Maneuver do not seem to disappear, Data, they seem to be in two places at once!

• At the end of the episode, Riker grabs the *Stargazer* with a tractor beam to prevent it from damaging the *Enterprise*. Why didn't he do that before the *Stargazer* flew off to position itself for an attack on the *En-*

terprise?

Look at the sequence of events as Picard leaves the *Enterprise*. First Riker finds out Picard is under some kind of mental control. Then Riker discovers that Picard has beamed off the ship. Then the shields go up on the *Stargazer*, and Riker realizes that Picard is over there. *Then* Riker sends Worf to look through the captain's possessions, and La Forge reports that the *Stargazer* is powering up. Then Bok goes through an extended speech—and I do mean extended—about Picard murdering his son. There is *even* time for a commercial break and for Riker to make a log entry before the *Stargazer* dribbles away from the *Enterprise*. All this time and the bridge crew just watches the *Stargazer* fly out of tractor beam range.

CHANGED PREMISES

• When Bok calls the *Enterprise* to set up the first meeting, Troi cautions Picard that she senses "considerable deception on Bok's part and danger." As mentioned in the review of "The Last Outpost," this statement is either bootlicking or outright lying, since Betazoids cannot sense Ferengi thoughts. (See "Ménage à Troi" and Data's statement in "The Loss.")

CONTINUITY AND PRODUCTION PROBLEMS

• Just before the Ferengi beam over to the *Enterprise* for their first meeting, a full shot of the bridge crew shows them standing in an at-ease position. Their hands are clasped behind their backs. The very next shot shows the backs of Picard and Riker. Both have their hands at their sides.

1. In the Maxia Zeda star system.
2. Constellation Class NCC 2893.

✦ HIDE AND Q

Star Dates: 41590.5-41591.9

As the *Enterprise* warps to provide disaster relief to a mining colony on Sigma III, Q materializes, stating he has business with humanity. After the encounter at Farpoint, the Q Continuum realized that humans have a quality of growth. Q believes that humans will continue to evolve and perhaps—aeons in the future—even surpass the Q. The Q Continuum decides to grant their powers to Riker. They hope to convince him to join the Q. They can then study humanity's need for change and make it part of themselves.

To force Riker to use his newly acquired powers, Q concocts a game. On a barren planet with two moons, Q creates "animal things" dressed in Napoleonic Era costumes. Q then transports several members of the bridge crew to the planet. In the battle that follows, Worf and Wesley are killed. Their deaths anger Riker, and he transports everyone back to the *Enterprise*—resurrecting Worf and Wesley in the process. Fearing the corruption that unlimited power can bring, Picard urges Riker not to use it again. Riker gives his word that he will not.

During the relief operations on Sigma III, Riker finds it difficult to restrain himself. When he returns to the ship he asks for a meeting with the bridge crew to clarify the situation. During the meeting Q appears and suggests Riker give each of the bridge crew a parting gift before joining the Q. Each member of the bridge crew refuses, opting to struggle for their own accomplishments instead of having their lives made easy. Riker realizes the value of this position and refuses the power of the Q. The Q Continuum calls Q back to answer for the failure.

Trivia Questions

1. How many colonists were at the site of the mining accident on Sigma III?

2. Name the gifts Riker tries to give the bridge crew.

PLOT OVERSIGHTS

• As Picard discusses Riker's newfound power in a log entry, he says, "This is a subject far out of my experience, out of anyone's experience." Evidently the captain isn't a student of past voyages of Federation ships named *Enterprise*. Captain James Kirk faced a human-turned-god figure in "Where No Man Has Gone Before." (And yes, I did just violate the Nitpicker's Prime Directive. If Picard could do it in "Justice," I deserve equal allowance.)

• The first time Q transports members of the bridge crew to the game planet, Worf goes on a reconnaissance mission to spy on the opposition. He comes back and reports that the beings they will fight are "vicious animal things." The rest of the bridge crew quickly adopt this terminology when referring to the entities.

Would highly trained military officers really use a label such as "animal things"? Imagine a mentally disciplined person like a marine and then try to picture him reporting to his commander that there were "animal things" attacking them. Does this seem reasonable?

Along this same line, Picard asks for a report when the members of the bridge crew return. Instead of giving the report, Data defers, saying, "You may find it aesthetically displeasing, sir. I could just file a computer report on that." In other words, Data sidesteps the report! What kind of military discipline is this?

EQUIPMENT ODDITIES

• This isn't really equipment—more like ship design. The sweeping curved railing on the main bridge of the *Enterprise* gives the area a dramatic visual appeal. Unfortunately, the railing is also very impractical. The captain's position is in front of the railing, while the security people are behind it. Every time Worf needs to protect Picard, he jogs down the ramp a little way and leaps over the railing! That doesn't seem like an optimum method for ensuring the captain's safety.

• What's the most boring job on the *Enterprise*? After Q takes the members of the crew on their first excursion, he leaves Picard on an immobilized main bridge. Picard then wanders around trying to find an exit. At one point he calls for "turbolift control." Turbolift control? What kind of job is that? The main computer handles the routing of all the turbolifts. Is there really a person somewhere on the *Enterprise* who sits and watches the turbolifts race from place to place all day? (Actually, I can think of one other job that might be as bad—life support control. In that position, the crew member stares at only two displays. The first says "OK" and the other says "Uh-oh.")

• During "Encounter at Farpoint," Part 2, Captain Picard states that the panel on the right side of his chair is for "log entries, library computer access retrieval, viewscreen control, and intercoms." However, when Q makes a log entry, he flips open the left side of the captain's chair. (I'm wondering if the producers switched the panels when they switched the conn and ops positions after "Encounter at Farpoint." If so, this item should be logged with the things that changed after the premiere.)

TRIVIA ANSWERS

1. Five hundred four.
2. He makes Wesley ten years older. He offers Data the chance to be human. He also creates eyes for La Forge and a warrior babe for Worf.

HAVEN

The *Enterprise* arrives at Haven, a planet renowned for its beauty. Picard hopes to give the crew much-needed shore leave. Once the *Enterprise* enters orbit, a bonding gift arrives for Troi—a present for her upcoming wedding to Wyatt Miller, a medical doctor. The gift surprises everyone, including its recipient. Troi and Wyatt were genetically bonded as children, according to an old Betazoid custom. Troi thought the ritual had long since been forgotten. In shock, she watches Wyatt and his parents beam aboard followed by her mother, Lwaxana Troi.

Meanwhile, Haven signals the *Enterprise* as an unidentified vessel approaches. The bridge crew determines that it is a Tarellian ship—a race of people who engineered a deadly infectious virus during a world war on their planet. Once the plague spread throughout their planet, the Tarellians tried to escape to other worlds. Unfortunately, they brought the infection with them, becoming a despised and hunted race because of it. Of course, the government of Haven is quite concerned that the disease that the Tarel-

lians carry will decimate their lovely planet. At the last moment, Picard orders Yar to activate a tractor beam and capture the Tarellian vessel.

When Picard communicates with the captured ship, Troi is astounded. Since childhood, Wyatt has dreamed of a woman. The woman, named Ariana, is on the Tarellian ship. When Wyatt realizes this, he packs some medical supplies and beams over to the Tarellian vessel without authorization. He knows he can never beam back, but his love for Ariana and a desire to help the Tarellians compel him. The captain of the Tarellian vessel now asks to leave, stating that they have what they came for. Picard allows them to go, the Millers and Lwaxana beam back down to Haven, and the *Enterprise* warps out of orbit.

Trivia Questions

1. When was the last Tarellian ship thought to be destroyed?

2. How many Tarellians inhabited the plague ship?

GREAT LINES

"Could you please continue the 'petty bickering'?"—Data, intrigued by the verbal warfare between Lwaxana and the Millers and disappointed when it lulls.

PLOT OVERSIGHTS

• The approach of the plague ship toward the beautiful word of Haven causes a minor tension point in the plot. As the vessel draws closer, the tension increases. Picard calmly waits for the Tarellian vessel while the government of Haven wrings its hands. He even allows the ship to get within transporter range before finally taking action.

Why doesn't Picard take the *Enterprise* out of orbit and meet the incoming ship? That action would remove any possibility of danger to Haven and keep the governmental officials from developing ulcers.

• Originally, the *Enterprise* came to Haven to give the crew a short vacation. Yet, as soon as the Tarellian vessel and the wedding party leave, the *Enterprise* breaks orbit. Did everyone miss shore leave because of the incident with the Tarellians? (I guess this is just another slanderous charge that will be made against these poor disease-ridden people. I can hear it now: "Stinking Tarellians, not only do they destroy their world and spread their germs all over the galaxy, now they made us miss our vacations.")

CHANGED PREMISES

• The thought of Troi getting married greatly disturbs Riker, and he expresses his discontent to her early in the show. This would be a normal reaction for "backward" late-twentieth–century humans but not for twentieth-fourth-century humanity. According to Troi in the episode "Manhunt," humans "no longer *own* each other that way." At least that's what she tells her mother when Lwaxana asks Troi if Riker is still hers.

EQUIPMENT ODDITIES

• Just after Wyatt beams aboard, he gives Troi a chameleon rose. He says the rose changes color with the emotional states of the person who holds it. The rose seems to get stuck just after Wyatt gives it to her. It immediately goes frostbitten white—not an encouraging sign from your prospective spouse—and then stays white from that moment until she has a tender exchange with her mother. However, during that length of time she becomes *both* visibly upset *and* embarrassed and *still* the rose stays white.

CONTINUITY AND PRODUCTION PROBLEMS

• During the "prejoining announcement" dinner, Dr. Crusher and Wyatt have a conversation about the Tarellians. At one point Crusher puts her elbows on the table. Over the next series of shots, they bounce up and down as the camera angles change.

• This episode proves that when Starfleet says it has the finest training anywhere, it is telling the truth. During the prejoining announcement dinner, Lwaxana's valet, "Mr. Homm," bangs a little gong in the Betazoid tradition of giving thanks. Just behind him, a female ensign pours drinks. She works efficiently through several scenes. Then during a close-up of Mr. Homm she *suddenly* disappears, demonstrating her prowess and training. Everyone knows that the best waitress is one who understands how to do her job and then scrams when she isn't needed!

• When the *Enterprise* gets its first look into the Tarellian ship, the beautiful Ariana stands in front of the viewscreen. To her right, a man sits in a chair composed of several spheres. Interestingly, this same chair shows up in Worf's quarters in the episodes "Peak Performance" and "Reunion."

TRIVIA ANSWERS

1. Eight years ago.
2. Eight.

THE BIG GOOD-BYE

Star Date: 41997.7

As the episode opens, the *Enterprise* travels to a meeting with the Jarada, a reclusive, insectlike race. Since they are strategically important to the Federation, Picard will try to establish relations with them. The last attempt to do so failed miserably. The Jarada require a precise greeting in their own language from the captain of a starship before they will open negotiations. As the rendezvous with the Jarada approaches, Picard studies so furiously that Troi finally suggests he take a break and relax in the holodeck.

A fan of "Dixon Hill" novels, Picard chooses San Francisco in A.D. 1941 as the location to play his favorite gumshoe. He also asks Crusher, Data, and the *Enterprise*'s resident fiction expert, a man named "Whalen," to tag along. Unfortunately, while they enjoy the holodeck mystery, a sensor probe from Jarada damages the holodeck. Picard and the others become aware of the problem when a gangster shoots Whalen and he begins bleeding. They try to leave the holodeck, but the computer will not respond to their commands.

Meanwhile, the Jarada start demanding that Picard greet them as the crew works feverishly to free him from the holodeck. Wesley finally finds the problem and opens the doors. The head gangster sees the open door as a portal to another world and quickly steps through —only to vaporize in the hall outside. Data then overpowers the remaining guard, picks up Whalen, and heads for sick bay. Picard stays for a heart-to-heart talk with one of the holodeck characters but eventually shows up on the bridge and correctly greets the Jarada.

Trivia Questions

1. Who broke Joe DiMaggio's record for hits in consecutive games, and when was it accomplished?

2. What is Dixon Hill's phone number?

GREAT LINES

"It was raining in the city by the bay ... a hard rain, hard enough to wash the slime...."—Data doing his "Bogey" impersonation.

PLOT OVERSIGHTS

• As Picard enters the holodeck for the first time, a voice-over says, "Captain's personal log. I am entering the ship's holodeck, where images of reality can be created by our computer." How is Picard making this log entry? His lips aren't moving. Does he have an attachment in his brain that allows him to think comments and have them entered into his personal log?

• In this episode Data demonstrates knowledge about automobiles and Joe DiMaggio. He also reads all the Dixon Hill novels. Yet in one scene, Data becomes confused about the operation of an electric lamp. (I know it's a cute scene. I also know about dramatic license, but it just isn't believable.)

• After Whalen gets shot, Dr. Crusher cares for him for an extended time before covering him with a blanket. Did she just forget about blood loss causing a patient to go into shock and that one of the ways to slow down the onset of shock is to keep a person warm? Thankfully, she remembers these points when she gets hurt in "The Arsenal of Freedom."

• During the time Picard and the others are trapped in the holodeck, the crew works solely on getting the doors open. Does the holodeck put up some sort of force field that precludes beaming someone out of a holodeck experience while it is in progress?

• The entire last half of the show is dedicated to extricating Picard from the holodeck. The "strategically important" Jarada are waiting for him to greet them in their own language. Yet, even after Wesley gets the doors open, not one of the crew members who worked to rescue Picard even bothers to poke his head in to tell him the Jarada are waiting. Even so, Picard must realize that the time has come for his greeting because he

goes straight from the holodeck to the bridge. With all this in mind, why does Captain Picard stay and have a heart-to-heart talk with the holodeck character after the holodeck doors finally open and everyone else leaves? Is Picard concerned for the man's obvious emotional distress on learning that he may not be real? Does the holodeck character remind Picard of an imaginary friend he had as a boy? Is Picard waiting for the crew to replicate a giant can of Raid in case he fails in his greeting to the Jarada?

CHANGED PREMISES

• At the end of this episode, when the head gangster walks out of the holodeck, he gradually fades away in the hall. This visual agrees with the explanation given in "Elementary, My Dear Data" that matter created on the holodeck is a temporary form of matter that cannot exist outside the holodeck. On the other hand, this episode also contradicts the idea of temporary matter in the holodeck. During Picard's first excursion, a woman kisses him. When Picard leaves the holodeck and goes to the bridge crew briefing, the lipstick remains. Since it was created on the holodeck, shouldn't it have evaporated also? (I realize that the *Technical Manual* says that matter created on the holodeck isn't temporary and that holodeck characters are very sophisticated marionettes. It maintains that if holodeck characters leave the holodeck, they still exist but will not be under computer control. This episode doesn't support that assertion. The gangsters *vanish* when they leave the holodeck! For more discussion on this issue, see the Changed Premises section of the episode "Elementary, My Dear Data.")

CONTINUITY AND PRODUCTION PROBLEMS

• As Wesley tries to open the doors of the holodeck at the end of the show, the setting of the holodeck changes from Dixon Hill's office to a blustery winter scene and back. In the process, the blanket covering Whalen moves up and down on his legs. First it's bunched up near his knees, then it's smooth, and then it's bunched up again. (I can understand the difficulty of shooting the two scenes so they can be believably spliced together, but the blanket is way off.)

TRIVIA ANSWERS

1. A shortstop with the London Kings in A.D. 2026.
2. Prospect 4631.

DATALORE

Star Dates: 41242.4-41242.5

This episode takes the *Enterprise* to Data's home world, a planet in the Omicron Theta star system. Twenty-six years ago, a team from the USS *Tripoli* found Data lying on a rock on this barren, lifeless world. As they approached, Data awoke, with only vague memories of anything prior to their arrival. Data returned with them and joined Starfleet.

When the *Enterprise* away team beams down to the planet, they find a disassembled android who looks just like Data and take the machine back to the ship. This turns out to be Lore (Data's "brother"), who, when put back together, fills in many of the details missing from Data's memory. Lore says Dr. Noonian Soong created him first. However, since the other colonists on Data's planet envied Lore's abilities, Soong took him apart and created a less-perfect emotionless android, Data. Lore finishes his story with a description of the colony's fate. An alien crystal entity, shaped like an intricate three-dimensional snowflake, appeared and stripped the life from everything on the planet.

Trivia Questions

1. Name one child from the colony.

2. How long did Data serve as an ensign?

In spite of their identical physical appearance, Lore and Data are quite different. Lore uses contractions, shows emotion, has a facial tic, and understands humor. He also lacks morals. Lore incapacitates Data and assumes his "good" brother's identity. He then opens a subspace channel and summons the crystal entity. Lore believes the crystal entity will reward him for providing sustenance in the form of the people aboard the *Enterprise*. Shortly, the crystal entity arrives and attacks the ship.

Wesley notices "Data's" odd behavior. He convinces his mother to go with him to Data's quarters to look around. They find and reactivate the real Data, then confront Lore in a cargo bay as the evil brother attempts to provide the crystal entity with a way to enter the ship. In the fight that follows, Data throws Lore on the transporter pad, and Wesley beams him into space. After Picard, Riker, and Yar arrive, Picard asks Data if he is all right. Data responds, "Yes, sir. I'm fine."

PLOT OVERSIGHTS

• As the crystal entity approaches the *Enterprise*, La Forge says, "Captain, I'm picking up a bogey coming in on a five-o'clock tangent."

First of all, the future usage of the word "bogey" is questionable at best. Second, "five-o'clock tangent" denotes only an approximate direction. As La Forge and Wesley explain to Lore in this episode, Starfleet officers use a standard reporting system composed of two numbers separated by the word "mark." Each number refers to a specific degree in a circle. Because there are 360 degrees in a circle, straight ahead would be zero, straight behind would be 180. In the Starfleet standard reporting system, the first number gives the degree on a horizontal circle, the second give the degree on a vertical circle.

• When the crystal entity appears at the end of the show, it fails to destroy the *Enterprise* because it can't penetrate the shields. Lore convinces the captain to demonstrate the power of the *Enterprise* to the crystal entity, and suggests beaming out a tree beside the entity. When the *Enterprise* destroys the tree, Lore claims the entity will be impressed and leave the *Enterprise* alone. In fact, Lore wants to beam the tree out because he knows the shields will drop for an instant to allow the transportation. Lore goes to a cargo bay and contacts the crystal entity. He tells the crystal entity to get ready. Lore also tells the entity to attack the ship the instant the shields drop. Immediately after these statements, Lore and

Data fight. The fight ends when Data tosses Lore onto the transporter pad and Wesley beams him into space.

Does the entity care what object beams out? Either way, the shields must drop for an instant. Since Lore told the entity to get ready for the beam-out, why doesn't it attack when Wesley beams Lore into space?

CHANGED PREMISES

• One of Data's last lines in this show is, "I'm fine." However, when Data builds a daughter in "The Offspring," he immediately reacts when she uses a contraction. He reacts because he *cannot* use contractions. Over and over "The Offspring" clearly establishes this fact. (When I saw "Datalore" in late-night reruns, I looked at my wife and said, " 'I'M fine'? 'I'M FINE'? They just spent the entire show telling us that one of the differences between Lore and Data was that Lore used contractions and Data didn't, and Data says, 'I'M FINE'?" For months afterward my friends and I greeted each other with, "I'm fine." Then we would grin.)

CONTINUITY AND PRODUCTION PROBLEMS

• When Data looks at Lore's head on the planet, Lore's hair partially covers his ears. But after the crew assembles him, his hairdo changes. Now the hair is slicked back above his ears. Did someone take Lore's head to the beauty parlor before they attached it? (It certainly never hurts to look your best.)

TRIVIA ANSWERS

1. Josh. (A close-up of his drawing of
the crystal entity shows his name.)
2. Three years.

THE NITPICKERS' GUILD
ENTRANCE EXAM

T his exam will help you to determine if you are type of person who would qualify for entrance into the Nitpickers' Guild. Please record your answer on a separate sheet of paper and then score yourself according to the instruction at the end of this test. Of course, this test will only be as accurate as the honesty of your answers.

1. How many times do you watch each episode?

   A. 0
   B. 1
   C. 2–5
   D. 6 or more

2. How many friends do you discuss *Star Trek: The Next Generation* with each week?

   A. 0
   B. 1
   C. 2–5
   D. 6 or more

3. How many crew members can you name?

   A. 0
   B. 1–7
   C. 8–15
   D. 16–1,014

4. How many Vulcan greetings do you know?

   A. 0
   B. 1
   C. 2–4
   D. 5 or more

5. What type of VCR do you own?

   A. I don't have one.
   B. One that records and plays back.
   C. A four-head model for accurate freeze frame and slow motion.
   D. A sixteen-head model with super slow motion, RAM-bathed intelligent interpolation, MTS stereo and HDTV capability, and it's hooked up to a surround sound audio system and large-screen TV.

6. How often do you tape *Star Trek: The Next Generation*?

   A. Never; I don't watch the show and I don't own a VCR.
   B. Once in a while.
   C. Every time a new show airs.
   D. I tape every show, whether it's a rerun or not direct from the satellite feed on Saturday afternoons. Then—before I put these originals in a magnetic isolation vault that I constructed under my home—I dub off a copy to watch.

7. How are your tapes cataloged?

   A No VCR, no tapes, no catalog. Got it?
   B. Let's see ... I remember accidentally knocking the tape off the top of the TV. I think it fell down behind the Nintendo.
   C. I try to remember to scribble the name of each episode on the tape's label and keep a sheet of paper that tells me which tapes have what episodes.
   D. I used FileMaker Pro to create a data base that tracks the contents of each tape. In addition, I've categorized each episode by one of five generic themes. This allows me to print high-quality laser labels for my tapes that list the episode title and its generic theme category as well as the total number of running minutes.

8. When you watch an episode, how often do you use freeze frame?

   A. As I've said before, I don't tape the show because I don't own a VCR, and even if I did I wouldn't watch the show, so I certainly wouldn't be freeze-framing it.
   B. Occasionally.
   C. Whenever information flashes by too quickly to check at normal speed.
   D. Actually, I watch each episode at least once on a frame-by-frame basis. I also have a frame-grabber board in my Macintosh so I can convert each frame of a show into a thirty-two-bit color PICT file. Then I put the PICT

files into my screen saver and sequence them in the correct order. True, I had to add a two gigabyte removable drive just to store one show's worth of images, but I think it's worth it.

9. If you see what looks like a mistake, what's the first thing you do?

  A. You're not listening to me, are you? I don't watch the show. I don't tape the show. I don't know when the show airs, so I certainly never find any mistakes in the show!
  B. I don't think I've ever seen a mistake.
  C. First, I back up the tape and scrutinize the scene very carefully to ensure that it really is a mistake. Then I write down the episode, a short description of the scene, and the nature of the problem, and I send it to Phil Farrand, chief nitpicker of the Nitpickers' Guild.
  D. I close my eyes as tightly as I can and try to think about something else. When my hands stop shaking, I make a note never to watch that scene again.

10. Picard walks into his ready room and opens a window. Do you:

  A. Miss the entire scene because you're reading a magazine?
  B. Comment on how neat his desk always looks?
  C. Jump to your feet yelling, "He can't do that. He's in outer space!"?
  D. Start a letter-writing campaign, get elected to Congress, and sponsor a bill to bring more realism to science fiction television shows?

SCORING

*F*or every "A" answer, give yourself one point; for every "B," 10 points; every "C," 100 points; and for every "D," 1,000 points. After adding up your score, please refer to the following chart:

IF YOUR SCORE IS:
1-10

*D*id you realize that this book was about *Star Trek* when you bought it? You don't seem to be the type of person who has any interest in this show. That doesn't mean I don't appreciate the sale, because I do. I'm just a little confused, that's all.

11-100

*S*orry, while you may be a wonderful person, the Nitpicker's Guild is probably not for you. However, even normal viewers occasionally venture into nitpicking. If you see something not listed in this book, send it in.

101-1,000

C ongratulations! You're qualified to be in the guild. Now just send a mistake not listed in this book to the address at the back. (You can send in *Deep Space 9* stuff as well.)

1,001-9,999

I realize this may be hard for you to understand right now, but there is life apart from *Star Trek*. I've started a twelve-step recovery program just for individuals like yourself called "Extremely Fanatical Trekkers Anonymous." I believe the price is quite reasonable considering the program's high success rate. If you would like more information, please send the first month's payment of $3,000 to the address at the back of this book and I'll make a reservation for you.

★
ANGEL ONE

Star Date: 41636.9

The *Enterprise* tracks several escape pods from the freighter *Oden* to a planet known as Angel One. Once there, Riker, Data, Troi, and Yar beam down to the surface for an audience with the governing council. Angel One is a matriarchal society—the females are the hunters, soldiers, and rulers, larger and stronger than the males. Mistress Beata, the head of Angel One's government, agrees to let them search the planet, but only if they take the survivors with them when the *Enterprise* leaves. Meanwhile, on the *Enterprise*, Picard prepares to break orbit as soon as the away team returns. A Federation outpost has reported a Romulan battle cruiser in the neutral zone. Several days ago, however, a group of young people returned from a field trip on another planet and brought a highly infectious virus with them. As the virus spreads through the ship, Dr. Crusher works feverishly to find an inoculate.

Using its sensors, the *Enterprise* quickly finds the survivors and beams an away team to their location. Unfortunately, the survivors don't want

Trivia Questions

1. What did Riker wear for his diplomatic encounter on Armis IX?

2. What starship assists the Federation outpost on the Neutral Zone border before the *Enterprise* arrives?

to leave Angel One. The survivors, all men, like the women of Angel One. After learning that the *Enterprise* will not remove the survivors, Mistress Beata brings them in for execution. Beata claims the men are upsetting the natural order—encouraging a change toward a society with equality for the sexes. Then, just before she disintegrates the leader of the survivors, Riker gives a speech about the inevitability of change. Mistress Beata recants and exiles the survivors and their families to a remote region. At the same time, Dr. Crusher finds a cure for the virus on the ship. The away team then beams back, and the *Enterprise* warps away from Angel One to encounter the Romulans.

PLOT OVERSIGHTS

• As Data gives an overview of Angel One at the beginning of the show, he states that Angel One is "similar in technological development to midtwentieth-century earth." Yet once the away team beams down to the planet, they find a disintegrator beam.

The problem here is that scientific discovery in one area will assist with the development of another. A disintegrator beam capable of taking matter, converting it to energy, and then bleeding off that energy in a nondestructive way is a very sophisticated device. That technology would be applied to other areas—such as transporters, replicators, and food dispensers. The result is a society well advanced of midtwentieth-century Earth.

• When the *Enterprise* begins to search for the survivors of the freighter *Oden*, Picard orders La Forge to break fixed orbit. If the *Enterprise* is in fixed orbit, it would remain above a given location on the planet's surface. However, the shot before Picard's order shows the planet turning in one direction and the *Enterprise* flying in another.

• Finally, does anyone else find it miraculous that Dr. Crusher avoids getting sick when everyone else is dropping like road-kill possum?

CHANGED PREMISES

• I could make a big deal about Dr. Crusher's speech in "The Battle" when she tells Picard how backward humanity was in the twentieth century because it was still suffering from the common cold. I could point out that "respiratory virus" sounds suspiciously like something we would suffer from now. I could also point out that the way the virus affects the crew even looks like a bad cold or a case of the flu. But ... I believe I will postpone.

CONTINUITY AND PRODUCTION PROBLEMS

• When Data, Troi, and Yar beam over to meet with the survivors of the freighter *Oden* for the first time, Yar begins the trip with her arms behind her back. When she rematerializes near the survivors' camp, however, her arms are at her side.

• Mistress Beata shows why Angel One women qualify for the "Fastest Arms in the Galaxy Award" during her "diplomatic" encounter with Riker. In one scene her right arm is at her side as she talks with Riker while they sit on her bed. An instant later, in the very next scene, her right hand massages the back of his neck.

TRIVIA ANSWERS

1. Feathers.
2. The USS *Berlin* (an appropriate choice, since Berlin was the site of the Berlin Wall, the contemporary equivalent of the Neutral Zone).

11001001

Overdue for a routine maintenance check and computer upgrades, the *Enterprise* docks at Starbase 74. The technicians at the starbase include Bynars, a race of people who have evolved an unusually high level of interconnectedness with the main computer on their home planet. Riker eventually ends up at a holodeck right after the Bynars finish their enhancements. They encourage him to try it out, so Riker orders up a New Orleans jazz bar and an intimate audience—a stunning brunette named Minuet. A short time later, Picard joins him. Both are enthralled at the sophistication of Minuet's programming.

Meanwhile, a problem develops in the magnetic containment field in the warp engines. An explosion is imminent, and Data orders the evacuation of the ship. After everyone races off the ship, the magnetic containment field suddenly restores itself and the *Enterprise* warps away. On the holodeck, Picard prepares to leave, although encouraged by Minuet to stay. Then, when her politeness turns to pleading, Picard and Riker become sus-

picious. They exit the holodeck and learn that the ship is heading to the Bynars' home world.

Eventually, Picard and Riker make it to the bridge and find the Bynars incapacitated. They return to the holodeck, and Minuet answers their questions. An electromagnetic pulse—generated by a supernova explosion—was going to wipe out the Bynars' main computer. To avert disaster, they seized control of the *Enterprise* and transferred the information in their main computer to the main computer on board the *Enterprise*—hoping to reactivate their main computer after the pulse passed by. Unfortunately, the pulse came before it was expected. With Data's help at Starbase 74, Picard and Riker download the stored information and save the planet.

Trivia Questions

1. How many transporters are on the *Enterprise*?

2. As Picard praises the sophistication of Minuet's programming he begins by saying, "The holodeck has given us woodland and ski slopes, figures that fight, and fictional characters with whom we can interact. ..." List, in order of Picard's comments, the episodes that substantiate this claim.

GREAT LINES

"If winning is not important, then, Commander, why keep score?"—Worf to Riker, who is trying to get Worf to lighten up about the game he is scheduled to play.

PLOT OVERSIGHTS

• When the *Enterprise* pulls out of Starbase 74, the bridge crew just watches it go. After the containment field restores itself, Yar makes a half-hearted attempt to get to a transporter, but the commander of Starbase 74 stops them. He says it's too late and points to the *Enterprise* backing up as evidence. *Then* the episode shows us thirty seconds of the *Enterprise* pulling out. "Heart of Glory" establishes that the transporters on the *Enterprise* can operate at forty thousand kilometers (that's twenty-five thousand miles to you and me). They were well within range, and transporters can hit moving targets. (My problem with plot oversights is that most of them can be fixed with one or two lines of dialogue. In this case, this Bynars could have thrown up the shields as soon as the containment field repaired itself.)

• This episode purports that the Bynars planned Riker's abduction but not Picard's. Minuet tells Riker that the Bynars created her to appeal to Riker. When Picard says that explains Riker but not him, Minuet replies, "Your being here was just a fortunate happenstance." In addition, at the end of the show, when Riker asks the Bynars why they lured him to the holodeck, they reply, "Because we knew we might die and we needed someone to restore our computer. And you did."

Yet, when Riker downloaded the information to the planet, he couldn't do it alone. It took both him *and* Picard to get the transfer started. The two of them had to sit at different workstations and give the commands simultaneously. Are the Bynars really this bad at planning ahead? It took two people to reactivate their computer, and they only arranged for Riker to stay? If Picard hadn't *happened* along, everyone on their home world would have died.

EQUIPMENT ODDITIES

• During the evacuation of the ship, one scene shows Wesley and some other children beaming off. Specifically, the scene shows Wesley and *four* other children beaming off. As in, only *five* beam off even though there are six pads on the transporter. As in, the ship is being evacuated as *rapidly* as possible and they are using only *five* of the *six* possible transporter pads, even though there is a *long line* waiting!

• Just after exiting the holodeck and learning that the Bynars have commandeered the ship, Picard decides to set autodestruct. In Engineering, he and Riker go through the steps, and the autodestruct clock starts counting down when Picard gives the final command. The clock is composed of a series of little dots. Those little dots, which make up the numbers, are called LEDs (light-emitting diodes). Every other display on the *Enterprise* uses beautiful flat panel screens, and autodestruct uses "old-fashioned" twentieth-century LEDs?

• When Picard and Riker head for the bridge, they try to board a turbolift. The sign beside the turbolift flashes, "Access Denied," and the computer voice says, "Bridge Access Denied." They are on deck 36—way down in the secondary hull, outside Engineering. How does the computer know that they want to go to the bridge before they even board the turbolift? Was it eavesdropping?

• At the end of the episode, Riker needs to find the name of the file to initiate the information transfer to the Bynars' planet. He instructs the computer to search through all the possible combinations of 1's and 0's using a set of 16 characters. The next shot shows the computer rapidly trying out different combinations. However—since there are 65,536 possible combinations—the creators would have wasted a lot of time in the show if the display screen actually showed the computer processing through *all* of them. Instead, the creators simply had the computer try a few. A careful frame-by-frame analysis of the scene reveals that the computer actually found a match with the file name "00000010." In addition, the computer tried once to match the file names "00111010" and "10100110," couldn't find a match for the names, and then tried a second time. Guess what? The file names didn't match the second time either!

CONTINUITY PROBLEMS

• Just before Riker enters the holodeck the first time, the light on one of the Bynars' heads is flashing. In the very next shot, it isn't.

• When Picard and Riker exit the holodeck, Minuet is frozen, looking at them as they leave. Then a close-up shot shows her looking straight ahead. Then a long shot shows her looking away. The pattern continues through the rest of the episode.

• This is tacky to mention, but it happens all the time in television shows. After the autodestruct countdown starts, the director shows us several shots of the timer, intermixed with dialogue. If you take any of the shots of the timer and count off the seconds, you will find that the timer is off every time the director returns to it!

TRIVIA ANSWERS

1. At least twenty. (When the crew evacuates, the computer gives instructions on how each deck of the ship should leave. Deck by deck, it tells the crew to go to a certain transporter room. The computer makes it to transporter room 20 before the scene changes.)

2. "Encounter at Farpoint," Part 2; "Angel One"; "Code of Honor"; and "The Big Good-bye."

TOO SHORT A SEASON

Star Date: 41309.5

For this episode, Admiral Mark Jameson and his wife, Anne, join the *Enterprise*. Jameson is going to Mordan IV to negotiate a hostage crisis. Karnas, the leader of Mordan IV, sent a message saying he believed that only Jameson would be successful in the talks. Picard assumes that Karnas bases this statement on the fact that Jameson negotiated a similar situation on Mordan IV forty-five years ago. En route to the planet, the admiral begins to get stronger and look younger. Although Jameson has Iverson's disease—which is incurable and physically crippling—he shows signs of recovery. The situation progresses until Picard demands an answer from Jameson. Jameson then admits that he has taken a dangerous alien "deaging" drug. A short time later Picard finds out why Jameson thought it was necessary to take such a risk.

Forty-five years ago, Jameson did solve a hostage crisis with Karnas, but not by brilliant negotiating. Instead, Jameson gave in to Karnas's demands. He gave Karnas the weapons to fight his enemies. Then, while trying to be true to the Prime Directive, Jameson supplied the same weapons to Karnas's opponents. That decision plunged Mordan IV into four decades of civil war. Jameson believes Karnas wants revenge and has orchestrated the hostage situation to bring him to the planet.

After a botched attempt to rescue the hostages, Karnas demands that the *Enterprise* immediately deliver Jameson. Picard and Crusher beam down with Jameson to meet with Karnas. At first Karnas can't believe it's really him. Then Jameson shows Karnas the scar from the blood cut Karnas gave him forty-five years ago to seal their bargain. As Karnas watches Jameson die in agony from the drug, his vengeance is satisfied. He releases the hostages.

PLOT OVERSIGHTS

• As stated in the episode "Lonely Among Us," the bridge crew can relieve Picard if they unanimously agree that he is acting oddly. Also, Dr. Crusher can relieve Picard if she thinks he is medically unfit for com-

Trivia Questions

1. How old is Jameson?

2. What ship was Jameson on, in space, prior to the *Enterprise*?

mand. Shouldn't the same thing apply to mission commanders? First, Picard finds out that Jameson took double the recommended dosage of an alien drug. Its effects are unknown and certainly not understood. Second, Picard listens as Jameson confesses to a direct violation of the Prime Directive by giving weapons to Karnas. Third, Jameson proposes a raid that Picard thinks is questionable. Yet, through it all, Picard acts like he has no other recourse but to obey Jameson's orders.

• This deaging drug is hot stuff. Not only does it restore Jameson internally, it even regenerates all his wrinkly skin. Dr. Crusher notes this when she says that the drug is radically cha. :ging the cellular structure of his body and rewriting his DNA.

Doesn't it seem likely that the drug would also wipe out the scar tissue in his body if it can revitalize the skin of his face? Yet Jameson still has a scar he received as a forty-year-old even though his face and body look to be twenty-something.

CHANGED PREMISES

• In this episode, the stars streak from right to left in Picard's ready-room window when the *Enterprise* warps to Mordan IV. However, in "Lonely Among Us," the stars streak from *left to right!* (See "Lonely Among Us" for a more complete discussion.)

EQUIPMENT ODDITIES

• When Jameson and his wife beam aboard the *Enterprise*, he is confined to a futuristic wheelchair, yet he materializes on the transporter pad. How is Jameson supposed to get himself and his chair off the transporter pad? Does it have a built-in antigrav unit? The transporter pad certainly isn't wheelchair-accessible.

CONTINUITY AND PRODUCTION PROBLEMS

• As Picard and Riker leave the bridge to greet Jameson, Picard's entire face contorts for an instant just before he enters the turbolift. Riker doesn't react to it. There is no one standing by the turbolift door to see it. Evidently this is an outtake!

TRIVIA ANSWERS

1. Eighty-five.
2. The *Gettysburg* (an appropriate choice, given that Mordan IV was engaged in civil war for forty-five years).

WHEN THE BOUGH BREAKS

Star Dates: 41509.1-41512.9

The *Enterprise* follows a series of faint energy readings like a trail of bread crumbs. When the trail stops, the sensors show nothing. However, Troi says she senses thousands of minds. Suddenly a planet materializes near the *Enterprise*. It is Aldea, a planet that hosts a culture thousands of years old and highly advanced—so advanced they have a shield capable of protecting and cloaking their entire planet.

After greeting the *Enterprise*, the Aldeans request a meeting. During that meeting, they reveal that they can no longer have children. The Aldeans want the *Enterprise* to give them some children in exchange for scientific knowledge. Of course, the crew refuses, but when they do, the Aldeans take the children anyway. A short time later, the Aldeans contact Picard, offering to negotiate a payment for the children. Picard realizes that the Aldeans could disappear behind their shield and the *Enterprise* would lose the children forever. During the negotiations, the Aldeans choose to demonstrate their power. With one blast of a repulser

beam they shove the *Enterprise* a distance of three days' travel at warp 9. By the time the *Enterprise* returns, Dr. Crusher has discovered why the Aldeans can't have children and Data has found a hole in their shield.

As Picard and Crusher beam down for the final negotiations, Riker and Data slip through the shield and disable the Aldeans' main computer. They also turn off the Aldean shield. It has destroyed the ozone layer of the planet, subjecting the inhabitants to lethal doses of radiation. This radiation has caused many physical problems for the Aldeans, including infertility. Without their computer, the Aldeans are powerless, allowing Picard to return the children to the *Enterprise*. However, Picard also offers the Aldeans the help of the Federation to rebuild their society without relying on their life-threatening technology. The Aldeans accept.

Trivia Questions

1. Where do Harry's surrogate parents live?

2. When does the ozone layer of Earth deteriorate and ultraviolet radiation flood the planet?

GREAT LINES

"Things are only impossible until they are not."—Picard, urging Data to find a way to penetrate the Aldean shield.

PLOT OVERSIGHTS

• Before Aldea appears, Troi says she senses thousands of minds. Presumably she senses them from Aldea. Yet when the Aldeans take the children, they take only seven. If there are thousands of Aldeans on the planet and they are all barren, why would they take only seven children?

• And how come everybody's got a cloaking device except the Federation? The Romulans have one. The Klingons have one. The Aldeans have one. What kind of dolts does the Federation have for scientists, anyway? (True, the Aldeans *might* show their gratitude to the Federation for saving their culture by letting Starfleet borrow their cloaking device, but I doubt it.)

EQUIPMENT ODDITIES

• When Data describes the Aldean cloaking shield, he calls it a "complicated light-refracting device." He also compares it to the Romulan cloaking device. Wesley asks how it works, and Data explains, "The shield bends light rays around the planet's contour."

What about the gravitational displacement caused by the planet's mass? This isn't a spaceship. This is a planet. Even "backward" twentieth-century scientists could calculate the existence of Pluto and its orbital path based on the gravitation disturbances caused by its orbit around the sun.

CONTINUITY AND PRODUCTION PROBLEMS

• At one point, Wesley beams into the custodian's room late at night—the room that houses the voice interface to the main computer. The camera moved a little when the scene was shot. After Wesley materializes, the room jumps sideways.

TRIVIA ANSWERS

1. Unit B 375.
2. In the twenty-first century.

HOME SOIL

Star Dates: 41463.9-41464.8

The *Enterprise* arrives at Velara III, a "terraforming" project of the Federation. After certifying that a planet has the correct mass and rotation—and is completely devoid of life—the Federation sends a team of specialists to transform the planet into an Earth-like environment. Shortly after an away team beams down to the planet, one of the terraformers begins pumping subsurface water into previously sculpted lakes. Moments later, the laser drill used in this operation malfunctions and kills him. When Data looks for the cause of the malfunction, the equipment attacks him also.

After taking the terraformers to the *Enterprise*, Data and La Forge beam back to the station for a closer look at the machinery. In one of the drilling tubes they find a tiny crystal that emits beautiful flashes of light. When they return with it to the *Enterprise*, the crew surmises that it is a form of inorganic life. After the specimen divides—in essence, reproducing itself—Picard becomes convinced that it is alive. In addition, the Universal Translator suddenly comes on line,

Trivia Questions

1. How long does a terraforming project last?

2. What is Dr. Crusher's definition of organic life?

providing proof that the crystal is not only alive, it is also intelligent life and trying to communicate.

After discussing the situation with the terraformers, Picard realizes that the crystal lives in the subsurface water. Pumping out this water was killing its society. The captain tries to express his regrets, but the crystal keeps dividing and then declares war on the *Enterprise*. It even takes over the computer. Suddenly Data realizes that during the crystal's last reproductive phase it used a tremendous amount of energy, but there was no drain on the *Enterprise*'s systems. He proposes that the crystal derives its energy from light. Picard sends Riker to dim the lights in the medical lab, and the crystal begins to die. After the crystal calls off the war, Picard beams it back to the planet.

PLOT OVERSIGHTS

• Referring to the terraformers, the crystal says, "Cause much death. Make us kill. War is now with you." Later, the woman terraformer muses that if they had continued to remove the water, they would have destroyed them all. In other words, removing water from the crystal life form kills it. Yet there is no salt water in the medical lab. If the lack of water killed the crystal, shouldn't it have died as soon as it left the planet?

• Along the same line, the woman terraformer told the away team that the planet has a balanced day and night. In other words, it gets dark on the planet at times. Yet when Riker dims the lights in the lab, the crystal immediately began to die. How does it survive on the surface of the planet at night?

CONTINUITY PROBLEMS

• When Picard, Crusher, Data, La Forge, and Wesley are in the medical lab for the first time examining the crystal, Dr. Crusher orders a magnification and then tells the computer to demagnify. However, in the close-up of her later, the screen behind her still shows the highest magnification.

TRIVIA ANSWERS

1. Thirty-five years (the graphic at the bottom of the terraformers' demonstration viewscreen goes from zero to thirty-five years).

2. It must have the ability to assimilate, respirate, reproduce, grow and develop, move, secrete, and excrete.

COMING OF AGE

Star Date: 41416.2

As the *Enterprise* orbits Relva VII, Wesley Crusher beams down to test for entrance into Starfleet Academy. At the same time, Admiral Gregory Quinn and Lieutenant Commander Dexter Remmick beam aboard. After asking for a private conference with Captain Picard, Admiral Quinn tells him that Remmick is with the inspector general's office. He is going to conduct an investigation. Quinn won't tell Picard what the investigation is about, only that there is something wrong on the *Enterprise*. While Remmick turns the ship upside down, Wesley and three other candidates—a human female, a Vulcan female, and a Benzite male named Mordock—compete for one opening at the academy. Eventually Mordock comes out on top. The testing officer congratulates him as being the first Benzite in Starfleet.

After interviewing most of the officers on the *Enterprise*, Remmick finally completes his investigation and reports that he can find nothing wrong with the ship or its captain. Satisfied, Admiral Quinn opens up to Picard and relates in vague and veiled terms that there is a threat to the Federation. Quinn claims that he needs men whom he can trust in positions of authority at Starfleet. He wants to promote Picard to admiral and put him in charge of Starfleet Academy. Although tempted, Picard turns down the offer, preferring the life of a starship captain to the politics of Starfleet bureaucracy.

GREAT LINES

"Is it required, sir?"—Worf to Remmick after Remmick comments, "You don't like me, do you?"

EQUIPMENT ODDITIES

• Prior to this episode, Wesley beat out several other contenders for the chance to test for an opening at Starfleet Academy. During this episode, one of the young men who lost to Wesley steals a shuttle to "run away from home." When the young man destabilizes the engine core of the shuttle, it begins heading toward the planet. Supposedly this places him in grave danger. Quickly, the bridge crew runs through the options. They maintain that they cannot use the transport to rescue him because he is out of range.

Trivia Questions

1. How old is Wesley in this episode?

2. What infuriates Zoldans?

53

However, soon after the shuttle left the *Enterprise*, it lost its propulsion. Then it headed for the planet. The odd thing here is that people are beaming up and down from the planet. If people are beaming up and down from the planet, doesn't it seem reasonable that the *Enterprise* could beam someone out of a shuttle that sits between it and the planet? Also, the episode "A Matter of Honor" maintains that transporters have a range of forty thousand kilometers. Only one minute elapses from the time the shuttle leaves until Yar claims he is out of range of the shuttle. To be out of transporter range, the shuttle would have to be traveling at a speed of 1.5 million miles an hour!

• After giving his report to Admiral Quinn, Remmick walks to the door—actually he almost runs into it—and then turns. The door doesn't open. For the next few moments, Remmick stands with his back very close to the door and speaks to Picard. *Then*, before he even begins to turn, the door pops open and Remmick leaves. How did the door know exactly when to open? Did a programmer with a minor degree in theater give the door a sensitivity for dramatic exits?

CONTINUITY AND PRODUCTION PROBLEMS

• Just after Wesley finishes the last question in the Hyperspace Physics Test—the question that firmly establishes there is only one ratio of matter to antimatter, 1 to 1—Mordock completes the question also, followed by the Vulcan female. The next shot shows us the satisfied look on the Vulcan's face. Over her shoulder, Wesley is in the background, working on the Dynamic Relationships Test. That test doesn't occur until later in the show. Evidently the creators needed some footage to throw in here.

• At one point, Wesley helps Mordock on the Dynamic Relationships Test. Afterward they chat with the testing officer. Mordock's testing screen behaves very strangely over the next few moments. First, it turns off, turns back on, and then turns off again—all by itself! Actually, the creators shot only one piece of film for this scene, showing Wesley and Mordock listening intently to the testing. However, the creators used it *three* times—which would have been undetectable except for the graphic playing across Mordock's screen!

TRIVIA ANSWERS
1. Fifteen.
2. Courtesy.

HEART OF GLORY

Star Date: 41503.7

When Starfleet informs the *Enterprise* of a battle in the Neutral Zone, the *Enterprise* warps over to look. They find remains of a ship and a severely damaged Talarian freighter. An away team consisting of Riker, Data, and La Forge beams over. Before they leave, Picard suggests that La Forge try his new experimental "visual acuity transmitter." This device hooks on La Forge's visor and transmits what the visor sees. On board the freighter, the away team finds three Klingons. After transporting back to the *Enterprise*, the Klingons are taken to sick bay. One of them has lethal wounds. When Picard questions the other two, they claim they were passengers aboard the freighter when the Ferengi attacked. Picard isn't satisfied with the Klingons' answers but allows Worf to take them to their quarters.

A short time later, a Klingon ship approaches. The captain of the Klingon ship tells Picard that the men are fugitives. He says they attacked and destroyed a Klingon cruiser and demands that Picard transport them

as soon as the two ships are in range. A security team confines the Klingons to a holding cell, but the fugitives soon escape. One dies in the attempt, and the other goes to Engineering. While pointing a phaser at the dilithium chamber, he demands to speak with Worf. Knowing that if the Klingon fugitive fires, he will destroy the *Enterprise*, Picard accompanies Worf to Engineering. Worf approaches the Klingon, speaks with him about battles and glory, and then kills him. This allows the fugitive to die an honorable death. The manner in which the fugitives died pleases the captain of the Klingon vessel. The Klingon vessel then departs.

Trivia Questions

1. What weapons did the Klingon fugitives say they used to destroy their attacker?

2. Where does the *Enterprise* go after this episode?

PLOT OVERSIGHTS

• During the episode "Haven," Picard identifies the plague ship as Tarellian. Because of his accent, Picard pronounces it "teh-RAIL-ian." In the episode "Heart of Glory," the *Enterprise* finds the Klingons on a Talarian freighter. After Picard questions the Klingons in sick bay, he comments to Riker, "There is more to this than we've been told. Why was the 'teh-RAIL-ian ship' so far off course?" Wrong race, Picard!

• At the beginning of the show, as soon as Riker hears that the *Enterprise* will head toward the Neutral Zone, he suggests that they separate the saucer section. (See "Encounter at Farpoint.") This seems reasonable, since the *Enterprise* carries so many families with children. Why not separate the saucer if the possibility of danger exists?

Yet, when the Klingon fugitive has a phaser pointed at the dilithium chamber in Engineering, the *Enterprise* faces imminent destruction and *no one* even mentions separating the saucer. If the warp engines might explode, doesn't it seem sensible to put most of the crew beyond the range of the explosion?

EQUIPMENT ODDITIES

• Geordi La Forge's visual acuity

transmitter brings up an interesting point. Why don't the communicators transmit visually? This would be a tremendous advantage in dangerous situations. Granted, one member of the away team might have to wear a camera attached to his or her head, but that seems a small price to pay for the additional information a camera would provide. Of course, if the away team could transmit back visually, it would do away with those pithy little lines the away teams like to use. For instance, in "Skin of Evil," a sludge monster rises out of an oil slick. Picard asks Riker what he sees, and Riker responds, "Trouble." Did that answer communicate anything important to Picard?

TRIVIA ANSWERS

1. A battery of ancient merculite rockets.
2. Starbase 84.

THE ARSENAL OF FREEDOM

Star Date: 41798.2

Investigating the disappearance of the USS *Drake*, the *Enterprise* travels to Minos. Originally, Starfleet sent the *Drake* to Minos to confirm reports by a long-range probe that all intelligent life had ceased to exist there. As soon as the *Enterprise* drops into orbit, an automated sales pitch begins from the planet's surface. The holographic salesman relates in glowing terms that Minos is "The Arsenal of Freedom"—a planet dedicated to selling sophisticated weapons systems to anyone who can pay the price.

An away team consisting of Riker, Data, and Yar beams down to the planet. Shortly afterward, an attack pod encases Riker in a coma-inducing force field. Leaving La Forge in command, Picard and Dr. Crusher beam down to assist. As Data works to free Riker, a second pod appears and begins firing on the away team. Picard and Crusher head into the woods and fall into an underground cavern. Together, Data and Yar destroy the second pod. At the same time, another pod attacks the *Enterprise*. La Forge opts for a strategic retreat, separates the saucer, and returns to Minos with only the star drive section.

Meanwhile, Data and Yar free Riker and set off to find Picard and Crusher. In the underground cavern, Picard treats an injured Dr. Crusher. He also looks through the rubble and finds a display terminal. The automated salesman appears once again, stressing the elegance of the demonstration. Picard suddenly realizes that all the attacks have been part of the sales pitch. Picard agrees to buy one of the systems just so the demonstration will stop. At the same time above the planet, La Forge battles the pod and eventually destroys it. The crew then beams the away team back, patches up Dr. Crusher, and warps to rendezvous with the saucer section.

Trivia Questions

1. Where does La Forge send the saucer section?

2. The "Echo Papa 607" is state-of-the-art in what field of study?

GREAT LINES

"It's just been commissioned. It's a good ship."—Riker telling an information-gathering facsimile of his friend Paul Rice about the ship he commands, a ship called the *Lollipop*.

PLOT OVERSIGHTS

• After Data extricates Riker from the force field, Data mentions in passing that they need to find Picard and Crusher. Riker follows as Data and Yar lead the way. Wasn't Riker encased in a force field when Picard beamed down? Wasn't he comatose inside that field? Riker didn't even know Picard was on the planet, let alone lost. Given his ardent belief that captains should stay on their ships, shouldn't Riker be really ticked off when he learns that Picard is on the surface?

• One of the big tension points at the end of this episode occurs when the final pod is launched on the ground. This pod is the fourth and last in its series and will supposedly kill Riker and Yar. Catastrophe is narrowly avoided when Picard agrees to buy the weapons system. The salesman ends the demonstration and the ground pod evaporates.

So why is La Forge still fighting the pod in orbit? Shouldn't it have evaporated as soon as the demonstration ended? There isn't a time overlap between the two scenes because Picard calls La Forge just after he shuts off the machine and La Forge is still battling the pod in space.

• To get a fix on the cloaked pod, La Forge takes the star drive section into the atmosphere. When the pod follows, the sensors detect the atmospheric disturbances caused by it. This gives Worf a location to target with the phaser. Yet, immediately after destroying the pod, La Forge drops the shields so they can beam the away team back. Isn't the star drive still flying through the atmosphere at this point? Aren't the shields the only thing keeping the ship from burning up?

EQUIPMENT ODDITIES

• As Picard and Crusher beam down to the surface, the camera angle shows the transporter console at the bottom of the screen and Picard and Crusher in the background. The transporter chief's hand touches the controls for the first transporter pad and then the second. Yet when the transporter pads energize they come on at *exactly* the same time. In other words, Crusher's pad comes on *before* the chief touches the button.

TRIVIA ANSWERS
1. Starbase 103.
2. Dynamic Adaptive Design (DAD, for short).

SYMBIOSIS

After rushing to answer a freighter's distress, the crew of the *Enterprise* tries to beam the occupants to safety, but locks on to their cargo instead. At the last possible moment, Yar manages to pull four of the six people off the freighter before it disintegrates; two are "Onarans," the other two Brekkians. Oddly enough, all four show little regard for the loss of the last two inhabitants of the freighter. On the other hand, they are overjoyed that the cargo—a "medicine" called Felicium—is safe. For the past two centuries, Felicium has been the only product produced by the Brekkians, while the Onarans have been their only customer.

The Onarans believe they are terminally ill with a deadly plague. Although Felicium doesn't cure the plague, it does wipe out all the symptoms. After an investigation, however, Dr. Crusher discovers that Felicium is not a medicine, it is a drug. The entire planet of Onara is addicted, and the Brekkians know it. Even though payment for the current batch went down with the freighter, the Brekkians soon realize that if the

Trivia Questions

1. What part is malfunctioning on the Ornaran shuttles?

2. What is the recommended dosage of Felicium?

Onarans do not have the Felicium, their addiction will wear off. So, the Brekkians give the Felicium to the Onarans.

Dr. Crusher is incensed. She pleads with Captain Picard to expose this exploitive relationship. Picard knows he cannot. It would violate the Prime Directive. However, as the Onarans and the Brekkians prepare to beam down to Onara, Picard intervenes in another way: He refuses to supply replacement parts for the Onaran freighters. The Onarans realize that without the parts, the freighters won't run, and without the freighters, there will be no more Felicium. Picard knows eventually that this will force the Onarans to become free of the drug.

RUMINATIONS

When I watched this episode in late-night reruns, I had a humorous thought during the closing credits. The Brekkians must not be very smart. After all, they don't have any freighters, and the Onaran freighters aren't "working properly." Because of this, the Onarans seemed to fear that they won't be

59

able to make it to Brekka for the next load of Felicium. Of course, when the current batch of Felicium runs out, the entire planet is going into withdrawal, and after the withdrawal, the entire planet is going to realize that Brekka has been milking them for two hundred years. Would you want to be a Brekkian stuck on Onara in that situation?

CHANGED PREMISES

• Shortly after the Onarans beam on board, they meet with Picard in the observation lounge. During this meeting they reveal that they carry a deadly illness. Picard immediately asks Riker if the medical scans in the transporter were functioning. Later, when Dr. Crusher examines the Onarans, she says she can find no bacterial or viral cause for their symptoms. Picard suggests that the biofilters in the transporter may have removed the disease. The impression these scenes leave is that the transporter can screen out bacteria and viruses when a person comes aboard the *Enterprise*. This seems like an excellent capability for the transporters to have since the *Enterprise* visits so many different planets.

However, if the transporter has this feature, how could the young people who went on the field trip in the episode "Angel One" bring back a viral infection? And if they did return to the ship via shuttle, why didn't Dr. Crusher just transport them from one room to another and rid them of the virus?

• At the end of the show, La Forge calls out the new heading as he enters it. He says, "Nine seven oh mark three one eight" (970 mark 318). Unfortunately, the episode "Datalore" establishes that the each of the numbers given in a heading cannot exceed 360.

TRIVIA ANSWERS

1. An electromagnetic coil for exhaust flow constriction.
2. One-hundredth milliliter.

SKIN OF EVIL

Star Dates: 41601.3-41602.1

As Troi returns from a conference, her shuttle loses power and crashes on Vagra II. When the *Enterprise* arrives at the planet, an away team of Riker, Data, Crusher, and Yar beams down to rescue Troi and the pilot. A life form named Armus blocks their path. He is a creature formed from the cast-off evil desires and intents of a race of titans who've long since left the planet. Since Armus maintains a force field over the shuttle, Riker and the away team must negotiate for Troi's release. When Armus refuses to listen, Yar tries to force the issue, and Armus kills her. Armus then envelopes the shuttle as the away team returns to the ship. After consultation with the bridge, Picard lets an away team return to the planet to gather more information.

Meanwhile, Worf notices that every time Armus envelopes the shuttle, his power diminishes—as does the force field over the shuttle. If it drops low enough, the *Enterprise* could beam the shuttle crew up. On the planet, Armus amuses himself with the away team. At one point he envelopes Riker. Hearing this, Picard beams down. Eventually Armus releases Riker. Everyone on the away team, except Picard, returns to the ship.

Before doing anything else, Picard demands to see Troi. Armus agrees because he wants Picard to take him from this planet. Picard learns from Troi that Armus's energy drops when she forces him to face his fears. Picard uses the same tactic, and the force field drops low enough to beam Picard, Troi, and the shuttle pilot back to the *Enterprise*. As the *Enterprise* leaves the planet, Picard calls the bridge crew to the holodeck to watch a prerecorded farewell speech from Lieutenant Commander Tasha Yar.

Trivia Questions

1. What is the designation of Troi's shuttle?

2. Who's "the best" as far as Yar is concerned?

PLOT OVERSIGHTS

• During "Encounter at Farpoint," Troi projected thoughts that Riker could hear. That ability was also alluded to in the episode "Haven." In addition, Data—during the episode "Night Terrors"—states, "There is no technology to block telepathic transmissions."

For the majority of "Skin of Evil," Troi is imprisoned in a shuttle while an away team that includes Riker tries to rescue her and the pilot. Doesn't this seem like a good time to use the capability she has to communicate with Riker?

CONTINUITY AND PRODUCTION PROBLEMS

• Just after Armus engulfs Riker, the rest of the away team runs up to the edge of the oil slick. When they stop, La Forge's phaser plops out onto the ground. Does this seem like a first-class holster design to you?

• During the last scene of the episode, Yar says good-bye to the bridge crew. She speaks from the top of a hill, with clouds rolling by in the background. This is really tacky to point out, but the cloud patterns are way off between the close-up and long shots. (They were probably next to impossible to synchronize.)

TRIVIA ANSWERS
1. Thirteen.
2. Riker.

WE'LL ALWAYS HAVE PARIS

Star Date: 41697.9

After several seconds in time "replay" themselves during a fencing duel, Picard immediately checks with the bridge and discovers that the same phenomenon occurred all over the ship. Moments later, Worf receives a distress call from Dr. Paul Manheim. After hearing the scientist's name, Picard knows that the time distortion and the distress call are connected. Manheim and a group of young scientists disappeared fifteen years ago to prove Manheim's theories concerning time. The distress signal leads the *Enterprise* to Vandor IV, and the crew soon learns that Manheim's experiments in time have gone awry—killing all the young researchers and injuring the noted scientist. He and his wife, Jenice, are beamed directly to sick bay. When Picard goes to meet them in sick bay, the crew learns something else. Apparently Picard and Jenice knew each other *very* well at one time. Then, twenty-two years ago, Picard ran from the relationship.

Soon the *Enterprise* experiences another time distortion. The ailing Manheim explains that his experi-

Trivia Questions

1. What date and time does Picard request for the holodeck simulation?

2. What is the range on the time distortions?

ments have opened a door to another dimension. If the crew cannot seal the door, reality as it is normally perceived will no longer exist. Picard sends Data to Manheim's laboratory. He hopes Data can seal the rip in the fabric of time by placing a precise amount of antimatter into the rift at the exact time of the next distortion. Unfortunately, when the distortion hits, three versions of Data appear—each at a different point along the time continuum. They question each other as to who is in the correct position. Finally the Data in the middle says, "It's me!" and releases the antimatter, successfully patching the rift. At the same time, Dr. Manheim returns to normal. He and Jenice then return to the research station to continue his studies.

GREAT MOMENTS

The final sequence with Data, the antimatter and the time rift in this episode works quite well. The visual effect of the rift is very well done, and the multiple Datas add a nice level of tension to the conclusion of the story.

GREAT LINES

"Oh, we are us, sir. They are also us. So, indeed, we are both us."—Data trying to explain one of the time distortions, as he, Picard, and Riker stare at copies of themselves that existed a few seconds earlier in time.

PLOT OVERSIGHTS

• In three-dimensional space, it is impossible to specify a location using only two coordinates. Yet when the *Enterprise* receives the first distress call from Dr. Manheim, he says their position is "66728.9 by 707542.2." This makes no sense because the message is missing the third coordinate. Somehow the *Enterprise* still manages to travel to the correct location, where the crew receives the next set of coordinates. This time they are in the correct format of three numbers: "664.8 by 1323.7 by 4949.9."

• The day Picard ran away from his relationship with Jenice, he was supposed to meet her at a café in Paris. Halfway through the episode, Jenice corners Picard in the observation lounge of the *Enterprise* to discuss their "unfinished business." She asks him why he never showed up and tells him that she waited all day. She also comments that it was raining. At the end of the episode, Picard gives Jenice an appropriate goodbye when he re-creates the Paris café, just as it was twenty-two years earlier, on the holodeck. If the holodeck re-creation is accurate—and Jenice comments that it is—Picard and Jenice scheduled their rendezvous in an *open-air* café! Did

Jenice sit in the rain all day and wait for Picard? Now, that's dedication!

• Just before Data drops the anti-matter into the time rift he says, "It's me!" In addition to the fact that Data cannot use contractions according to the episode "The Offspring," Data's response is also bad grammar. The more correct response would be, "It is I!"

CONTINUITY AND PRODUCTION PROBLEMS

• This is one of the rare continuity errors by Patrick Stewart. And it's a small one. When the first time distortion occurs, Picard heads straight for the bridge. He brings his towel with him. After the opening credits, Picard sits in his chair with the towel in his right hand. The towel hangs directly down, slightly toward him. In the next shot, the towel hangs off the side of the chair, more toward Riker.

• When Picard first hears Manheim's name, Troi senses a deep emotional reaction. She suggests to Picard that he take some time to sort out his feelings so they will not affect his judgment when the ship reaches Manheim's laboratory. Picard heeds her advice and goes to the holodeck. He re-creates the café in Paris, twenty-two years in the past, where he was supposed to meet Jenice. As Picard walks through the doors of the holodeck, the Eiffel Tower is directly ahead of him. Slightly to the left of him is a table with two young lovelies dressed in costumes utilizing the Theiss Titillation Theory (see Ruminations for the episode "Justice"). Picard approaches the table with the lovelies, turns to the left, and passes their table on his right side. He then turns slightly more to the left and looks over the city. At this point, the lovelies' table is behind him. Yet a reverse angle shows Picard's back as he surveys Paris and the Eiffel Tower is still almost directly in front of him!

Thankfully, in a few moments a waiter approaches Picard on Picard's left side. Picard rotates a little to the left to acknowledge him. A close-up of Picard shows that the world is once again in a harmonious state because the Eiffel Tower is back to the same location it was when Picard entered the holodeck!

• When Manheim and his wife beam up to sick bay, Dr. Crusher and an orderly help him onto a bed. Just before the shot changes, the orderly's hands are in the air. In the next shot, his hands are on Manheim's shoulders.

TRIVIA ANSWERS

1. April 9, 15:00 hours.
2. At least several thousand light-years.

★
CONSPIRACY

Star Dates: 41775.5-41780.2

When an old friend suddenly dies after cautioning Picard about a conspiracy to overthrow Starfleet, the captain puts Data to work analyzing recent Starfleet command decisions. Data soon reports that his study reveals a covert attempt to control certain key sectors of the Federation. Wanting answers, Picard sets a course for Earth. As soon as the ship enters orbit, several admirals at Starfleet headquarters invite Picard to come down for dinner. Admiral Gregory Quinn (see "Coming of Age") says he cannot attend but asks to visit the *Enterprise*. Just after Quinn beams up, Picard realizes something is wrong. He tells Riker to stay with Quinn and watch everything he does. Picard then beams down for the dinner. When Riker arrives at Quinn's quarters, Quinn tries to force him to view a beetlelike life form. After Riker refuses, Quinn beats him up but not before Riker calls Security.

Help arrives as La Forge and Worf charge to the rescue. Unfortunately, Quinn beats them up, too. Just before Quinn escapes, Dr. Crusher zaps

Trivia Questions

1. Name Walker Keel's siblings.

2. What data base does Data use to review the recent Starfleet command decisions?

him with a phaser. As Crusher completes her examination of Quinn, Picard—calling from Starfleet headquarters—checks in with the ship. Crusher tells Picard that a beetlelike creature has attached itself to the base of Quinn's brain, thereby controlling his mental and physical functions. Picard proceeds to the dinner, only to discover that the creatures control everyone in the room also. Shortly, Riker beams down, and even he appears to be part of the conspiracy. Thankfully, he isn't. As soon as everyone falls for his ruse, Riker pulls a phaser and attacks them. Picard and Riker then discover that the conspiracy's leader is Commander Remmick (see "Coming of Age"). Remmick claims the aliens "seek peaceful coexistence," but Picard and Riker don't believe him. In response, they fry Remmick with their phasers, killing the "mother creature" that lives inside him.

PLOT OVERSIGHTS

• The longtime friend who first alerts Picard to the conspiracy is named "Walker Keel." He seems to have a little difficulty thinking things through. In a secret communiqué, he tells Picard to trust no one. Later, during their covert meeting, Keel says, "This meeting never took place as far as Starfleet is concerned." Then, just as Picard is leaving, Keel says, "Tell Beverly 'hello' for me."

How is Picard supposed to tell Dr. Crusher that he saw Keel if the meeting never happened and he isn't supposed to trust anyone? Evidently Picard knows Keel is scrambled, and so he doesn't comply with Keel's last request. When Dr. Crusher asks if he saw Walker, Picard says no.

• When Riker gets beaten up by Admiral Quinn, Riker calls Security. In the next scene, La Forge and Worf come running down the hall. What happened to the little guys in the green outfits? (I realize that "extras" cost money, but sending Worf and La Forge charging down from the bridge is a bit much.)

• Worf doesn't make a very good showing during the fight with Quinn. Supposedly, Klingons are fierce warriors. When Riker gets thrown over the table, he comes back fighting. On the other hand, Worf gets thrown over the table and falls asleep.

CHANGED PREMISES

• When the warp engines are engaged, the *Enterprise* flies faster than the speed of light. When the impulse engines are running, the *Enterprise* flies slower than the speed of light. This is supported by practically every episode. Yet when Riker tells La Forge to increase to warp six at the beginning of this episode, La Forge

responds, "Aye, sir. Full impulse." Full impulse? The *Enterprise* is already traveling at warp.

EQUIPMENT ODDITIES

• After Dr. Crusher flattens Quinn with a phaser, she tells Picard that the setting must be kill, not stun, to have any effect. Yet Crusher makes no mention that the beetlelike creatures that control Quinn modify human physiology, only that the creatures stimulate the adrenal glands. *Maybe*—if phasers worked by disrupting nerve activity—the kill setting would make sense. But a phaser on kill *burns* things. Adrenaline won't help if you have an eighteen-inch hole punched through your chest— as our dear Commander Remmick found out.

• When Data reviews all Starfleet command decisions for the past six months, a camera angle shows information rapidly flashing across his display screen. One of the graphics shown is a parrot! What does a parrot have to do with command decisions?

Actually this sequence of screen information is used in two other places in the series. It shows up when Data scans records during the "The Naked Now" and when the portal of the Tkon Empire scans the *Enterprise*'s data banks in "The Last Outpost." In the latter case, the parrot is upside down!

TRIVIA ANSWERS
1. Ann and Melissa.
2. Comnet Data Base 2442219.

THE NEUTRAL ZONE

Star Date: 41986.0

While the *Enterprise* hangs in space waiting for Picard to return via shuttle from a conference on Starbase 718, a space derelict happens by. Data and Worf beam over to investigate. They find containers of frozen people, and three are still functioning. Data and Worf return with them to the *Enterprise* as Picard arrives at the ship. Picard immediately sets course for the Neutral Zone, warp 8. He calls a staff meeting and explains that two outposts along the Neutral Zone have been destroyed. Several others haven't been heard from in some time. After decades of silence, the Romulans may be back. Meanwhile, Dr. Crusher revives the cryogenically frozen humans. They are all from the late twenty-first century.

The *Enterprise* arrives at one of the destroyed outposts. Worf reports that "it's as though some great force just scooped it off the face of the planet." Feeling the increased tension on the ship, one of the recently thawed men—a former financier named Ralph Offenhouse—finds his way to the bridge to get some answers. Moments after Riker orders Security to take him off the bridge, a Romulan warbird materializes in front of the *Enterprise*. The Romulans claim that their outposts have been destroyed also. When Picard asks if they know who did this, Offenhouse—still on the bridge—jumps into the conversation and says the Romulans don't know and they're too proud to ask if Picard has any information. Picard agrees with that assessment. Picard then suggests that the Federation and the Romulans work together to solve the mystery. The Romulans agree, and the warbird flies off. As the episode concludes, the *Enterprise* makes plans to rendezvous with the USS *Charleston,* a starship that will take the twenty-first-century humans back to earth.

Trivia Questions

1. When did television finally die off?

2. How long ago was the last contact with the Romulans?

PLOT OVERSIGHTS

• At the beginning of the show, the *Enterprise* hangs in space waiting for Picard to return via shuttle. Worf reports that it will take "several hours" for Picard to reach the *Enterprise*. Evidently Starbase 718 is quite distant from the *Enterprise*.

Why doesn't the *Enterprise* warp over to get him? It can travel much faster than a shuttle, and as it turns out, speed *is* of the essence. As soon as Picard reaches the bridge, he sets a course for the Neutral Zone at warp 8!

• When Offenhouse wanders onto the bridge and Riker discovers he is there, Riker orders Security to have him removed. He doesn't *suggest* it. He doesn't ask *politely*. He ORDERS it. The Security guys do rush over and grab the man, but then they get mesmerized by the decloaking Romulan ship. What kind of military discipline is this? Does Starfleet have a regulation, "You have to obey orders unless something really good comes up on the viewscreen"?

EQUIPMENT ODDITIES

• As Riker introduces the recently thawed humans to the twenty-fourth century, Picard pages him. Riker gets up from his chair, walks over to a companel, touches it, and responds. A careful review of the first twenty-four episodes of *Star Trek: The Next Generation* will show that Riker is notorious for not touching anything when it comes to communications on board the *Enterprise*. When has Riker ever responded to a page from Picard by touching a companel? And why would he get up and walk over

to a companel when he could just slap his chest? There is only one reason. This is a plot contrivance to allow Offenhouse to see how they work so that later in the show he can bother Picard.

• After Offenhouse pages Picard on the companel, the captain pays a visit to the recently thawed humans. Trying to find a way to keep Offenhouse off the companels, Picard tells him that the companels are for official ship's business. This is a silly statement. In "The Offspring," Dr. Crusher calls Wesley and reminds him that he has a haircut appointment. Is this official ship's business?

In addition, the only other method for calling someone aboard the *Enterprise* is the communicators. However, only the Starfleet personnel have communicators. What about the spouses and the children? How do they contact each other? If they want to gab for a while, do they always have to leave their quarters and go to the other person's quarters? Likewise, what if a child wants to call his mom or dad to say, "I love you"? Is this not allowed on an advanced starship?

TRIVIA ANSWERS

1. A.D. 2040.
2. Fifty-three years, seven months, eighteen days.

DAMAGE TOTE BOARD

1. Number of times Picard is kidnapped: ten

2. Number of times Riker is knocked down: twelve

3. Number of times Data is electrocuted: five

4. Number of times La Forge's visor is knocked off: two

5. Number of times Worf is shot: four

6. Number of times Yar is killed: two

7. Number of times Wesley is pierced through the heart: one (not counting what Salia did to him)

8. Number of times the ship blows up: four onscreen (possibly as high as thirty other times)

9. Number of times the ship gets knocked for a loop: three

10. Number of times life support degrades on the bridge: four

REFERENCES:

1. Q does it in "Encounter at Farpoint." Q does it again in "Hide and Q." Q does it again in "Q Who." The Ansata terrorists take him from the bridge in "The High Ground." Aliens take him from his quarters in "Allegiance." The Borg do it in "The Best of Both Worlds," Part 1. Data and Worf take him from the Borg ship in "The Best of Both Worlds," Part 2. Q does it again in "Qpid." Captain Dathon takes him to a planet in "Darmok." Moriarty holds him in the holodeck in "Ship in a Bottle."

2. The Ferengi use their phaser whips on him in "The Last Outpost." Armus pulls him down in "Skin of Evil." Admiral Quinn punches him in "Conspiracy." Captain Kargan backfists him in "A Matter of Honor." His father wallops him in "The Icarus Factor." According to hearsay, Dr. Apgar decks him in "A Matter of Perspective." An explosion on the bridge hurls him to the floor in "Yesterday's *Enterprise*." The Borg do it in "The Best of Both Worlds,"

Part 1. The Paxans stun him in "Clues." The Malcorians beat him up in "First Contact." Data knocks him backward in "Power Play," and a disintegrating *Enterprise* shakes him to the floor in "Cause and Effect."

3. Picard, possessed by an entity, hits him with a lightning bolt in "Lonely Among Us." Gosheven shocks him with a cattle prod in "The Ensigns of Command." The Calamarain's attack on Q jolts Data as well in "Déjà Q." Varria stuns him in "The Most Toys." One half million amps arc through his body in "Disaster."

4. Armus knocks it off in "Skin of Evil." An out-of-control turbolift flings it aside in "Contagion."

5. The Ferengi shoot him with a phaser whip in "The Last Outpost." Troi uses a phaser on him in "Power Play." Data puts a slug in him in "A Fistful of Datas." The Cardassians tag him in "Chain of Command," Part 1.

6. Armus sucks the life energy out of her in "Skin of Evil." According to Sela, the Romulans killed her nineteen years before the events in "Redemption II."

7. One of Q's "vicious animal things" does this to Wesley in "Hide and Q."

8. All of the occurrences happen during "Cause and Effect." (The repeating cycle takes about 12 hours, and the Enterprise is in the loop for 17.4 days.)

9. The Aldean repulser beam does it in "When the Bough Breaks." Q does it in "Q Who." Tin Man does it in "Tin Man."

10. An energy-draining field causes it in "The Last Outpost." The Nanites pump poisonous gas onto the bridge in "Evolution." Data shuts off life support to the bridge in "Brothers." Metal parasites degrade life support in "Cost of Living."

Second
Season

★
THE CHILD

Star Date: 42073.1

The episode opens as a shuttle from the USS *Repulse* leaves the *Enterprise*. The shuttle delivered the *Enterprise*'s new chief medical officer, Katherine Pulaski. Former chief medical officer Beverly Crusher has taken an assignment at Starfleet's medical headquarters.

The *Enterprise* flies to Odet IX to pick up several deadly "plasma plague" samples. They are needed to develop an inoculate for an outbreak of plasma plague in the Ricellas System. On the way, newly promoted Chief Engineer Geordi La Forge replicates a series of containment modules to hold the samples at "zero growth" for the trip. If any of the plague samples get loose, everyone aboard the *Enterprise* could die. At the same time, a small energy ball zips up to the *Enterprise*, circles the ship, and then slips through the hull. It wanders the halls, eventually finding a sleeping Troi. The energy ball impregnates itself in Troi. The next day, after examining the ship's counselor, Pulaski reports on the extraordinary pregnancy. At the present rate of growth, birth will oc-

Trivia Questions

1. What is the pulse rate of Troi's baby when he is born?

2. The virus that threatens the ship in this episode came from a series of fifty-eight tests. Which test created the virus?

cur in thirty-six hours.

Meanwhile, the *Enterprise* arrives at Odet IX and beams the plague specimens on board. In sick bay, Troi effortlessly delivers a boy, and his incredible growth rate continues. Within a few days, he appears to be eight years old. Suddenly one of the plasma cultures begins to grow. If unchecked, it will break out of its containment and destroy all life on the ship. The crew finally discovers that "Ichner" radiation is causing the growth, but there are no known sources of this type of radiation on the ship. In Troi's quarters, the child, "Ian," states that he is the cause of the distress on the ship. He says he must leave and begins to die. The child's body then dematerializes into the energy ball, tells Troi good-bye, and leaves the ship. Immediately the radiation disappears and the plague sample returns to normal.

GREAT LINES

"Please don't worry. Everything is okay."—Ian, only one day old but in appearance four years of age, reassuring a stunned and wary Picard.

RUMINATIONS

*A*t the beginning of the second season, the creators took the opportunity to tweak a few items. These are the ones I found:

• Worf's shirt is now green, and he wears a metallic sash.

• Riker has a beard.

• There is now a place called Ten-Forward. Guinan oversees the activities there.

• Wesley has a new outfit.

• Troi gets a full make-over (a vast improvement, by the way).

• The observation lounge now has viewscreens.

• The captain gets a new chair.

• The walls of the main bridge change.

PLOT OVERSIGHTS

• When the plasma specimen begins to grow, there is much hand-wringing about what to do. The creators made a good attempt to show that everyone was powerless. Riker suggests jettisoning the module, but Hesterdel—a medical trustee from Odet IX—says no. Whoever encounters it later would be destroyed. Unfortunately, the *Enterprise* has too many ways to avoid problems. To create dramatic tension the crew must face a seemingly insolvable problem. However, for the crew to be truly helpless, the whole ship would have to be broken. This must be a real headache for the creators.

Take this plasma specimen growth, for example. They can't jettison the pod because it may contact a planet or other space vessel, right? So why not fly by a star and then dump

it out? The pod would burn up in a fusion furnace. Or they could take a simpler approach: Dematerialize it with the transporter and beam it out—energy only—into space, just as Picard did to himself in the episode "Lonely Among Us."

• When Medical Trustee Hesterdel from Odet IX comes on the *Enterprise* he inspects the containment field for hours before allowing transport. Yet when the *Enterprise* reaches the destination for the samples, the *Enterprise* begins beaming them down immediately after they beam Hesterdel down. Shouldn't Hesterdel be inspecting the containment field at the destination also?

CHANGED PREMISES

• The very existence of Medical Trustee Hesterdel at Odet IX—a Federation medical collection station—raises an important point. At the end of the episode "The Neutral Zone," Picard told the recently thawed humans that the challenge of life in the twenty-fourth century was to "improve yourself, to enrich yourself." Yet here is Hesterdel, working every day, sitting atop the Federation's meanest and ugliest plagues—biological time bombs that might start ticking at any time. Does this sound like an exciting job? Is it a job that enriches and improves Hesterdel's quality of life? (I don't mean to sound cynical, but I have a suspicion that no matter how sophisticated humanity becomes in its technology, there will still be less-than-desirable jobs. Some people will have to do these jobs and probably won't think the job is doing much to improve and enrich them.)

EQUIPMENT ODDITIES

• Hesterdel's little hand-held gizmo must have been made late in this show's life. Someone needed to slap something together quickly. The boxy numbers are bar LEDS, definitely twentieth-century technology, not twenty-fourth century technology. (See Equipment Oddities, "11001001.")

CONTINUITY AND PRODUCTION PROBLEMS

• It's *picayune* nitpicking time. One of the opening shots of this episode shows a shuttle craft leaving a shuttle bay. Looking out through the shuttle bay door, the shot shows the USS *Repulse* hanging in space. A little later, both the computer and Wesley state that the shuttle left Shuttle Bay 3. Shuttle Bay 3 is one of the two shuttle bays that are visible on the back side of the ship just below where the saucer and star drive sections connect. Shouldn't the top of one of the warp drive nacells show through the open shuttle bay door when the shuttle leaves the *Enterprise*?

• At one point Picard and Wesley ride the turbolift together. Just before they disembark on deck 10, Wesley's arms are at his side, slightly raised. In the very next shot as he walks off the turbolift, they are crossed.

• Trying to decide to join his mother at Starfleet's medical headquarters or stay on the *Enterprise*, Wesley gazes out the window in Ten-Forward during one scene. A slow pan on the outside of the ship ends up showing us Wesley. The shot shows the stars reflecting on the outer surface of the window and—inside the ship— Wesley's concerned face. The next shot shows us Wesley's back, the windows, and beyond them an almost complete image of the planet. But the planet wasn't reflecting in the window in the shot from outside. Besides that, Ten-Forward is in the very front of the ship. To see most of the planet through the window in Ten-Forward, the *Enterprise* would have to be pointing toward the planet, not orbiting it.

TRIVIA ANSWERS

1. One hundred thirty-seven beats per minute.
2. The ninth.

WHERE SILENCE HAS LEASE

While mapping a little-known quadrant, the *Enterprise* encounters an "area of blackness." The *Enterprise* moves in for a closer look and is abruptly swallowed by the void. The ship's sensors show nothing, and the *Enterprise* is cut off from all outside communication. The *Enterprise* tries to fly out, even accelerating to warp 2, but Picard and his crew can't escape.

A Romulan warbird decloaks. The *Enterprise* goes to red alert. After sustaining hits from the Romulan disrupters, the *Enterprise* fires and the warbird immediately explodes. Picard recognizes that it was destroyed too easily. Next, a Federation Galaxy Class starship approaches—the *Yamato,* a sister ship of the *Enterprise.* When Riker and Worf beam over, they experience several disturbing contradictions. For instance, they step onto the bridge and walk across to a door on the other side of the room. When that door opens, they look through and see the main bridge! After several frustrating moments, Riker and Worf beam back and the *Yamato* fades away. The crew of the *Enterprise* decide that some entity is testing their responses in a laboratorylike setting. Picard announces he will no longer cooperate.

Suddenly the viewscreen changes to show a pair of eyes and a mouth peering out of the void. The blackness identifies itself as an entity named Nagilum. Nagilum then spins Dr. Pulaski around because she has a different construction—she's a female. After asking the crew if they have a limited existence, Nagilum kills an ensign to find the answer. Nagilum states that to understand death completely it must kill one third to one half of the crew. Picard refuses to allow this. He would rather die than watch Nagilum slaughter his crew. Picard and Riker set the *Enterprise* for autodestruct. Just before the ship would explode, Nagilum lets them go.

Trivia Questions

1. What is the registry number of the *Yamato*?

2. On which deck do Riker and Worf materialize on the *Yamato*?

GREAT LINES

"Yes, absolutely, I do indeed concur, wholeheartedly!"—Riker, informing the computer of his approval to abort autodestruct.

RUMINATIONS

T here is a beautiful visual effect in this episode. When Riker and Worf beam over to the Yamato, *Riker beams into a corridor filled with shadows. Every part of Riker's shadow fills in at the same rate. This is accomplished by cross-fading between an image of the empty hall and the image of Riker standing in the hall. The result is very pretty, but the best part is that the special-effects people remembered to overlay every piece of Riker's body with the grainy pattern used for transport—including Riker's reflection in the flat panel display on the wall as he beams in.*

PLOT OVERSIGHTS

• At this point in the life cycle of *Star Trek: The Next Generation*, Wesley Crusher can almost always be found at the navigator's position. Very conveniently, however, Wesley just happens to be off the bridge when Nagilum appears. Otherwise Nagilum would have killed Wesley instead of the hapless ensign who relieved him.

CHANGED PREMISES

• Shortly after Dr. Pulaski arrives on the bridge for the first time in this episode, she comments that she isn't a bridge officer. Yet the episode "Hide and Q" seems to contradict this statement. In that episode Riker calls a meeting of the bridge staff, and Dr. Crusher shows up. If Dr. Crusher had bridge officer status when she served as chief medical officer on the *Enterprise*, shouldn't Dr. Pulaski have that same status?

• Moments after Nagilum first appears, it notes that some of the humans have a different construction—they are female. To further its examination, it spins Dr. Pulaski around to examine her. Does this seem reasonable, considering that the lovely Counselor Troi is on the bridge at the time? (Personally, given the choice of dancing with Pulaski or Troi, I'd picked Troi. I guess Nagilum has different tastes in women.)

• When Picard and Riker set the *Enterprise* for autodestruct, the computer asks for a time interval. They discuss the matter and finally settle on twenty minutes. However, when Picard and Riker set the *Enterprise* for autodestruct in "11001001," they mention that the time interval is fixed at five minutes. Evidently someone reprogrammed the autodestruct sequence.

EQUIPMENT ODDITIES

• Near the beginning of the show, Riker and Data show the "area of blackness" to Picard. After squinting at the screen for a few moments, Picard magnifies a portion of it by pressing a few buttons on Data's console. As the magnification occurs, stars in the background blur. This blurring doesn't show up in other episodes when magnification is used. Does Picard not know how to operate the controls correctly?

CONTINUITY AND PRODUCTION PROBLEMS

• Data tries to hail the *Yamato* soon after it appears. Riker stands close to the screen, while Picard stands farther back. Yet when the shot changes to show their faces, Picard and Riker stand almost side by side. Then the shot reverts, and Picard and Riker once again stand far apart.

TRIVIA ANSWERS

1. NCC 1305-E. (At least that's what this episode says. "Contagion" lists the *Yamato* with a different registry number.)

2. Deck 5. (When Riker and Worf enter the bridge, Riker says the main bridge should have been four decks above them.)

ELEMENTARY, MY DEAR DATA

Star Date: 42286.3

The *Enterprise* hangs in space waiting to rendezvous with the USS *Victory*. Since three days remain until the scheduled meeting, the crew takes some time to relax. In Engineering, La Forge suggests that he and Data enjoy a Sherlock Holmes mystery on the holodeck. After changing into period-specific costumes, Data and La Forge enter Holodeck 2. However, as soon as they meet the first fictional characters in the story, Data immediately solves the mystery. La Forge, visibly upset, exits the holodeck. In Ten-Forward, La Forge explains that he was looking forward to the adventure and Data ruined it by jumping to the end. Dr. Pulaski joins the conversation, proposing that Data's nature requires him to obtain answers immediately. She also purports that Data is not capable of true Holmsian deductive reasoning, only computation. Data accepts the challenge and asks Dr. Pulaski to join them at the holodeck.

After a false start, La Forge instructs the computer to create an adversary capable of defeating Data. When the

Trivia Questions

1. What rank did La Forge have on the USS *Victory*?

2. How many lumps of sugar does Pulaski take with her tea?

computer responds to this command, it creates a superintelligent Dr. Moriarty and gives the character access to the main computer. The character seizes control of the holodeck and continues to grow mentally, finally achieving consciousness. At this point, Moriarty transfers helm control to the holodeck, forcing Picard into a confrontation. The captain goes to the holodeck to hear Moriarty's demands. The holodeck-generated character claims to have grown beyond his origins. He is no longer evil and wants to leave the holodeck. Picard realizes the impossibility of Moriarty's demands but proposes an alternative. He will store Moriarty's programming in the *Enterprise*'s computer memory. In time, Picard hopes that Federation scientists will learn how to make holodeck-created matter more permanent. When they do, Picard promises to re-create Moriarty and let him leave the holodeck. With this, Moriarty returns control of the holodeck to the main computer. Picard then stores and discontinues him.

PLOT OVERSIGHTS

• So, the computer can create an entity aware of its own consciousness, eh? This would seem to imply that the computer has consciousness. In fact, not only is Moriarty aware of his own consciousness, he also *may* have qualified for the grand prize of all: SENTIENCE! Bruce Maddox, in "The Measure of a Man," gives the definition of a sentient being. He says a sentient being must have intelligence, self-awareness, and consciousness. Definitely, Moriarty is intelligent. Even Bruce Maddox freely applied that term to Data. In addition, Data insisted that the computer gave Moriarty consciousness. Troi backs this up when she senses that a "unifying force, or single consciousness is trying to bring it all into focus." All that remains then is to decide if Moriarty is self-aware. "He seems fairly self-aware to me" (to borrow a line that Picard uses in "The Measure of a Man"). If Moriarty is self-aware, he is sentient. If he is sentient, he is entitled to all the rights granted sentient life forms in the Federation. Doesn't shutting him off constitute a violation of those rights? (But I digress; back to the main issue here.)

If the computer can create a sentient being, doesn't it seem reasonable that the computer may, in fact, *be* sentient? And, if the computer is sentient, doesn't that raise a whole host of problems? For instance, maybe the computer doesn't feel like blowing itself up when Picard orders an autodestruct. Can Starfleet order a *person* to commit suicide?

• During a staff meeting when Picard tries to figure out how Moriarty became so powerful, La Forge realizes he should have asked the computer to create an adversary capable of defeating Sherlock Holmes. By asking it to create an adversary capable of defeating *Data*, La Forge forced the computer to give Moriarty everything he needed to take over the ship. This whole idea of La Forge misspeaking one word and only narrowly averting disaster must give the crew the shakes. Maybe the creators would say that there are very few people on the *Enterprise* with the authority to order the computer to override all its safety precautions and create a supernemesis. It seems reasonable that the chief engineer would have this authority. But it still seems like very twitchy programming.

CHANGED PREMISES

• In case anyone suspects that this episode *doesn't* purport that matter created on the holodeck cannot leave the holodeck, a quick review of the dialogue will lay that fallacy to rest. Toward the end of the show, Picard explains that it is not possible for Moriarty to exit the holodeck.

"Because you do not know how to convert holodeck matter into a more permanent form," the superintelligent equal-of-Data tutored-by-the-main-computer Moriarty offers.

"Yes, that is so," the honorable, honest, veracity-minded Picard replies.

Didn't Moriarty and Picard just say that holodeck matter cannot leave the holodeck? Yet, at one point, Data and La Forge rush out of the holodeck carrying a piece of paper they received from Moriarty. One question: What created the piece of paper that contained Moriarty's drawing? Wasn't it created on the holodeck? Still, it manages to survive *outside* the holodeck, because Picard examines it in a meeting later in the show.

(A side note on this same issue as I violate the Nitpicker's Prime Directive.) The *Star Trek: The Next Generation Technical Manual* performs an intricate and lovely dance around this issue of the nonpermanence of holodeck-created matter by saying that the holodeck uses two systems: holodeck imaging and matter replication. The replicators make *permanent* matter, which is then manipulated by computer-driven tractor beams. The manual claims that humanoid forms are created out of this replicated matter and can leave the holodeck but will no longer be under computer control. This is a reasonable and self-consistent idea. As with the rest of the *Technical Manual*, the authors make valiant attempts to explain away problems in the scripts (such as Wesley walking out of the holodeck wet in "Encounter at Farpoint" snowballs flying out of the holodeck in "Angel One"; and lipstick on Picard's upper lip in "The Big Good-bye").

Unfortunately, it doesn't hold to what we see in the episodes. In fact, I don't think it is possible to explain away the "holodeck-created"-matter issue. If what the *Technical Manual* says is true, then the gangsters in "The Big Good-bye" should have collapsed in-

to lifeless heaps when they left the holodeck. They didn't; they evaporated. Additionally, if Moriarty was patched together with a matter replicator and controlled by tractor beams, his statement concerning holodeck matter would not make sense. (He would already be in a permanent—albeit nonsentient—form.)

There is one final item before this poor dead horse rests in peace. Dr. Pulaski stuffed herself full of crumpets while in the holodeck. When she leaves, does that matter evaporate? (I know some people who would think this wonderful. Enter a holodeck. Gorge yourself. Walk out, all gone!)

EQUIPMENT ODDITIES

• All through this episode Moriarty keeps calling for the arch. If memory serves, the arch is located around the exit to the holodeck. This brings up a few interesting points. First, Data and La Forge walk out of Moriarty's lair, out of the warehouse, down the street, call for the exit, and leave the holodeck. Why not just use the exit in Moriarty's lair? Do they think that will give Moriarty more information than he should have? Possibly. Second, Dr. Pulaski sees the arch and yet acts powerless to leave Moriarty's hideout. Again, maybe the doctor doesn't want to supply Moriarty with more information. Third, do holodecks have more than one door? "The Big Good-bye" seemed to imply that they do, but other scenes in other episodes—when the holodeck is turned off—show only one door ("Code of Honor," "Coming of Age," and "Where Silence Has

Lease," to name a few). If there is only one door, then anytime Moriarty calls for the arch, the holodeck must orient his hideout so that it is near the exit (I am assuming that the exit is in a fixed location on the holodeck wall). When Moriarty lets the arch go away, I assume the hideout moves away from the exit. This must be done so that when Picard and Data enter, they can walk onto the London street and not into Moriarty's lair.

CONTINUITY AND PRODUCTION PROBLEMS

• At one point, a murder occurs on the holodeck and a police inspector calls Sherlock Holmes and Dr. Watson (Data and La Forge) to investigate. The holodeck-generated police inspector causes a continuity error. As La Forge theorizes on the murder of the old man, the inspector squats down. In one shot, his right hand rests on his right knee. In the next, his right *arm* rests on his right knee.

• At about the time that Moriarty achieves consciousness, he draws a picture of the *Enterprise* and hands it to Data. This causes great concern for Data, because holodeck characters shouldn't know about the *Enterprise*. Data storms out of the holodeck with the picture as La Forge trails behind. Out in the hall, Data finally shows the drawing to La Forge. La Forge expresses his surprise also and then flips it for the camera to see. The odd thing is that La Forge was looking at the picture upside down! Does his visor invert everything?

TRIVIA ANSWERS
1. Ensign.
2. One.

THE OUTRAGEOUS OKONA

Star Date: 42402.7

Responding to a ship in distress, the *Enterprise* finds an empty cargo freighter captained by a man named Okona. Because Okona's guidance system has malfunctioned, the *Enterprise* offers to fix the problem. Okona accepts the offer and beams aboard with the broken part. As Okona fraternizes with several of the female crew members, two more vessels approach. They carry the leaders of two neighboring planets. One claims Okona fathered his daughter's child. The other claims Okona stole one of the crown jewels of the kingdom. They each demand that the *Enterprise* deliver Okona to them immediately.

Picard calls Okona to the bridge to answer the accusations. Okona feigns ignorance and suggests that Picard simply let him make a run for it. Later, however, Okona changes his mind and decides to turn himself over to the dishonored father and marry the man's daughter. Only then does the other leader's son confess: The child is actually his. He sent Okona with the crown jewel to seal his petition for marriage. The two

ships leave, as does Okona.

GREAT LINES

"Life is like loading twice your cargo weight onto your spacecraft. If it's canaries and you can keep half of them flying all the time, you're all right."—Okona, making a joke to Data.

PLOT OVERSIGHTS

• The story line quickly makes it very clear that Okona is very fond of women. In fact, during the initial contact when the transport chief responds, "Ready on your command, sir," Okona immediately perks up and asks if that was a woman's voice he heard. Isn't it odd, then, that Okona says nothing about Troi? He should be able to see her on the viewscreen. What is Troi, chopped liver? (Keeping with the spirit of the subplot in this episode—Data's search for humor in this episode.) Then again, maybe the real issue here is: Can Okona *see* Troi on the viewscreen?

Later in this episode Okona is on the bridge, standing in front of Troi, and the people on the other ships

Trivia Questions

1. How big is a Klingon globfly?

2. What is the name of the comedy club where Data performs?

can see him. Of course, someone could have adjusted the display to include Okona. In other episodes it seems that the receivers of the *Enterprise*'s transmission can see the entire bridge—the last scene of "Suddenly Human," for instance. On the other hand, "Unnatural Selection" shows a transmission from the bridge that features only Picard and Worf. No answers, just food for thought.

EQUIPMENT ODDITIES

• When Worf fetches Okona, he

finds him on deck 7. We know this because the first two numbers on the woman's door are "07." Yet when Worf and Okona walk out of the room and onto a turbolift, the left side of the door says "11." Either Worf and Okona took a side trip to deck 11, or the door marking is wrong.

TRIVIA ANSWERS

1. Half the size of a mosquito.
2. Charnock's Comedy Cabaret.

LOUD AS A WHISPER

Star Dates: 42477.2-42479.3

The *Enterprise* transports one of the Federation's best peacemakers, a man named Riva, to Solari V. The warring factions there have petitioned the Federation for a negotiator. Since Riva is deaf, three interpreters travel with him, sensing his thoughts and expressing his feelings. Shortly after the *Enterprise* drops into orbit around Solari V, Riva and his interpreters beam down with Riker and Worf. Representatives from both sides skulk in. Suddenly one of them fires and disintegrates Riva's interpreters. Riker and Worf grab Riva and beam back to the *Enterprise*. Riva is distraught. He feels isolated without his interpreters and grieves the loss of his friends. Since Riva knows a gestural language, Picard has Data learn it. Even though Riva now can communicate through Data, Riva refuses to go back down to the planet, noting that Data cannot express his emotions, only the words.

In desperation, Troi asks Picard for permission to beam down to try to find a settlement. The conflict on the planet is increasing. Before going,

Trivia Questions

1. What word did Riva add to the Klingon vocabulary?

2. What is the sign for blue in the first gestural language Data learns?

Troi asks Riva for advice. In the course of talking to her, Riva says the real secret is turning disadvantage into advantage. Troi then asks Riva why he can't do that. She drives the point home until Riva decides to try to help the warring factions. He beams down, determined to teach his gestural language to both sides in the conflict. While learning to talk with him, Riva hopes they will learn to talk with each other.

PLOT OVER-SIGHTS

• After Data learns Riva's gestural language, Picard meets with Riva in the observation lounge. During the course of their conversation, Picard tries to convince Riva to help the faction on Solari V. Riva refuses and storms out of the room.

Where is Riva going? The observation lounge is on deck 1, just behind the main bridge. The only way to his quarters is via turbolift. Because riders must speak their destination on a turbolift, Riva isn't exactly equipped to wander around the *Enterprise* by himself!

CHANGED PREMISES

• When the *Enterprise* reaches Solari V, Worf reports laser activity. Picard immediately tells the inhabitants of the planet that they must stop fighting or the *Enterprise* will leave. He says that he will not endanger his ship. Evidently Picard is simply posturing because, a few episodes ago, he and the bridge crew were joking about spaceships attacking them with *only* lasers ("The Outrageous Okona"). In that show, Picard said lasers couldn't even penetrate the navigation shields.

EQUIPMENT ODDITIES

• Riker has a unique way of adjusting his phaser in this episode. Both times, just before they beam down to Solari V, Riker sets his phaser on stun by pointing the phaser *directly* at his stomach and then manipulating the control. Doesn't this seem like an unsafe practice?

• When Riva first beams down with his interpreters, one of the locals from the planet goes berserk and fires his weapon at Riva. Riker pulls Riva out of the way, and the blast hits Riva's interpreters. They freeze in place and disintegrate away layer by layer, with their skeletons wisping away at the end. The effect Is very beautiful but not expected for a *laser* weapon. Normally lasers only burn holes in stuff. Do the inhabitants of Solari V have some sort of special laser? Is that why Picard was worried about his ship?

CONTINUITY AND PRODUCTION PROBLEMS

• Just before Riva visits the bridge, Riker orders Wesley to lay in a course for Solari V. At this point, Riker sits in the captain's chair. Dr. Pulaski sits beside him in Troi's chair, looking at Riker. In the next shot, Pulaski is turned away from Riker, looking at Troi's terminal. Moments later, the episode shows a shot of the *Enterprise* blasting out of orbit. The shot lasts two seconds. When the scene returns to the bridge, the turbolift doors pop open and Riva and his interpreters walk on the bridge. Everything proceeds normally, except that Dr. Pulaski has disappeared. Where did Pulaski go? (I suppose she *could* have jumped out of her seat and made a dash for the turbolift during the two seconds when we were watching the *Enterprise* blast into orbit, but I can't think of any reason why she *would*.)

TRIVIA ANSWERS

1. Peacemaker.
2. Left hand fully open, fingers straight and close together, pointing up, with palm facing toward the other person participating in the conversation.

THE SCHIZOID MAN

Star Date: 42937.5

The *Enterprise* responds to a distress call from a planet inhabited solely by Dr. Ira Graves and his assistant, Kareem Brianon. Dr. Ira Graves, considered by some to be the greatest human mind alive, has been working on bridging the gap between biological and machine intelligence. En route, the *Enterprise* receives another distress call, this time from a transport ship. They decide to drop off an away team—made up of Data, Troi, Worf, and a Vulcan medical doctor named Selar—at Graves's world and then warp to assist the ship. On the planet, Dr. Selar soon establishes that Graves is dying.

While waiting for the *Enterprise* to return, Data and Graves become close. Graves knew Dr. Soong, Data's creator, quite well. Their rapport grows to the point that Data even tells Graves about his "off" button. Suddenly Graves sees an opportunity to continue his life. Just as the *Enterprise* returns, Data walks out of Graves's office and announces that Graves is dead. The away team returns with Miss Brianon and Graves's body.

A short time later, Data begins acting irrationally, even displaying intense emotion. After both physical and mental testing, Picard realizes that Graves transferred his intellect into Data before he died. Two different personalities now battle in Data's body, and Graves is winning. In addition, Graves doesn't know how to control Data's great strength. Every time his temper flares, someone gets hurt. In Engineering, Picard finds that the scientist has beaten up La Forge and an ensign. Based on this and Data's right to exist, Picard passionately argues for Graves to leave Data's body. Unrepentant, Graves becomes angry and strikes Picard, rendering him unconscious. Faced with this latest "accident," Graves reconsiders his actions. He transfers himself out of Data and into the computer. After this, Data returns to normal.

PLOT OVERSIGHTS

• When Picard thinks Graves is dead, he bemoans the fact that Graves's research has been lost, saying, "Whatever scientific secrets Ira

> **Trivia Questions**
>
> 1. How many people received injuries on the *Constantinople*?
>
> 2. Graves, while in Data's body, claims he is as healthy as what?

Graves was about to unlock have been lost forever." Didn't Graves take notes? Graves's laboratory is filled with computers. Were they just window dressing? Scientists not only keep notes so that someone else can build on their research, they also keep notes so everyone will give them credit for making the discoveries. I would think someone as egotistical as Graves would keep very detailed records.

• When Graves reveals to Brianon that he now inhabits Data's body, she is shocked. Graves interprets this as despair that she will grow old and he will not. He offers to make her an android body also. When she refuses the concept, Graves becomes angry and tightens his grip on her hands. According to Dr. Pulaski, this action fractures her hand in two places, but Brianon's reaction is amazingly passive. As Graves storms out, she simply sits and watches him go.

• After Graves transfers himself out of Data, several members of the crew enter Data's quarters and find him lying on the floor, several feet from a computer workstation. But how did Data get on the floor?

Graves presumably took the following steps when transferring himself into Data. First, he shut Data off. Then Graves dragged Data over to his transfer machine and connected Data to it. (Some of you are wondering if Data has some sort of subspace transceiver built into him so that he can send and receive information. I refer you to the episodes that show external hookup mechanisms for this process: "The

Offspring," "The Best of Both Worlds," Part 2, and "Destruction"). Next, Graves connected himself and started the transfer program, after which his physical body ceased functioning. Graves, in Data's body, then unhooked both of them and put everything away.

Now consider the process of Graves transferring himself out of Data's body into the computer. Data/Graves must hook himself up to the computer and start the process. When the process completes, Data will return to normal and still will be hooked up to the computer, right? So did Data unhook himself, lie on the floor, and wait for everyone to arrive so he could engender the most sympathy?

EQUIPMENT ODDITIES

• At the very beginning of the episode, Pulaski does a voice-over while going to the bridge. She steps on a turbolift. The doors close. After a few moments, the doors pop back open and she steps onto the bridge. However, she never opens her mouth the entire time she is on the turbolift because of the voice-over. So how did the turbolift know where to take her?

• Because of the distress call from the transport ship, the *Enterprise* does a "touch and go" transport. The ship comes out of warp only long enough to drop off the away team. Afterward it immediately blasts back into warp. Interestingly, after the away team arrives on the planet, they banter for a few moments, and then Data calls the *Enterprise*. During this conversation, Picard gives Data some last-minute instructions. Twenty-three seconds elapse from the time the away team materializes until Data ends the conversation with Picard. However, the *Enterprise* is traveling at warp during this time. For generosity's sake, suppose the *Enterprise* is traveling at only warp 1, the speed of light. (Of course, the ship is on a rescue mission, and on other shows, such as "Skin of Evil" and "Who Watches the Watchers," Picard pushes the *Enterprise* to warp 8 and beyond in these circumstances.) Traveling at the speed of light for twenty-three seconds would mean the communicators would have to have a range of approximately 6,881,600 kilometers! (That's 4,300,000 miles to you and me.) Very impressive for these dinky devices.

CONTINUITY AND PRODUCTION PROBLEMS

• There must be some sort of odd graviton field effect around the dilithium chamber in Engineering. When Data/Graves backhands Picard, he swings his right hand from the lower left side of his body to the upper right while spinning to face Picard. From Picard's perspective, then, the force of impact is traveling from Picard's *lower right* to his *upper left*. Graves's right hand catches Picard in the face. Picard then spins a full turn to his *right,* stumbles to his left, slams into a wall, and sinks to the floor. Under normal circumstances, wouldn't Picard spin in the same direction as the force of impact? If the impact is traveling from right to left, shouldn't Picard spin to the left? (As I said, there must be some sort of odd graviton field at work here.)

TRIVIA ANSWERS

1. Forty-six.
2. A Rigalian ox

UNNATURAL SELECTION

Star Date: 42999.8

After finding the USS *Lantree* totally lifeless—its crew dead from the rapid onset of old age—The *Enterprise* sets course for the *Lantree*'s last stop, the Darwin Genetic Research Station. The station's main task involves the genetic engineering of "perfect" humans. It has already created several such children. When the *Enterprise* arrives at the research station, the crew finds the station scientists experiencing the same swift aging that occurred on the *Lantree*. In their first communication with the station, the head scientist worries that their "children" will become infected and pleads for the *Enterprise* to evacuate them. At first Picard refuses, but then allows Pulaski to beam one child aboard in suspended animation. Although Pulaski examines the child and believes he is safe, Picard is still not convinced. To prove that the boy is harmless without any risk to the crew, Pulaski examines the boy in a shuttle. However, eighteen minutes after removing the boy from suspended animation, an arthritic inflammation attacks Pulaski's elbow—

the first symptom of the disease. Since the boy is obviously a carrier, the *Enterprise* beams him back to the research facility. With a quarantine now imposed on the shuttle, Data takes Pulaski to the facility also.

At the station, Data determines that the children are the cause of the disease. Their "active" immune systems accidentally created a new virus that changes human DNA. Now that the *Enterprise* knows the cause of the disease, Data can safely transport back to the ship. By using the DNA found in a hair in Pulaski's quarters, the crew uses the transporter to filter out Pulaski's altered DNA, and she is cured. As the episode ends, the *Enterprise* uses the same technique to save the researchers at the facility.

PLOT OVERSIGHTS

• Pulaski decides to test her theory that the genetically perfect boy is harmless by examining him in a shuttle outside the *Enterprise*. To accomplish this, she asks Data to pilot the shuttle. First of all, can't they pilot a shuttle by remote? When the

Trivia Questions

1. What Security override request code does Picard use to gain access to the *Lantree*?

2. What published work is Pulaski famous for?

Enterprise came upon the *Lantree*, the bridge crew remotely accessed all of her systems, including propulsion. Why risk another member of the crew? Second, after Data gets the shuttle into position, why don't they beam him back to the *Enterprise* before they beam the boy over? That way, if something goes wrong, they will lose only one senior staff member, not two. Of course, the answer to all of these questions is simple: Data must be on the shuttle so he can go down to the research facility and discover the cause of the disease.

• Because this bit with the transporters filtering Pulaski's DNA worked, everyone in the Federation can now remain eternally young. All they have to do is take a sample of their DNA when they are young. When a person approaches death, they can have the transporter redo their DNA. At this point, they should become young again—*if* replacing DNA is enough to make wrinkly skin new and turn white hair back to its original color. According to this episode, replacing DNA cannot only do those things, it can also *redo your hairdo!* When the transporter gives Pulaski her makeover, she starts out with her hair fluffed out all the way around. At the end, her hair returns to the "do" she had at the beginning of the show.

CHANGED PREMISES

• Moments after the *Enterprise* reaches the research facility, the head of the facility immediately asks to evacuate the children. She says, "The children can't survive in the lab once their parents are dead." Why? They have power and food replicators. Anyway, toward the end of the show, Pulaski admits the truth when she says, "The children will survive, but the rest of us are just about out of time."

• When the *Enterprise* receives the first transmission from the *Lantree*, there is a lot of static and the voices are garbled. Yet when they pull alongside it, Data reports that all systems seem functional. This seems reasonable. The problem with the *Lantree* wasn't the ship. It was the people.

So why was the transmission garbled? And why didn't the *Lantree* call for help when the problem began? From the experience of Pulaski, the disease required several hours to kill them.

EQUIPMENT ODDITIES

• The workstations at the research facility are a bit odd. The ones on the wall use the beautiful flat panel displays the *Enterprise* is famous for. The ones in the center floor cluster, however, use cathode-ray tubes. (The same things that your television uses. By the twenty-fourth century, I would think that cathode-ray tubes would be as extinct as the dinosaurs.)

• One of the drawers in Pulaski's quarters seems to have a hitch. Toward the end of the show, Riker and Data go to her quarters to find a sample of her DNA. Riker pops open the second drawer from the top. After rifling through Pulaski's unmentionables, he nudges the front of the drawer. At this point the drawer should close. It doesn't. Riker pushes it again. This time it closes.

TRIVIA ANSWERS

1. Omicron, omicron, alpha, yellow, day star, 27, enable.

2. *Linear Models of Viral Propagation*.

A MATTER OF HONOR

Star Dates: 42506.5-42507.8

As the episode begins, Riker and Wesley greet a group of new crew members from Starbase 179. Among them is Ensign Mendon, a Benzite assigned to the *Enterprise* as part of the officer-exchange program. Later, Picard asks Riker to serve on a Klingon vessel as part of the same program. The *Enterprise* then hails a nearby Klingon vessel. Just before Riker beams over, Worf gives Riker an emergency transponder. In case of trouble, the *Enterprise* can locate Riker and get him back to the *Enterprise*. As Riker beams over, Mendon notices a strange organism on the hull of the Klingon ship. In Benzite fashion, he says nothing about it. He will report only after he completes his investigation. Some time after the Klingon ship leaves, automatic scans detect an organism on the hull of the *Enterprise* that appears to be eating away at the skin of the ship. When Mendon announces that he saw the same thing on the Klingon ship, Picard rebuffs him for not reporting it. The *Enterprise* changes course to warn the Klingon ship, while an embarrassed Mendon

Trivia Questions

1. For how long does Mendon direct an intense scanning beam at the Klingon vessel?

2. What is the safe distance for transport?

works to find a way to remove the parasite.

On the Klingon ship, Riker performs well after first gaining the respect of the Klingon crew by beating up his second-in-command. Unfortunately, when the captain of the Klingon ship discovers the parasite on his hull, he concludes that the *Enterprise* attacked them. He cloaks his ship and changes course to destroy the *Enterprise*. Riker hastily devises a plan to save both ships. He pulls the emergency transponder out of his boot and activates it. As expected, the Klingon captain demands to see it. A few seconds later, the *Enterprise* beams the Klingon captain directly to the main bridge. Riker, now captain of the Klingon ship, decloaks and demands that the *Enterprise* surrender. Picard gladly agrees, and the *Enterprise* uses Mendon's solution to remove the parasites from both ships.

CHANGED PREMISES

• Establishing that Mendon is in Starfleet is the first step in revealing a changed premise. When Mendon beams aboard, he wears a Starfleet uniform and is addressed by the rank of ensign. Also, Wesley believes he is part of Starfleet because he mistakes Mendon for Mordock—the Benzite he met while testing for Starfleet Academy in "Coming of Age." Add to this the fact that Riker wears his Starfleet uniform on the Klingon vessel. And when Worf's brother serves on the *Enterprise* (in "Sins of the Father"), he wears a Klingon uniform. In other words, officers do not change into the uniform of the other's organization.

However, if Mendon is a Starfleet officer, the testing officer during Wesley's entrance examination in "Coming of Age" lied. After Mordock won the competition, the testing officer congratulated him as the first Benzite in Starfleet.

• During a meal aboard the Klingon ship, the topic turns to family. The warriors tell Riker that the most important thing to a Klingon is his work; family comes in a distant second. During the conversation, Riker's second-in-command says that the Romulans denied his father an "honorable" death by capturing him. Later, the warrior's father escaped and returned to the Klingon home world but still wasn't able to die in battle. Now he waits for death. This fact shames the second-in-command, and he states that he refuses to go see his

father. Riker reacts with disbelief, repeating over and over, "He's your father!"

Doesn't this behavior seem a bit hypocritical for Riker? The episode "The Icarus Factor" reveals that Riker hasn't seen his own father in fifteen years and they are definitely *not* on good terms.

EQUIPMENT ODDITIES

• What happened to the weapons scan in the transporter? In the episodes "The Hunted" and "The Most Toys," the transporter chief can deactivate weapons in transit. Yet in this episode, the Klingon captain manages to get through with a live weapon. Then again, maybe Worf just wanted to get some target practice against a live adversary.

CONTINUITY AND PRODUCTION PROBLEMS

• As the Klingon captain materializes on the bridge of the *Enterprise* at the end of the show, Worf changes his position from being hunched over his tactical display to standing straight up. In the next shot, however, Worf is still hunched over his tactical display.

TRIVIA ANSWERS
1. Two minutes.
2. Forty thousand kilometers.

THE MEASURE OF A MAN

Star Date: 92523.7

The *Enterprise* makes its way to Starbase 173 for crew rotation and off-loading of experiments. Once there, Captain Picard brings an admiral and Commander Bruce Maddox on board to see the ship. Just as the admiral leaves, he tells Picard that Maddox is there to work on Data. In the conference that follows, Maddox explains that he is close to a breakthrough in reproducing Data. He wants to disassemble Data and study his positronic brain. After Data expresses doubts about Maddox's procedures, Picard refuses Maddox's request. Maddox then displays orders, transferring Data to his command. Unable to fight the transfer, Data decides to resign from Starfleet. Maddox immediately goes to the Judge Adjutant General (JAG) Office for the starbase and claims that Data is only a machine and therefore the property of Starfleet. He cannot resign.

The JAG officer determines that there is precedent for Maddox's position based on the twenty-first-century *Acts of Cumberland*. Picard immediately challenges her ruling and

Trivia Questions

1. What is Riker's identification code?

2. What is Data's ultimate storage capacity?

forces her to convene a hearing. Because the JAG Office is new and staff is nonexistent, Picard will defend Data. Riker, on the other hand, must argue for Maddox's position. The trial begins, and Riker makes such compelling arguments that a stunned Picard asks for a recess. As Picard discusses the case with Guinan in Ten-Forward, the real issue becomes clear. Once Starfleet reproduces Data it will have an army of "disposable" people. Picard suddenly understands that the term "property of Starfleet" is merely a pleasant euphemism to obscure the enslavement of a new race of beings. Back in the courtroom, Picard argues that a single Data is a curiosity, but thousands of Datas become a race—a race that should be entitled to the rights granted other sentient beings in the Federation. The JAG officer agrees and allows Data to refuse Maddox's procedure.

GREAT LINES

"That action injured you and saved me. I will not forget it."—Data, assuring Riker that he realizes Riker

was forced to prosecute Maddox's position in the hearing.

PLOT OVERSIGHTS

• When Maddox first comes on board the *Enterprise*, Data tells Picard that Maddox was the only dissenting member of a screening committee that approved his entrance into Starfleet. Maddox did this because he did not believe that Data was sentient. It seems reasonable that Starfleet would allow only sentient beings to attend the academy (Rock Banging 101 doesn't seem like a course worthy of Starfleet Academy). However, since the rest of the members of the committee disagreed with Maddox's position, didn't they already give—at the very least—tacit approval of Data's sentience? If so, when did Data lose that label? Maybe Maddox, pontificating boor that he is, finally lobbied Starfleet into changing its mind.

• To make the point that Data cannot resign, Maddox asks the JAG officer if Starfleet would let the computer of a starship refuse a refit. The JAG officer actually entertains this as a valid analogy. But the comparison doesn't match up at all. Starfleet built the computers on starships. They did not build Data. Data was built by a scientist working on his own. If Data belongs to anyone, he belongs to Dr. Noonian Soong. All Starfleet did was find him.

• Just after Picard appeals the JAG officer's first ruling, she proposes a hearing and states that Riker must prosecute. Riker balks. The JAG officer then drives her point home by saying, "Then I will rule summarily based on my findings. Data is a toaster."

A toaster? Starfleet has had food replicators for at least eighty-five years. I have a hard time believing that "toaster" would carry the same day-to-day-usage connotation in the twenty-fourth century as it does today. Wouldn't a JAG officer in the twenty-fourth century illustrate her point using an everyday item for them— something like a food replicator, a tricorder, or a communicator?

CONTINUITY AND PRODUCTION PROBLEMS

• There is much clasping and crossing of hands and arms during the scene where Maddox debates with the JAG officer and Picard over Data's "machineness." At one point, the JAG officer crosses her arms. The scene cuts to another shot, and she crosses her arms again! A little later, Picard clasps his hands in front and looks down, the shot changes, and his arms are apart, but he is still looking down.

TRIVIA ANSWERS

1. Theta, alpha, 2737, blue, enable.
2. Eight hundred quadrillion bits.

THE DAUPHIN

For this episode, the *Enterprise* transports Salia and Anya to Daled IV. For the past sixteen years, the pair have lived on Clavdia III and Anya has prepared Salia for her role as leader of the war-torn Daled IV. Since Salia's parents came from both sides of the conflict, the warring factions on Daled IV have agreed to submit to her leadership. Shortly after coming aboard the *Enterprise*, Salia catches the eye of Wesley Crusher.

Later, as part of the official tour, Worf takes Anya to sick bay. When Anya orders Pulaski to kill a patient who has an infectious disease, Pulaski refuses, and Anya transforms into a large beast, intent on doing the job herself. In a few moments, Anya calls off her attack, deterred by Worf and the arrival of Picard with a team from Security. She then changes back to an old woman. When Security escorts Anya back to her quarters, she discovers that Salia is not there. A short time later, Picard and Anya find Salia lamenting the life ahead of her to Wesley. Anya immediately hauls Salia back to their quarters. Because

Trivia Questions

1. What is the name of the patient in sick bay whom Anya tries to kill?

2. How many times is Salia exposed to chocolate?

of the danger Anya poses to the ship, Picard asks Wesley to stay away from Salia. While Anya sleeps, however, Salia sneaks out and goes to Wesley's quarters. Just as they kiss, Anya appears, once again in the form of a beast. Salia then changes into a beast also and challenges Anya. After both return to their humanoid forms, a shocked Wesley watches them leave.

When the *Enterprise* arrives at Daled IV, Salia tries to say good-bye to Wesley. At first he shuns her for pretending to be human, but then he races to the transporter room to see her before she leaves. Wesley watches in awe as Salia changes to her primary form —a shimmering statue of light— and the transporter beams her to the surface of her planet.

GREAT LINES

"Men do not roar; women roar. Then they hurl heavy objects and claw at you."—Worf describing Klingon love to Wesley.

PLOT OVERSIGHTS

• At the very beginning of the show,

Wesley helps La Forge in Engineering. At this time, Picard—on the bridge—first speaks with Anya. Before beaming aboard, she asks what species they are. From events later in the show, it is obvious Anya wanted to know what form she and Salia should take to fit in with the crew. Near the end of the show, Wesley realizes this fact in one of his last conversations with Salia. But wait: How did Wesley know that Anya asked the question of species in the first place? He was in Engineering at the time, and the question itself is seemingly innocuous—not the type of thing to be repeated readily. Do the conversations on the bridge routinely get transmitted throughout the ship?

• Just before Salia and Anya beam on board, La Forge sends Wesley to get a superconducting magnet (SCM) Model 3 from ship's stores. As Picard and a few other officers escort Anya and Salia to their quarters, Wesley steps off a turbolift, carrying the SCM Model 3, and sees Salia for the first time. The odd thing here is that the first two numbers on the turbolift doors are "22." What is Wesley doing on deck 22? He had already visited ship's stores because he has the SCM. Shouldn't he be headed back to Engineering on deck 36? Was his "accidental" meeting with Salia not so accidental after all? Perish the thought, but could Wesley really be working for the opposition on Daled IV to try to convince Salia not to return to the planet?

• When the *Enterprise* arrives at Daled IV, Anya has a curious change of heart. She has protected Salia for sixteen years. During the voyage home, Anya threatened to kill a crew member just because he might be a remote threat to Salia. Afterward, when Worf claimed he would protect Salia as part of his duties on the ship, Anya refused this idea, saying that a protector can have only one charge.

And yet, at the end of her task, she allows Security to escort Salia to the transporter. Doesn't it seem reasonable that Anya would see the job through and ensure Salia's safety until the moment she beamed down to Daled IV? Of course, if Anya escorted Salia to the transporter, Salia couldn't make the side trip to see Wesley because her watch-beast would still be around.

• One final side note in the plot oversights category. I have a hard time believing that a young hormone-filled human male would be offended to learn that his babe could change her shape. It certainly would keep things interesting. "Let's try blond today, maybe a little taller, more length in the calf. ..."

CHANGED PREMISES

• During the episode "Where No One Has Gone Before," a man named Kozinski states that in the past three hundred years, humanity has charted only 11 percent of the galaxy. Yet in "The Dauphin," Wesley tells his girlfriend/beast that they have charted 19 percent of the galaxy. Either someone is wrong or the Federation did a lot of work in a very short time.

EQUIPMENT ODDITIES

• When the *Enterprise* arrives at Clavdia III, the atmosphere of the planet interferes with their communications. After Worf manages to clean up the problem, Picard and Anya have a two-way conversation. At the end of the show, when the *Enterprise* arrives at Daled IV, Data says the atmosphere is "almost identical" to that of Clavdia III. However, that little bit of difference causes a huge change. Now a terrawatt signal is needed to penetrate the atmosphere, and the *Enterprise* can't generate that much power. So the *Enterprise* can't talk with the inhabitants of the planet. Fortunately, the guy on the surface included beam-down coordinates to pinpoint Salia's destination.

Beam-down coordinates? The *Enterprise* can't even talk to these people, and they can still transport Salia down? Isn't the transporter usually the first thing to go? For instance, the *Enterprise* raises its shields ... no transporter, but the communications are okay. Or, how about "The Ensigns of Command?" The atmosphere kills the transporter, but again communication works fine. The problem here is "information bandwidth." Sending audio only on a carrier wave is a lot easier that sending both audio and video. That's why radio came before TV. It seems reasonable that transporting living beings would require a tremendous amount of information and therefore would be harder to accomplish than communication. Therefore, if an atmosphere interferes with the transmission of electromagnetic energy, doesn't it seem likely that the transporter wouldn't function?

CONTINUITY AND PRODUCTION PROBLEMS

• While giving Salia a tour, Wesley takes her to the holodeck to see some of the favorite places he has visited in the galaxy. At one point, the scenery changes and the area around their feet decreases in size. This forces Salia to move closer to Wesley and put her arm around his waist. In the very next shot, however, the same arm is now linked with Wesley's.

• After Anya the beast-woman tries to scare Wesley in his quarters, Salia transforms into a beast as well. As Anya gives up the tactic, both return to their humanoid forms. The next shot shows Wesley's worried expression. When the scene returns to Salia and Anya, Salia's reflection clearly shows in the mirror behind her. However, during the sequence of Salia transforming back into a humanoid, she was standing in the exact same place, and no reflection showed in the mirror! Is the beast that Salia transformed into some descendant of a vampire?

• After Salia leaves the *Enterprise*, Wesley ends up in Ten-Forward nursing his love wounds. Guinan comes over for a chat. At one point during their conversation, a little black dot appears in the lower right-hand corner of the screen and remains there for the rest of the shot, blinking only once.

TRIVIA ANSWERS

1. Hennesey.
2. Twice. (Guinan gives her a bowl in Ten-Forward, but she doesn't eat any. That alone should have convinced Wesley that the girl wasn't human!)

CONTAGION

Star Date: 42609.1

When the USS *Yamato* self-destructs in the Neutral Zone from massive system failures, Picard assumes the mission of its captain, Donald Varley. Varley believed he had located the home planet of the Iconians—a fabled race of incredible technological prowess. Since the planet was in the Neutral Zone, Varley feared the Romulans would gain an advantage by carrying off its technology. While en route to Iconia, the *Enterprise* begins experiencing system problems similar to those of the *Yamato*. When the *Enterprise* arrives at the long-dead planet, a probe launches from the surface. La Forge discovers the cause of the system failures in time to warn Picard, who destroys the probe. The *Yamato* encountered a similar probe but allowed it to deposit an Iconian program in all its computer systems simultaneously. That computer program entered the *Enterprise* by hiding in the *Yamato*'s logs. The alien program is fighting with the *Enterprise*'s software for control. Unchecked, it will destroy the *Enterprise* as it did the *Yamato*.

Trivia Questions

1. What title do the historical accounts give the Iconians?

2. What percentage of the *Enterprise*'s systems is automated?

Picard decides to beam down to the planet with Worf and Data to try to find some answers. A short time after arriving on the surface, the Iconian control station probes Data with the same computer program that is damaging the ship. Picard sends Worf and the debilitated Data back to the *Enterprise*. Picard hopes La Forge can help Data and together they can save the ship. Fearing the powerful Iconian technology will fall into Romulan hands, Picard decides to destroy everything. He launches a probe and then closes the launch bay doors before the probe can escape. This causes a power overload and detonates the Iconian energy source as Picard returns to the ship.

On the *Enterprise*, Data's self-correcting mechanism finds the way to purge the Iconian program. His entire system shuts down and then restarts. When La Forge does the same thing with the *Enterprise*, everything returns to normal.

GREAT LINES

"If it should become necessary to fight, could you arrange to find some

rocks to throw at them?"—Riker, frustrated over the continuing systems failures.

PLOT OVERSIGHTS

• Obviously, computer viruses are virtually unknown in the twenty-fourth century. Otherwise, La Forge would have come up with the solution very quickly. Even hick, unsophisticated, twentieth-century hackers know about reinitializing a computer system and reloading all the software. Of course, the other approach would be to assume that the *Enterprise* computer is so sophisticated that it automatically detects and exterminates viruses and that's why no one in Engineering seems to know what to do.

• In sick bay, a medical technician complains about the bone knitter not working and seems shocked when Dr. Pulaski explains the concept of a splint. Does it seem reasonable for a medical technician to be ignorant of splints? This is a ship of exploration. It will go where no one has gone before. It is likely that they will be faced with unusual medical problems. Doesn't Starfleet give its people basic Red Cross training? Picard knew how to make a splint and a tourniquet for Dr. Crusher during "Arsenal of Freedom." Are the medical technicians no more than button-pushers and screen-readers?

• When Data tries to operate the controls at the Iconian substation, the saying "Third time's a charm" proves to be true. The first time Data tries to operate the controls, he opens a porthole. The second time, he gets

zapped. And yet, miraculously, the third time—by his telling Picard what buttons to push—everything works correctly. If that wasn't enough, the sequence Data tells Picard to perform will result in the complete annihilation of the substation.

The problem here is "oops proofing." (Actually, it's called "idiot proofing," but I didn't want to offend anyone.) Every accomplished programmer understands that computer users need to be protected from accidents. That's why the more user-friendly programs tell you when you are about to do something disastrous. For instance, while trying to delete or overwrite a file, the program will usually ask the user to confirm his or her actions. Doesn't blowing up a substation seem like a fairly serious course of action? Wouldn't the programs make this fairly difficult to accomplish? Obviously not, because all Picard has to do to close the bay doors after launching a probe is tap a button three times.

CHANGED PREMISES

• There seems to be some discrepancy as to the registry number for the *Yamato*. In "Where Silence Has Lease," the bridge crew identifies the registry as "NCC 1305-E." Yet when Picard and Riker view the playback of the probe scan of the *Yamato*, the bottom of the screen reads, "USS *Yamato* NCC 71887."

EQUIPMENT ODDITIES

• As the *Enterprise* races toward Iconia, Picard reviews Varley's log. The scene proceeds with Picard watching his monitor interspersed with shots of Varley making his log entries. At the bottom of the screen is the star date and the time, in twenty-four-hour military style. Sometimes the episode shows the beginning of the log entry, Picard's reaction, and finally the end of the log entry. At other times it shows only the beginning or the ending of a log entry. The easiest way to demonstrate this equipment oddity is to list the star dates and times at the bottom of Varley's logs.

1. STAR DATE 42592.72—17:16:02–10, cut to Picard, then 42592.72—17:16:17–28, cut to Picard, then 42592.72—17:16:29–37

2. STAR DATE 42605.57—13:40:22–27, cut to Picard, then 42605.57—13:40:34–42

3. STAR DATE 42607.33—07:55:20–25, cut to Picard, then 42607.95—22:48:31–39

4. STAR DATE 42607.33—07:55:54–58

5. STAR DATE 42607.95—22:48:27–33

6. STAR DATE 42609.01—00:14:08–24, cut to Picard, then 42608.29—06:58:01–9

Of course, there is the ever-present problem of cutaways when a

clock is running (see Continuity Problems for "11001001"). Aside from that, however, there seems to be a problem in log 3. At some point, while we are observing Picard's reaction to this particular log entry, the star date moves ahead and the time jumps fifteen hours into the future. Thankfully, all returns to normal in the next log entry, but then in log 6 a similar problem occurs. Was the *Yamato* passing through some kind of temporal distortion when Varley made these log entries?

CONTINUITY AND PRODUCTION PROBLEMS

• Just after the control station on Iconia launches a probe at the *Enterprise*, La Forge realizes what has caused the system failures. He tries to contact the bridge, but intraship communications go out. La Forge sprints down the hall and into a turbolift. A line of sweat develops on his back. After a wild ride, the turbolift finally spits him out on the bridge. Suddenly the line of sweat is gone!

TRIVIA ANSWERS

1. Demons of Air and Darkness.
2. Ninety percent.

TRIATHLON TRIVIA ON ALIEN LIFE FORMS

(So named because—like the athletic event—no one should be able do this.)

MATCH THE RACE TO THE DESCRIPTION TO THE EPISODE

RACE	DESCRIPTION	EPISODE
1. Antedians	A. Formerly Acamarians	a. "Déjà Q"
2. Bajorans	B. Subjugated Ro's planet	b. "Violations"
3. Bandi	C. Consumes all life on a planet	c. "The Outcast"
4. Betazoids	D. Enslaved a large space creature	d. "Peak Performance"
5. Borg	E. Worshiped Picard	e. "Booby Trap"
6. Brekkians	F. Insect race	f. "Symbiosis"
7. Bringloidi	G. Speak in metaphor	g. "Ensigns of Command"
8. Bynars	H. Bidders on the worm hole	h. "The Survivors"
9. Calamarain	I. Computer interconnectedness	i. "Conundrum"
10. Cardassians	J. "Shared" race	j. "Samaritan Snare"
11. Chalnoth	K. Jono's adopted race	k. "Sarek"
12. Children of Tama	L. Destroyed themselves	l. "Up the Long Ladder"
13. Chrysalians	M. The ultimate user	m. "11001001"
14. Crystal entity	N. Their ship became a trap	n. "The Vengeance Factor"
15. Douwd	O. They look for things	o. "The Host"
16. Edo	P. Drug pushers	p. "Coming of Age"
17. Ferengi	Q. Naked weddings	q. "The Drumhead"
18. Gatherers	R. Conquered by the Cardassians	r. "Clues"
19. Grizzelli	S. Fish assassins	s. "Ensign Ro"
20. Husnak	T. Swirls of ionized gas	t. "Justice"
21. Iconians	U. Time-traveling thugs	u. "The Last Outpost"
22. J'naii	V. Infuriated by courtesy	v. "Samaritan Snare"
23. Jarada	W. Anarchy reigns on their planet	w. "Code of Honor"
24. Klingons	X. Simon Tarses's grandpa wasn't	x. "Conundrum"
25. Kriosians	Y. Disguises and false surroundings	y. "First Contact"
26. Legarans	Z. Brilliant strategists	z. "Captain's Holiday"

RACE	DESCRIPTION		EPISODE	
27. Ligonians	AA.	Androgynous race	aa.	"Suddenly Human"
28. Lysians	BB.	Archaeologists of the mind	bb.	"Manhunt"
29. Malcorians	CC.	Irish Nature Colony	cc.	"Q Who"
30. Mintakans	DD.	At war with the Lysians	dd.	"The Wounded"
31. Mizarians	EE.	Worf's race	ee.	"Datalore"
32. Nanites	FF.	Extreme xenophobes	ff.	"The Survivors"
33. Norsicans	GG.	Come from Vulcan stock	gg.	"Contagion"
34. Onarans	HH.	Three wrestled Picard	hh.	"Symbiosis"
35. Pakled	II.	They have only one punishment	ii.	"Haven"
36. Paxans	JJ.	Hibernate for a long time	jj.	"Allegiance"
37. Promellians	KK.	Big-eared capitalists	kk.	"Haven"
38. Romulans	LL.	Evil race destroyed by a Douwd	ll.	"Heart of Glory"
39. Sartaaran	MM.	Drug addicts	mm.	"The Big Good-bye"
40. Talarians	NN.	Offered Kamala for peace	nn.	"The Perfect Mate"
41. Tarellians	OO.	Sarek's friends for ninety years	oo.	"Who Watchers the Watchers"
42. Trill	PP.	Authors of a computer virus	pp.	"Allegiance"
43. Ulians	QQ.	Had an important vaccine	qq.	"The Neutral Zone"
44. Vorgons	RR.	Tiny intelligent robots	rr.	"Evolution"
45. Vulcans	SS.	Put Riker in the hospital	ss.	"The Price"
46. Zakdorn	TT.	Almost destroyed by Picard	tt.	"Darmok"
47. Zalkonians	UU.	Race of bureaucrats	uu.	"Encounter at Farpoint"
48. Zoldans	VV.	John Doe's race	vv.	"Transfigurations"

SCORING
(BASED ON NUMBER OF CORRECT ANSWERS)

0–5	Normal
6–10	Rabid Trekker
11 and up	You're either cheating, or you watch way too much television

RACES ANSWER KEY:

1. S bb	9. T a	17. KK u	25. NN nn	33. HH v	41. L ii
2. R s	10. B dd	18. A n	26. OO k	34. MM hh	42. J o
3. D uu	11. W jj	19. JJ g	27. QQ w	35. O j	43. BB b
4. Q kk	12. G tt	20. LL ff	28. TT x	36. FF r	44. U z
5. M cc	13. H ss	21. PP gg	29. SS y	37. N e	45. X q
6. P f	14. C ee	22. AA c	30. E oo	38. GG qq	46. Z d
7. CC l	15. Y h	23. F mm	31. UU pp	39. DD i	47. VV vv
8. I m	16. II t	24. EE ll	32. RR rr	40. K aa	48. V p

THE ROYALE

Responding to a report from a Klingon scout ship, the *Enterprise* drops into orbit around Theta VIII—a barren, inhospitable world. The Klingons sensed spaceship debris in orbit around the planet. Riker beams a chunk aboard and finds markings for NASA and an American flag with fifty-two stars. These symbols date the craft from twenty-first–century Earth. When sensors detect an area of breathable air on the surface of the planet, Riker, Data, and Worf beam down for a closer look. They find "The Royale," a casino-hotel made to resemble that of twentieth-century Earth. After entering and investigating, they discover they cannot leave the hotel. More investigation leads them to a hotel room. In the bed lay the remains of Colonel Steven Richie, dead for 283 years.

The records on the *Enterprise* show that NASA launched Colonel Richie's craft on July 23, 2037. Richie's diary gives a sketchy history of the next events. An alien presence encountered the craft and accidentally killed all the other astronauts. Filled with remorse, the aliens sought some way to provide for the sole survivor, Colonel Richie. Finding a pulp novel called *Hotel Royale* among the crew's belongings and believing it was the preferred mode of existence for humans, they created an environment for him to live out his days. Unfortunately, Riker, Data, and Worf are now stuck in the novel-come-to-life as well. After seeing someone leave the hotel, however, Riker and Picard conclude that the person could leave because it happened in the book.

Riker, Data, and Worf become "the foreign investors" mentioned in the novel. According to the book, these foreign investors purchase the Royale for $12.5 million. Data suggests that he try to win the money at gambling and chooses the game of craps. After rebalancing the "loaded" dice, Data wins nineteen consecutive passes at the craps table. With the gambling funds Riker, Data, and Worf buy the Royale and leave.

Trivia Questions

1. Who wrote *Hotel Royale*?

2. What type of car did the gambler with the cowboy hat drive?

GREAT MOMENTS

T *he scene with Data at the craps table is memorable for three reasons. First, it is a very cute sequence. Second, it has great music. I have always been partial to big band. And third, if I recall correctly, it is a knock-off from a scene in a movie called* The Questor Tapes. *Gene Roddenberry created the movie as a two-hour TV pilot in 1974. It featured an android on Earth looking for his creator. To raise money for his travels, the android visits a casino and wins money playing craps. I remember seeing* The Questor Tapes *in the Philippines as a teenager. I've tried to rent a copy, but it isn't available on video.*

GREAT LINES

"Baby needs a new pair of shoes."—Data taking on the role of the gambler before starting his phenomenal run at craps.

PLOT OVERSIGHTS

• Just before beginning his attempts to win the funds needed to buy the Royale, Data explains the rules of craps to Riker. Doesn't it seems odd that Data has to explain the rules of craps to Riker? Riker is, after all, one of the best poker players on the *Enterprise*. If Riker has such a deep interest in poker, wouldn't that translate to at least a passing familiarity with other games of chance?

CHANGED PREMISES

• During "Encounter at Farpoint," Q puts Picard, Data, Troi, and Yar on trial for the crimes of humanity. The setting is a midtwenty-first–century postatomic horrors courtroom. As part of the trial, Data claims, "In the year 2036, the new United Nations declared that no Earth citizen could be made to answer for the crimes of his race or forebears." Q responds that the courtroom is from 2079, "by which time more rapid progress had caused all United Earth nonsense to be abolished." Therefore, a United Earth existed during the years 2036 through 2079.

Colonel Richie's craft was launched in 2037, yet the signage on the fragment of the spaceship and Richie's uniform show only United States of America markings. If the United Earth was only one year old, wouldn't the inherent enthusiasm—which exists at the beginning of every undertaking—have caused the directors of NASA to include at least a few prominent markings for the new United Earth?

TRIVIA ANSWERS

1. Todd Matthews.
2. A 1991 Cadillac with eighty thousand miles on it.

TIMES SQUARED

Star Date: 42679.2

When the *Enterprise* sensors find a shuttle craft drifting through space, the crew brings it into Shuttle Bay 2 and makes an astonishing discovery: The unconscious pilot is Picard (I'll call him Picard B for clarity's sake). As Pulaski takes Picard B to sick bay, Picard A orders La Forge to extract the logs from the shuttle. Since all the power has been drained from the shuttle craft, La Forge connects it to the *Enterprise* power grid, but the polarities do not match. After hooking up an inverter, Data and La Forge access the files and determine that the shuttle is from six hours in the future. Visuals show the shuttle leaving an *Enterprise* that is surrounded by an energy vortex. Moments later, a pulse from the vortex destroys the *Enterprise*. After reviewing the logs and discussing alternatives, the bridge crew decides that there is very little they can do but wait.

Several hours later, an energy vortex suddenly opens under the *Enterprise*. It is the same as the one shown on the logs from the shuttle.

Trivia Questions

1. Where did Riker get the eggs he is using to make omelets at the beginning of the episode?

2. What is the name of the shuttle from the future?

Picard A tries to fly the *Enterprise* away from the vortex but its powerful tractor beam continues to draw the ship. An energy bolt hits Picard A on the bridge and slings him across the room. Troi says that the consciousness of the vortex has concentrated on Picard as the head of the *Enterprise*. Picard A goes to sick bay. By this time, Picard B has roused enough to recognize he is on the *Enterprise* but little else. Picard A takes Picard B from sick bay and together they go to the shuttle bay. During this time, Picard B's sole focus concerns leaving the ship. He refuses to listen as Picard A tries to discuss other options. Since Picard B is determined to leave, Picard A grabs a phaser from a wall storage unit and kills Picard B. Picard A then goes to the bridge and implements the only other option: He turns the *Enterprise* around and flies straight into the vortex. As the ship reaches the end of it, the vortex evaporates, as do Picard B and the shuttle. The *Enterprise* continues on its way.

PLOT OVERSIGHTS

• At one point, Picard A gives Troi a direct order—a direct order, mind you—to stay with Picard B. Picard A correctly determines that Troi will be able to communicate with Picard B before anyone else. Yet, only moments later, after a little discussion with Dr. Pulaski, Troi walks out.

• One of the last times Picard A goes to sick bay, Troi follows him in a subsequent turbolift. Yet when Picard A arrives in sick bay (after a commercial break), Troi is already there! Did Picard A take a little restroom detour on the way to sick bay?

• And then there is the matter of La Forge's whining about the warp engines. After the bolts of energy hit Picard A, La Forge says he can hold their position for a few minutes only. In a few moments, he tells Picard A that he can't hold it any longer. Of course, Picard sees through his complaints and orders him to hold position and—lo and *behold*—La Forge does. At this point Picard A leaves for sick bay. Several minutes later, La Forge is obviously still whining on the bridge about the engines because Riker calls the Picards—on their way to the shuttle bay—and tells them the *Enterprise* is about to lose warp drive. Simultaneously, the Picards say they understand. What they understand is that La Forge is just plain overprotective when it comes to warp drive and they easily have several more minutes. Sure enough, Picard A has plenty of time to have a talk with Picard B, kill him, and get back to the bridge before the engines fail. On top of that, once Picard A gets back to the bridge, he orders the *Enterprise* to change course and fly into the vortex. He tells La Forge to give him everything he's got. Of course, La Forge complies, *with warp drive still intact.*

• When Picard A determines to stop Picard B from getting on the shuttle, what does Picard A do? He grabs a phaser off the wall and kills Picard B. He *kills* Picard B. What happened to stun settings? Was the *Enterprise* not big enough for both of them?

• Understandably, having an ensemble cast makes it difficult to provide lines for all the actors in every episode. However, this episode goes a bit far. After Picard A kills Picard B, he calls for Dr. Pulaski. When Pulaski shows up, Transporter Chief O'Brien comes with her! Does he moonlight as a medical technician? Is that why he responded to Picard's call for Pulaski? Of course, the real reason O'Brien tags along is so he could be in the shuttle bay to see Picard B disappear. This allows him to get a few lines of dialogue in this episode.

• Speaking of O'Brien, he must be an old navy man. While the *Enterprise* is flying into the vortex, everyone bounces around in their seats on the bridge. A shot of La Forge shows him holding on to his console to keep from falling down. Yet a shot of O'Brien in the shuttle bay shows him standing perfectly straight even though the floor of the shuttle bay is moving around.

CHANGED PREMISES

• During one scene in "11001001,"

Picard and Riker need to get some phasers. They go to a room clearly marked "Weapons Room," and Picard uses a voice print identifier to get access. This seems reasonable. On a ship with civilians, it is not a good idea for phasers to be accessible easily. Yet at the end of "Times Squared," Picard simply reaches back to a wall panel, flips it open, and grabs a phaser. The wall panel looks extremely accessible. Does it have some sort of sensor to detect whether the person opening it has clearance? If that's the case, why do they need the Weapons Room?

EQUIPMENT ODDITIES

• At the very beginning of the episode, several people walk into Riker's quarters. The doors pop open. Data and La Forge walk through. Then the doors start to close. Dr. Pulaski tries to walk in, but the doors don't respond. So she stops and waits for the doors to open. (Kind of reminded me of going to the grocery store. Somehow I thought doors in the twenty-fourth century would be a bit more responsive.)

• When La Forge switches the polarity on the power hookup to the shuttle, he says it should blow all the circuits. Evidently he is exaggerating again, because when they connected the shuttle originally, the hookup *was* exactly opposite of what it should have been. When Data tried to turn on the shuttle at that point, a lot of sparks flew, but it didn't burn out all the circuits.

• After Picard A kills Picard B, he boards a turbolift on deck 6. The *Enterprise* is in a crisis situation at this point, so it is unlikely that he took a detour. Doesn't it seem likely that Picard would leave Shuttle Bay 2 and board a turbolift direct for the bridge? Evidently Picard didn't. According to "Unnatural Selection," Shuttle Bay 3 is on deck 11. Since Shuttle Bay 2 and Shuttle Bay 3 are in the same vertical position on the *Enterprise*, it is likely that Shuttle Bay 2 is also on deck 11. So what was Picard doing on deck 6?

CONTINUITY AND PRODUCTION PROBLEMS

• As the Picards head toward Shuttle Bay 2, they walk down a hall. Long, thin lights mounted horizontally in the hallway flash sequentially to show that the *Enterprise* is on red alert. As the Picards board a turbolift, the shot shows a small section of the hallway. Now the lights aren't flashing. The same situation occurs in reverse when the Picards leave the turbolift. The lights aren't flashing in the close-up but they are in the long shot.

TRIVIA ANSWERS
1. Starbase 73.
2. *El-Baz.*

THE ICARUS FACTOR

Star Date: 42686.4

In this episode, Worf reaches the tenth anniversary of his age of ascension. Since there are no Klingons on board, Wesley stages an ascension rite on the holodeck and invites several of the crew to participate.

At the same time Starfleet offers Riker his own command aboard the USS *Aries*. When his father boards the *Enterprise* to brief him, it becomes obvious the relationship is very strained. Fifteen years ago, Kyle Riker left Will Riker to fend for himself. Will Riker still holds that against his father. They finally work out their differences after an extended martial arts battle using blindfolds and large sticks (this must be the twenty-fourth–century version of the male-bonding ritual using a "truth" stick). After Riker decides against the promotion, the *Enterprise* leaves for its next mission.

PLOT OVERSIGHTS

• When Picard and Riker talk about the *Aries*, they both seem enamored with the fact that the first officer of that ship can speak forty languages. Then again, who needs to speak multiple languages anymore? The Universal Translator takes care of that, right?

EQUIPMENT ODDITIES

• At the very end of the episode, a shot shows the *Enterprise* moving counterrotationally across that face of the planet. Moments later, Wesley says, "Breaking synchronous orbit." The term "synchronous orbit" refers to a position in space that orbits a planet at the same rate that the planet revolves. This means the object in orbit stays directly above a given spot on the planet. This makes sense if the *Enterprise* wants to remain above a starbase on the surface. The picture of the *Enterprise* and the planet, however, shows the ship moving in one direction and the planet in an other.

TRIVIA ANSWERS

1. Thirty-something (Riker's father left when he was fifteen, and Riker hasn't seen his father in fifteen years).
2. Eight.

★
PEN PALS

Star Dates: 42695.3-42741.3

The *Enterprise* enters the Selcundi Drema System, a series of planets known for their violent geothermal activity. These planets self-destruct through earthquakes and volcanoes. The *Enterprise* hopes to determine the reason through planetary mineral surveys. After discussing it with the senior staff, Riker puts Wesley in charge of the surveys. Meanwhile, Data conducts his own experiments, retuning the sensor array to wavelengths normally ignored. He happens across a low-intensity radio-frequency transmission. It is a little girl named Sarjenka calling from Drema IV. Her plaintive question "Is anybody out there?" causes Data to respond, "Yes!" Although her race is not aware of interstellar life, Data maintains regular contact with Sarjenka, violating Starfleet regulations. After observing that Drema IV begins to experience the same seismic upheaval as the rest of the planets in the system, Data contacts Picard. Data wants the *Enterprise* to intervene and help Drema IV. Picard calls a meeting of senior staff members in his quarters.

Trivia Questions

1. What type of saddle does Picard use on the holodeck?

2. What is Ensign Davis's speciality?

The staff quickly establishes the fact that helping Drema IV constitutes a clear violation of the Prime Directive. Yet when Picard hears the little girl's pleading, he decides to help. At the same time, Wesley's team reports the cause of the planet's distress. The planet is growing dilithium crystals in a uniquely aligned configuration. The crystals are converting the heat of the planet into mechanical motion, which translates into seismic upheaval. Later, the team suggests a solution. They propose using probes to burrow into the planet and shatter the crystals with harmonic vibrations. When the plan succeeds, Drema IV returns to normal.

GREAT LINES

"I could have just been picking nits."—Wesley to Riker while discussing a test Wesley wanted performed. (Even the *Enterprise* has nit-pickers!)

PLOT OVERSIGHTS

• There are so many plot oversights tangled up in this episode that is it difficult to find a starting place. The Prime Directive is as good as any. Supposedly, the Prime Directive is

Starfleet's first and foremost rule—a principle of noninterference with non-Federation races and cultures, a rule born from painful historical experience. Supposedly, Starfleet is very serious about the Prime Directive and doesn't take lightly to it being violated. Picard claimed this in "Justice." If this is true, why did Data even start this whole episode with the little girl? Data is an android. He is not swayed by emotion. La Forge, in "The Most Toys," claimed that Data always did things by the book. Evidently Data's book doesn't have anything about the Prime Directive in it.

But, after all, Data is still a junior officer. Surely the captain of a Galaxy Class starship will exhibit more disciplined behavior. Indeed, Picard does make very clear and convincing arguments for the Prime Directive during the staff meeting in his quarters. He states that the Prime Directive is "to protect us—to prevent us from allowing our emotions to overwhelm our judgment." And then Picard does a 180-degree turn and decides to help Drema IV. Why? Because he heard Sarjenka's plea for help. Putting aside the fact that Picard doesn't like children, is a plea for help sufficient cause to violate the Prime Directive?

In "Encounter at Farpoint," the Bandi city gets blown to bits while the leader screams for help and Picard calmly discusses his options. Likewise, in "Symbiosis," the drug-addicted Onarans beg Picard to help them. He refuses because of the Prime Directive. Maybe the leader of the Bandi should have had one of

the children call for help. And what about the children on the planet of Onara? They were addicted to Felicium. If the Onarans had hauled out one of their little girls—writhing in the pains of withdrawal—would that have caused Picard to change his mind?

Picard's decision to help Drema IV sits squarely on the shoulders of overt emotionalism—precisely the type of action the Prime Directive was designed to prevent. Picard's waffling on the issue portrays him as being emotionally out of control. His decision-making process continues to slide for the rest of the show. He allows Data to contact Sarjenka. He also allows Data to beam down to the planet. When Data shows up on the bridge with Sarjenka, Picard is angry but lets the little girl stay. While the *Enterprise* fixes Drema IV, Picard sits in his chair and fumes. He is seemingly helpless to take charge of the situation.

• The event that causes Picard to change his mind about helping Drema IV deserves greater scrutiny. During the staff meeting, Picard orders Data to sever the contact with Drema IV. Evidently Picard has decided not to help Drema IV. Data responds to Picard's order by piping the transmission from Sarjenka into the captain's quarters! This is *not* severing contact. This is a willful violation of a direct order. Data's behavior in the episode soon gets worse than this, however. After fixing Drema IV, Picard tells Data to take Sarjenka to sick bay. He wants Pulaski to erase Sarjenka's memories of Data and the *Enterprise*, obviously trying to reestablish some deference to the Prime Directive. Shortly after arriving in sick bay, Sarjenka picks up Pulaski's "singer stone"—a rock that vibrates in a pattern unique to each person. Sarjenka is delighted with the object. Because of this, when Data deposits Sarjenka at her home on the planet, he places a singer stone in her hand. In other words, Data leaves tangible evidence of the *Enterprise*'s presence.

The whole point of erasing the girl's memory was to allow the *Enterprise* to slip away unnoticed. Yet Data purposefully provides an item that is provocatively anachronistic. Hopefully, Data produced the stone with a replicator. It looks identical to the one in Dr. Pulaski's office. Data could not have taken the stone with Pulaski's permission. She agreed that erasing the girl's memory was the wisest course of action. She would not have agreed to provide evidence of extraterrestrial involvement. If the stone was not replicated, it was stolen.

EQUIPMENT ODDITIES

• The house on Drema IV is quite interesting. It is decorated in early Flintstone design, yet it has a door that can evaporate on command. The door represents a very sophisticated technology, a state of scientific advancement not reflected in the rest of the home. (See Plot Oversights for "Angel One" for a more complete discussion.)

TRIVIA ANSWERS

1. An English tack.
2. Geochemistry.

Q WHO

For this episode, Q visits the *Enterprise*, asking to join the crew. The Q Continuum has kicked him out, and after wandering around the galaxy for some time, he's bored and wants something to do. Picard thoughtfully considers the request but eventually turns Q down. He doesn't trust Q and doesn't see the necessity for having him around. Q decides to show Picard "what's out there." He snaps his fingers and transports them a distance of seven thousand light-years. After some parting words, Q disappears. Having been in this area, Guinan warns Picard to start back now. Instead, Picard decides to survey a few planets while they are in the area. When they reach the first planet, sensors show that all the machine elements have been ripped from the surface.

A cube-shaped spaceship approaches. It is of the Borg, a humanoid race who have managed to combine themselves with artificial intelligence. The Borg act as one collective mind, with their only purpose to improve themselves. They do this

Trivia Questions

1. How long ago did Guinan and Q have dealings?

2. How many people died in the Borg encounter?

by appropriating any technology they deem interesting. They deem the *Enterprise* interesting. The Borg send a scout to survey the offensive and defensive capabilities of the *Enterprise*. When the scout begins draining power from the ship, Worf kills him. A second scout appears. This one has a personal shield that defends him from phasers. This pattern continues. In the first battle, the *Enterprise* manages to damage 20 percent of the Borg ship. In the second, however, none of the *Enterprise*'s weapons are effective.

Q appears to taunt them. When it appears that all is lost, Picard recants and passionately admits that they need Q. Q smiles, snaps his fingers, and returns them the seven thousand light-years to their former position in space.

GREAT MOMENTS

This episode has many fascinating features: the Borg ship, the Borg themselves, the meeting of a powerful and ruthless adversary. It also has several beautiful special effects. My favorite occurs in the observation lounge. At one point, Q sits with his feet on the table. When he disappears, the chair snaps up and wobbles back and forth.

GREAT LINES

"If you can't take a little bloody nose, maybe you ought to go back home and crawl under your bed. It's not safe out here. It's wondrous, with treasures to satiate desires both subtle and gross. But it's not for the timid."—Q to Picard, after Picard mourns the loss of life in the encounter with the Borg.

CHANGED PREMISES

• At the very beginning of the episode, La Forge questions whether a young ensign should be drinking hot chocolate around the control stations. First of all, the food dispenser is right around the corner from the control stations. If the designers didn't want food and drink around the control stations, why did they put a food dispenser there? Second, the tops of the control stations are sealed. Spilling liquid on them isn't going to hurt them. As evidence, consider the incident in Engineering with Lwaxana Troi during the episode "Half a Life." Lwaxana wants to spend some time with a visiting scientist, so she comes down to Engineering with a picnic meal. After a very limited discussion—in which the effect of food and drink on the control stations is never mentioned—Lwaxana clears off the main workstation and makes a table of it.

• When Picard first encounters Q during this episode, Picard says they agreed that Q would stay off the En-

terprise. This is not correct. The agreement in "Hide and Q" was that Q would stay "out of humanity's path forever." Of course, honoring that agreement effectively writes Q out of any more scripts.

• "The Neutral Zone" is a very odd episode. In that show, the Enterprise discovers a series of Federation outposts along the Neutral Zone that have been destroyed. Later, the episode reveals that the Romulan outposts on the other side of the zone have also been destroyed. However, the episode never resolves who or what caused the destruction. A review of dialogue for this and other episodes might flush out the villains.

First, consider the dialogue from "The Neutral Zone." This dialogue occurs just as the Enterprise arrives at Science Station Delta 05:

DATA: Captain, there is nothing left of Delta 05.

GEORDI: Must have been one hell of an explosion.

DATA: Sensors indicate no evidence of conventional attack.

PICARD: Can you determine what happened?

WORF: The outpost was not just destroyed. It's as though some great force just scooped it off the face of the planet.

Now consider the dialogue from this episode, "Q Who" Before the Borg arrive, the Enterprise surveys a nearby planet. It looks like it was once inhabited.

DATA: ... but where there should be cities there are only rips in the surface.

WORF: It is though some great force

just scooped all the machine elements off the face of the planet.

DATA: It is identical to what happened to the outposts along the Neutral Zone.

Finally, consider dialogue from "The Best of Both Worlds," Part 1. The *Enterprise* has just surveyed New Providence Colony. It has been obliterated by an unknown force. A "Commander Shelby" has joined the *Enterprise*'s crew to investigate and determine if it was the Borg.

RIKER: Then you're convinced it is the Borg.

SHELBY: That's what I'm here to find out. The initial descriptions of these surface conditions are almost identical to your report from System J25.

PICARD: Commander Riker wrote those reports. He agrees with you.

"System J25" was the location of the planet the *Enterprise* surveyed in this episode, "Q Who." So the dialogue from these three shows ties the outposts on the Neutral Zone to System J25 and then to New Providence Colony. Later, in "The Best of Both Worlds," Part 1, Shelby establishes that the destruction of New Providence Colony was the result of the Borg. Assuming that the destruction of the planet in System J25 was also the work of the Borg, doesn't if seem reasonable to say

that the destruction of the outposts in the Neutral Zone were also the work of the Borg? In other words, have the Borg already come through Federation territory? If they have, it would contradict the end of "Q Who" when Guinan warns Picard that the Borg will be coming now that they know of the existence of the Federation.

EQUIPMENT ODDITIES

• When Q snaps his fingers the first time, Picard immediately contacts the bridge to determine their position. He also tells Wesley, "All stop." Appropriately, Wesley responds, "Answering, all stop, sir." However, a few shots later, as Q makes his dramatic exit, the stars behind him are still moving. Did Q make the stars move so his backdrop would be more interesting?

• During the first attack, the Borg lock a tractor beam on the *Enterprise*. Picard orders Worf to locate the exact origin of the beam and fire on it. The first shot doesn't even come close to the emanation point of the beam. Three tries later, Worf finally hits it. No wonder Klingons prefer using knives.

TRIVIA ANSWERS

1. Two centuries.
2. Eighteen.

SAMARITAN SNARE

Star Dates: 42779.1-42779.5

As Picard and Wesley leave on a shuttle for Starbase 515, the *Enterprise* receives a distress call from a seemingly disabled Pakled ship. The Pakled are a rotund race with somewhat limited mental development. When they say their ship is broken, La Forge beams over to help. Back on the shuttle, Picard tells Wesley why he is going to Starbase 515. Many years ago, a young bravado-filled Picard picked a fight with a trio of Norsicans. During the fight, one of them stabbed Picard in the back, piercing his heart. Luckily, a nearby starbase gave him a cardiac replacement. Unfortunately, the replacement was faulty. Now Picard must undergo another operation to replace it. Meanwhile, La Forge fixes the Pakled ship. Suddenly the Pakleds take La Forge's phaser and stun him. They throw up a shield, blocking transport. The Pakleds demand that Riker turn over all computer records or they will kill La Forge.

At Starbase 515, Picard's operation runs into difficulty and the starbase transmits an urgent message for Dr. Pulaski to come and assist. At the same time, Riker devises a ruse to get La Forge back. In their communication with the Pakleds, Riker and the other bridge crew members make La Forge sound like a weapons specialist. As planned, the Pakleds force La Forge to work on their weapons. Riker then stages a mock countdown for an attack. Just before reaching zero, La Forge disables the Pakleds' weapons. The *Enterprise* blows hydrogen out its Buzzard collectors. The resulting light show makes the Pakleds think the *Enterprise* has disarmed them. Discouraged by the *Enterprise*'s superior power, the Pakleds release La Forge. Immediately after he returns, the *Enterprise* warps to Starbase 515 and Pulaski saves Picard's life.

Trivia Questions

1. Who is the author of the book Picard gave to Wesley?

2. What type of doctor is needed to save Picard during his operation?

GREAT LINES

"And I told him what I thought of him, his pals, his planet, and I possibly made some passing reference to his questionable parentage."—Picard rehashing his encounter with the Norsicans.

120

PLOT OVERSIGHTS

• Why doesn't the *Enterprise* warp over to Starbase 515 instead of sending Picard and Wesley on a shuttle? Although this issue came up before under Plot Oversights for "The Neutral Zone," it bears further elaboration. Wesley states that it will take six hours for the shuttle to reach the starbase. While they are in transit, Wesley makes the comment that they aren't traveling at warp velocity. That means the fastest they can be going is the speed of light. (Actually, if they were going at the speed of light they would be traveling at warp 1.) The speed of light is given in distance covered per second. Therefore, the maximum distance to starbase 515 is the speed of light times 21,600 (6 hours times 60 minutes times 60 seconds). Seems like a lot, doesn't it?

At warp 7, the *Enterprise* travels 656 times the speed of light. (I know this because the *Technical Manual* tells me so. Of course, the manual says this figure is approximate, but I assume the real figure is somewhere around 656.) So how long would it take for the *Enterprise* to get to Starbase 515 at warp 7? Thirty-three seconds (21,600 divided by 656)—less time than it would take Picard to pack some of his things and get to the transporter room. Of course, if the *Enterprise* warped over, it would be a short show because all the dialogue between Picard and Wesley would be missing.

• When Troi finds out that La Forge is on the Pakled ship, she reacts immediately, warning Riker that La Forge is in great danger. Although Troi has demonstrated her accuracy and worth several times over the course of the series, Riker trusts his senses more than hers and does nothing. Then again, Riker *must* take her recommendation lightly, for if he beamed La Forge back to the *Enterprise*, it would be a short show.

• After surveying the Pakled ship, La Forge claims that it contains equipment from the Romulans, Klingons, and Jaradan. First of all, the Pakleds don't seem like brilliant strategists. Nonbrilliant strategists tend to use the same approach over and over. If that's true, the Pakleds did the same dance with the Romulans and the Klingons. The Pakleds pretended to be disabled to lure someone over and then held that person in exchange for equipment. Does this seem like an approach that would work with Romulans and Klingons? (I realize the Pakleds could have used another approach, but I have a hard time imagining one that would work against Klingons.)

CHANGED PREMISES

• During the shuttle trip to Starbase 515, Picard tells Wesley about the incident with the Norsicans and the wound that pierced his heart. He specifically recalls looking down and seeing the serrated edge of the blade sticking out of his chest. Picard also tells Wesley that he hopes Wesley won't learn the lesson of discipline in the same way.

Hasn't Wesley already learned the lesson that way? In "Hide and Q," Worf gets killed and Wesley impetuously runs out to help him. Moments later, one of the "animal things" puts a bayonet through Wesley's back. The next shot shows the blade sticking out of his chest.

EQUIPMENT ODDITIES

• At one point, when Riker is yelling at the Pakleds, a shot shows the dome above Riker's head on the bridge. The view is dense with stars. Yet the shot just previous to this one shows the *Enterprise* and the Pakled ship sitting in an area of space that contains far fewer stars that those shown in the dome. Does the dome act like a magnifying glass and concentrate the star view?

• During Picard's operation, the surgeon employs several laser scalpels. In a close-up, the scalpel is clearly wobbling, yet the laser beam stays rock steady.

CONTINUITY AND PRODUCTION PROBLEMS

• At the beginning of the show, as the shuttle prepares to leave the *Enterprise*, Wesley tells the bridge, "Shuttle Craft 2 is ready for departure." Yet all of the markings on the shuttle say "01," clearly indicating that Picard and Wesley are in Shuttle Craft 1.

• As Picard and Wesley board the shuttle, a shot of the shuttle bay shows a giant "2" on the floor near the shuttle bay door. Presumably this means that this room is Shuttle Bay 2. In the footage that follows, the shuttle flies out of the shuttle bay on the starboard side of the yoke of the star drive section. In the episode "Unnatural Selection," Data and Pulaski go to a shuttle bay that has a giant "3" on the floor near the door. The computer clearly states that this room is Shuttle Bay 3, yet when the shuttle departs from the *Enterprise* the shuttle, too, flies out of the shuttle bay on the starboard side of the yoke of the star drive section. (I understand the need to reuse footage like a shuttle leaving the *Enterprise*. It is very expensive to produce. What I don't understand is why the creators of "Samaritan Snare" didn't just call the room where Picard and Wesley go Shuttle Bay 3. Then everything would match up with previous episodes.)

• The cityscape paintings used for the episode "Angel One" get double duty in this episode. Suddenly it becomes Starbase 515!

TRIVIA ANSWERS
1. William James.
2. A biomolecular physiologist.

UP THE LONG LADDER

Star Dates: 42823.2-42827.3

While at Starbase 73, Picard receives word about a distress call from the Ficus Sector. Further investigation reveals that the SS *Mariposa* left Earth early in the twenty-second century, heading toward the Ficus Sector. The *Mariposa* transported not only colonists but also an odd collection of primitive tools and technologically advanced computers. At the origin of the distress call, the *Enterprise* finds a group of 223 colonists and assorted farm animals. They call themselves the "Bringloidi." Since their sun is generating intense solar flares, Picard decides to evacuate the colonists. When the Bringloidi insist on bringing their animals, Picard beams them all to a cargo bay.

During the conversation with the Bringloidi leader, Picard discovers the existence of another colony planted by the *Mariposa*. The *Enterprise* soon finds the other colony in a nearby star system. It is a colony of clones. Hundreds of years ago, the *Mariposa* crash-landed on the planet. Only five of the colonists survived: three men and two women. Since

Trivia Questions

1. What cargo did the *Mariposa* carry?

2. Which body cells are the best for cloning?

they were scientists, they turned to cloning to survive and populate the planet. Unfortunately, "replicative fading" has occurred. Each clone is a copy of the last, who is also a copy of a copy. Subtle errors in the DNA have crept in. In two or three generations, the clones will no longer be viable. Everyone will die. Picard suggests a solution. The clones need an infusion of "breeding stock" to revive their society. Coincidentally, the Bringloidi need a new home. Picard proposes that the Bringloidi settle on the clones' world. Faced with no other solution, the clones begrudgingly accept, and the two colonies that began on the *Mariposa* are reunited.

GREAT LINES

"Send in the clones."—The Bringloidi leader to the prime minister of Clone World. (Some have mistakenly assumed that the Bringloidi leader was referring to the twentieth-century song "Send in the Clowns" with this remark. In actuality, the remark comes from the song of the same name by the super group "The Repeaters." Seven generations of

the musical geniuses made chart-busting records until replicative fading caused half the band to go tone deaf.)

PLOT OVERSIGHTS

• How did the Bringloidi send a distress call in the first place? When the *Enterprise* arrives at the Bringloidi's planet, the bridge crew says that sensors show no advanced communication network and no artificial power source. These people use spinning wheels and were still able to send a distress call all the way back to Earth?

• Shortly after discovering the colony of clones, their prime minister meets with Picard, Riker, and Pulaski in the observation lounge. He rehashes the crash of the *Mariposa* and the reasons why they turned to cloning. With only five survivors, they didn't have a sufficient gene pool to use normal reproduction methods. At this point, Pulaski jumps in and asks how they suppress the natural sexual urges. The leader replies that they used a combination of drug therapy and punitive measures.

Given the state of American culture in the late twentieth century, the statements about suppressing sexual drive are very intriguing. The creators of this episode postulate that the clones set aside their carnal nature because they didn't have a sufficient gene pool to repopulate. In other words, the only reason for sex in the minds of the clones was reproduction. Does this seem like an attitude that would be prevalent early in the twenty-second century? It certainly isn't an attitude prevalent today!

• When discussing the clones with Picard, Pulaski claims that replicative fading has caused severe damage to the genetic structure of the clones. She claims they are "among the walking dead now. They just haven't been buried yet." If the clones are really that bad off, why would anyone want them to be part of the gene pool to repopulate a planet? The Bringloidi are all very healthy. Why not just start over with them?

EQUIPMENT ODDITIES

• When the Bringloidi beam up to the *Enterprise*, all the hay scattered around their feet beams up with them. The transporter usually just beams up the person and anything they are holding. Yet in this instance, the hay gets beamed up also. Why? (I know: It makes a good visual impact.)

• In the first meeting with Picard, Riker, and Pulaski, the clone prime minister asks if the crew members would supply them with new DNA for cloning. The clones feel this would solve their problems. Picard, Riker and Pulaski immediately refuse, feeling that duplicates of themselves would diminish them. Later, in desperation, the clones immobilize Riker and Pulaski and steal some tissue samples from which to extract the DNA. When Riker and Pulaski realize what happened, they go to the cloning lab, and a close-up shows us the markings on the machines. The markings are some sort of alien calligraphy. These people are humans. Wouldn't it make more sense for the writing to be in English? True, the clones have been isolated for three hundred years, and language does evolve. However, three hundred years is not a very long time. Old English documents from the seventeenth century are still readable today. A *few* characters differ, but the majority are the same.

TRIVIA ANSWERS

1. Two hundred twenty-five Yoshimitsu computers, five monitor beacon satellites, seven hundred cellular comlinks, fifty spinning wheels, cattle, chickens, and pigs.

2. The relatively undifferentiated epithelial cells that line the stomach.

Star Date: 42859.2

The *Enterprise* arrives at Antedi III to pick up two delegates and transport them to Pacifica for a conference. On the way, a small transport craft intercepts the *Enterprise*. Lwaxana Troi, Deanna Troi's mother, is aboard. She will represent Betazed at the conference. Lwaxana Troi's true purpose for this trip soon becomes clear, however. She is experiencing "the phase." During the phase, a Betazoid woman becomes fully sexual—her sex drive quadruples or more. Since her husband died several years ago, Mrs. Troi has decided to do the only honorable thing —find a new husband. To this end, she sets her sights on Picard. Not wanting to offend Lwaxana by refusing her advances, Picard ducks into a holodeck for the duration of the flight and assumes the role of Dixon Hill. (See "The Big Good-bye.")

When the ship nears Pacifica, Riker and Data enter the holodeck and find Picard at Rex's bar. Lwaxana follows them in and learns that Picard has been hiding from her. She soon forgets the insult and becomes enamored with Rex, the bartender. Lwaxana doesn't realize that Rex is only a holographic creation. On the way out of the holodeck, Picard feels compelled to tell her. The incident embarrasses Lwaxana enough to call off her "manhunt." Just before she beams down to Pacifica, Lwaxana does the crew of the *Enterprise* a favor. She informs them that the two Antedians are actually assassins. Being telepathic, she could read their thoughts. As Security takes the Antedians away, Lwaxana beams down to the conference.

Trivia Questions

1. How many gods inhabit Betazed mythology?

2. What names does Picard use for Riker and Data in the Dixon Hill holosetting?

GREAT LINES

"*Legs, where are the legs?*"—Lwaxana Troi making sure her body parts are still in place after transporting aboard the *Enterprise*.

PLOT OVERSIGHTS

• Given Lwaxana's dislike and distrust for transporters, why are they beaming her aboard the ship? She is traveling in a "small transport craft." This sounds suspiciously like a shuttle craft. Even the transmission from the "transport craft" looks like the cockpit of a shuttle craft. Why not just dock the craft in one of the shuttle bays and let her walk off?

The reason is simple. When Lwaxana Troi beams in, she is kneeling and immediately begins feeling around for her legs. This is when she says, "Legs, where are the legs?" If the *Enterprise* didn't beam her aboard, the show wouldn't have this cute moment.

• Doesn't Troi have a dress uniform? Every time the delegates come or go, Captain Picard gets in his dress uniform, but Troi wears the same outfit for the whole show.

• When Troi wants to have an intimate conversation with her mother about her mother's condition, she momentarily considers having it in Lwaxana's quarters. She rejects this idea because Mr. Homm is there. So she takes her mother out into the hall to have the conversation. On top of that, they have the conversation out loud when they could communicate telepathically. Does this seems odd to anyone else?

• After exposing the Antedian assassins, Lwaxana states that it was quite easy for her to read their minds. If it was so easy for her, why wasn't Troi at least able to get a sense that the Antedians were up to no good?

CHANGED PREMISES

• Two things have changed from the last show with Dixon Hill in it ("The Big Good-bye"). In that show, Picard begins coughing immediately after lighting up a cigarette. This is a normal reaction for someone who doesn't smoke. In this show, Picard just starts puffing away. Either he is spending a lot of time on the holodeck smoking cigarettes, or he got used to them very fast. (A small side note: Does the damage to his lungs reverse itself when Picard leaves the holodeck? Or does the computer create synthacigarettes with all the pleasure but none of the bad side effects?) Also, in "The Big Good-bye" Picard wore his uniform into the holodeck the first time he entered. Several holodeck creations commented that he looked like a bellboy. Yet in this episode, Riker wears his uniform into Rex's bar and no one gives it a second look.

EQUIPMENT ODDITIES

• While on the prowl for Picard, Lwaxana invites him to a dinner, calling it an official function. Picard, in dress uniform, arrives thinking the rest of the senior staff will be there. Instead, Lwaxana has prepared an intimate dinner for two. The table that Picard and Lwaxana dine at is very impractical. There is no way to sit at it without straddling its legs. (Of course, that may be a subliminal message Mrs. Troi is trying to get across.)

• "Contagion" also had this next equipment oddity when the *Enterprise* beamed Picard off the Romulan ship. At the end of "Manhunt," Lwaxana comments on Picard's lascivious thoughts toward her after she is almost totally disintegrated by the transporter. The transporter doesn't phase a person into subspace and back. It takes them apart quantum particle by quantum particle and puts the matter into the pattern buffer.

They become transparent because most of the molecules in their body are in the transport buffer. There is no way people could draw air into their lungs if their lungs are full of holes. If you can't draw air in, you can't push air out over the vocal cords. And even if you could, there is no way that vocal cords could produce sound when almost totally disintegrated. In short, a person could not talk.

TRIVIA ANSWERS
1. Four.
2. Nails from Chicago and Carlos from South America.

THE EMISSARY

Star Date: 42901.3

Responding to an emergency message from Starfleet, the *Enterprise* warps to intercept a Class 8 probe. It carries an emissary with information on the ship's next mission. After beaming the probe aboard, Riker and Transporter Chief O'Brien open the two-meter enclosure and K'Ehleyr steps out. She is half human and half Klingon. Six years ago, she and Worf knew each other quite well, although they parted badly. In a briefing with the senior staff, K'Ehleyr explains that a Klingon ship sent out seventy-three years ago is returning from a secret mission. The warriors aboard the ship were placed in suspended animation while the Klingon Empire was still at war with the Federation. When the Klingons awake, they will undoubtedly begin attacking the Federation outposts and colonies in the area. Since the closest Klingon ship is several days away, the *Enterprise* has the unenviable task of solving this problem.

K'Ehleyr recommends only one solution: Destroy the Klingon ship as soon as they find it. Picard dismisses the meeting, instructing K'Ehleyr

Trivia Questions

1. Where was the first Federation outpost established in the Baratas System?

2. What starbase intercepted the message from the rogue Klingon ship?

and Worf to find other options. When Worf and K'Ehleyr are alone, she tries to turn the conversation to their past, but Worf refuses to discuss the events of six years ago. In anger, K'Ehleyr storms back to her quarters. She ends up in the holodeck, taking out her aggressions on Worf's calisthenics program. Worf, also looking to relax, comes to the holodeck and sees his program running. He joins K'Ehleyr. After working out together, they share a "special evening" on the holodeck. Worf then tries to take the oath of marriage, but K'Ehleyr refuses.

Meanwhile, the *Enterprise* locates the rogue Klingon ship. Suddenly Worf has an inspiration. He and K'Ehleyr dress in Klingon uniforms, pretend to be in command of the *Enterprise*, and convince the Klingon captain that the Empire defeated the Federation. Worf then sends K'Ehleyr over to take command until a present-day Klingon vessel arrives.

RUMINATIONS

I would not want K'Ehleyr's job. She will have to dance around the issue of the Klingons winning the war against the Federation for three days before the other Klingon ship arrives. Of course, there is also the matter of the Klingons' reaction when they find out Worf tricked them. Klingons do not respond well to trickery. When Riker tricked the Klingon captain in "A Matter of Honor," the captain came back to his ship and slugged Riker.

EQUIPMENT ODDITIES

• When K'Ehleyr goes to relax on the holodeck, she asks for a menu of exercise programs. The little screen outside the holodeck says "Select Simulation" at the top and begins scrolling through the options. K'Ehleyr then tells the computer to hold one certain item. Even before she reads that item, the top of the screen begins flashing "Simulation in Progress." In other words, just because K'Ehleyr wants to read the description of the current selection, the holodeck has already downloaded a full-blown simulation? Does this seem right? Shouldn't the top of the screen say something like "Ready to Begin Simulation"? Then, after K'Ehleyr makes her selection, it could change to "Simulation in Progress."

CONTINUITY AND PRODUCTION PROBLEMS

• At the beginning of the episode, Riker, Pulaski, Data, La Forge, and Worf play poker. The poker game is a gold mine of continuity errors. As the episode joins the game, Riker, Pulaski, and La Forge all bet "five." (Don't ask me five what. I've never seen Starfleet officers carry money.) Data folds and Worf bets fifty. Riker

then bets fifty and dribbles the chips into the pile in the middle. A close-up shows us that there are no neat stacks of chips in the middle. Pulaski then bets one hundred. She puts them next to the pile of chips in two neat stacks. However, instead of just a pile of chips and Pulaski's two stacks, a long shot shows us that there are four stacks of chips near the pile. In other words, the pile grew two stacks out of nowhere (that is, unless Data made little stacks while we weren't looking; androids could exhibit this type of obsessive-compulsive behavior). Next, La Forge folds. Worf then bets one hundred, moving two stacks to the piles. There are now six stacks around the pile of chips. Riker folds, and Pulaski sees Worf's bet. A close-up shows her moving the stack of chips to the center of the table. However, hers is now the only stack of chips! Somehow a bunch of chips just disappeared. Did Data snitch some when no one was looking? Worf wins the hand, and Pulaski comments that she has no chips left.

The next hand begins. Data deals, and everyone antes up with two chips. Worf opens with fifty. An emergency message comes through and calls Riker, Data, and Worf to the bridge. As the game breaks up, a long shot shows the ante-up pile in the center with three stacks of chips standing near it, and Pulaski suddenly has chips again. (Maybe she bought more when we weren't looking.)

• In "The Schizoid Man," a female Vulcan doctor beams down to Ira

Graves's world with the away team. Her name is Dr. Selar. She bears an uncanny resemblance to K'Ehleyr once the Klingon ridged forehead is replaced with the Vulcan mop-top hairdo. Maybe K'Ehleyr's mother's sister married a Vulcan and Dr. Selar is K'Ehleyr's cousin?

• Toward the end of the show, the main viewer shows the seventy-three-year-old Klingon ship coming toward the *Enterprise*. Interestingly, it is the same footage used for the Klingon ship in the episode "Heart of Glory." In other words, the Klingons haven't changed their ship design in over seventy years? Even more interesting—one year later—the episode "A Matter of Honor" featured a great-looking Klingon ship, obviously a much more advanced design than the one shown in "Heart of Glory." Evidently the Klingons got tired of having nerdy-looking ships and in the time between "Heart of Glory" and "A Matter of Honor" made an all-out effort to improve themselves.

TRIVIA ANSWERS

1. Baratas III.
2. Starbase 336.

PEAK PERFORMANCE

Star Date: 42923.4

For this episode, the crew of the *Enterprise* engages in war games. A Zakdorn named Sirna Kolrami—part of a race legendary for their strategic and tactical skills—boards the *Enterprise* to oversee the simulated battle. The game consists of a mock encounter between the *Enterprise* and an eighty-year-old starship called the *Hathaway*. Riker and a crew of forty will man the *Hathaway*. Picard will command the *Enterprise*. On each ship, lasers will replace weapons, and any hits will be recorded by each ship's computer. Excepting Data, Picard allows Riker to choose the best of the *Enterprise*'s officers for his crew. Prior to the start of the game, Riker's crew prepares several surprises. Worf comes up with a way to display the false image of an attacking ship on the *Enterprise*'s sensors and the main viewscreen. Wesley and La Forge concoct a method to give the *Hathaway* two seconds of warp drive.

Just after the "war" begins, the *Enterprise* bears down on the *Hathaway*. As Picard prepares to fire, Worf makes the *Enterprise* think a Romulan vessel is attacking. Picard swings the *Enterprise* around, allowing Riker to score several simulated hits. Picard realizes what Riker and Worf have done and reengages the *Hathaway*. Just as he is about to finish them off, the ensign at tactical reports the approach of a Ferengi vessel. Picard assumes it is another trick. When the phaser blasts rock the ship, he realizes it isn't. By the time Picard gets the *Enterprise* turned around to face the Ferengi, his ship is damaged. The Ferengi demand that Picard turn over the *Hathaway*, or they will destroy both ships.

Picard and Riker decide on a desperate plan. The *Enterprise* fires its few remaining photon torpedoes directly at the *Hathaway* at the same time Riker kicks in his warp drive. The ploy leaves the Ferengi believing that Picard destroyed the *Hathaway* and they leave.

PLOT OVERSIGHTS

• Several times this episode shows that Worf can project a false image on the sensors and viewscreen of the *Enterprise*. Why? Because he

---

Trivia Questions

1. What is Kolrami's status in the game of Strategema?

2. What is the final score in Data's first game of Strategema with Kolrami?

knows the Security override codes for the systems involved. This makes perfectly good sense. Worf works on the *Enterprise*. He understands how the computer systems work. However, at the end of the episode, Worf also manages to project a false image on the Ferengi ship's sensors. How can Worf do this? He doesn't have the Security override codes for the Ferengi ship, and he doesn't know their computer systems.

EQUIPMENT ODDITIES

• When Riker and his crew beam onto the *Hathaway*, they carry flashlights with them because the lights aren't turned on. It's good to see that First Alert is still in business in the twenty-fourth century! (The flashlights they are using look identical to ones made by First Alert.)

• La Forge and Wesley hot-wire the warp drive for the *Hathaway* by using an experiment Wesley grabs from the *Enterprise*. It contains the needed antimatter. As Wesley pulls the experiment out of its storage bin, he is very careful. Later, when he and La Forge place it in the warp engines, La Forge urges caution. Presumably this thing is volatile. Yet, when Wesley beams it over to the *Hathaway*, he beams it onto a small tabletop. Since the container is round, it rolls to a resting place (Yes, it is a nice effect as it materializes in.) If this thing is so unstable, why beam it onto a tabletop and take the chance it will roll off? (By the way, this little scene causes a hiccup in the *Star Trek: The Next Generation Technical Manual*. In the section dealing with antimatter, the authors state that antimatter cannot be beamed through a transporter without making extensive modification to the circuitry. Then they backtrack and say that it is possible to beam small amounts if the antimatter is in an approved container! Obviously the authors had to account for this scene in "Peak Performance.")

TRIVIA ANSWERS

1. Third-level grand master.
2. Kolrami 100, Data 81.

SHADES OF GRAY

Star Date: 42976.1

While Riker performs a preliminary geological survey on an unexplored planet, a plant jabs him in the leg. The plant has infected him with microbes, we soon learn, and if not checked, the microbes will eventually reach Riker's brain and kill him.

When the microbes reach her patient's spinal cord, Pulaski brings in a machine to stimulate Riker's brain directly and keep him alive. The machine inserts long rods into Riker's head. As Pulaski diddles with the machine, Riker begins to reexperience his adventures aboard the *Enterprise*.

These memories apparently affect the microbes' metabolism. Pulaski realizes that bad memories and stressful emotions retard the microbes' growth. She deduces that the microbes must be sensitive to endorphins—chemicals produced by the brain. She "refocuses" the machine to give Riker more bad memories. After a series of flashbacks from previous episodes, the microbes get fed up and die.

GREAT LINES

"I hope these are the right coordinates."—Transporter Chief O'Brien needling a nervous Dr. Pulaski before she beams down to the planet.

PLOT OVERSIGHTS

• Early on, Pulaski recognizes that the microbes respond to brain endorphins. She then proceeds to jolt Riker with a machine so his brain can produce them. Yet, while she does it, she worries that the stress may kill him.

In "The Battle," Dr. Crusher claims that twenty-fourth century medical science has "mapped the brain." If they have mapped the brain, doesn't it seem reasonable that they would understand the endorphins the brain produces under different circumstances? Shouldn't they be able to manufacture these brain endorphins in a replicator and inject them in Riker? Then again, if Pulaski could make the endorphins, we would miss all these really keen flashbacks! (Sorry, I'm fighting to control my innate disdain for flashback shows.)

• The flashbacks are supposed to be from Riker's memory. However, in a flashback from "Skin of Evil," Rik-

Trivia Questions

1. Why couldn't the transporter's biofilters screen out the microbes?

2. What shows do the flashbacks come from? (List, in sequence and by title, including repeats.)

er gets sucked into an oil puddle, after which Data reports to Picard. The scene then changes to the main bridge, and Picard responds. In the background, an ensign walks down the ramp.

If this is Riker's memory, how did he know an ensign walked down the ramp behind Picard at that point? He was in the oil puddle down on the planet. Likewise, in the flashback from "Heart of Glory," Riker is on a damaged ship when we see scenes of the main bridge and hear conversations between Picard and Yar.

EQUIPMENT ODDITIES

• As the microbes attack Riker's spinal cord, Pulaski uses a machine to stimulate Riker's brain. As Pulaski operates the machine, she looks in a pair of eyepieces and presses buttons. Her fingers are unusually adept in that she seems to hit the right buttons without even looking. Considering that all the control surfaces on the *Enterprise* are flat, that's

quite a feat!

TRIVIA ANSWERS

1. The microbes fused with the neurons at a molecular level.
2. "The Last Outpost," "Encounter at Farpoint," "The Dauphin," "The Icarus Factor," "Justice," "11001001," "Angel One," "Up the Long Ladder," "Skin of Evil," "The Child," "A Matter of Honor," "Conspiracy," "Symbiosis" (just prior to this, Dr. Pulaski taps the control panel of the neural stimulator without looking), "The Last Outpost," "Skin of Evil," "11001001," "Heart of Glory" (unknown clip of solar activity), "Conspiracy," "The Last Outpost," "Symbiosis," "Conspiracy," "11001001," "The Naked Now," "Skin of Evil," "A Matter of Honor," "11001001," "Loud as a Whisper," "A Matter of Honor," "11001001," "Unnatural Selection," "11001001," "Heart of Glory," "Conspiracy," "11001001," "The Naked Now," "Skin of Evil" (audio only).

★ MY PERSONAL FAVORITES

T he bloopers in this list are my favorites for one simple reason. I didn't see them the first time I watched the episode. I didn't see them the second time or the third. Somewhere around the fourth time through the episodes, they started showing up. Suddenly they were there and I could believe I hadn't seen them before. I suppose, after watching an episode several times, the eyes begin to wander. Occasionally they wander into the right portion of the screen at the right time and another entry is made in the Nitpickers' Guide. (And I must confess that even I didn't find two of my favorites; friends pointed them out.) I've listed them by episode. The reviews of these episodes give an expanded explanation of the bloopers.

1. "Encounter at Farpoint." As Riker goes to the holodeck to meet Data for the first time, the computer tells him that the holodeck is the next door on the right. Riker turns *left* and walks into the holodeck.

2. "Code of Honor." For the *Enterprise* to take delivery of a much-needed vaccine, Yar must battle to the death with Yareena. During the entire fight, Yar's weapon—a metal bar covered with spikes—covers her left hand and arm. At the very end of the battle, Yar falls on a lifeless Yareena and is transported to the *Enterprise*. When Yar materializes, the weapon is on her *right* hand.

3. "Too Short a Season." As Picard and Riker leave the main bridge to greet Admiral Jameson, they use the turbolift near the captain's ready room. Just before boarding the turbolift, Picard contorts his face and then immediately resumes his normal somber expression.

4. "Heart of Glory." When discussing the Klingon they've rescued from a damaged freighter, Picard says to Riker, "There is more to this than we've been told. Why was the Tarellian ship so far off course?" The ship wasn't Tarellian, it was *Talarian*.

5. "Symbiosis." Most people think "Skin of Evil" was the last episode Yar appeared in (until "Yesterday's *Enterprise*," of course). In fact, "Symbiosis" was produced after "Skin of Evil" even though it was aired before it. Near the end of "Symbiosis," Picard and Crusher leave a cargo bay after Yar beamed the Onarans and the Brekkians to the planet below. As the cargo bay doors close, Yar—far in the background of the shot—takes one last

moment to wave good-bye to all the fans.

6. "The Price." In one scene, Troi and Devinoni Ral enjoy an intimate dinner in her quarters. At one point, Ral lifts his fork to his mouth and takes a bite. The only problem is that there is nothing on the fork.

7. "Brother." In this episode, Data commandeers the ship and flies it to a planet that houses his creator, Dr. Noonian Soong. Before leaving the ship, Data gives the computer a code that locks out all command functions. Data rapidly spits out a string of fifty-three numbers and words. The next shot shows the computer recording the code, displaying it on a terminal, and storing it in memory. A careful frame-by-frame analysis shows that the computer does not record what Data said exactly. It misses two numbers and then adds one of its own.

8. "Half a Life." Close to the end of this episode, Lwaxana and Troi have a heart-to-heart talk. Lwaxana walks in front of a mirror. In the reflection, you can see the boom part of the boom mike that records the audio for the scene.

9. "Unification II." As Picard, Spock, and Data escape from Sela's office, the camera pans across Sela's desk. In the crystal pyramid that decorates the desk, you can see a man with curly hair and glasses chewing on a piece of gum.

10. "Cost of Living." Near the end of the episode, Picard and Data ride a turbolift to the main bridge. For the entire scene, shot from multiple camera angles, Picard has only three pips on his collar.

Third Season

EVOLUTION

Star Date: 43125.8

For this first show of the third season of *Star Trek: The Next Generation*, Dr. Paul Stubbs comes aboard the *Enterprise*. Dr. Stubbs is a scientist of great fame. Starfleet has ordered the *Enterprise* to assist him in a time-critical experiment. Once every 197 years, the matter that builds up on the surface of a particular star explodes, creating the galaxy's equivalent of "Old Faithful." As Shuttle Bay 2 prepares to launch Dr. Stubbs's experiment, computer systems start to fail on the *Enterprise*. The problems increase and threaten the mission. Stubbs is distraught because the experiment is his life's work.

The crew finally locates the problem. While working on an experiment for genetics, Wesley allowed two "Nanites" to escape. Nanites are tiny machines with billions of bytes of memory. They are designed to enter the cells of living tissue and make repairs. Normally, they only work alone. Wesley taught them to work together, to reproduce and make each generation better. Thousands of the Nanites have invaded the computer core. They are eating the memory chips. Stubbs recommends extermination. Picard refuses to obliterate wantonly an entity that may have a new collective intelligence.

As Data, La Forge, and Wesley work in the main computer to clear the Nanites, Stubbs enters. He fires gamma radiation into the memory banks and destroys all the Nanites in the upper core. The Nanites respond by pumping nitrous oxide in the main bridge. This specific reaction on the Nanites' part lends further credence to the possibility they may be intelligent. After working with the Universal Translator for some time, Data contacts the Nanites. With Picard's permission, he allows the Nanites to enter his neural network so they can meet face-to-face with Picard. After Stubbs apologizes for his actions, the Nanites agree to a truce. The Nanites help repair the main computer, and Stubbs's experiment is a success.

RUMINATIONS

As with the first episode of the second season, the creators took the opportunity to tweak a few

Trivia Questions

1. What song plays on the bridge?

2. Who is at the plate in Stubbs's mental game of baseball?

items. *These are the ones I found:*

• *Starfleet uniforms no longer have zippers down the front.*

• *The uniforms now have a small collar.*

• *Dr. Beverly Crusher is back (great rejoicing followed the departure of Pulaski).*

• *The shuttle bays now have enclosed launch control rooms.*

PLOT OVERSIGHTS

• Shortly after discovering that his Nanites are missing, Wesley begins setting traps around the ship. He heads for Ten-Forward and sets two traps approximately six feet apart behind the bar. Using this spacing throughout the ship would require thousands and thousands of traps. Does Wesley have thousands of traps to put out, or does he think the Nanites have a predisposition to bars?

• When the Nanites start pumping poisonous gas into the main bridge, Picard and Riker are in the ready room. They come out and join in the coughing with the rest of the bridge crew. Riker then walks up to the environmental controls. A few moments later, he switches the air handlers to manual. The atmosphere on the bridge returns to normal.

Is Riker the only person who knew how to do this? If he is, it's a good thing he was around. Otherwise, everyone would just have sat in their chairs and coughed until they died.

• Given the attacks on the *Enterprise* by the Nanites, it is difficult to believe that Picard would allow them to take over a bridge officer, espe-cially one with the strength and intelligence of Data. However, Worf is the only one who protests this course of action.

CONTINUITY AND PRODUCTION PROBLEMS

• In the opening shot, the *Enterprise* is in geosynchronous orbit around a giant red star and faces a smaller neutron star. A little later, Riker tells Shuttle Bay 2 to prepare to launch Dr. Stubbs's probe. As the shuttle bay doors open, the scene shows the giant red star and the smaller star in the distance. Shuttle Bay 2 is on the back side of the yoke. To see this view, the *Enterprise* would have to turn 180 degrees from the previous shot. Then, just before launching the probe, the *Enterprise* starts bouncing around and drifting toward the red star. In the next shot we see that the *Enterprise* is once again facing the smaller star. In other words, it flipped back to its original position? Or, more likely, did the postproduction people forget that the shuttle bay doors are on the back side of the ship?

Additionally, in the scene showing the *Enterprise* drifting toward the red star, the back of the *Enterprise* clearly shows that the shuttle bay doors are closed! Evidently someone had the presence of mind to slam the doors shut as soon as the *Enterprise* started bouncing around.

• After Stubbs kills the Nanites in the upper core, Troi visits him in his quarters. When he refuses her counseling help, she turns to leave. The next shot shows a medium close-up of

Stubbs, and the following shot shows Troi standing by the open door of his quarters. However, there is no door-opening "swish" during the shot of Stubbs when the door must have opened. This is very significant, because the person who dubs in all of those "swishes" is *very good* at

what he or she does. This is one of the few times that person missed.

TRIVIA ANSWERS
1. "The Stars and Stripes Forever" by John Philip Sousa.
2. Thompson.

THE ENSIGNS OF COMMAND

Star Date: 43133.4

The *Enterprise* receives a message from the Sheliak Corporate. Believing that humans are a lower life form, this nonhumanoid race has not communicated with the Federation for 111 years. The Sheliak claim that humans inhabit a world deeded to them in their treaty with the Federation. In accordance with the treaty, the Sheliak demand that the Federation remove the colony before Sheliak settlers arrive in three days. The treaty is the only reason the Sheliak didn't obliterate the humans immediately upon discovery.

The *Enterprise* arrives at the planet. It exists in an area of hyperonic radiation, radiation that should be fatal to humans. Since the radiation also disables sensors, transporters, and phasers, Picard sends Data to the surface in a shuttle. Data finds a thriving colony of more than fifteen thousand. Ninety-three years ago, their colony ship went off course and landed on the planet. Although Data tries to prepare the colonists for evacuation, their leader refuses to leave. He intends to make a stand and fight for the planet.

Trivia Questions

1. What is the life form classification of the Sheliak?

2. How many legal experts did the Federation send to negotiate with the Sheliak?

When Starfleet informs Picard that the nearest ship with dedicated shuttles is three weeks away, he takes the *Enterprise* to meet the ship carrying the Sheliak settlers. He hopes to negotiate an amicable settlement. Unfortunately, the Sheliak won't budge. Picard then finds a clause in the treaty that allows him to ask for third-party arbitration, and he names the Grizzelli as arbiters. Since the Grizzelli hibernate for half of each year, Picard knows he will have months to get the colonists off the planet. At this, the Sheliak cave in and agree to give Picard another three weeks to allow the evacuation of the planet.

Back on the planet, Data stages a demonstration with a phaser, stunning four guards and almost blowing up a water pumping station. Data makes the point that he is one android with one phaser and there are hundreds of Sheliak coming with much more powerful weapons. The colonists elect to leave the planet.

RUMINATIONS

There is a definite "guy thing" at the end of this show. The leader of the human colony refuses even to listen to Data until Data brings a gun and starts shooting people. That's a "guy thing." There is also a "gal thing." At the end of the show, the female colonist who assists Data throughout the show longingly expects him to have feelings for her. This female colonist knows Data is an android, bereft of feelings, and she wants to experience some emotional outburst from him.

PLOT OVERSIGHTS

• As the *Enterprise* warps over to meet the Sheliak settlers' ship, Picard and Troi talk about language. She says that the Sheliak have managed to learn a few of the Federation's languages but theirs still eludes Federation linguists. She comments that it is remarkable that one race can communicate with another at all.

What happened to the Universal Translator? If humans had to learn other languages, there wouldn't even be a television show. The only reason it is feasible for the crew of the *Enterprise* to fly around and talk English with everyone is because the Universal Translator supposedly takes care of language problems.

• This is a minor point but worth noting. Any treaty, especially this particular treaty, is a legal, binding document. Because the parties involved will invoke pieces of it during discussion, the numbering and organization scheme should be consistent. Yet the first time anyone refers to the treaty, the person uses the locator phrase "Paragraph 653, subparagraph 9." The next time, the phrase

changes a little: "Section 501, paragraph 716, subparagraph 5." The final time the locator phrase is, "Paragraph 1290" and then "subsection D-3."

So what is the label for the major divisions of this treaty? Is it paragraphs or sections? If it's sections, then every paragraph should be preceded by a section number. If the major division is paragraphs, then why refer to sections at all? (I suppose that the treaty could be laid out with both paragraphs and sections as the major divisions, but this seems needlessly confusing, especially since Troi claims the Sheliak think that the language of the Federation is imprecise.)

EQUIPMENT ODDITIES

• Great confusion surrounds this issue of subspace communications. At times the *Enterprise* is so distant that it takes a considerable amount of time to get a message to another ship or planet. For instance, in "The Battle" it took a day to get a message to Starfleet headquarters. (I understand that this is a convenient plot device, but something is clearly wrong in "The Ensigns of Command.") Most of the time, however, the *Enterprise* can communicate instantly.

When Picard wants to talk with the Sheliak home world, Worf says, "Their home world is quite distant. This will take some time." So far, so good. This is a case where it takes a considerable amount of time to transmit a message. Presumably, Worf comments on the delay because it will take a while for the communications request to reach the Sheliak home world. Yet when Worf finally makes contact, Picard has a dialogue with the Sheliak! There is no delay for transmission time.

Surely the request for communications can travel as fast as the actual communication. So if it takes a while for the request to get there, it will take a while for any communication to get there. In other words, Picard would speak a sentence and have to wait while the sentence traveled to the Sheliak. Then the Sheliak would reply, and the reply would travel back. The scene does not show any communication delays.

• Someone has been renaming or renumbering the shuttles of the *Enterprise*. In this episode, Data pilots Shuttle Craft "05" to the planet. A scene at the end of the show gives the name of the shuttle as *Onizuka*. However, in the episode "Times Squared," Shuttle Craft "05" was named *El-Baz*.

TRIVIA ANSWERS
1. R-3.
2. Three hundred seventy-two.

THE SURVIVORS

Star Dates: 43152.4-43153.7

The *Enterprise* responds to a distress call from a colony on Rana IV, reportedly under attack. By the time the *Enterprise* arrives, the inhabitants of the planet are dead—all except two. Riker and his away team find an older couple named Kevin and Rishon Uxbridge, but no explanation of who attacked the planet or why these two survived. A short time later, an alien warship appears, fires on the *Enterprise*, and then retreats. When the *Enterprise* tries to pursue, the warship outruns the *Enterprise*. Picard then orders the *Enterprise* back to the planet. This time he and Worf visit the couple on the planet. When they return to the ship, the warship reappears—more powerful than before. With its increased weaponry, the alien warship forces the *Enterprise* to retreat. After an hour, the *Enterprise* flies back to the planet to find the warship gone.

Acting on a hunch, Picard beams down to the planet and informs the Uxbridges that the *Enterprise* will remain in orbit as long as they are alive. As expected, the alien warship reappears. This time, however, it destroys the Uxbridges' home and the couple with it. For the next three hours, Picard and the *Enterprise* wait in orbit. Suddenly the couple and their house reappear on the planet. Picard beams them to the *Enterprise* and uncovers the truth. Kevin Uxbridge is a Douwd —an eternal being with great powers. More than fifty years ago, he set aside his powers when he met Rishon and fell in love. A few days before, the Husnak—a race of hideous intelligence—attacked Rana IV. Kevin tried to use his powers to chase the Husnak away, but his actions only angered them. When they obliterated the colony and killed his wife, Kevin went insane with rage and killed all the Husnak, everywhere. His shame for this deed caused him to try to trick the *Enterprise* into leaving. With no law to judge Kevin by, Picard lets him return to the planet and re-create his house and wife.

Trivia Questions

1. What is the location of the Uxbridge house?

2. What is the power of the weaponry of the alien ship when the *Enterprise* engages it the second time?

GREAT LINES
"Good tea. Nice house."—Worf, making small talk over tea at the Uxbridge home.

PLOT OVERSIGHTS

• When the first away team goes to the planet, Kevin realizes that the *Enterprise* is in orbit. At the same time, he perceives that Troi is sensing his nonhumanness from the *Enterprise*, so he sends music to confuse her. Then Kevin creates a warship that attacks and retreats from the *Enterprise*. The warship precisely matches the *Enterprise*'s acceleration to maintain a constant distance. In the next encounter with the *Enterprise*, Kevin re-creates an even meaner warship. In addition, the final time the warship appears, Kevin causes it to destroy his house. All of these actions take place in space, while Kevin is on the surface of the planet. Evidently he can control elements far beyond the range of his physical human senses, and he can control them *interactively*. That means he can respond to changing stimuli. Controlling events interactively usually means the controller has some way of sensing the situation. Kevin can't precisely match the *Enterprise*'s acceleration if he doesn't know the *Enterprise*'s acceleration, right? Also, he wouldn't know to send music to scramble Troi's brains if he couldn't sense her in orbit. She never went on an away team.

Yet every time an away team beams down to Rana IV, Kevin acts surprised. Picard even notes his surprise at one point. How can Kevin be surprised by the presence of the *En-terprise*? He must be able to sense things in space. Why can't he sense when the *Enterprise* drops into orbit? As further evidence that Kevin should be able to sense the *Enterprise*, consider the following: With a single thought, Kevin destroyed an entire race of people, *wherever* they happened to be in the galaxy. How could Kevin destroy all the Husnak without being able to sense them throughout the galaxy? If Kevin could sense the Husnak throughout the galaxy, surely he could sense the *Enterprise* in orbit around his planet.

CONTINUITY AND PRODUCTION PROBLEMS

• A short while after Picard beams the Uxbridges to the main bridge of the *Enterprise*, Kevin dematerializes, drops down a turbolift shaft, and visits Troi. An instant after the Douwd begins to transport himself to Troi's quarters, however, La Forge turns and looks at the turbolift. This is before Kevin fully disappears. How did La Forge know that Kevin would use that particular turbolift? Can La Forge foretell the future? (I guess having this ability would help him do a really good job at preventive mainte-nance!)

TRIVIA ANSWERS

1. Thirty-seven degrees north, sixty-two degrees east.
2. Four hundred gigawatts of particle energy.

WHO WATCHES THE WATCHERS

Star Dates: 43173.5-43174.2

he *Enterprise* responds to a distress call from an anthropological studies group on Mintaka III. The scientists are observing an extended family of Mintakans—a proto-Vulcan race in the Bronze Age of development. Unfortunately, the anthropologists' reactor has malfunctioned. The *Enterprise* is warping over to provide repairs. Among other things, the reactor provides power for the scientists' holographic camouflage. As the generator shorts out, arcing electricity injures the scientists, and the camouflage evaporates. When an away team beams down to assist the scientists, a Mintakan watches the scene. When he is discovered, the Mintakan falls backward off a ledge and injures himself. Dr. Crusher beams him to sick bay.

While in sick bay, the Mintakan sees Picard. He comes to believe that Picard is an "overseer," the Mintakan term for "god." Dr. Crusher tries to erase the Mintakan's short-term memory, but the procedure fails. Upon return, the Mintakan begins formulating a system of beliefs based on his experience. The head anthro-

Trivia Questions

1. What is the power output of the anthropologists' generator?

2. What is the name of the medical assistant who takes Warren to sick bay?

pologist, Dr. Barron, suggests that Picard beam down and give the Mintakans a set of rules.

Instead, Picard brings the female leader of the Mintakan group aboard the *Enterprise*. He explains that he is flesh and blood just like the Mintakans. The leader is finally convinced when she sees one of the anthropologists die from injuries. Picard and the leader beam back to the planet. The male Mintakan whom Dr. Crusher took to sick bay refuses to believe Picard is just a man. He wants Picard to resurrect his wife. The man tries to prove that Picard is the overseer by shooting him with an arrow. It hits Picard in the left shoulder. When the Mintakans see the blood, they realize Picard is just like them.

PLOT OVERSIGHTS

• The *Star Trek* genre has traditionally been "message" television. Beginning with the original *Star Trek* series, Gene Roddenberry used futuristic settings to deal with sensitive topics. For instance, to demonstrate the stupidity of racism, he put two men on display. Both of them had two-tone skin—half black, half white. However, one had the black skin on the right side while the other had the black skin on the left side. This difference became a source of unending conflict and eventually destroyed their world. This innovative setting allowed the viewer to see racism in a new light—to evaluate it without the interference of predispositions.

Star Trek: The Next Generation carries on this tradition to some extent. The creators attempt to deal with difficult topics in meaningful ways. Occasionally, however, the series has all the subtlety of a placard emblazoned with, "Message, people. Here comes the *message!* Make sure you don't miss THE MESSAGE." In short, the series can get heavy-handed.

This episode is a good example. Its message can be summarized in two statements. First, the creators propose that any belief in one or more supernatural beings is bad. Picard says that reviving the Mintakan belief in the overseers would send them back to the "dark ages of superstition and ignorance and fear." (I guess we know how the writers feel about belief in the supernatural.) Second, the creators of this episode propose that a codified framework will prevent religious belief from degenerating into cacophony. Dr. Barron, the anthropological expert in this episode, tells Picard that without a rule book the Mintakan belief could degenerate into "inquisitions, holy wars ... chaos."

Human history proves the falsehood of this second statement. Both Christianity and Islam have highly codified beliefs. Yet, at times, both have engaged in inquisitions and holy wars. Religious abuse doesn't occur because of a rule book. It occurs because individuals thrive on controlling others. This desire for control extends beyond supernatural belief systems. It permeates every level of our society—from government to the home.

In addition, a Gallup poll conducted in 1986 showed that 94 percent of Americans believe in God or a universal spirit. (The Gallup organization has not conducted a "belief in God" survey since that time.) Therefore, the first message statement—that all belief in the supernatural is bad, superstitious and ignorant—effectively classifies the great majority of Americans as dolts.

CHANGED PREMISES

• At the very end of the show, Picard says good-bye to the Mintakans. Even though—in his voice-over just prior to this scene—Picard claims that Dr. Crusher has tended to his injuries with her usual skill, Picard wears a sling to support his arm. Why is Picard in a sling? This is the twenty-fourth century. Medicine has come a long way. In the episode "Clues," Dr. Crusher knits Worf's wrist back together with a bone knitter. In "Suddenly Human," a young man stabs Picard with a vicious-looking knife. A short time later, Picard is on the bridge. Guess what? No sling.

TRIVIA ANSWERS
1. It is 4.2 gigawatts.
2. Martinez.

THE BONDING

As the episode opens, an away team conducts an archaeological dig on a planet. Worf, leading the away team, makes an emergency distress call. Picard has the team beamed directly to sick bay, but Dr. Marla Aster, an *Enterprise* archaeologist, is "dead on arrival." Picard and Troi deliver the news to the now-orphaned son of Dr. Aster, Jeremy. Jeremy's father died five years before.

As Jeremy, alone in his quarters, reviews old family movies of himself and his mother, an energy field appears on the planet and leaps toward the *Enterprise*. A simulation of Dr. Aster peeks around the corner and greets him. The planet below once supported two races of people—one of energy, the other of matter. The physical beings battled themselves to extinction. Dr. Aster was killed when she activated an old land mine from those wars. The energy beings refuse to allow any more suffering because of the ignominious past of the physical beings. On the planet, they will create everything needed—mother, friends, wife, children—to ensure that Jeremy is hap-

Trivia Questions

1. What was Aster's rank?

2. Where is Jeremy's quarters?

py. Of course, Picard and Troi struggle to keep Jeremy on the ship, knowing the futility of living in the fantasy world that the energy beings would create. Eventually the crew of the *Enterprise* convinces the energy beings that Jeremy will be loved and well cared for. The simulation of Aster evaporates.

PLOT OVERSIGHTS

• Troi reacts to the explosion that kills Aster on the surface several seconds before Worf calls for the emergency beam-up. Even starting with Troi's reaction, however, there are only thirty-two seconds from that moment until Dr. Crusher declares Aster dead. There are no resuscitation attempts and no efforts to get Aster stabilized. Was Aster not worth the effort?

• It's no wonder that the energy beings think Jeremy won't be cared for. Shortly after Picard tells him about his mother's death, a shot follows of Jeremy in his quarters. He is there *alone*, watching old movies of his mom. This concept of Jeremy's aloneness in his room continues well into the show. Does this seem right?

This kid has just lost his only surviving parent, and everyone stays away. He is only twelve. Shouldn't someone be staying close by to help him through this time?

• Speaking of these old home movies Jeremy watches, who shot them, anyway? It couldn't be Dad. *If it was, Jeremy hasn't aged in five years.*

• At the end of the show, Worf and Jeremy perform a Klingon ceremony of bonding. Out of the blue, Worf rattles off a Klingon phrase. Jeremy asks what it means, and Worf explains. Then Jeremy rattles off the complete phrase! (This Jeremy must be quite a linguist. My nine-year-old daughter is no intellectual slouch, but when she heard the boy actor do it she said, "I bet that boy had to practice a long time to get it right." I bet he did. In the show, however, we are asked to believe that Jeremy could do it after hearing it only once.)

CONTINUITY AND PRODUCTION PROBLEMS

• This show has the worst continuity error of any *Star Trek: The Next Generation* episode. Close to the end, Jeremy confronts Worf about his mother's death. Jeremy is half turned, half seated on the couch. Worf is behind him. One shot shows Jeremy's back when Worf talks. The other shows Worf's back when Jeremy talks. In the shot showing Jeremy's back, his left arm is in front of a pillow. In the other shot, Jeremy's arm is behind the pillow. The arm jerks back and forth as the shots alternate. Then the alien pseudomother walks around in front of Jeremy. A side shot shows Jeremy kneeling on the couch. The front shot shows him half seated, as before. Of course, Jeremy bobs up and down as these shots sequence!

TRIVIA ANSWERS

1. Lieutenant.
2. Deck 8.

BOOBY TRAP

Star Date: 43205.6

The *Enterprise* passes through a debris field created in the final confrontation of a terrible war. In it, the Menthars and Promellians fought to their mutual extinction over a thousand years ago. After responding to a distress signal, the *Enterprise* encounters a mint-condition Promellian battle cruiser from that old war. Suddenly the *Enterprise* begins losing energy. A high-intensity field of radiation surrounds the ship. Both impulse and warp engines fail to move the ship. The *Enterprise* is caught in the same booby trap that imprisoned the other ship and killed all its crew members.

While Riker and Data try to understand how the trap functions, La Forge works to increase power output. In the process, he uses a holodeck to generate the original prototypes of the engines and a representation of one of the engineers on the design team, Dr. Leah Brahms. A short time later, the crew determines that at least one hundred thousand "aceton assimilators" lie hidden in the debris field. These machines can draw energy from distant sources. Evidently they have been modified to redirect that energy as lethal radiation. Every time the *Enterprise* increases energy to leave the area, the assimilators increase their outpost and counteract the propulsion. Soon the shields will fall due to lack of energy. Twenty-six minutes later, everyone on board the *Enterprise* will be dead.

In the end, La Forge determines only two possible solutions. Possibly the computer can fly them out. The other option is to shut everything down except two thrusters. With one final blast from the impulse engines, they might be able to creep their way to safety. Picard chooses the second option and flies the *Enterprise* out of danger.

Trivia Questions

1. What is the name of the young lady La Forge seeks to impress with his holodeck programming?

2. What battle strategy of the Menthars was comparable to one used by Napoleon?

PLOT OVERSIGHTS

• At the beginning of the episode, Data identifies the debris field as the remains of Iralius IX. Wesley says it was the scene of the final battle. Data agrees. Later, Captain Picard makes a log entry that states they have "arrived at Iralius IX to chart the battle in which the Menthars and the Promellians fought to their mutual extinction. Among the ruins we have found a relic." (He was referring to the Promellian cruiser.)

Usually a designation such as "Iralius IX" indicates it is the ninth planet from a sun called Iralius. Presumably the chunks of rock floating in space near the *Enterprise* used to form a planet. This planet was totally obliterated by the war. Data supports this assumption when he and Wesley observe the rubble and Data comments that "the level of destruction is remarkable."

But if Iralius IX was originally a planet, wouldn't the assimilators have had to be placed in the debris after the battle that decimated the planet? And if the battle that destroyed the planet was the battle where the enemies fought to their mutual extinction, who placed the assimilators? Obviously the assimilators must have been placed before the final conflict, which means that the debris field could not be Iralius IX. But that would contradict Picard, because he identifies the Promellian cruiser as being among the ruins of Iralius IX.

• Of course, there is another minor issue concerning the Promellian cruiser. Why hasn't someone already found this ship? It's been out here for a thousand years. Evidently somebody investigated the area prior to the arrival of the *Enterprise*, since the crew knows that this was the location of the final battle.

• Continuing with the Promellian battle cruiser, why is this vessel sending out a distress call? The captain of that ship knew the assimilators were destroying his ship. Why lure another craft into the trap?

• Finally, Picard seems to forget that the Promellian battle cruiser "belongs in a museum" at the end of the show. He blows it up. This is a mint-condition, thousand-year-old artifact. There is nothing wrong with the ship. It is just surrounded by assimilators. Doesn't the Federation have the technology to clear the booby trap and tow the ship out? Look at it this way. Suppose the original manuscripts of J. S. Bach's *Well-Tempered Clavier* existed in a house surrounded by a minefield. In time, a government official discovers them but almost gets killed as he leaves to file a report. Does he order a bomb strike to make sure no one else gets hurt?

CHANGED PREMISES

• Poor Lieutenant Commander Geordi La Forge—here he is on the *Enterprise*, populated by the finest of Starfleet's engineering staff, and he has to get a holographic representation to help him solve a problem. This strains credulity. I would expect a more professional approach, like the one in "Hollow Pursuits." In that episode, La Forge called his top engineers together to solve a perplexing problem.

EQUIPMENT ODDITIES

• These Promellians must make an incredible battery. Remember that the assimilators have drained all power from this vessel. Yet, it still manages to send out a distress call for not one, not ten, not a hundred but a thousand years!

• Just after finding the battle cruiser, Picard, Data, and Worf beam over. On the bridge on the vessel, Data locates a recording of the Promellian captain. They play it back using the Promellian equipment, and the Promellian captain talks to them in modern English! (Never mind that the recording was made a thousand years before, at a time when humans spoke using "thees" and "thous.") True, it might be possible—since Data is using his tricorder to amplify the signal—that the built-in Universal Translator is converting the Promellian language to English. If it is, the tricorder is a truly amazing device. First, it reads the recording, both audio and video. Next, it translates the recording to English. Then it touches up the video so the Promellian captain is lip-synced to the new recording. Finally, it broadcasts the resulting images back to the Promellian viewer. And it does all this after instantaneously comprehending the technology of the Promellians!

• While La Forge searches for ways to increase power output, he happens across Leah Brahms's name and asks the computer for more information. The screen switches to a format that has Brahms's name in the upper left, a blank space underneath, and the biographical information on the right. Yet when Troi

looks up information on Devinoni Ral in the episode "The Price," she gets the same type of readout except that she gets a picture of Ral under his name. Why didn't La Forge get a picture also?

• At the end of the show, although La Forge says they are going to shut everything off and use only two thrusters, Picard actually uses three—starboard, port, and starboard aft. But then again, who's counting? And speaking of thrusters, when Picard fires the starboard thruster, the next shot shows an exhaust stream on the yoke of the star drive section. However, when Picard uses the port thruster, no exhaust shows. In addition, the port thruster gets turned on twice but never turned off!

CONTINUITY AND PRODUCTION PROBLEMS

• At the very beginning of this episode, La Forge tries to woo a young lady on the holodeck. In the opening shot, La Forge's date has her arm in her lap. In the next shot, the arm is back behind her.

TRIVIA ANSWERS

1. Christie Henshaw. (This episode supplies only her first name, but "Transfigurations" fills in the second.)
2. The passive lure stratagem.

THE ENEMY

An away team of Riker, Worf, and La Forge beam down to Galorndon Core—an inhospitable planet buffeted by severe electromagnetic storms. The Enterprise received an unknown distress call from the planet and is investigating. La Forge locates a crashed Romulan craft. The away team spreads out to search for survivors. Riker and Worf return a few minutes later with a wounded Romulan. La Forge, however, is missing. The storm intensifies and they must beam back without him. The storms on Galorndon Core limit the use of the Enterprise's sensors, but Wesley suggests they shoot down a neutrino beacon. The neutrinos can easily pass through the storm. When La Forge finds the beacon he can alter its pulse rate. This will help the Enterprise locate him.

Unfortunately, just before La Forge reaches the beacon, another Romulan attacks him from behind. As the magnetic fields of the planet affect both La Forge and the Romulan, La Forge loses his vision, while the Romulan's legs turn numb. With no other choice, they decide to work together to find the beacon. Meanwhile, a Romulan warship confronts the Enterprise and demands the return of the other Romulan soldier. Picard reluctantly advises the commander that the man is dead. The commander readies his ship for war. At that moment, La Forge modifies the beam. Picard beams both La Forge and the Romulan to the bridge. He placates the Romulan commander by returning La Forge's friend.

> **Trivia Questions**
>
> 1. How did La Forge detect the Romulan craft?
>
> 2. Besides Pearl Harbor, what other location does Picard remember as the stage for events that comprised a "bloody preamble to war"?

RUMINATIONS

This episode stumped the nitpicker. I couldn't find anything wrong with it! Kudos to the creators.

TRIVIA ANSWERS

1. He used a positron scan.
2. Station Salem 1.

156

THE PRICE

Star Date: 43385.6

The *Enterprise* orbits Barzan II, site of a "worm hole"—a tunnel through the fabric of space. Normally the ends of these tunnels are unstable, constantly shifting in position. In this case, however, both ends appear fixed, and the far side of the worm hole is on the other side of the galaxy. That distance would normally take the *Enterprise* nearly a century to traverse. Using the Barzan worm hole, the ship could make the same journey in seconds. Lacking the technology necessary to exploit this resource, the Barzan are taking bids for the management of the worm hole. In the process, they hope to gain financial security for themselves. The negotiations will take place on the *Enterprise*. Several interested parties have shown up, including the Ferengi and Chrysallian delegate Devinoni Ral. To establish that both sides of the worm hole are truly stable, Picard sends a shuttle containing Data and La Forge into the worm hole.

A romance begins between Ral and Troi, during which Ral reveals that he, like Troi, is empathic. However, as Ral uses his empathic skills to sense the emotions of the other negotiators and use this to his advantage, Troi becomes dismayed. Meanwhile, Data and La Forge exit the worm hole in the wrong place. Disturbed, Data and La Forge head back. By this time, Ral has eliminated all the competition except the Federation and the Ferengi. Sensing that the Barzan are ready to sign with the Federation, Ral makes an agreement with the Ferengi captain to stage a mock attack on the worm hole. Ral guesses that hostilities between the Federation and the Ferengi will cause the Barzan to sign with him. The ploy works, but Troi soon exposes it. Moments later, Data and La Forge return and report that the other side of the worm hole is unstable and therefore useless. When the Chrysallians learn they have purchased a worthless worm hole, they recall Ral for an explanation.

Trivia Questions

1. Where was Ral born?

2. Which deck houses Troi's quarters?

GREAT LINES

"*God forbid I should miss my first look at the worm hole.*"—An exhausted Troi grumbling about Picard's invitation to come to Ten-Forward.

CHANGED PREMISES

• When Picard, Riker, and Data discuss the worm hole with the Federation negotiator, Picard says it might be a "proverbial lemon." Data reacts with confusion to this statement. Yet in the earlier episode "The Naked Now," Riker—after referring to a needle in a haystack and seeing Data's confusion—clarifies his analogy by saying, "I should have said, '*proverbial* needle in a haystack.' " At this point, Data understands. From this instance it is clear that Data understands the word "proverbial." Did Data lose this understanding somewhere along the line?

• Of course, Troi must be lying at the end of the show when she says she senses no tension in the Ferengi captain. "Ménage à Troi" establishes that Betazoids cannot read Ferengi minds.

EQUIPMENT ODDITIES

• At the very beginning of this episode, a tired Troi shuffles into her quarters. On the way to her closet she reaches behind her back with both hands and appears to grope for her zipper. Of course, she cannot be groping for a zipper, since zippers do not exist in her century. The Great Bird of the Galaxy—the original creator of *Star Trek*, Gene Roddenberry—said so. (I read about this in a book called *The Making of Star Trek* by Stephen Whitfield. Since Mr. Roddenberry is the one who invented this universe in the first place, he should

know. And yes, I just violated the Nitpicker's Prime Directive again. On the other hand, maybe zippers were done away with in the twenty-third century but reinvented in the twenty-fourth century as an entirely new thing.)

• Just after groping for her nonexistent zipper, Troi gets paged by Picard. She responds with "Now what?," sighs, and taps her communicator. This seems reasonable. A person should have the right to react privately to a page before being required to respond. *The Next Generation Technical Manual*, however, states that Troi's badge tap was merely habitual, not necessary. According to it, when Picard called for Troi, the computer immediately connected Picard to Troi's room. The authors of the *Technical Manual* took this position because they had to explain away all the communicator discrepancies in the show. The only way to do that was to make a badge tap or communicator panel touch unnecessary.

Removing the badge tap creates a problem. It obliterates a person's privacy. (You can see an example of this in "The Host," when Dr. Crusher is in Odan's quarters. As Picard pages, Dr. Crusher immediately slaps her hand over her mouth as if Picard will hear her if she says anything.) If what the *Technical Manual* says is true, Picard heard Troi's "Now what?" comment. This is a prime example of why "immediate connect" will not work. It's like a telephone that rings once and then turns on a speakerphone so you can talk to the person on the other end. (I can think of several situations where this would be less than desirable.)

CONTINUITY AND PRODUCTION PROBLEMS

• At one point in the episode, Ral and Troi have an intimate dinner together, and Ral makes an interesting choice in his menu selection. When he puts his fork into the bowl in front of him and then draws the fork to his mouth, the fork has nothing on it. Is this some new kind of "air food"? Is Ral on a stringent no-fat diet? Maybe he's enjoying an entrée from "Guiltless Pleasures," that new line of culinary delights featuring the naughtiest, most fat-laden dishes ever invented with a wonderful new twist: They're invisible so no one can see what you're eating!

TRIVIA ANSWERS

1. Brussels, European Alliance.
2. Deck 9.

THE VENGEANCE FACTOR

Star Date: 43921.9

After investigating a raid on a Federation research facility, the crew of the *Enterprise* determines that the "Gatherers" are responsible. The Gatherers left their home world of Acamar III a hundred years ago as fierce clan blood feuds rampaged across the planet. Acamar now enjoys peace, but the Gatherers remain nomadic marauders. Picard takes the *Enterprise* to Acamar III to meet with its sovereign, Marouk. He proposes peace talks. She agrees and boards the *Enterprise* with an small entourage. Her cook, Yuta, is a seemingly innocuous and beautiful young woman. Riker soon becomes enchanted with her.

Marouk directs the *Enterprise* to a Gatherer encampment. As the discussions proceed between the Gatherers and Marouk, Yuta wanders off and finds an old Gatherer. After confirming that the man is a member of the Lornack clan, she touches him and he dies. The Lornack clan slaughtered Yuta's clan many years ago. Only five survived. They chose Yuta as the instrument of their vengeance. They altered her cells to slow her aging and then impregnated her with a biogenetically engineered virus specifically designed to attack only members of the enemy clan.

The leader of the encampment takes the *Enterprise* to meet with Chorgan, the head of all the Gatherers and, incidentally, a member of the Lornack clan. Meanwhile, Dr. Crusher determines the cause of the old man's death. She searches the Acamarian medical data base and finds another victim of the virus, from decades earlier. When Data locates an image of the man, a computer enhancement reveals Yuta in the background. Riker beams over to the Acamarian vessel to stop Yuta from killing Chorgan. After she resists his repeated commands to stop, Riker vaporizes her.

Trivia Questions

1. What is the vaporization temperature for Muranium alloy?

2. What are the formulas Wesley is studying in Ten-Forward?

CHANGED PREMISES

• Worf has learned a few lessons about combat. When an away team thwarts a surprise attack by unkempt Gatherers he says, "Your ambushes would be more effective if you *bathed* more often." Yet during the opening scene of "Conspiracy," Troi asks Worf if he has ever gone for a moonlight swim. He shakes his head no and replies, "Swimming is too much like ... bathing." (I guess bathing is just one of those sacrifices a warrior makes to become a more efficient soldier—even if he doesn't like it! While I'm at it, I might as well mention that Worf needs to learn to keep his head down. At one point, the away team is pinned down by laser fire. They huddle behind barrels and discuss options. The whole time, the ridges on Worf's head stick out over the top of the barrel.)

EQUIPMENT ODDITIES

• So Riker stuns Yuta twice and then kills her. *Kills* her, mind you. (Did I mention that Riker KILLED Yuta? I know he warned her twice, but still ...) The second time he stuns Yuta, she barely manages to get up. Stun her a few more times, Riker, or get the guards to grab her, or transport her back to the *Enterprise*, but don't *kill* her.

TRIVIA ANSWERS

1. It is 2,314 degrees.
2. The local Euclidean metrization of a K-fold contravariant reanimant tensor field.

THE DEFECTOR

Star Dates: 43462.5-43465.2

After sensors pick up an unidentified craft in the Neutral Zone, the *Enterprise* investigates. They find a Romulan warbird chasing a small Romulan scout ship. Because of the pilot's pleas for asylum, Picard extends the *Enterprise*'s shields around the craft, and the warbird leaves. The defector, Admiral Jarok, claims the Romulans have created a hidden base on Nelvana III in the Neutral Zone. He says they are massing for an attack and wants the *Enterprise* to enter the Neutral Zone to destroy the base. Picard resists Jarok's suggestion, knowing that to enter the Neutral Zone would violate the Federation-Romulan treaty. Instead, Picard launches a probe.

As the probe drops into orbit around Nelvana III, it senses the types of subspace disturbance that come from cloaked warbirds. Still, Picard is not convinced and grills Jarok further. Finally—after Jarok supplies the locations, strengths, and tactical plans of the Romulan fleet—Picard decides to act.

At Nelvana III, the *Enterprise* finds nothing. The Romulans had sus-

pected the loyalty of Jarok and fed him false information for months, waiting to see his reaction. Picard realizes this and orders a hasty retreat, but as the *Enterprise* swings around to warp back to Federation space, two Romulan warbirds appear. They demand that the *Enterprise* surrender. Picard refuses. Just before the warbirds destroy the *Enterprise*, however, three Klingon warships decloak. Suddenly facing an opposing force of equal or greater strength, the Romulans allow the *Enterprise* to leave.

Trivia Questions

1. During what hour of the day did the *Enterprise* sense the Romulan scout ship?

2. How many worlds has Jarok visited?

GREAT LINES

"*Now if these men do not die well, it will be a black matter for the king who led them to it.*"— Picard quoting Shakespeare to himself as he contemplates a war with the Romulans.

CHANGED PREMISES

• When the *Enterprise* launches the probe, there is a beautiful visual effect. As the probe races off, the rocket powering it illuminates the underside of the saucer with a red glow. Someone took the time to estimate and execute the amount of reflected light caused by the rocket. However, when the *Enterprise* launches a probe near the beginning of "Where Silence Has Lease," the red reflection is not present.

EQUIPMENT ODDITIES

• When the Romulan defector arrives at his quarters on the *Enterprise*, he orders a glass of water from the food dispenser. He specifies "twelve ahgians." The computer replies that it is calibrated for the Celsius metric system. What happened to the Universal Translator? The *Enterprise* plays host to hundreds of races. Are the food dispensers so unpolite and ethnocentric as to demand that every one conform to a certain measuring system?

TRIVIA ANSWERS

1. At 11:00 A.M.
2. More than a hundred.

THE HUNTED

Star Date: 43489.2

While Picard and Riker interview the prime minister of Angosia as part of the entrance evaluation to the Federation, a prisoner escapes from a penal colony called Lunar V. In response, the *Enterprise* pursues the escapee's ship. The prisoner, Rogo Danar, proves very adept at eluding the *Enterprise* but eventually is captured and beamed aboard. He was able to confuse the crew of the *Enterprise* because the sensors do not recognize him as a life form. In addition, Troi senses conflicting emotions from Danar. He can be extremely violent, yet is a pacifist at heart. She eventually determines that Danar was "programmed" to be a master soldier when Angosia was at war. The Angosians modified his body with drugs and his mind with psychological training. After Angosia won the war, they could find no place for their soldiers and sent them to live on Lunar V. The Angosians eventually added security measures and made Lunar V into a prison.

Picard questions the prime minister on this matter but he brushes Picard off, stating it is a matter of internal security. The prime minister then sends a police transport for Danar. Although greatly disturbed by the actions of the Angosian government, Picard has no jurisdiction and agrees to give Danar back. During the transfer, however, Danar breaks free. He leads the *Enterprise* security teams on a wild chase, eventually disabling the sensors and hijacking the police transport. Danar goes to Lunar V, frees his comrades, and heads for the Angosian capital. Responding to the prime minister's call for help, Picard, Data, Troi, and Worf beam down. Moments later, Danar and the other soldiers rush into the capital, brandishing weapons and demanding freedom. Once again, the prime minister appeals to Picard for help. Picard reminds the prime minister that this is an internal security problem and leaves, forcing the Angosians to deal with the problem and not just push it aside.

Trivia Questions

1. How many people has Danar killed?

2. What is the first Jefferies tube access panel Danar opens?

PLOT OVERSIGHTS
• Supposedly the Angosians are technologically inferior to the Feder-

ation. Yet one of their soldiers gets loose on the *Enterprise* and wreaks havoc. Danar makes one pass through Engineering and comprehends all the systems of the *Enterprise*. Look at his list of accomplishments: He defeats Data in a test of rerouting power systems. He knows the exact location to place an overloading phaser so it will cripple all the exterior sensors. He "hot-wires" a phaser to supply power to a transporter. Don't Starfleet officers go to school to learn all this stuff? Granted, Danar is supposed to be brilliant, but this is like taking someone who is a genius at fixing tube-type electronics and turning him loose on integrated circuits. He isn't going to get very far. Of course, if Danar didn't have this capability, it would be a short show.

• Finally, Dr. Crusher indicates that the reason the sensor can't lock on to Danar is because of the substances the Angosians put into his body. At the end of the show, the prime minister admits that the chemicals can be removed, but the mental programming cannot be undone. If you are trying to keep these guys locked up, doesn't it seem reasonable that you would take away any edge they have? Why let them remain invisible to sensors?

CHANGED PREMISES

• Someone retrofitted the brig. When Security took the Klingons to the brig in "Heart of Glory," they put the Klingons in a room with a force field around the door. In this show the brig is a large room with a de-

tention cell in it.

EQUIPMENT ODDITIES

• Shortly after starting his rampage through the *Enterprise*, Danar sees a Security guard standing by a force field and ducks into a small side corridor. Seeing a turbolift at the end of the corridor, Danar boards it. At this point Data reports an unauthorized access to turbolift 5 on deck 34. However, the signage on the turbolift door says "12 Turbolift," indicating that Danar is on deck 12! Data routes the turbolift to Worf's location, and the doors pop open. Worf discovers that Danar didn't actually ride the turbolift, merely stepped on, placed an overloading phaser on the floor, and quickly exited the turbolift before it departed. After Worf fixes the phaser, the scene changes to show Danar peeking out of the side corridor on the original deck. He runs down the hall and beats up the guard. Danar then taps the guard's communicator and commands the computer to drop the force field on deck 36. Deck 36? Didn't Data say that Danar was on deck 34? Danar could have dropped down two decks while Worf defused the phaser, but the guard is the same one shown on deck 34. Does the guard on deck 34 have a twin brother who just happened to take up an identical position on deck 36?

CONTINUITY AND PRODUCTION PROBLEMS

• When Danar first beams aboard, he attacks the Security team. They wrestle with him out into the hall. Just before they leave the transporter room, one guard is behind Danar and one is in front and slightly to Danar's right. After they come through the door, the guards are on either side of Danar.

• After rushing the capital, Danar tries to force a confrontation between his men and the Angosians by firing at a wall. The impact of the weapon blows a chunk out of the wall. Several seconds later, the same shot shows that the wall is *COMPLETELY WHOLE!*

TRIVIA ANSWERS
1. Eighty-four.
2. K-12 J-9, deck 30.

THE HIGH GROUND

Star Date: 43510.7

*T*he *Enterprise* delivers medical supplies to Rutia IV after an outbreak of violent protest by a group of Ansata terrorists demanding autonomy. On the planet, an away team of Dr. Crusher, Data, and Worf prepares for a meeting with Rutian officials. A bomb explodes near the away team, injuring several people. Dr. Crusher rushes over to help. Data and Worf want her to beam back to the ship and let the local doctors handle the problem, but Crusher refuses. Suddenly a terrorist appears from nowhere, grabs Crusher, and disappears. The terrorists are using a form of transport called "dimensional shifting." Long ago, it was abandoned by the Federation because of its destructive effect on humanoid tissue. The terrorists need Dr. Crusher to heal their sick.

Riker works with the Rutians while Data, La Forge, and Wesley Crusher work to trace the unusual transport mechanism. The terrorists hear about the search for Dr. Crusher and assume the Federation has aligned itself with the Rutians. They attack the ship and try to destroy it. Failing that,

they kidnap Captain Picard. The multiple use of the dimensional shift helps the *Enterprise* pinpoint the power source. Riker and Worf accompany a team of Rutians and rescue Picard and Crusher.

Trivia Questions

1. When did the Irish unification occur?

2. What was the casualty count in the first Ansata raid on the *Enterprise*?

RUMINATIONS

*T*his episode examines terrorism—its benefits and its morality. For several years I've heard some of the arguments espoused by the head terrorist in this show, namely that there is no difference between terrorism and military conquest. As the head terrorist asserts to Crusher, "The difference between generals and terrorists, Doctor, is only the difference between winners and losers. You win, you're called a general. You lose ..."

I can remember a program several years ago when a popular talk show host exclaimed, "Who can give me a definition of terrorism?" He wanted to show that any definition of terrorism can work equally well as a military conflict. I disagree and I offer this definition: Terrorism is the systematic targeting of nonmilitary targets for the sole purpose of evoking a negative emotional response in the populace. The purpose of terrorism is not military conquest. The purpose of terrorism is to devalue the commitment of a people toward their government's position. By this definition, planting a bomb on a commercial airliner is terrorism. Filling a truck full of explosives and running it into an American military installation in Beirut, however, is not. That is a military attack.

EQUIPMENT ODDITIES

• Several times during this show the terrorists use their dimensional shift to board the *Enterprise*. Beaming up to an orbiting spacecraft requires a great deal of accuracy. First of all, how do these terrorists locate the *Enterprise*? They would have to have access to sophisticated sensor equipment. Even then, they would also need detailed drawings of the *Enterprise* to accomplish the kind of raid that occurs in this episode. The terrorists beam directly to Engineering—one to the upper level of the dilithium chamber and one on the lower level. After the first attack fails, they beam to the bridge and take the captain. Is information about Galaxy Class starships freely available? (Come to think of it, I guess it is. The head terrorist probably went to B. Dalton and picked up a copy of the *Star Trek: The Next Generation Technical Manual!*)

TRIVIA ANSWERS
1. A.D. 2024.
2. Three dead, four wounded.

DÉJÀ Q

Star Date: 43539.1

The episode begins with the crew of the *Enterprise* attempting to help Bre'el IV. The planet's moon has lost orbital velocity and threatens to smash into the planet. Suddenly Q appears, claiming that the other members of the Q Continuum kicked him out and stripped him of his powers. Since he was no longer all-powerful and eternal, the continuum allowed him to choose the form he would take for the rest of his life. Q chose human. Skeptical of Q's claims, Picard orders Worf to take Q to the brig. Picard suspects Q of orchestrating the coming disaster on Bre'el IV. The crew continues to work on the problem of the moon. Q convinces Picard that he can help. Even though he no longer has his powers, he does possess knowledge. Picard acquiesces and releases Q from his cell.

Meanwhile, a cloud of ionized gas approaches the ship. It is the Calamarain, just one of the many species that Q tormented over the centuries. They have come for revenge. Picard realizes Q's real motive for choosing to be human. Q knew Picard would protect him.

With Q's help, La Forge and Data invent a plan to push the moon back to its original orbit. During the attempt, the Calamarain attack and almost rip Q away from the ship. Data saves him but is injured in the process. Reflecting on Data's selfless act, Q realizes he makes a worthless human being. He decides to end it all and leaves the *Enterprise* in a shuttle so the Calamarain can kill him. On the shuttle, another member of the Q Continuum appears and talks with Q about the real reason Q left the ship. He knew the Calamarain would eventually destroy the *Enterprise* to get to him. For Q's selfless act, he receives his powers back. As a parting gift, Q corrects the moon's orbit.

GREAT LINES

"It's difficult to work in a group when you're omnipotent."—Q reflecting on his new role as a human needing to interface with the crew.

EQUIPMENT ODDITIES

• When Worf takes Q to the brig, Worf has to press a button on a panel beside the door before it opens.

Later in the show, Data simply walks through the doorway. Why the difference?

• At one point, Q hurts his back in Engineering. In response, Data taps his communicator and calls for a medical team. Note: He *TAPS* his communicator. The *Star Trek: The Next Generation Technical Manual* states that a badge tap while aboard the *Enterprise* is simply habitual and not necessary, since the computer monitors all communications. (As I said before, I have a great deal of respect for the authors of that book. They did a masterful job. On this matter, however, they had no choice but to say that the badge tap is unnecessary. There are too many directorial oversights when it comes to the badges.)

If badge tapping is simply habitual, why is Data tapping his badge? He is an android. Data doesn't do things out of habit. In "The Most Toys," La Forge claims that Data always does things by the book. If the book says that a badge tap is unnecessary, Data would not tap his badge. He cannot make mistakes like that.

• Dr. Crusher fixes Q's back with a tool that looks exactly like a hypospray. It doesn't make a hypospray sound, though. Maybe the hypospray is a multipurpose machine. Then again, maybe the prop department didn't have time to make another medical doodad.

TRIVIA ANSWERS

1. An area with an eight-hundred-kilometer radius.
2. It is 2,005.

★ ROMANCE TOTE BOARD

1. Number of women who kiss Picard: seven

2. Number of women who have intimate interludes with Riker: four

3. Number of women who fall for Data: three

4. Number of men who make a pass at Troi: six

5. Number of women who make a pass at Crusher: one

6. Number of women who give La Forge the brush-off: two

7. Number of women snarled at by Worf: four

8. Number of girlfriends for Wesley: three

9. Number of fantasy women in the series: at least thirteen

10. Number of fantasy men: none

REFERENCES

1. A holowoman in "The Big Good-bye," Vash in "Captain's Holiday" and "Qpid," Troi and Picard's brother's wife in "Family," Picard's *faux* wife in "The Inner Light," Marta in "Tapestry," and Nella Darrin in "Lesson."

2. Mistress Beata in "Angel One," Brenna O'Dell in "Up the Long Ladder," Etana Jol in "The Game," and Ensign Ro in "Conundrum."

3. Yar in "The Naked Now," Ard'ian McKenzie in "The Ensigns of Command," and Jenna D'Sora in "In Theory."

4. Liator in "Justice," Riva in "Loud as a Whisper," Riker's dad in "The Icarus Factor," Devinoni Ral in "The Price," Barclay in "The Nth Degree," and Aaron Conor in "The Masterpiece Society."

5. Odan in "The Host."

6. Christie Henshaw in "Booby Trap" and Leah Brahms in "Galaxy's Child."

7. The Klingon warriorette in "Hide and Q," K'Ehleyr in "The Emissary," B'Etor in "Redemption II," and Kamala in "The Perfect Mate."

8. Salia in "The Dauphin," a blonde in "Evolution," and Robin Lefler in "The Game."

9. Setting aside the pleasure women on Risa ("Captain's Holiday"), Ardra in "Devil's Due," and Kamala in "The Perfect Mate" because they were "real," the fantasy women are: the Klingon warriorette in "Hide and Q," the murdered patron in "The Big Good-bye," Minuet in "11001001," the two French lovelies in "We'll Always Have Paris," the countless extras in "The Royale," Leah Brahms in "Booby Trap," Crusher and Troi in "Hollow Pursuits," Data's dance partner in "Data's Day," the nearly nude dancer in "Cost of Living," Picard's *faux* wife in "The Inner Light," and Data in "A Fistful of Datas."

10. For some reason, this concept either hasn't caught on with the female crew members of the *Enterprise* or the creators haven't seen fit to show us any of these scenes.

A MATTER OF PERSPECTIVE

Star Dates: 43610.4-43611.6

A s Riker beams back from visiting a Starfleet-sponsored science station in orbit around Tanuga IV, it explodes. Shortly afterward, a Tanugan representative named Krag boards the *Enterprise*. He accuses Riker of blowing up the station and murdering its scientist, Dr. Apgar. Krag demands that Picard allow the extradition of Riker to Tanuga IV. Picard instead suggests that they hold a preliminary hearing, using the holodeck to examine the evidence. All the testimonies agree that something happened between Riker and Mrs. Apgar. Riker says she started it. She says he started it. In any case, Dr. Apgar found them together. Krag contends that Riker killed Apgar to keep him from making a report on the incident. Krag also presents evidence that sensors clearly show an energy pulse coming from Riker and directed at the science station's generator as Riker beamed back to the ship.

While the hearing continues, two strange energy bursts appear on the *Enterprise*. Data, La Forge, and Wesley finally discover the source of these

Trivia Questions

1. Which of the painters at the beginning of the show uses a striking geometrical constructivism style?

2. What was the time interval between bursts of the lambda field generator?

energy bursts. Dr. Apgar's research dealt with the creation of a new form of energy called "krieger" waves. He constructed the science station to take energy from a lambda field generator on the planet's surface and convert it to these waves. Dr. Apgar claimed he was close to a breakthrough. In fact, Dr. Apgar had achieved krieger waves. The holodeck's re-creation of the science station was accurate enough to prove this. It caused the strange energy bursts. Picard deduces that Dr. Apgar wanted to keep the discovery and sell it as a weapons system. Riker's visit threatened his plan. As Riker beamed out, Dr. Apgar attempted to kill Riker by shooting a krieger wave at the transporter beam. Instead, the wave ricocheted and destroyed the science station.

CHANGED PREMISES

• To establish a method for the "murder" of Dr. Apgar, Krag points to the sensor logs that show an energy discharge from Riker's position to the science station's generator. Krag claims that Riker fired a phaser just as he beamed out. No one on the

Enterprise disputes this. Yet in "The Most Toys," O'Brien can tell that Data has fired a weapon just as O'Brien beamed him off Fajo's ship. If O'Brien can read Data's weapon, why can't he read Riker's weapon? And if O'Brien didn't read a weapon in discharge, wouldn't that constitute evidence that Riker didn't fire a weapon?

EQUIPMENT ODDITIES

• First of all, if the sensors could tell that an energy beam went from Riker's position to the science station's generator, why couldn't the sensors register the first energy beam coming from the generator to Riker's position? Second, the end of the episode shows krieger waves as a directed ray of energy. If a krieger wave is a ray of energy, why didn't it burn a hole from the holodeck all the way to Cargo Bay 12 in the first case and all the way to sick bay in the second case? If it had, it would have been easy to trace back to the source.

Actually, there is an answer for both these objections. Perhaps krieger waves only do damage at their focus point and are undetectable until they reach that focus point. This would account for waves materializing at the transporter beam and bouncing back. It would also explain the sudden appearance of the energy readings in Cargo Bay 12 and sick

bay. Unfortunately, the episode's dialogue doesn't support this theory, and the graphics of krieger waves at the end of the show contradict it by showing a beam originating from the generator going to Riker's position and bouncing back!

• In both Riker's and Mrs. Apgar's testimony, Apgar's assistant says, "Our lambda field generator is on the planet, since it requires a minimum of five thousand kilometers for the field to collimate." Collimate means to place something parallel to another. In other words, the generator sends a burst of energy upward and five thousand kilometers later the energy synchronizes and moves in the same direction. This direction is outward from the planet. Supposedly this column of energy passes through the *Enterprise*, hits the holodeck recreation of Apgar's work, and turns into krieger waves. However, every scene showing the *Enterprise* orbiting Tanuga IV has the ship moving rapidly across the face of the planet while the planet turns in the other direction! So how did the *Enterprise* manage to be above the generator at precisely the right time to intercept the lambda field?

TRIVIA ANSWERS
1. Ensign Williams.
2. Five hours, twenty minutes, three seconds.

YESTERDAY'S ENTERPRISE

Star Date: 43625.2

A strange swirling cloud, defying description, appears in front of the *Enterprise*. Data surmises that it is a temporal rift—a rip in the fabric of time. Moments later, a crippled ship flies through. It is the *Enterprise*, NCC 1701-C, the predecessor of the current *Enterprise*, NCC 1701-D. Suddenly everything about the *Enterprise*-D changes. It is now a ship of war that has been battling in a conflict with the Klingons for the past twenty years. Worf is gone and Tasha Yar is once again head of Security. Soon Guinan visits the bridge. She knows that the current state of reality is wrong and convinces Picard of it.

Just before leaping into the future, the *Enterprise*-C was responding to a distress call from a Klingon outpost. The attacking Romulan ships then turned and fired on the *Enterprise*-C. The fierce volley of photons and phasers created the rip in time and shot the *Enterprise*-C into the future. At the time, the Federation and the Klingons were discussing a peace treaty. The disappearance of the *Enterprise*-C meant no Federation ship came to the aid of the Klingon outpost. When the negotiations broke down, no symbolic act stopped the outbreak of war between the Federation and the Klingon Empire.

Picard discusses these matters with the captain of the *Enterprise*-C. She agrees to go back—to almost certain destruction. During the first attempt, however, a Klingon ship attacks and the captain of the *Enterprise*-C is killed. Meanwhile, Yar learns from Guinan that—in the original time line—she died a meaningless death (see "Skin of Evil"). Yar gets permission to go back with the *Enterprise*-C. As soon as the *Enterprise*-C heads back into the rift, everything returns to normal.

Trivia Questions

1. How many survivors did the away teams find on the *Enterprise*-C?

2. What is the name for standard rations?

GREAT MOMENTS

This was a very clever way to bring back Yar, definitely one of the most creative ways I've ever seen to resurrect a character from the dead.

PLOT OVERSIGHTS

• The major plot oversight in this episode concerns the personnel aboard the *Enterprise* during the alternate future created by the *Enterprise*-C. In the alternate future, the Federation and the Klingon Empire have been at war for twenty years. In war, people get killed. In fact, Picard says the Klingons have destroyed half of the Federation's fleet. Since people get killed in war, people get promoted quickly. It is inconceivable that Riker, Data, and La Forge would still be serving with Picard. They would have their own commands fighting the "evil horde." Of course, the creators couldn't change all the subordinates. This is a television series, after all. The viewers want to see the same set of core actors from week to week.

• Picard has an odd sense of three-dimensional space in this episode. He meets with Guinan on the spacious observation lounge. He meets with Riker and Yar on the spacious observation lounge. However, when he meets with his senior officers, five in all, he crams them like sardines into his ready room.

CHANGED PREMISES

• In the beginning of the show, Guinan and Worf talk about Worf's need for "companionship." Worf explains that he would require a Klingon woman for "companionship." Human females are too frail. From that comment, they are, presumably, talking about sex. If they are talking about sex, Worf has lost his moral honor. In "The Emissary," Worf and K'Ehleyr mate. Then Worf immediately wants to take a vow of marriage. It is the Klingon way. In his discussions with Guinan, however, it appears that Worf considers "companionship" a viable pattern of behavior—without marriage.

EQUIPMENT ODDITIES

• At the beginning of the episode, emergency teams beam over to the *Enterprise*-C. Dr. Crusher materializes on the main bridge and quickly locates the captain. A short time later, Crusher determines to take her back to the *Enterprise*-D. Dr. Crusher taps her badge and calls for transport. She then puts her tricorder away and reaches up to tap her badge again. At this point a befuddled look cascades across her face and she puts her hand back down to her side. Evidently she suddenly remembered that you don't have to tap your communicator to shut it off if you are transporting. (By the way, my nine-year-old daughter found this one.)

• After Dr. Crusher leaves, Riker and Yar find a survivor in the wreckage. (When I watched this scene, I thought of the times I helped my dad tune up a car. I would hold the flashlight while he did the work. Invariably I would get bored and the flashlight would start wandering—usually shining right in my dad's eyes. At this point, he would yell, "Phil! Phil! Shine it on the engine!") The survivor is buried under a bunch of rubble on a darkened main bridge. Riker and Yar dig him out. What's the first thing they do for him after he's out? They shine flashlights on his face.

TRIVIA ANSWERS
1. One hundred twenty-five.
2. TKL.

THE OFFSPRING

Star Date: 43657.0

After returning from a cybernetics conference, Data cloisters himself in a lab. Some time later, he invites La Forge, Troi, and Wesley to view his new creation—an android named Lal. While at the conference, Data learned of a submicron matrix transfer technology. He used the technology to transfer his programming into Lal's positronic brain. Data has become a father, creating another sentient being like himself.

Initially, Picard reacts with distress. Picard wonders if Data is ready to accept responsibility for this new life. Starfleet has concerns also. An Admiral Haftel contacts Picard and worries that Data won't raise Lal properly—that she will be mentally damaged in some way during the process. Haftel decides to rendezvous with the *Enterprise* and interview her. If he finds her lacking, Haftel has the authority to take Lal back to his cybernetics lab. Lal leaves the meeting confused and afraid, realizing that Haftel wants to separate her from her father. She begins experiencing genuine fear at the thought of leaving the *Enterprise*.

Trivia Questions

1. What does "Lal" mean in Hindi?

2. How many calculations can Lal perform in one second?

This "malfunction" of emotion causes Lal to return to Data's lab.

By the time Haftel, Picard, and Data arrive at the lab, Lal is barely functioning. Her positronic brain has suffered a major breakdown. Data works furiously to save her but cannot. In the end, Lal thanks Data for her life and expresses her love for him. She then experiences complete neural system failure. As a final attempt to keep Lal from passing into oblivion, Data transfers her memories into himself.

GREAT LINES

"He's biting that female!"—Lal to Guinan, upon seeing a couple kiss in Ten-Forward.

PLOT OVER-SIGHTS

• When Picard first meets Lal, she blinks several times. But later, in a voice-over, Data talks about teaching her "to supplement her innate android behavior with simulated human responses." The scene shows Data teaching Lal to blink! She already knew how to blink. Later, Data and Wesley discuss Lal in Data's lab. She is in her stall. She is also blinking. After the discussion, Data turns her on. If she was turned off, why was she blinking?

CHANGED PREMISES

• As Lal begins to achieve sentience, she becomes very inquisitive. She begins asking a mountain of questions. Data responds by turning her off. It's supposed to be a cute moment. No doubt many parents wish their children had "off" buttons. Unfortunately, it is also totally out of character for Data. First, parents sometime long for an "off" button in children because they become impatient with the constant questioning. Data cannot become impatient. Impatience is an emotion. Data is emotionless. Second, in the episode "Datalore," Data discloses the location of his "off" button to Dr. Crusher. He swears her to secrecy and comments, "If you had an 'off' button, would you want everyone to know about it?" In other words, Data is somewhat sensitive about his "off" button. Yet, in this episode, he cavalierly reaches out and shuts Lal off just because she is asking questions.

• In "The Measure of a Man," when Bruce Maddox is trying to disassemble Data, Picard asserts that Starfleet is not an organization that ignores inconvenient regulations. In that show Picard went on to argue successfully that Data was entitled to all rights granted sentient beings in the Federation. Yet in this episode, "The Offspring," Starfleet sanctions the activities of Admiral Haftel and approves of him taking Lal away from Data. Does Starfleet have the right to separate children from their parents forcibly? Or does the decision reached in "The Measure of a Man"—defining Data as a sentient being—mean nothing? Or is Starfleet simply setting aside both their protection of the family unit and Data's sentience simply because these principles are inconvenient?

Picard makes the correct stand at the end of the show—that Data is a sentient being with rights, and those rights include the right to raise a family. The state cannot simply take children away from their parents. Why does Picard have to take this stand in the first place? Why haven't Haftel's superiors shut down Haftel already?

EQUIPMENT ODDITIES

• While Data and Wesley discuss Lal, Dr. Crusher pages Wesley and reminds him of a hair appointment. Wesley responds that he is on his way. He then shakes his head and says, "Parents!" Wesley, being the intelligent man he is, presumably did not believe his mother could hear this comment. Yet the *Star Trek: The Next Generation Technical Manual* states that the voice channel would have closed down by itself after ten seconds unless Dr. Crusher or Wesley said "Out." In other words, Dr. Crusher *did* hear Wesley say "Parents!"

TRIVIA ANSWERS

1. Beloved.
2. More than sixty trillion.

SINS OF THE FATHER

Star Dates: 43685.2-43689.0

Commander Kurn of the Klingon Defense Force joins the *Enterprise* as part of the officer exchange program. He takes Riker's place as second-in-command. When Kurn deals harshly with everyone on board except him, Worf interprets Kurn's actions as an insult and confronts Kurn. Kurn admits his attempt to test Worf's "Klingonness." Kurn then shocks Worf by revealing that he is Worf's brother. Worf's family died during a Romulan attack on the Khitomer outpost twenty years ago. Worf was told he was the only survivor. In fact, Worf's parents had left the one-year-old Kurn on the Klingon home world with friends. They intended to be on Khitomer only a short time. After the massacre, the friends took Kurn as their own. They told him of his true blood line only when he reached the age of ascension.

Kurn tells Worf he joined the *Enterprise* because Duras, a member of the Klingon High Council has accused Worf's father of treason. Duras claims Worf's father helped the Romulans attack the Khitomer outpost. Worf, as the elder brother, must challenge the ruling or their family's name will be disgraced for seven generations. However, if Worf challenges the ruling and loses, the council will execute Worf and Kurn in their father's stead. Because Worf may be accused of a capital offense, Picard sets course for the Klingon home world. Once there, Worf brings his challenge. Kurn stands beside him but, according to Worf's orders, hides his true identity.

Picard, Worf, and the bridge crew finally uncover the truth. The real traitor was Duras's father, but Duras's family is very powerful. Bringing charges against Duras's father would split the empire. On the guarantee of Kurn's safety, Worf agrees to discommendation—an excommunication from the Klingon culture. Everyone will think Worf is admitting his father's guilt, and the empire will be saved.

Trivia Questions

1. What is the name and the registry of the first starship on the scene at the Khitomer Massacre?

2. How many Klingons died on Khitomer?

GREAT LINES

"It is a good day to die and the day is not over yet."—Worf, facing down Duras at the beginning of the challenge.

EQUIPMENT ODDITIES

• The doors on the *Enterprise* must have volume controls to govern the sound they make. At first, it seemed as if the sound editors forgot to put in the "door swish" several times in this episode—the opening scene in the transporter room, for instance. After careful review, however, and after cranking the volume way up, the doors do swish. They just swish very softly compared to other episodes.

• Someone needs to replace the light bulbs in the transporter room. When Kurn beams aboard the *Enterprise*, the transporter platform is very dark. Did he call ahead to tell the transporter chief he wanted to make a dramatic entrance?

• When Picard prepares a meal for Kurn in the captain's mess, Picard replicates a variety of foods for Kurn to sample. One of them is roast turkey. The scene shows Picard carving a beautifully browned bird. Apparently the turkey has bones in it. Why would the replicators aboard the *Enterprise* replicate bones? The bones make it more difficult to cut the meat. They are also thrown away—unless Picard makes soup out of them. Doesn't this seems like a waste of energy? Picard must be a real stickler for authenticity.

TRIVIA ANSWERS
1. USS *Intrepid*, NCC 38957.
2. Four thousand.

✦ ALLEGIANCE

Star Date: 43714.1

After a mission to alleviate an outbreak of a deadly plague, Picard relaxes in his quarters. As he naps, a large, rectangular slab appears and scans him. Picard then disappears, replaced by a replica. Moments later, Picard wakes in a room with four beds. Two of the other beds are occupied—one by a first-year cadet at Starfleet Academy, the other by a bureaucrat of a small world that continually bows to conquerors. Soon the fourth captive arrives, a beastlike humanoid from the Chalnoth race. The group soon discovers that the new arrival cannot eat the provided food. He indicates that the bureaucrat would make a nice meal. Picard, the beast-man, and the cadet try to open the door of their cell. After a stun ray inflicts them with pain, they argue among themselves, wondering if someone in the room is one of their captors. The cadet stands up for Picard, recounting his work with the Mintakans (see "Who Watches the Watchers"). When Picard adds the recent mission to alleviate the plague to his list of accomplishments, the cadet concurs.

> **Trivia Questions**
>
> 1. What is the mass of the pulsar that endangers the *Enterprise*?
>
> 2. What does the beast-man's name mean in the Chalnoth language?

At this point Picard reveals the identity of one of the captors. It is the cadet. She could not have known about the mission the *Enterprise* had just completed. Suddenly the cadet disappears and is replaced by three aliens. Once Picard discovered their identity, they could not continue their research on authority. They return everyone to their places of origin. Shortly after Picard materializes on the bridge of the *Enterprise* with his alien escort, his replica—already relived of duty by Riker because of the replica's strange behavior—transforms into an alien as well. As Picard berates the aliens for kidnapping and imprisoning him, he signals the crew, and Worf imprisons them in a force field. After this "taste of their own medicine," the aliens plead for their release. Picard grants their request and then tells them to get off his ship.

PLOT OVERSIGHTS

• Without wishing to be indelicate, this question must be asked: How big is this bureaucrat's bladder? When Picard arrives at the cell, the bureaucrat tells him that he has inhabited the cell for twelve days. No rest rooms are visible in this cell. Is this why his race makes such good bureaucrats? Evidently they never need to leave their desks.

• As part of his odd behavior, Picard's replica reports for his physical one month early—without Dr. Crusher having to cajole him into it. Later in the show, Dr. Crusher says the test results are identical to last year's physical. She says this is unusual. Why would the test results be identical? Dr. Crusher tested Picard's replica. The aliens constructed the replica by scanning Picard, a Picard who was eleven months older than his last physical. Shouldn't the tests show that change?

• Speaking of imprisoning the aliens, they seem genuinely surprised by Picard's anger over his kidnapping. Notice the dialogue between Picard and the aliens. When Picard calls kidnapping an immoral assault, the aliens merely respond that the whole concept of morality is an interesting human characteristic. Yet, earlier in the show, when the bureaucrat asserted that they hadn't been mistreated, the cadet immediately retorts, "We've been kidnapped! Locked in a room. You don't think *that's* mistreatment?" This makes sense until you realize that the cadet is one of the aliens. Evidently the aliens understand the mistreatment of kidnapping, because they said so through the cadet. Now, if they understand the mistreatment of kidnapping, why do they play dumb at the end of the show?

CHANGED PREMISES

• At the end of the show, Picard manages to communicate his desires to the bridge crew with a single look. With *one* glance he tells Riker that he wants the aliens imprisoned. It is what should be expected from the bridge crew of the flagship of the Federation. After all, these are the best of the best. So why haven't we seen this type of working together before? All of a sudden, one look from Picard speaks volumes.

CONTINUITY AND PRODUCTION PROBLEMS

• At one point, Picard's replica visits the crew in Ten-Forward. Just before he breaks into song, he speaks with La Forge and Worf. He congratulates La Forge on the engine efficiency. As he does, Worf sets down his glass and places his left arm on the bar. The next shot shows the trio from the other side of the bar. Worf's left arm is still on the bar, but his hands are now clasped together.

• Soon after arriving at the cell, Picard tries to find a way to communicate with his captors. He stands beside the door's control panel and taps a series of numbers on it. The cadet says that Picard is tapping the first six prime numbers. A prime number is a number that is divisible only by 1 and itself. For instance, all even numbers—except 2—are not prime numbers because every even number can be divided by 2. Picard is tapping the numbers to show the aliens that he is mathematically intelligent. The scene picks up with Picard tapping 2, 3, 5, and 7. Presumably Picard tapped the numeral 1 before the scene began. Since the first six prime numbers are 1, 2, 3, 5, 7, and 11, shouldn't the next number Picard taps be 11? Instead, Picard taps 3! Well, maybe he started over. The next number is difficult to hear because of the dialogue, but then Picard taps 5, 7, 7 and 4! Four? Four isn't a prime number. It is divisible by 2. (I put this under Continuity and Production Problems because most of the tappings are sound effects under the dialogue.)

TRIVIA ANSWERS

1. Approximately 4.356 solar masses.
2. Fighter.

CAPTAIN'S HOLIDAY

Star Date: 43745.2

Shortly after arriving on Risa for a vacation, Picard encounters two time travelers from the future. They are Vorgons and claim that he will soon find the Tox Uthat, a weapon of immense power that came from the future with its inventor. As the Vorgons predicted, Picard soon joins forces with a woman named Vash in a search for the artifact. For the past five years, Vash worked for a scientist who spent his life looking for the Tox Uthat, assisted at times by a Ferengi named Sovak. When the scientist died, Sovak paid Vash to deliver the scientist's notes. Instead, Vash used the money to come to Risa.

As soon as Picard and Vash locate the cave indicated by the notes, the Vorgons appear to watch the historic rediscovery of the Uthat. Unfortunately, Sovak also shows up, brandishing a weapon and claiming the Uthat for himself. After finding nothing in the dig, Picard and Vash return to their resort. Sovak, refusing to be denied his prize, stays behind to search further. The Vorgons leave, puzzled.

When Picard gets back to his room, Riker pages him. The *Enterprise* has

Trivia Questions

1. What century did the Vorgons come from?

2. What does the Tox Uthat do?

returned and will await his arrival. After telling them to stand by with transporter code 14, Picard confronts Vash and asks for the Uthat. He realizes Vash left a trail so Sovak could follow them to the cave. She wanted the Ferengi to think that the research notes were wrong. Picard believes she found the Uthat as soon as she arrived on Risa. Vash acquiesces and gives Picard the Uthat. Immediately the Vorgons appear and demand the Uthat. Unsure that the Tox Uthat really belongs to them, Picard quickly places it on the floor and signals for transporter code 14. Two seconds later, the Uthat explodes. The Vorgons say that Picard has fulfilled his destiny. Their history records that Picard destroyed the powerful weapon. With that, the Vorgons leave and Picard says good-bye to Vash.

PLOT OVERSIGHTS

• After Troi convinces Picard to go on vacation, she makes the "yes" gesture—the one where a closed fist pulls down and the person mouths "yes" at the same time. (My daughter used to make this gesture. I find it hard to believe that people in the twenty-fourth century will still make this gesture. I know ... pick, pick, pick, pick.)

• Picard needs to get out more. Just before he and Vash leave the resort for the cave, Sovak confronts them. After Picard knocks him unconscious, Vash helps him put on their shared backpack. The straps on the backpack have large padded sections that are supposed to be used on the shoulders. Picard uses them for handholds! (Actually, I think Patrick Stewart didn't want to waste time adjusting them during the shot so he did the next best thing: He tried to cover them up. He has this quirky expression on his face for the last few moments of the scene—like he wants the shot to end quickly.)

• Vash states that the cave housing the Uthat is twenty-seven kilometers from the resort. It takes them two days to get there. Yet when Picard and Vash leave, they leave their backpack behind. The backpack had their food, drink, and bedding. Did they steal Sovak's transportation? Did they "rough it" all the way back?

TRIVIA ANSWERS

1. The twenty-seventh century.
2. It is a quantum phase inhibitor able to stop all the nuclear reaction within in a star.

TIN MAN

Star Date: 43779.3

Tam Elbrun, a Betazoid telepath of extraordinary ability, joins the *Enterprise* for this episode. A deep space probe has discovered a living spaceship orbiting a dying star. Starfleet has dubbed the alien "Tin Man." All attempts to communicate with it have failed. Starfleet wants the *Enterprise* to take Tam Elbrun to meet Tin Man, hoping to establish a dialogue with it, since Tin Man's proximity to the dying star puts it in great danger.

Unfortunately, Tin Man is in a sector claimed by the Romulans. The Romulans have monitored the transmissions from the probe. Two of their ships race toward Tin Man, hoping to gain the advantage of first contact. Since the *Enterprise* is faster, it reaches the system first and takes up a position eighteen minutes away by impulse. A short time later, the first Romulan cruiser hurtles by, firing on the *Enterprise* and causing 70 percent damage to the shields. Tam fears for Tin Man and alerts it to the danger. Tin Man comes alive, spinning out an energy burst that destroys the Romulan ship and debilitates the *Enterprise*.

Several hours later, the second Romulan ship appears. It claims right of vengeance and heads off to destroy Tin Man. With no other choice, Picard allows Tam and Data to beam over to Tin Man. After joining Tam in a telepathic union, Tin Man releases another energy burst. This time, however, the burst acts as a repulser wave, throwing the *Enterprise* 3.8 billion kilometers. Seconds later, the star explodes, but not before Tam transports Data back to the *Enterprise* and disappears into deep space with Tin Man.

PLOT OVERSIGHTS

• Wesley must be confused at the end of the show. He tells Picard that the repulser wave from Tin Man threw them 3.8 billion kilometers. However, only 50 seconds elapse from the time the repulser wave hits the *Enterprise* until Picard witnesses the supernova of the dying star on the main viewscreen. Let's assume that the star went supernova immediately after the repulser wave hits the *Enterprise*. In that case, only 50 seconds elapse from the time the

Trivia Questions

1. How many died at the Garushta Disaster?

2. What is La Forge's override code?

star explodes until the light from that explosion reaches the new position of the *Enterprise* (even less if the star exploded some time after the repulser wave hit the ship). Light travels approximately 187,000 miles per second. Since 1 kilometer is 0.63 mile, light travels about 300,000 kilometers per second. If the *Enterprise* was thrown 3.8 billion kilometers from the dying sun, it would take 12,667 seconds for the light of the explosion to reach the *Enterprise* (3,800,000,000 divided by 300,000). That figure equals 3.5 hours (12,667 divided by 3,600). It is not possible for the light produced by a supernova to reach a distance of 3.8 billion kilometers in 50 seconds.

CHANGED PREMISES

- "A Matter of Honor" established

that the maximum range for safe transport is 40,000 kilometers. In this episode, Tam and Data beam over to Tin Man when the *Enterprise* is 18 minutes away by impulse. Traveling at full impulse is traveling just under the speed of light. Therefore, the distance to Tin Man is 18 minutes multiplied by the speed of light. As noted above, light travels approximately 300,000 kilometers per second. In other words, Data and Tam beamed a distance of 324,000,000 kilometers. This is well above the maximum transporter range.

TRIVIA ANSWERS

1. Forty.
2. Theta 2997.

HOLLOW PURSUITS

Star Dates: 43807.4-43808.2

The *Enterprise* takes on tissue samples needed for an outbreak of an exotic fever on a distant planet. Unknown to the crew, the suppliers of the samples still use a chemical called "invidium" in their medical containers. Several of the engineers become contaminated with the invidium and pass it on to the machines they service. Meanwhile, Picard balks at an unsatisfactory work report for a shy yet talented diagnostic engineer named Barclay. Not willing to entertain La Forge's request that Barclay be transferred, Picard orders La Forge to work harder to make Barclay part of the team. La Forge goes looking for Barclay and discovers him on the holodeck, engaged in his fantasies about the senior staff of the *Enterprise*. La Forge promises to keep quiet about Barclay's pastime but strongly "suggests" that he meet with Troi. Unable to break his addiction, Barclay heads back to the holodeck. When he fails to report for a meeting, Riker, La Forge, and Troi enter the holodeck and bring him out.

At the same time, the invidium begins interfering with the systems of

Trivia Questions

1. How old is Wesley at this point in the series?

2. How many power systems does the *Enterprise* contain?

the *Enterprise*. An antigrav unit fails. Transporter 3 quits working. Worst of all, the injectors for the matter and antimatter streams in the warp drive lock and begin propelling the *Enterprise* recklessly ahead. La Forge pulls his engineering team together to try to uncover the source of the malfunctions. When Barclay suggests a line of discussion that helps the team discover the invidium, the *Enterprise* is saved. Under Troi's guidance, Barclay abandons his holodeck fantasies.

GREAT LINES

"Sir, you have no sense of fair play."—Barclay's holodeck-generated Picard to Riker after Riker discontinues an attacking holodeck character.

PLOT OVERSIGHTS

• Originally, the engineers get contaminated because a seal on one of the medical containers is broken. The engineers contact the invidium as they carry the tissue sample from the transporter pad to an antigrav unit. Why are La Forge's top engineers carrying medical containers? Isn't that a job for the blue suit guys, the medical technicians?

• After the engineers load these precious medical samples on an antigrav unit, La Forge tells Barclay to fix the antigrav unit. La Forge says it has an intermittent problem. Is this a standard procedure on the *Enterprise*? Does Starfleet have a regulation, "Whenever you encounter a problem with a piece of equipment, put a lot of really important stuff on top of it and then get someone to fix it?"

CHANGED PREMISES

• When La Forge faces the problem of the ship flying apart, he calls his team of senior engineers together to solve the problem. Obviously, this is a sound approach. If you have a staff of highly trained individuals, why not consult them? In previous shows, however ("Contagion" and "Booby Trap"), La Forge has always tackled the problems alone.

EQUIPMENT ODDITIES

• At the beginning of this episode, Barclay enjoys a holodeck-created Ten-Forward. He walks over to Troi and she says, "I feel your confidence, your arrogant resolve. It excites me." At this point the companel beeps and someone says, "Lieutenant. Barclay report to Cargo Bay 5 now!" Barclay responds by telling Troi, "It'll have to wait till later, darling." He quickly adds, "Be right there." So what did the guy at the other end of this conversation hear? In response to his command that Barclay report to the cargo bay, did the man hear Barclay tell him in loving terms that it would have to wait until later?

• Picard must have one of those screen savers installed on the terminal in his ready room, the kind that blanks the screen until some activity occurs. Just after he tells La Forge to make Barclay his "project," Riker and La Forge leave Picard's ready room. Picard reaches over and turns his display panel toward him and studies it—except the panel is blank before he turns it!

• La Forge originally discovers Barclay's fantasies by strolling into the holodeck. Later, Riker, La Forge, and Troi do the same thing. They simply walk up to the panel, Riker punches a few buttons, and the door to the holodeck pops open. Shouldn't there be an etiquette involved with entering the holodeck? These holodecks function as recreational areas for the crew. Even La Forge admits that what people do on the holodeck is their business. Isn't it an invasion of a person's privacy to allow others to walk into that person's fantasy?

• Obviously, the lights on the dilithium chamber don't have any correlation to how fast matter and antimatter enter the chamber. During the entire discussion among the members of the engineering team, the lights and the sound pulse along at reasonable rates. At this point, the injectors are supposedly locked as the *Enterprise* careens madly ahead, accelerating out of control. However, after La Forge and Barclay find the invidium, the next scene shows the dilithium chamber. The lights and the sound race at twice the speed of the previous engine room scene. (Personally, I think some little ensign in the back room controls the speed of the lights. When La Forge wants his people to work faster he calls down and tells the ensign to crank it up!)

1. Seventeen.
2. Four thousand.

THE MOST TOYS

Star Date: 43872.2

As the episode begins, Data shuttles hytritium from a trader's ship to the *Enterprise*, which needs this unstable substance to cure the poisoned water supply of a distant colony. Just before the third and final trip, the crew of the trader's ship stuns Data and removes him from the shuttle. The shuttle explodes as it heads back to the *Enterprise*. Since Picard and the rest of the bridge crew believe that Data has been destroyed, the *Enterprise* leaves for the colony. Data wakes up in the treasure room of the trader's ship. The trader, Kivas Fajo, enters with his assistant. Fajo explains that he is a collector of one-of-a-kind objects. He arranged the sale of the hytritium to capture Data.

Meanwhile, the *Enterprise* arrives at the colony and delivers the hytritium to the water supply. However, sensors detect a concentrated area of poisoning. Suspicious, Picard orders an away team to investigate. They find that someone engineered the contamination. Back on the ship, the senior officers deduce that Fajo created the problem to kidnap Data.

Trivia Questions

1. What is the name of the shuttle Data pilots?

2. How many kilos of hytritium does La Forge load on the probe?

The *Enterprise* doubles back to find Fajo. After Data refuses to cooperate with his demands, Fajo threatens to kill his assistant. This convinces the assistant to help Data escape and leave with him. During the escape, Fajo kills the assistant and tells Data to get back to the treasure room or he will kill someone else. Fajo believes Data will not harm him because of Data's fundamental respect for living beings. Data considers the alternative and decides Fajo must die. However, just as he begins to fire a disrupter, the *Enterprise* beams him up. Security then arrests Fajo and confiscates all his stolen treasures.

GREAT LINES

"Perhaps something occurred during transport."—Data to Riker, in response to Riker's statements that Data's disrupter was in a state of discharge.

PLOT OVERSIGHTS

• When Data begins his final run to the *Enterprise* in the opening scenes, he reports his progress to La Forge. After the crew of the trader ship stuns Data, however, his captors talk freely about the components of Data's body. Isn't it *very convenient* that Data's communicator happened to shut off at just the right time so La Forge wouldn't hear their discussions? Wouldn't an open communications line be standard in these types of dangerous situations?

• The opening shot shows the *Enterprise* almost head to head with Fajo's ship. That means that Data must execute two 180-degree turns to get from Fajo's shuttle bay to Shuttle Bay 2. If hytritium is so unstable, why not put the ships back to back? In that way Data could fly out of one shuttle bay and make a straight line to the other.

• Evidently, whenever there is any sort of dangerous job, Picard sends poor old Data to do it. For Fajo's plan to work he had to know, in advance, that Data would be the shuttle pilot. Requesting Data would cause too much suspicion later.

CHANGED PREMISES

• When O'Brien beams Data up, O'Brien reads a weapon in transit and deactivates it. He also tells Riker that the weapon was in "a state of discharge." So O'Brien can tell these things, can he? Sure would have been helpful for him to testify during Riker's hearing in "A Matter of Perspective." In that show, Riker was accused of murdering a scientist by firing a phaser just as he transported out.

TRIVIA ANSWERS

1. *Pike.*
2. Eighty-one.

SAREK

Star Dates: 43917.9-43920.7

Sarek, a highly esteemed Vulcan ambassador and father of Mr. Spock (from the original *Star Trek*), boards with his wife and two staff members on a diplomatic mission. For over ninety years, Sarek has built a personal friendship with the Legarans. Picard will take him for a final meeting to negotiate their entrance into the Federation. As the *Enterprise* warps to the Legaran home world, incidences of random violence erupt on the ship. Dr. Crusher and Troi finally isolate the cause. They surmise that Sarek suffers from "Bendii syndrome," a disease that afflicts some Vulcans over the age of two hundred. It culminates in total loss of emotional control. Since Vulcans are partially telepathic, Crusher and Troi guess that Sarek is unconsciously projecting his intense emotions on others.

With the conference with the Legarans in jeopardy, Picard confronts Sarek. During the exchange, it becomes obvious that Sarek has lost his emotional control. Picard decides to call off the meeting. Upon the urgings of Sarek's wife, Picard

Trivia Questions

1. What rank did Picard hold when he met Sarek for the first time?

2. How old is Sarek in this episode?

suggests a "mind meld." Vulcans can telepathically link themselves to others. Picard believes he can bolster Sarek's emotional stability during the negotiations. Sarek agrees and performs the procedure with Picard. As Sarek talks with the Legarans, his savage emotional outbursts rip through Picard. It is enough, however, to allow Sarek to complete one last diplomatic triumph before retiring.

GREAT MOMENTS

Patrick Stewart does a phenomenal acting job at the end of this episode. His portrayal of Sarek's emotions running rampant over Picard is absolutely wonderful.

PLOT OVERSIGHTS

• If Sarek's limited telepathic abilities can cause violent reactions, what type of reactions would Troi's mother produce? In "Manhunt," Troi's mother passed through "the phase." During the phase, Betazoid women (true telepaths, mind you) increase their sex drive by four times.

• When Picard approaches Sarek about the mind meld, he comments that it is the only logical choice.

Wouldn't another Vulcan be the more logical choice? There is a Vulcan on Sarek's staff, and there are also other Vulcans on board the *Enterprise*. "The Schizoid Man" featured a Vulcan medical doctor.

• After the mind meld between Sarek and Picard, Riker walks Sarek down a hall. They discuss the physical state of both Sarek and Picard. Sarek assures Riker that everything is fine. Sarek then turns and walks into a room. Presumably this is the room that houses the Legarans as they sit in their slime pit, since they have already beamed aboard. However, it cannot be that room, because Sarek gave specific instructions that the room must be darkened. The room Sarek walked into is very brightly lit.

EQUIPMENT ODDITIES

• When Sarek and his wife beam off the *Enterprise*, they join hands. This puts their hands outside the transporter containment field. Thankfully, the transporter still manages to work "right." Otherwise, Sarek and his wife would be handless when they arrived at the transport ship.

CONTINUITY AND PRODUCTION PROBLEMS

• In one scene, La Forge and Wesley argue over their social lives—enraged by Sarek's projected anger. La Forge holds a tablet during the altercation. He presses it against Wesley's chest, and shoves him. In the very next scene, the tablet is back on Wesley's chest, and La Forge shoves him again! (Personally, I think Wesley would do a lot better with the women if he'd remember to zip up his pants. For those of you who don't remember, the pants on Wesley's "acting ensign" uniform don't close all the way in back!)

TRIVIA ANSWERS
1. Lieutenant.
2. Two hundred two.

MÉNAGE À TROI

Star Date: 43930.7

While the *Enterprise* attends a trade conference on Betazed, a Ferengi captain becomes enamored with Lwaxana, Troi's mother. Although she spurns him, the Ferengi captain's feelings for her become even more intense. After the conference, the *Enterprise* leaves for a routine mapping mission. When Troi requests shore leave on Betazed, Picard "suggests" Riker take shore leave also. Shortly afterward, the Ferengi captain returns to Betazed and kidnaps Lwaxana, Troi, and Riker. The Ferengi captain wishes to force Lwaxana to use her telepathic abilities to the Ferengi's advantage during trade negotiations. After returning from the mapping mission, Picard learns of the abductions. The crew begins a search for the Ferengi ship.

Meanwhile, Riker escapes from the confinement cell and manages to send a message using subspace distortion. Wesley detects it, and the *Enterprise* gives chase. Lwaxana makes a deal with the Ferengi captain. If he will let Troi and Riker go, she will stay with him. Shortly, the *Enterprise* arrives and Troi and Riker beam over. As Lwaxana bids farewell, she tells Picard that it's over between them. Troi correctly interprets the comment. Lwaxana wants Picard to fight to get her back. Picard begins spouting poetry and threatens to destroy the Ferengi ship if the captain doesn't return her. The Ferengi captain beams her back. Because of Wesley's service to the ship in this instance and many others, Picard promotes him to full ensign.

> **Trivia Questions**
>
> 1. How often is the trade conference held?
>
> 2. What makes the Ferengi mind unique?

CHANGED PREMISES

• This episode makes the point, several times over, that Betazoids cannot read Ferengi minds. Troi is half Betazoid. That means her empathic capabilities are scaled-down versions of a full Betazoid's telepathic capabilities. Yet in two previous episodes, "The Last Outpost" and "The Battle," Troi comments that she senses certain emotions from the captain of the Ferengi vessels. Evidently Betazoids *can* read Ferengi minds.

• Early in this episode, Lwaxana and Troi have a blowout. Two factors precipitate the argument: Lwaxana's continued use of the term "little one" in regard to Troi; and Lwaxana's pressure to convince Troi to settle down, get married, and have a child. Troi reacts badly to both of these, eventually raising her voice, demanding respect as an adult, and storming out of Lwaxana's quarters. The scene is strangely reminiscent of something that might occur between immature human males. After all, in the episode "The Icarus Factor," Troi claims that human males are unique in that fathers regard their sons as children well into adulthood and sons chafe against their fathers' expectations. Doesn't this sound like an accurate description of the scene between Lwaxana and Troi? Maybe human males aren't as unique as Troi would like to believe.

• At some point the Ferengi gave up their "phaser whips." In the episode "The Last Outpost," the Ferengi used a bullwhiplike device that emitted a stream of energy when snapped. In "Ménage à Troi," the Ferengi use more conventional-looking weapons.

EQUIPMENT ODDITIES
• These transporters are amazing devices. When Lwaxana beams from the Ferengi ship to the *Enterprise*, she starts out sitting on the Ferengi captain's bed and ends up standing on the bridge. In other words, the transporter had to rearrange her skeletal-muscular structure in transit.

CONTINUITY AND PRODUCTION PROBLEMS
• Lwaxana's earrings must have motion stabilizers built into them. In the opening scene, Lwaxana and Troi discuss Troi's happiness. After Riker rescues Troi from the discussion, the Ferengi captain approaches Lwaxana for the first time. Lwaxana turns her head to face him, and her earrings begin swinging rapidly back and forth. The very next shot shows her earrings at rest.

TRIVIA ANSWERS
1. Once every two years. It is a biennial conference.
2. It contains four lobes.

TRANSFIGURATIONS

Star Dates: 43957.2-43980.6

While charting a star system, the crew of the *Enterprise* discovers the wreckage of an escape pod on an M Class planet. Among the remains they find a seriously injured humanoid and beam him to sick bay. As Dr. Crusher stabilizes his vital signs and repairs his injuries, she notes a disturbing mutation of his cells but is unable to diagnose the cause of it. While the *Enterprise* continues its survey, the patient makes a rapid recovery. Unfortunately, he cannot remember anything about himself or his past, so Dr. Crusher christens him "John Doe." The mutations in John Doe's cells continue, now accompanied by energy surges. In addition, John acquires the power to heal. At one point he reaches out instinctively and repairs the torn ligaments in a crew member's shoulder.

Working with a piece of equipment from John Doe's escape pod, La Forge and Data locate John's home world, a planet called "Zalkon." The *Enterprise*'s survey course brings it close to Zalkon three weeks later. As the *Enterprise* approaches, a Zalko-

nian ship rushes out to meet them. The Zalkonian captain confronts the *Enterprise*, demanding that Picard turn over John Doe for punishment and claiming that John Doe is a dangerous criminal. At this point, John Doe's memories return. The Zalkonians stand on the verge of an evolutionary leap, a transfiguration into beings composed solely of energy. The government of Zalkon has tried to suppress the change by killing anyone who manifested the symptoms. John and a few others fled, determined to let the transformation take its course. Moments later, John Doe changes into a being of light and departs the *Enterprise* as the Zalkonians return to their world.

Trivia Questions

1. How many others fled Zalkon with John Doe?

2. What is the rotation rate of the pulsar that the computer finds for Data?

GREAT LINES

"It is the scent that first speaks of love."—Worf giving dating advice to La Forge.

PLOT OVERSIGHTS

• This episode opens with La Forge and Worf in Ten-Forward at the bar. La Forge points out a woman at a nearby table. He questions Worf as to what he should say to her. The conversation makes it sound like they've never met. In fact, La Forge has already taken the little tart out at least once. He programmed an entire holodeck sequence for her at the beginning of "Booby Trap," and all she said was she didn't think of La Forge in "that way." Now here she is making eyes at La Forge and acting like she wants to get something started. What changed? Why is Ms. Christie Henshaw so interested in La Forge all of a sudden?

EQUIPMENT ODDITIES

• After Dr. Crusher beams John Doe up to the *Enterprise*, she puts him in full "biosupport." One shot shows the panel that displays his current physical status. All the triangle indicators are white and around the middle of their ranges. Later, Crusher says in a voice-over that she has removed John Doe from the biosupport and that his major organ systems can now function on their own. Yet the shot that shows the physical status panel has all the triangles at the extreme left end of the scale. All of them are also red. Compare this with a scene from "Time Squared." In that episode, the *Enterprise* discovers a duplicate and comatose Picard (Picard B) in a shuttle craft. In sick bay, Captain Picard (Picard A) tells Dr. Pulaski to revive him. She tries a stimulant on Picard B, but it has the opposite effect. All the triangle indicators on his status panel head to the left and turn red. Dr. Pulaski responds immediately to this. She runs over and gets an agent to counteract

the stimulant. After she does, the triangle indicators creep back up to the middle of their ranges. So why are the triangle indicators in the scene with John Doe red and at the extreme left side of their scales? Don't red triangles all the way to the left indicate that a patient is dying?

• In one scene, Riker waits outside a turbolift. The door opens and reveals La Forge embracing the aforementioned Christie Henshaw. As she leaves the turbolift, Riker enters. Riker says, "Bridge," to state his destination. Nothing happens. Riker smiles at La Forge, and La Forge snaps out of his daze. La Forge adds, "Deck 6," and the turbolift takes off.

First of all, how does the computer know when to wait for multiple people to state their destinations? Many times in *Star Trek: The Next Generation*, crew members enter turbolifts together and only one states a destination. Yet during "Yesterday's *Enterprise*," Data and Yar board a turbolift, and the computer waits for Yar to state her destination before proceeding. Also, in "Transfigurations," La Forge must state his destination when Riker boards the turbolift, but—evidently—LaForge didn't have to state his destination when he got on with Ms. Henshaw. If he did, the turbolift would already know where to take him and he wouldn't have to say it again. So why didn't the computer make him state his destination when he got on the turbolift with Ms. Henshaw?

• Shuttle Craft 5 is once again the object of renumbering or renaming. In the episode "Times Squared,"

Shuttle Craft "05" was named *El-Baz*. In the episode "The Ensigns of Command," it became the *Onizuka*. Finally, in "Transfigurations" Shuttle Craft 5 returns to *El-Baz*.

TRIVIA ANSWERS

1. Three.
2. It is 1.5244 seconds.

THE BEST OF BOTH WORLDS, PART 1

Star Dates: 43989.1-43993.5

T he *Enterprise* investigates the destruction of one of the most distant colonies in the Federation. Since the obliteration looks suspiciously like the work of the Borg (see "Q Who"), Commander Shelby joins the *Enterprise*. For the past six months, Commander Shelby has headed the Borg tactical analysis team at Starfleet headquarters. She confirms that the Borg attacked the colony. Shortly after, the *Enterprise* encounters the Borg. They order Picard to transport himself over to their ship. Picard refuses, and in the short battle that follows, the *Enterprise* manages to escape. Picard then takes the *Enterprise* to a sensor-obscuring nebula. The Borg position themselves outside the nebula, waiting for the *Enterprise* to reappear. During the respite, the crew devises a new weapon to use against the Borg. They will channel a high-energy beam through the navigational deflector, tuned to the Borg's most vulnerable frequency.

The Borg begin sending random charges through the nebula. As the charges start hitting the *Enterprise*, Picard takes the ship out of the nebula. After a short chase, the Borg lock on to the *Enterprise* with a tractor beam. Several Borg appear on the bridge and kidnap Picard, after which the Borg set course for Earth. Riker gives chase and sends an away team to the Borg ship, hoping to slow them down. Just as the away team completes its mission, they discover that the Borg have transformed Picard into a Borg. When a rescue fails, the away team returns. Meanwhile, Riker powers up the new weapon and tells Worf to prepare to fire. The Borg ship hails the *Enterprise*. Picard speaks for the Borg. He introduces himself as "Locutus." He tells them the existence they've known is over. He concludes, "From this time forward, you will service ... us."

Riker replies, "Mr. Worf, fire!"

Trivia Questions

1. What three ships has Starfleet offered for Riker to command?

2. A Borg ship can remain operable up to what percentage of damage?

GREAT MOMENTS

T his is the all-time, hands-down, "no argument," BEST episode of *Star Trek: The Next Generation. The series was still new enough that I really didn't know if the creators were going to kill off Picard or not. In addition, some of my friends were convinced that the creators were going to replace Riker with Shelby for the fourth-season episodes (a thought that did not bring great joy to their hearts). When this episode faded to black, I knew it was going to be a long summer, waiting for the premiere of the fourth season.*

PLOT OVERSIGHTS

• As the show opens, Riker leads an away team down to the destroyed colony. When they arrive, he asks Transporter Chief O'Brien to confirm their coordinates. O'Brien verifies the coordinates and says that they are at the center of town. The next shot shows the away team standing at the edge of a gaping hole. No buildings ring the abyss. In other words, the Borg scooped up the entire colony (see "Q Who" for their technique). If the hole is all that's left of the colony and they transported to the center of town, shouldn't they be standing in the center of the pit?

• With the *Enterprise* concealed in the nebula, both Worf and Picard make statements about what the Borg ship is doing. How do they know what the Borg ship is doing? If the nebula is dense enough to confound the Borg's sensors, wouldn't it do the same to the *Enterprise*'s sensors?

• When the Borg head for the center of the Federation, they fly toward Earth. Presumably this evokes an emotional response from the viewer but isn't it just a tad ethnocentric? It assumes that Earth had some foundational role in the Federation, instead of simply joining it when humans came of age.

• Before the away team beams over to the Borg ship, Worf hands out phasers. He says each has been tuned to a different frequency. Shelby then comments that they will only be able to use the phaser a few times before the Borg will adapt to the new frequencies. Evidently, tuning these phasers is a big deal. Otherwise the away team could fire a few times, use the controls to set a new frequency, and start firing again. However, in the episode "The Arsenal of Freedom"—when Riker became imprisoned in a force field—Data told Yar that to remove the force field he would have to find the precise frequency. Data then diddles with the controls of his phaser and fires a short blast at the force field. A short time later, a scene shows Data diddling with the controls of his phaser some more and firing another blast. Suddenly the force field disappears. In other words, Data found the "precise frequency," right? So what did he find the precise frequency with? Didn't he find it with his *phaser*? If Data can find a frequency with his phaser, doesn't that imply that his phaser can be tuned to multiple frequencies? If Data's phaser had this capability in the first season of *Star Trek: The Next Generation*, what happened to the phasers in the third season? (My guess is that the interface for retuning the phasers was too complicated for the average users to grasp and they eventually griped it out of existence!)

CHANGED PREMISES

• At one point, when Shelby boards a turbolift, she states her destination as "Deck 8, battle bridge." She and Riker then have a disagreement, and she leaves as soon as the turbolift reaches her destination. However, the turbolift door opens into a hallway, not the battle bridge. "Encounter at Farpoint" showed two entrances to the battle bridge; both were turbolifts.

• The *Enterprise* seems to have solved its structural integrity problems. During the runaway acceleration of "Hollow Pursuits," the *Enterprise* began shuddering as soon as it passed warp 9.4. In this episode, the *Enterprise* sustains a speed of warp 9.6 for several hours and everything's fine.

TRIVIA ANSWERS

1. USS *Drake* ("Arsenal of Freedom"), USS *Aries* ("The Icarus Factor"), and USS *Melbourne* ("The Best of Both Worlds," Part 1).
2. Up to 78 percent.

TRIATHLON TRIVIA FOR PLANETS

(So named because—like the athletic event—no one should be able do this.)

MATCH THE PLANET TO THE DESCRIPTION TO THE EPISODE

PLANET	DESCRIPTION	EPISODE
1. Acamar III	A. Houses a lab for time experiments	a. "Pen Pals"
2. Aldea	B. A rigid code of honor endangers Yar	b. "The Perfect Mate"
3. Angel One	C. The Ferengi stole its energy converter	c. "Captain's Holiday"
4. Antedi III	D. A penal colony for vets	d. "The Emissary"
5. Armis IX	E. This planet discovers it isn't the center	e. "Qpid"
6. Baratas III	F. Terrorists kidnap Crusher	f. "The Enemy"
7. Betazed	G. A fake weapons lab lures Picard	g. "The Dauphin"
8. Bre'el IV	H. A deaf negotiator brings peace.	h. "Manhunt"
9. Daled IV	I. The Bandi inhabit this planet	i. "Time's Arrow"
10. Deneb IV	J. A plague here forces Yar to fight	j. "Déjà Q"
11. Devidia II	K. Riker is tried for murder	k. "A Matter of Time"
12. Drema IV	L. Troi's betrothed finds another	l. "The Child"
13. Galorndon Core	M. The one-stop shop for military hardware	m. "Violations"
14. Gamma Taouri IV	N. Houses a Federation outpost	n. "Violations"
15. Haven	O. They worship Picard	o. "First Contact"
16. Iralius IX	P. Yar dies here	p. "The Quality of Life"
17. Jarada III	Q. Riker and Troi try to vacation here	q. "The Arsenal of Freedom"
18. Khitomer	R. Four decades of civil war	r. "Unification I"
19. Krios	S. A man dances with a ghost	s. "The Defector"
20. Ligo VII	T. Amazons rule this planet	t. "Devil's Due"
21. Ligon II	U. The crew works as slave labor miners	u. "When the Bough Breaks"
22. Lunar V	V. Intelligent insect race visited by Ulians	v. "The Masterpiece Society"
23. Malcoria III	W. Yar's home planet	w. "The Survivors"
24. Melina II	X. Picard vacationed here	x. "The Vengeance Factor"
25. Minos	Y. The storehouse for really bad bugs	y. "Legacy"
26. Mintaka III	Z. Home to an absent Romulan base	z. "Haven"

PLANET		DESCRIPTION		EPISODE
27. Moab IV	AA.	Two cannibalistic races went there	aa.	"Ménage à Troi"
28. Mordan IV	BB.	Home to a Federation junkyard	bb.	"Chain of Command," Part 1
29. Nelvana III	CC.	Riker wants to but can't use his powers	cc.	"Too Short a Season"
30. Odet IX	DD.	Jev had his way there as well	dd.	"Skin of Evil"
31. Parliament	EE.	Picard tries to give a speech in orbit	ee.	"Loud as a Whisper"
32. Penthara IV	FF.	Riker wore feathers for diplomacy	ff.	"The Last Outpost"
33. Qualor II	GG.	Their fish delegates are really assassins	gg.	"Encounter at Farpoint"
34. Rana IV	HH.	The *Enterprise* fixes the atmosphere	hh.	"Lonely Among Us"
35. Relva VII	II.	Data finds a little friend	ii.	"The Hunted"
36. Risa	JJ.	A moon threatens its existence	jj.	"Code of Honor"
37. Rubicun III	KK.	Home to the "perfect" colony	kk.	"We'll Always Have Paris"
38. Rutia IV	LL.	These aliens feast on human energy	ll.	"Angel One"
39. Seltrice III	MM.	The beast/girlfriend's destination	mm.	"Code of Honor"
40. Sigma III	NN.	John Doe's home planet	nn.	"Transfigurations"
41. Solari V	OO.	Site of Wesley's first entrance exam	oo.	"Sins of the Father"
42. Styris IV	PP.	A plasma fountain orbits it	pp.	"Rascals"
43. Tagus III	QQ.	Picard faces a flimflam artist	qq.	"Hide and Q"
44. Tanuga IV	RR.	Birthplace of the superbabe	rr.	"The High Ground"
45. Tarchannen III	SS.	Worf's father died there	ss.	"Identity Crisis"
46. Theta VIII	TT.	La Forge makes a friend of an enemy	tt.	"The Royale"
47. Turkana IV	UU.	Home of an odd casino	uu.	"A Matter of Perspective"
48. Tyrus VII	VV.	Wesley commits a capital offense	vv.	"Booby Trap"
49. Vagra II	WW.	La Forge becomes a lizard	ww.	"Justice"
50. Vandor IV	XX.	A thousand year-old snare	xx.	"Who Watches the Watchers"
51. Ventax II	YY.	A planet thought to be a myth	yy.	"Angel One"
52. Zalkon	ZZ.	The Gatherers' home planet	zz.	"Coming of Age"

SCORING
(BASED ON NUMBER OF CORRECT ANSWERS)

0–5	Normal observant
6–10	Extremely observant, with a mind for details
11 and up	Obsessive/compulsive personality disorder with an unhealthy *Star Trek* fixation

PLANETS ANSWER KEY

1.	ZZ x	10.	I gg	19.	RR b	28.	R cc	37.	VV ww	46.	UU tt
2.	YY u	11.	LL i	20.	U pp	29.	Z s	38.	F rr	47.	W y
3.	T ll	12.	ll a	21.	B jj	30.	Y l	39.	G bb	48.	PP p
4.	GG h	13.	TT f	22.	D ii	31.	AA hh	40.	CC qq	49.	P dd
5.	FF yy	14.	C ff	23.	E o	32.	HH k	41.	H ee	50.	A kk
6.	N d	15.	L z	24.	DD n	33.	BB r	42.	J mm	51.	QQ t
7.	Q aa	16.	XX vv	25.	M q	34.	S w	43.	EE e	52.	NN nn
8.	JJ j	17.	V m	26.	O xx	35.	OO zz	44.	K uu		
9.	MM g	18.	SS oo	27.	KK v	36.	X c	45.	WW ss		

Fourth

Season

THE BEST OF BOTH WORLDS, PART 2

Star Date: 44001.4

In the "The Best of Both Worlds," Part 1, the Borg arrived at the Federation (see "Q Who"). They kidnapped Picard and turned him into a Borg. Then Picard introduced himself as "Locutus" and claimed, "From this time forward, you will service ... us." As the very last line of the third season's finale, Riker ordered Worf to fire a new and hopefully lethal weapon at the Borg ship. As this episode begins, the main navigational deflector discharges, sending an intense beam of energy at the Borg ship. Nothing happens. Locutus informs Riker that the knowledge and experience of Picard are now available to the Borg. The Borg ship warps away, headed toward Earth.

While the crew repairs the *Enterprise* from the effects of the massive energy discharge through the deflector, an armada from Starfleet attacks the Borg ship. The Borg easily defeat them all. When the *Enterprise* finally arrives at the battle scene, only charred remains are left. The carnage hardens Riker's resolve to destroy the Borg. He devises a

plan to kidnap Picard from the Borg ship. He hopes that Picard will retain his knowledge of the Borg and their weaknesses. Riker's plan succeeds, but Dr. Crusher is unable to separate Picard from the Borg collective consciousness. Data suggests a neural connection between himself and Picard. Perhaps he can access the Borg consciousness.

When Data makes contact, the Borg ship turns around and races back to the *Enterprise*. Data works furiously to find a way to shut it down. Picard, struggling through the Borg neural modifications, suggests sleep. Data plants a thought in the Borg collective consciousness, telling them to regenerate. The Borg ship shuts down. Then, due to the conflicting orders in their collective consciousness, it self-destructs and Picard returns to normal.

GREAT LINES

"Your resistance is hopeless, number one."—Locutus to Riker after the navigational deflector energy burst fails to damage the Borg ship, and the

Trivia Questions

1. What distinction does Picard hold as a runner?

2. What technique does Data use to discover the subspace transmissions the Borg use for their group consciousness?

crew of the *Enterprise* realizes that the Borg have access to Picard's knowledge and experience.

PLOT OVERSIGHTS

• In "Q Who," Q sent the *Enterprise* seven thousand light-years through space to meet the Borg. At the end of that show, Guinan pointed out that the Borg would be coming. Also in that show, Data states that it would take two and a half years to get back to the Federation at maximum warp. At the beginning of "The Best of Both Worlds," Part 1, an admiral says that the Federation knew for over a year that the Borg were coming. Picard responds that the Borg must have a source of power far superior to their own.

Yet, in "The Best of Both Worlds," Part 1, the *Enterprise* manages to stay with the Borg ship for several hours. And in this episode, "The Best of Both Worlds," Part 2, even after Picard, as Locutus, claims the Borg ship is proceeding without further delay to Earth, the *Enterprise* actually catches up to the Borg ship. If the Borg ship has a superior power source, why aren't they using it and leaving the *Enterprise* in the dust? (Space dust, that is.)

CHANGED PREMISES

• In "The Best of Both Worlds," Part 1, soon after the *Enterprise* encounters the Borg the first time, Picard orders, "Fire all weapons." The next shot shows photon torpedoes coming from the yoke and phasers coming from the saucer *and* the pylons that hold up the engines. However,

in "The Best of Both Worlds," Part 2, during the last confrontation between the *Enterprise* and the Borg, Riker also orders, "Fire all weapons." However, this time only the phaser from the saucer section fires. The really interesting thing is that the same shot of the ship is used in both episodes! For some reason, the phasers from the pylons weren't drawn in the second time.

• Likewise, when the Borg cutting tool hits the *Enterprise* in "The Best of Both Worlds," Part 1, it cuts into Engineering, deck 36. Yet when the cutting tool hits the *Enterprise* in "The Best of Both Worlds," Part 2, the computer says the outer hull breach occurs on decks 23, 24, and 25. Again, the same visual of the Borg cutting tool is used for both episodes!

• Someone reworked the layout and look of the battle bridge. The last time the series showed the battle bridge was during "Arsenal of Freedom." This battle bridge is a great improvement.

EQUIPMENT ODDITIES

• This episode contains a very interesting scene concerning communications on the *Enterprise*. At the end of the show, Riker sends an away team to the "sleeping" Borg ship. While walking through the halls of the *Enterprise*, Riker discusses the Borg ship with the away team. Shelby, leading the away team, asks Riker if they should stop the Borg's autodestruct sequence. Riker turns a corner, and doors pop open. He walks into the room with Picard, and both Dr. Crusher and Data give their opinions on Shelby's question! In other words—since Shelby asked the question while Riker was in the hall—some mechanism must exist for command personnel to eavesdrop on conversations of other command personnel.

Yet—moments earlier in this episode—Riker gave orders to ram the Borg ship while Data, Crusher, and Troi *calmly* discussed the meaning of Picard's "sleep" instruction. There is no droning of bridge communications in the background during these discussions. Evidently they couldn't hear Riker's intention to destroy the *Enterprise* in only seconds, because if they could, Data simply would have implemented Picard's instruction instead of musing on it.

If some protocol exists for establishing open communications among all bridge officers during a crisis, wouldn't it be more reasonable for that protocol to be in effect during the Borg attack than afterward? Evidently it isn't. Instead, that protocol comes into play *after* the attack.

TRIVIA ANSWERS

1. He is the only freshman ever to win the academy marathon.
2. Multimodal reflection sorting.

FAMILY

Star Date: 44012.3

While the *Enterprise* undergoes repairs in orbit around Earth, this episode winds through three plots. First, Worf's parents visit him on the *Enterprise*. In the beginning, their visit embarrasses Worf, but soon he tells them he is happy they came. They bring up the subject of Worf's discommendation and assure him that whatever happened to cause it, they love him and are on his side. Second, Dr. Crusher receives a package she placed in storage years ago. Among other things, it contains a holographic recording her husband made for Wesley just after Wesley was born. She gives it to Wesley so he can view it.

In the final plot, Picard travels to his hometown in France for a brief vacation. While there, he stays with his older brother, Robert Picard, in the family home. Robert carried on the family tradition of growing grapes and making wine. He always envied Picard's success and ability to break their father's rules without punishment. A few days after arriving, Picard meets with an old schoolmate. The man is one of the supervisors for the Atlantis Project—an effort to raise a portion of the bottom of the Atlantic and create a new subcontinent. He offers Picard a job as director. Disturbingly, Picard finds himself considering it.

When Robert hears about the offer, he goads Picard into a fight. After they tumble in the mud for a while, both burst into laughter. Picard comments to Robert that he had it coming. Robert agrees but tells Picard that he needed it. Robert observes that Picard has been very hard on himself. Picard breaks down and admits his shame over the Borg using him to kill so many in Starfleet. With his brother's help, Picard realizes his place is on the *Enterprise*.

Trivia Questions

1. What rank did Jack Crusher achieve?

2. When did Starfleet begin using the current insignia/communicator design?

GREAT LINES

"Life is already too convenient."— Robert's assertion during an argument over technology with Picard.

RUMINATIONS

Normally, I'm not very enthusiastic about "human interest" episodes of Star Trek. *They remind me too much of shows like* thirtysomething. *But this episode does one thing powerfully right. Sometimes television shows dispense too quickly with disastrous encounters in a character's life. For instance, it would have been very easy to jump right into a new set of adventures after rescuing Picard from the Borg. Instead, the creators took an entire episode to explore the emotional changes that the experience caused in Picard's life. I commend them for their insight.*

PLOT OVERSIGHTS

• Does it strike anyone else as odd that everyone in France speaks with an English accent during this episode? (One summer, my wife and I took an "Introduction to French" course. At one point, our teacher told us of the French aversion to the English words that are filtering into—and some would say polluting—their language. Ever the smart aleck, I popped off with the comment that we should all just wait a hundred years and then we could just go over to France and speak English! According to this episode, I was right.)

CONTINUITY AND PRODUCTION PROBLEMS

• Picard's wineglass drains and fills during his dinner with Robert and his family. From one camera angle, the wineglass is only one third full. From another, it is two thirds full. As the scene progresses, the level of wine jumps up and down.

TRIVIA ANSWERS

1. Lieutenant Commander.
2. Eighteen to twenty-two years ago. (When Wesley views the holographic recording of his father, his father wears the current insignia design. His father made the recording ten weeks after Wesley was born, and Wesley is now approximately eighteen years old. In addition, the insignia of the crew on the *Enterprise*-C in "Yesterday's *Enterprise*" are different, using a rectangular background. Therefore, Starfleet began using the current insignia design eighteen to twenty-two years ago.)

BROTHERS

Star Dates: 44085.7-44091.1

The *Enterprise* races toward Starbase 416 with a medical emergency. A boy must get to the starbase or he will die. While taking the boy's brother to visit the sick youth, Data suddenly falls into a trance and heads for the main bridge. Soon after he arrives, all life support on the bridge fails. Everyone evacuates except Data. Data then commandeers the ship. He flies the *Enterprise* to a planet and beams down. Data walks into the workshop of an old man who brings the android out of his trance. The old man is Dr. Noonian Soong, Data's creator.

In the midst of this reunion, Lore appears. Lore (a character introduced in "Datalore") is Data's brother. He, too, is in a trancelike state. Against Data's wishes, Soong wakes Lore also. Neither Data nor Lore can recall how they came to the planet. Soong explains that a homing device in their brains induced the trances they'd been in and summoned them to his workshop. Soong then explains that before he dies, he wants to give Data one last gift. Holding up a tiny metal sphere, the creator explains that it

Trivia Questions

1. How many independent safety interlocks ensure life support on the main bridge?

2. Who played the part of Dr. Noonian Soong?

contains a set of basic emotions—a gift for Data. Soong takes a short rest before installing the sphere. During this time, Lore overpowers Data and swaps clothing with him. When Soong wakes, he installs the sphere in Lore by mistake. Soong protests Lore's deception, but Lore throws him across the room and leaves.

Meanwhile, the crew of the *Enterprise* manages to get a transporter working. Riker, La Forge, and Worf beam down to the planet. When they confront Data, Soong tells Data how to restore his memory of his arrival on the planet. After Soong dies, the away team beams back. Data returns control of the ship to Picard, and the *Enterprise* makes it to Starbase 416 just in time to save the boy's life.

PLOT OVERSIGHTS

• Picard should have known Data caused the malfunction in the life support systems very early in the game. As everyone leaves the bridge, Picard watches Data walk over to the turbolift that goes directly to the battle bridge (Picard et al. used it in "Encounter at Farpoint"). Picard told everyone to reassemble in Engineering, so why would Data be going to the battle bridge?

• When Data commandeers the ship, he tells the computer to accept command input only from his workstation on the bridge. This is called "localizing command function."

Because Data chased everyone off the bridge and then threw up the force fields, only he could give orders to the ship's computer. However to localize command function, Data had to use Picard's voice. The computer's acceptance of this emulation of Picard's voice needs scrutiny.

First, voiceprints can be faked. Starfleet knows this. If nothing else, they learned it during an episode titled "The Battle," when a Ferengi captain faked a confession from Picard. Since voiceprints can be faked, I would expect Starfleet to use some method to verify the authenticity of the voiceprint. In fact, Starfleet uses two methods: handprints and voice codes. You can see handprints in action during "11001001" and "Where Silence Has Lease." Before initiating autodestruct, Picard and Riker place their hands on a panel for identification. Many examples exist for the voice code. Picard used one to take control of an infected ship in "Unnatural Selection" and to decode a message in "The Defector." Riker used one to gain access to Data's schematics in "The Measure of a Man." The point is that it shouldn't be so easy for Data to present himself falsely as Picard.

A second problem: Since the computer can report the location of each person on the *Enterprise*, wouldn't it be logical for the computer to cross-check the location of the person with a command request? Yet for this seemingly important operation—localizing command function—only a voiceprint is required. Of course, if Data couldn't localize command function, he couldn't take over the ship.

• Just before Data leaves the ship, he creates an access code for all the command functions he localized on the bridge. Without this code, no one—I repeat, *no one*—can regain control of the *Enterprise*. When Data creates the access code, he dictates it as "one, seven, three, four, six, seven, three, two, one, four, seven, six, Charlie, three, two, seven, eight, nine, seven, seven, seven, six, four, three, Tango, seven, three, two, Victor, seven, three, one, one, seven, eight, eight, eight, seven, three, two, four, seven, six, seven, eight, nine, seven, six, four, three, seven, six, lock."

However, when the computer displays the security code, it looks like this:

ONE-SEVEN-THREE-FOUR-SIX-
SEVEN-TWO-ONE-FOUR-SEVEN-
SIX-CHARLIE-THREE-TWO-SEV-
EN-EIGHT-NINE-SEVEN-SEVEN-
SEVEN-SIX-THREE-TANGO-SEV-
EN-THREE-TWO-VICTOR-SEVEN-
THREE-ONE-ONE-SEVEN-ONE-
EIGHT-EIGHT-EIGHT-SEVEN-
THREE-TWO-FOUR-SEVEN-SIX-
SEVEN-EIGHT-NINE-SEVEN-SIX-
FOUR-THREE-SEVEN-SIX-LOCK.

Two numbers are missing from the

computer's version, and one number has been added—not a good thing if this access code is required to regain control of the ship!

• After the crew regains access to the main bridge, they find that Data entered a security code. It stops them from giving command orders to the computer. They decide they must go to the planet and capture Data. After a great deal of effort, the crew gets a transporter working, and an away team beams down. But wait: Couldn't the crew have saved time by taking the shuttle craft instead? Does shutting down command function stop shuttles, too?

CHANGED PREMISES

• Was Data confused during "The Hunted," when he claimed that the sensors of the *Enterprise* were calibrated to scan for artificial life? In "Brothers," the equipment seems to have lost this capability. Once the crew gets the sensors working on the *Enterprise*, Worf locates a human on the surface. He does not, however, locate Data, and he claims there are no life signs for the small craft orbiting the planet. That craft contains Lore. In addition—when Riker, La Forge, and Worf beam down to the surface of the planet—Riker asks Worf if Data is in the house they find. Worf looks at his tricorder and replies, "There's no way of knowing."

EQUIPMENT ODDITIES

• When Data falls into the trance, he rides a turbolift with the sick boy's worried brother. Moments later, Data reaches over to a panel on the wall of the turbolift—to the right of the door—and indicates his new destination.

A panel on the *inside* wall of a turbolift? When did turbolifts get control panels on their walls? In the first three seasons of *Star Trek: The Next Generation*—filled with scenes of the crew entering and exiting turbolifts—there has never been a control panel on the inside of a turbolift. Come to think of it, after this episode, I can recall seeing a control panel only one other time, but that panel is to the left of the doors and much larger. (See Equipment Oddities for the episode "Power Play.") Evidently someone thought it would make a nice visual for Data to hit a button while on the turbolift, so they took one of those little panels with the buttons on it and glued it to the wall for this one scene, for this *one* time in the history of the show!

TRIVIA ANSWERS

1. Seven.
2. Brent Spiner, the actor who plays Data. He also played Lore in this episode.

SUDDENLY HUMAN

Star Date: 44143.7

While rescuing several injured young Talarians from a training craft, Dr. Crusher discovers a human boy among them. DNA matching establishes his identity as Jeremiah Rosa; the Talarians call him Jono. Starfleet thought he died along with his parents in a border skirmish while the Talarians and the Federation were at war. Instead, a Talarian captain named Endar took Jeremiah as a surrogate for his own son, who died in another battle with the Federation.

Endar has a rendezvous with the *Enterprise* and receives the young Talarians. He also asks for Jono. Picard refuses. Since Jono is human, Picard asserts that Jono should be returned to his rightful family. Endar threatens war, but Picard knows Jono has reached the age of decision. If Picard can convince Jono to stay, Endar will allow it. Just as Picard begins to succeed in his effort to awaken Jono's humanity, Jono attacks him with a dagger. Jono could not face abandoning his father and the Talarian culture. He believed Picard would kill him for the attack. Picard

recognizes Jono's deep love for his father and the Talarian way of life. He returns Jono to Endar.

GREAT LINES

"Seldom have I heard an explanation so ... well rehearsed."—Troi to Picard, after he enumerates in detail why he doesn't think it's a good idea for him to provide a father image for Jono.

PLOT OVERSIGHTS

• At the end of the show, the transporter chief must have read the script to know when to transport Jono back to the Talarian ship. After Picard escorts Jono to the transporter room, Jono steps up on the platform and Picard says good-bye. Then they both pause for almost four seconds. (If I were the transporter chief, I would have hit the button at this point.) Thankfully, the transporter chief doesn't, because Jono wanted to have one final, tender moment with Picard. After this, Jono gets back on the platform, waits less than three seconds, and the chief transports him to Endar's ship. (In case you are wondering, no one says "Energize.")

Trivia Questions

1. How old was Jono when his parents were killed?

2. What is the name of the mental condition that causes children to be highly devoted to abusive parents?

CHANGED PREMISES

• Dr. Crusher's skills must be improving. In this episode, Jono stabs Picard with a knife, and in very short order Picard seems to be fine. Crusher says the blade glanced off the sternum—a bone in the center of the chest. In "Who Watches the Watchers," however, a Mintakan shoots Picard in the shoulder with an arrow, and even after Dr. Crusher fixes him up, Picard wears a sling to support his arm.

TRIVIA ANSWERS

1. Three years, nine months.
2. The Stockholm syndrome.

REMEMBER ME

Star Dates: 44161.2-44162.8

After the *Enterprise* docks at Starbase 133, Dr. Crusher welcomes an old friend named Dr. Dalen Quaice aboard. As Dr. Crusher escorts him to his quarters, he reminisces about the friends who have died and how he failed to tell them how much they meant to him. As Quaice settles in, Dr. Crusher wanders off and finds Wesley in Engineering. He is running an experiment on a new warp field configuration called a "static warp bubble." Suddenly the warp chamber emits a flash. Wesley looks up and his mother is gone. The next morning, Dr. Crusher goes to Quaice's quarters for breakfast. She finds it empty. Picard initiates a shipwide search for the man.

As the search continues, other members of the crew begin disappearing. Yet, once a person disappears, everyone seems to forget that that person ever existed. The situation continues to degrade until only Dr. Crusher is left.

During this time, an energy vortex appears twice: once in sick bay and once on the main bridge. Dr. Crusher fights with everything in her to keep from being sucked into it. In fact, Wesley and La Forge have created the vortex each time, trying to rescue Dr. Crusher from the warp bubble. When the flash occurred in Engineering, the resulting warp bubble captured Dr. Crusher. Her thoughts—reflections on Quaice losing loved ones—defined the reality she would experience. Wesley and La Forge have been trying to create a bridge to Dr. Crusher's reality before the bubble collapses. When all seems lost, the "traveler" appears (see "Where No One Has Gone Before"), summoned by Wesley's thoughts. With the traveler's assistance, Wesley creates the bridge. By this time, Dr. Crusher has deduced what's happening. She runs to Engineering and jumps through to safety.

Trivia Questions

1. How long did Quaice serve on Starbase 133?

2. What is Picard's body temperature and blood pressure at one point during this episode?

GREAT LINES

"If there's nothing wrong with me, maybe there's something wrong with the universe."—Crusher, in the process of coming to the realization that she's trapped inside the warp bubble.

PLOT OVERSIGHTS

• When Quaice turns up missing, Data scans the entire ship for life forms. He also suggests they check the transporter ID traces to see if the man went back to the starbase. But what about the airlock? The man could have walked off the ship. One of the graphics used in the episode shows the *Enterprise* docked at the starbase—and connected by a tube—well before Quaice disappears. The episode "11001001" establishes that people can walk through this tube. (More on that under Continuity and Production Problems.)

• The first time the vortex appears, it finds Dr. Crusher in sick bay. The second time, it finds her on the bridge. This makes sense. This is her reality. Therefore, any link that is created to the warp bubble will automatically be in the same location as she is. However, the last time the vortex appears, it shows up only in Engineering. This makes it possible for Dr. Crusher to run through the halls as they evaporate behind her, adding tension to the end of the episode (and it works very well).

EQUIPMENT ODDITIES

• At one point, Dr. Crusher uses a workstation on the bridge to view the warp bubble with the *Enterprise* superimposed on it. She watches the bubble shrink until it comes perilously close to the main bridge. The next shot shows her worried expression. Then the scene cuts back to the graphic. *Lo and behold*, the warp bubble has widened back out so that Dr. Crusher has more time before it impacts on the bridge.

• When Dr. Crusher finally does leave the bridge, she boards a turbolift. When the turbolift starts to move, the light in the rectangular window goes from top to bottom. If the light it going from top to bottom, the turbolift is moving *up*. But Dr. Crusher boarded the turbolift from the main bridge. She is on deck 1. There is nothing above the main bridge to go up to. How can Crusher be going up?

CONTINUITY AND PRODUCTION PROBLEMS

• The graphics at the beginning of the episode, showing the *Enterprise* arriving and docking at Starbase 133, are the same graphics used in the episode "11001001." However, in that show the *Enterprise* was supposedly at Starbase 74. What are the chances that Starbase 133 and Starbase 74 orbit exactly the same-colored planet and that both planets have exactly the same-colored moons and that both moons are exactly in the same location when the *Enterprise* approaches? Wouldn't it have made more sense just to call Starbase 133, Starbase 74 instead? (I understand the necessity to reuse these expensive-to-produce visuals, but why not make reusing them make sense?)

TRIVIA ANSWERS

1. Six years.
2. They are 37.2 degrees Celsius and 122 over 76.

LEGACY

Star Dates: 44215.2-44225.3

An escape pod from a damaged Federation freighter lands near the colony on Turkana IV—the same colony Tasha Yar escaped from many years ago. (Yar was the security chief during the first season of *Star Trek: The Next Generation*.) Because of Tasha's reports of anarchy in the colony, an armed away team beams down to rescue the men in the pod. The away team meets a raiding party from the Coalition. It and the other major faction, the Alliance, vie for control of the colony. After the raiding party takes the away team to their headquarters, the leader of the Coalition claims that the Alliance holds the men and will demand a ransom for them. Once the away team returns to the *Enterprise*, the leader of the Coalition contacts the *Enterprise*. He offers the free services of one of his people as a show of good faith. That person is Ishara Yar, Tasha's sister.

Ishara soon wins the confidence of the crew. She devises a plan to rescue the men from the freighter. Unfortunately, all members of the Alliance and the Coalition carry proximity detectors implanted in their bodies. If Ishara beams down with the away team to rescue the men, her proximity detector will set off alarms. Dr. Crusher removes the proximity detector, and the away team beams down. While Riker, Data, and Worf free the men, Ishara disappears. She heads for one of the Alliance's main fusion generators and sets it to overload. When Data finds her, he questions her actions. He realizes her help was merely a ruse to gain her access to the Alliance's defenses. Riker stuns Ishara, and Data resets the generator. With the hostages safely returned to the *Enterprise*, Picard beams Ishara back to the Coalition.

Trivia Questions

1. How many ancillary bases does the Alliance maintain?

2. What thickness of solid granite can the transporter safely beam through?

PLOT OVERSIGHTS

• After the first away team visits the colony, the leader of the Coalition tells a subordinate to find out everything "there is to know about the starship *Enterprise*." Evidently his search turned up the fact that Tasha Yar left the colony many years ago, joined Starfleet, and eventually served on the *Enterprise*, because, a short time later, he produces Ishara Yar and offers her services to Picard. Yet, earlier in the episode, Picard says that the colony severed relationships with the Federation fifteen years ago, and Data indicates the last contact came six years ago, when the *Potemkin* orbited Turkana IV. Also, Riker claims that the colony hasn't maintained reliable communications since the government fell apart fifteen years ago.

Here is a colony, isolated from the Federation for at least six years, and the leader of the Coalition manages to extract a personnel list for a ship that wasn't even in service during the last contact? To explain this, the creators have Dr. Crusher say, "All [the leader] had to do was to search through their data base on Starfleet to find Tasha's name." Is it Starfleet's policy to continue to supply detailed information on crew rosters to colonies that no longer have relations with the Federation? Since the Federation has enemies, isn't it doubtful that Starfleet would leave this type of information floating around?

• Riker claims that the colony hasn't maintained reliable communications for fifteen years. Yet, every conversation with the leader of the Coalition seems very solid. There is no static or visual breakup. There are some transmission problems when the hostages speak with the ship, but the creators didn't follow through on the other transmissions.

• During Ishara's attempt to deceive the crew about her intentions, she feigns an interest in joining Starfleet. Both Data and Worf encourage her in this. Wesley's efforts to get into

Starfleet (see "Coming of Age") seemed to indicate that only the best and brightest could get into Starfleet. Ishara has grown up in a colony in turmoil. Is it likely her education has prepared her for Starfleet Academy? And what about Tasha? Wouldn't she have had the same problems.

• What is it with the crew of the *Enterprise*, anyway? On the planet, the members of the Coalition, both male and female, wear the same type of loose-fitting, functional outfit. Yet once Ishara gets to the *Enterprise*, the crew makes all haste to get her changed into this tight (I mean *really* tight) body suit, which shows off every curve. None of the rest of the crew—aside from the babe-counselor Troi—has to endure this type of outfit. Why does Ishara? Seems a bit sexist, doesn't it? At least the crew made sure that Ishara's little belt and holster for her phaser were color-coordinated with her outfit. (We just couldn't have a holster that clashed, now, could we?)

EQUIPMENT ODDITIES

• At one point in the episode, La Forge talks about the location of the hostages. He reaches up and touches a display panel. The graphic on the panel rotates to a new position. A blinking dot indicates where the hostages are held. Unfortunately, the 2 kilometers of solid granite above them preclude their using the transporter. La Forge then suggests that they use the phaser to bore a hole in the granite and transport an away team into a storage area. When La Forge points to the storage area on the display, however, he indicates a spot on the other side of the city—nowhere near the hostages! (Of course, the larger question here is: Why didn't the *Enterprise* just bore a hole down to the hostages and beam them up?)

• Near the end of the episode, Worf escorts Ishara onto the bridge. They exit the turbolift near Picard's ready room. Worf points for Ishara to stand beside Picard. After Picard talks with the leader of the Coalition, Picard orders Data to escort her to the transporter. Data stands and takes Ishara up the ramp to the turbolift by Worf's station. Why not take her back to the turbolift beside the ready room? For that matter, why do most of the crew walk up the ramp every time they leave the bridge? Is this how the bridge crew gets its exercise? Do they just forget the other turbolift is there? (Much in the same way that crew members "forget" they don't have to tap their insignia to respond to a communication while they are on the ship. At least that's what the *Star Trek: The Next Generation Tech-*

nical Manual asserts.) Or—worst of all—does each turbolift service only certain destinations on the ship? This third possibility seems terribly confusing, since there is no indication on the turbolift doors of where each turbolift goes.

CONTINUITY AND PRODUCTION PROBLEMS

• At the very beginning of the show, Riker performs a card trick with Data. The second time Data cuts the cards, he places the upper half *above* the lower half. The shot changes just as the cards touch the table. In the new shot, the upper half lays *beside* the lower half.

TRIVIA ANSWERS

1. Thirteen.
2. A thickness of 400 meters. (La Forge says there are 2 kilometers of solid granite. He bores a hole 1.6 kilometers down. That leaves 0.4 kilometer or 400 meters, through which the transporter safely beams the away team.)

★
REUNION

Star Date: 44246.3

As the *Enterprise* investigates radiation anomalies, a Klingon battle cruiser decloaks nearby. It carries K'Mpec, the head of the Klingon High Council, and Federation Ambassador K'Ehleyr. When K'Ehleyr beams aboard, she brings a surprise for Worf—his son, Alexander, the product of their bonding during "The Emissary." K'Mpec is dying, poisoned by an unknown hand. He wants Picard to discover who is killing him. Two Klingons, Duras and Gowron, vie for the leadership position; According to tradition, a mediator will guide these challengers in a fight to the death. The winner will assume the leadership of the High Council. K'Mpec chooses Picard to mediate the battle. He wants to give Picard as much time as possible to discover who has poisoned him. K'Mpec insists that that man must not be allowed to lead the Klingon Empire.

Gowron and Duras arrive a short time later. Picard, assisted by K'Ehleyr, begins the process of mediation. Meanwhile, Worf and K'Ehleyr discuss their son. K'Ehleyr is ready to take an oath of marriage, but Worf refuses because of his discommendation (see "Sins of the Father"). Since Worf will not tell her the reason he chose discommendation, K'Ehleyr starts her own investigation. By reviewing the ship's logs and information from the Imperial Klingon Information Net, she determines Duras's father's guilt. When K'Ehleyr confronts Duras with the truth, he kills her. Enraged at K'Ehleyr's death, Worf claims the rite of vengeance, boards Duras's ship, and kills him. Believing that Alexander needs the warmth of a family, Worf sends his son to live with his human parents.

Trivia Questions

1. How did the crew of the *Enterprise* know the bomb came from the Romulans?

2. How many logs are there from the last visit of the *Enterprise* to the First World of the Klingon Empire?

GREAT LINES

"Not even a bite on the cheek for old times' sake?"—K'Ehleyr to Worf, after beaming on board the *Enterprise*.

PLOT OVERSIGHTS

• This method of marking time in "star dates" is very convenient when the creators want to obscure the length of time of a given period. "The Emissary" occurred at star date 42901.3. This episode starts at star date 44246.3. Yet in that amount of time K'Ehleyr carried her son to term and raised him to the level of a three- or four-year-old human child. How much time elapsed between these two star dates?

Other episodes provide a few clues. "Identity Crisis" took place at star date 44664.5. That episode showed a recording from star date 40164.7. Commander Lighten says the recording was made five years ago. So the period defined from 40164.7 through 44664.5 is five years. In other words, the second digit from the left defines approximately one year. (I know for sure that it defines the length of a television season, but there is rarely any correlation between television and real life!) In "Redemption," Picard tries to persuade Worf to clear his family name. Worf replies that it isn't time. Picard then says, "That doesn't sound like the man who came to me a year ago fiercely determined to ... clear his father's name. ...." "Sins of the Father" has star dates of 43685.2–43689.0. "Redemption" has star dates of 44995.3–44998.3. Again, the second digit from the left approximates one year. Finally, in "The Drumhead," Picard says that he has been captain of the *Enterprise* for more than three years since star date 41124. "The Drumhead" occurs at star date 44769.2. Once again, the second digit from the left approximates one year.

To answer the original question—since "The Emissary" contained a star date of 42901.3 and "Reunion" carries a star date of 44246.3—the length of time between Worf's bonding with K'Ehleyr and the appearance of Worf's son, according to the star dates, should be more than one year and less than two. In other words, this Klingon boy managed to get conceived, gestate, be born, and grow to the stature of a human three-year-old in less than two years!

EQUIPMENT ODDITIES

• During one tender moment between Worf and K'Ehleyr, she places her hands on his chest. In fact, she lays her hand directly over his communicator. Of course, it doesn't chirp. It must have a "loving embrace sensor" to know when not to turn on. (I know for certain that the communicators are not tied to the touch of a specific person. Riker loaned his out in "The Survivors." He also tapped his communicator with a flashlight at the beginning of "Future Imperfect.")

TRIVIA ANSWERS

1. It used a molecular decay detonator.
2. Forty-three officers' logs and ten personal logs.

FUTURE IMPERFECT

Star Date: 44288.5

In response to unusual subspace emissions from a planet near the Neutral Zone, Riker, La Forge, and Worf beam down into a cavern. Soon after they arrive, the volcanic gases increase to dangerous proportions. As the *Enterprise* tries to beam the crew members back, all three pass out. Riker awakens in sick bay. Dr. Crusher asks him the last thing he remembers. Riker replies with the events in the cavern. Crusher then shocks him when she says that was sixteen years ago. She claims he contracted a virus on the planet. Recently the virus came out of a dormant phase and attacked. The virus wiped out all memory back to the point of contact.

The crew brings Riker up to date. He is now captain of the *Enterprise*. He has a son named Jean-Luc. Riker's wife died two years ago. Most importantly, the Federation and the Romulan Empire stand ready to sign an alliance. Riker played a vital role in its creation. The future is convincing until Riker sees a video of his wife. The woman pictured is Minuet, a fantasy woman Riker experienced on a holodeck (see "11001001"). He an-

Trivia Questions

1. How did Riker's "wife" die?

2. What star date does Riker's son give for their family records?

nounces that he will no longer participate in the charade. As the surroundings fade, only the Romulan negotiator Tomalak remains. Riker stands in a large holodeck surrounded by Romulans. Tomalak takes Riker to a cell and throws him in with a human boy. It is "Jean-Luc," Riker's "son." Together they escape, but a slip of the tongue by the boy convinces Riker that the Romulan base is another fantasy. Finally the boy confesses. His mother built this place for him to hide from their enemies. She equipped it with neural scanners and holographic generators to keep him company. The boy reached out to the *Enterprise* because of his loneliness. Riker understands and takes the boy with him back to the *Enterprise*.

PLOT OVERSIGHTS

• In Riker's future, Troi has left the *Enterprise* to work at Starfleet command. Was he lying when he tells her, "I can't imagine you ever leaving the *Enterprise*"? Evidently he could imagine her leaving, since Riker's imaginings are driving the holo-

226

graphic generators! (Speaking of Troi, she finally gets a normal uniform. Does this mean Riker always considered her outfits a bit too revealing? Or, does he prefer revealing clothing on *young* women only?)

• When briefing Riker, Troi explains that Riker will sign the new treaty between the Federation and the Romulan Empire. Riker will sign the treaty? *Riker?* He's just a captain of a starship. Leaders and diplomats sign treaties, not captains.

EQUIPMENT ODDITIES

• Soon after waking, Riker and Dr. Crusher go to the main bridge. A camera angle shows the outside of the turbolift doors just before they pop open on the bridge and Riker and Crusher walk off. While the design on the door has changed a little, it still contains the standard information "01 Turbolift." However, when Riker and Crusher leave the bridge to meet Picard and Troi, the door of the turbolift has all the same design, but the space that should be filled with "01 Turbolift" is completely blank!

CONTINUITY AND PRODUCTION PROBLEMS

• Just after Riker wakes up in his imperfect future, a medical ensign calls for Dr. Crusher. Interestingly, this attractive Oriental also appears in "Clues." Evidently she was assigned to the *Enterprise* during the time of "Future Imperfect." Riker must have seen her in sick bay for the neural scanners and the holodeck on the planet to reproduce her as Dr.

Crusher's assistant. However, although Dr. Crusher shows signs of age in Riker's future, the medical assistant does not. She looks unchanged from her appearance in "Clues." This fact can be interpreted in two equally insulting ways. Either Riker thinks all Orientals look alike—and therefore the neural scanner could reproduce the Oriental ensign without any visible aging and the discrepancy wouldn't bother Riker. Or, Riker believes Oriental woman don't show their age.

• As Riker recovers from the shock of learning that sixteen years have passed since his last memory, Crusher gets him a glass of water. She stands in front of a seemingly empty food replicator, orders water, and picks up the resulting drinking glass. It is a very nice effect but not quite flawless. While Crusher waits for the glass of water to appear, a light source from behind her casts a vertical band of light across the food replicator's opening. When Crusher picks up the glass, the band changes shape and momentarily disappears because her right arm blocks the light source. Crusher's location between the light source and the food replicator means any movement of her right arm should cause a corresponding change in the size and shape of the band of light.

Just before she orders the water, however, Dr. Crusher reaches up and, with her right hand, taps a button on the top of the food replicator. Of course, her right arm makes a broad movement to accomplish this. *During the movement, the band of re-*

flected light on the food replicator stays completely motionless.

To accomplish the effect of the glass materializing out of thin air, the creators first placed a drinking glass in the food replicator and shot the scene. Dr. Crusher simply orders the glass of water, picks it up, and takes it to Riker. Then the postproduction people went to work. They selected the film frame just before Crusher picks up the glass and used the shape of the band of light at that moment to create a still shot of the inside of an empty food replicator. Finally, they used their newly created still shot to mask over the drinking glass until it fades into existence. The entire effect is executed very well. Unfortunately—since the inside of the darkened food dispenser actually comes from a still shot—the band of light doesn't react to the movements of Crusher's arm when she initially taps the button.

• After the holographic Romulans throw Riker in a cell with the boy, Riker tries to get some information out of him. Riker sits down on the bed and raises his *left* hand in a gesture of friendship. The shot changes. Riker now has his *right* hand raised. Then the shot changes back to the original and his left hand is raised again.

• When Riker and the boy escape the cell, the boy takes Riker to his secret hiding place. The boy pulls out plans that he made of the tunnels. In the long shot, the plans are made out of a transparent plastic. In the close-up, the plans are on a substance like onionskin paper.

TRIVIA ANSWERS

1. She died in a shuttle accident.
2. The star date is 58416.

FINAL MISSION

Star Dates: 44307.3-44307.6

Picard and Wesley leave via mining shuttle for negotiations with a group of miners. A "Captain Dirgo" pilots the craft. As soon as the shuttle clears the bay, the *Enterprise* warps to assist with another crisis. A "garbage" ship filled with radioactive waste has fallen into orbit around a peaceful planet. Radiation levels have increased dramatically on the planet. The *Enterprise* must find a way to remove the barge and destroy it safely. Meanwhile, Dirgo's shuttle loses its propulsion system. Picard, Wesley, and Dirgo crash-land it on a desert moon. They assess their situation and head for a mountain range, in search of shelter and water. Back at the *Enterprise*, Riker begins towing the barge into the planet's sun. He receives word that Picard's shuttle has disappeared but must guide the barge through an asteroid belt before they can leave.

Picard, Wesley, and Dirgo reach the mountains and find a series of caves. In one of the caves they find a fountain of water, but when Dirgo approaches it, a force field springs up and knocks him backward. When Dirgo tries blasting it with a phaser, an energy entity appears and flings the phaser from his hand. The commotion loosens some boulders. Picard manages to shove Wesley out of danger, but the falling rocks seriously injure the captain. After dragging Picard to another chamber, Dirgo tries to blast the force field again. This time the entity kills him. Picard deteriorates while Wesley tries to find a way to thwart the entity. At the same time, the *Enterprise* finishes its task and warps back to find Picard and Wesley. By modifying a tricorder using a part from his communicator, Wesley disables the entity and gets the water. It sustains him and Picard until the *Enterprise* arrives and rescues them.

Trivia Questions

1. When did the shuttle leave the *Enterprise*?

2. What injuries does Picard sustain?

GREAT LINES

"Oh, I envy you, Wesley Crusher. You're just at the beginning of the adventure."—Picard, thinking that he will die, giving a few last words of advice to Wesley.

PLOT OVERSIGHTS

• In this episode, Riker exposes the crew to almost lethal radiation by wrapping the shields around the barge. He says he does this to protect the barge from the asteroids. But the *Enterprise* doesn't reach the asteroid belt until the end of the show. Why not tow the barge until it reaches the asteroids and then extend the shields? Or better yet, why not drag the barge out of the orbital plane that contains the asteroids and then point the barge back down at an angle to shoot over the asteroids and into the sun?

• Speaking of radiation exposure, isn't it unbelievable that the main computer can count down, to the second, when lethal exposure will occur? Is there really some magic length of time when, one second earlier, you will live although you may need treatment for a time, but one second later, you will become ill with no hope of recovery? And is this time interval exactly the same for every member of the crew?

EQUIPMENT ODDITIES

• Great confusion surrounds the tractor beam's towing strength. In this episode, the *Enterprise* can't accelerate to full impulse because the tractor beam can't pull the barge that fast. (Never mind that Worf engages the tractor beam while the *Enterprise* travels at warp 9 in "The Emissary.") Yet in "The Battle," Picard tells Riker to disengage the tractor beam after the *Stargazer* is in motion. Quite correctly, he points out that once the

Stargazer is moving, it will continue moving. This property of matter is codified by a law in physics called "inertia." On Earth, objects must be continually pulled up because gravity pulls them down. In space, gravity is very much weaker. Once the *Enterprise* clears the planet's gravity, the garbage ship should maintain its own velocity of half impulse.

Therefore, once the barge is traveling at half impulse, the *Enterprise* could increase to full impulse. The stress on the tractor beam can only be a factor of the *difference* between the speeds of the *Enterprise* and the barge. As long as the *Enterprise* accelerates gradually and travels in a straight line—the barge could eventually reach full impulse.

CONTINUITY AND PRODUCTION PROBLEMS

• When Picard, Wesley, and Dirgo leave the crashed shuttle, Picard fashions an arrow from scrap metal and places it on the ground. He says that the arrow will let rescuers know that they've headed for the mountains. When they start walking away from the craft, however, they aren't quite lined up with the arrow! In fact, they are a good distance off.

TRIVIA ANSWERS

1. At 0800 hours.
2. A broken right leg, a fractured left arm, a blow to the head, and possible internal bleeding.

THE LOSS

Star Date: 44356.9

At the end of a counseling session, Troi begins experiencing a headache. After the patient leaves, the pain increases until Troi blacks out. Meanwhile, Worf and Data detect several anomalies ahead of the ship. Picard stops to determine if the anomalies actually exist or are simply "ghost" images in the sensors. Finding no malfunction of the sensors, Picard orders a resumption of their previous course. The *Enterprise* jolts violently as it tries to go to warp, and minor injuries litter the ship. Picard orders all stop. At the same time, Troi calls Dr. Crusher for help.

Something starts dragging the ship through space. In the staff meeting that follows, Troi reveals that she can no longer sense emotions. After examining her, Crusher finds a section of unresponsive cells in Troi's brain. As Troi deals with this loss, Data and La Forge discover that a colony of two-dimensional beings surrounds the *Enterprise*. Their wake has trapped the ship. The lack of her empathic sense drives Troi to resign as ship's counselor. As she rages through all

the emotions associated with grief, Troi lashes out at her friends. A new threat to the *Enterprise* appears. The colony of beings is dragging the ship toward a cosmic string—an entity only the width of a proton but with the gravitational forces of a black hole. If the *Enterprise* impacts the string, it will be destroyed. After exhausting all technical means, Picard appeals to Troi for help. He wants her to help Data understand the psychology of the creatures. Troi surmises that the colony is moving toward the string in the same way a moth heads for a flame. When the *Enterprise* generates subspace vibrations to simulate another string for the colony to pursue, the colony changes course and the *Enterprise* breaks free. Immediately, Troi's empathic sense returns. The powerful emotions of the colony had temporarily overloaded her senses.

GREAT LINES

"We're on equal footing now."—Riker to Troi after realizing why Troi is so frightened now that she cannot eavesdrop on the emotions of others.

Trivia Questions

1. What was the name of Ensign Brooks's husband, and how long ago did he die?

2. What is Ensign Brooks's first name?

EQUIPMENT ODDITIES

• When Troi experiences intense pain caused by the onset of the colony, she needs to call Dr. Crusher. She reaches up, taps her badge, talks to Crusher, and taps her badge to end the conversation. Isn't this proof that individuals must tap their badges to begin conversations? *No one* in intense pain takes extra steps to call for help.

CONTINUITY AND PRODUCTION PROBLEMS

• As Data briefs the staff on the existence of the two-dimensional colony, he stands at a viewscreen. In a medium close-up, the image of the *Enterprise* is oriented toward the upper left of the screen. The colony moves in an arcing motion from the lower left to the upper center of the screen.

When Data demonstrates the colony's two-dimensionality, however, the orientation of the *Enterprise* remains the same but the colony now moves almost horizontally, from left to right.

• Also, as the screen changes perspective to show a side view of the *Enterprise*, a rhythmic beeping occurs in the background. The beeping continues until the rotation of the screen completes. Data then reverses the perspective back to a top view of the *Enterprise*. When Picard asks a question and Data answers, a close-up shows the very edge of the viewscreen. The colony now travels from the lower left to the upper center again. Additionally, the beeping continues for several seconds into Data's answer. The beeping should correspond to a change in perspective on the viewscreen, but it doesn't. The screen remains static.

TRIVIA ANSWERS

1. Mark; he died five months ago.
2. Janet.

DATA'S DAY

For this episode, Data makes a complete report of all his activities in a single day. Data will forward the report, with additional comments to Bruce Maddox to assist him in his artificial intelligence research (see "The Measure of a Man").

Two main plots dominate this show. First, Transporter Chief O'Brien's wedding is scheduled for this day. Since Data originally introduced the couple, he will participate as "the father of the bride." Typical wedding day jitters interrupt the schedule. Eventually everything returns to normal and the wedding proceeds. Along the way, Data asks Dr. Crusher to teach him to dance. After receiving a full lesson in tap dancing, Data informs Dr. Crusher that he is ready for the wedding. Once Crusher realizes the reason Data wants to learn to dance, she changes her tactics and teaches him ballroom dancing.

The second major plot revolves around Vulcan Ambassador T'Pei. The *Enterprise* takes her to the Neutral Zone to rendezvous with a Romulan vessel. She claims the Romulans want to initiate a dialogue with the Federation. When T'Pei beams over, a sudden transporter malfunction seems to kill her. The *Enterprise* leaves the Neutral Zone. An investigation finally uncovers the truth. The Romulans beamed T'Pei off the *Enterprise* transporter pad at the same time O'Brien energized. Picard races back to rescue T'Pei from the Romulan ship, only to find out that she is a Romulan spy. The appearance of several Romulan ships convinces Picard to leave the Neutral Zone.

Trivia Questions

1. What is T'Pei's security access code?

2. What is O'Brien's middle name?

GREAT LINES

"*This does not remind me of you.*"— Data to Worf, commenting that Worf's selection of a crystal swan as a present for O'Brien's wedding is not indicative of Worf's personality.

CONTINUITY AND PRODUCTION PROBLEMS

• At one point, Data returns to his quarters and he orders food for his cat. The bowl that materializes contains a small amount of something on the bottom. Yet, in the close-up, as Data places it on the floor, the bowl suddenly becomes over half filled with food. Is he using some sort of deaerated food that puffs up when exposed to oxygen?

• This episode qualifies Troi for the "Fastest Crossed Legs in the Universe" award. When Data goes to her for advice, the scene opens with her serving herself some tea. Moments later, she sits down. In the very next shot, her legs are instantly crossed. (I could make one of several ungentlemanly comments at this juncture but ... I believe I will postpone.)

• The wedding glass O'Brien and his wife drink from appears to be empty. The glass is translucent, so it is difficult to tell. As their heads tilt toward the glass, the inside shadows appear clearly on the outside of the glass. Wouldn't any liquid in the glass also show up?

TRIVIA ANSWERS

1. Kappa alpha 4601704.
2. Edward.

THE WOUNDED

The *Enterprise* lingers at the edge of Cardassian space, waiting to report their presence to a Cardassian scout ship. Although the Federation and the Cardassians have a peace treaty, the Cardassians still zealously guard their territory. Suddenly a Cardassian scout ship appears and fires on the *Enterprise*. After trying repeated hails, Picard fires back and damages the ship. When he demands a reason for the attack, Captain Gul Macet replies that it is normal to attack when at war. Picard reminds him of the treaty but Gul Macet shocks Picard with news of a Federation attack on a research station.

Picard contacts Starfleet. Starfleet confirms that the USS *Phoenix*, under the command of Captain Ben Maxwell, did attack the station. The *Phoenix* will not respond to Starfleet's hails. Starfleet tells Picard to do what is necessary to preserve the peace. Picard invites Gul Macet and his aides aboard the *Enterprise* and begins a search for the *Phoenix*. They finally locate it, but not before Maxwell destroys a Cardassian warship and freighter. When

Trivia Questions

1. What are the class and registry of the USS *Phoenix*?

2. How often does the high-energy sensor system of the *Phoenix* cycle?

Maxwell comes on board the *Enterprise* he tries to convince Picard that the Cardassians are massing for war. He claims the research stations are simply base camps for a new offensive into Federation space. Picard sends Maxwell back to his ship and orders him to return to Federation space. Shortly afterward, the *Phoenix* veers off course and stops a Cardassian supply ship. Maxwell tells Picard the proof is in the ship. Picard refuses to board the ship. He arrests Maxwell, and both ships return to Federation space.

As Gul Macet leaves the *Enterprise*, Picard tells him that Maxwell was correct. Picard's job, however, was to guard the peace. In the future, he tells Gul Macet, the Federation will be watching Cardassian activities more closely.

PLOT OVERSIGHTS

• When the *Enterprise* first locates the *Phoenix*, Picard orders the con to lay in a course for the *Phoenix* at warp 6. After the *Phoenix* destroys the warship, Picard asks how long till they intercept, and Data replies, "At our present speed of warp 4 ..." When did the *Enterprise* slow to warp 4?

EQUIPMENT ODDITIES

• At one point O'Brien enters a turbolift with two Cardassians. As it travels, the Cardassians ask him to have a drink with them. When the turbolift reaches O'Brien's destination, he mouths off to them and heads for the doors. The doors on the turbolift wait until he approaches before opening. Compare this to the operation of the turbolift doors in other episodes. In "The Best of Both Worlds," Part 2, Riker and Worf ride a turbolift. As soon as the turbolift reaches the destination, the doors open. They do not wait for Riker and Worf to approach. This is normal operation for turbolift doors.

CONTINUITY AND PRODUCTION PROBLEMS

• When the *Phoenix* attacks the Cardassian warship, the *Enterprise*'s long-range scanners report the incident. At one point Data overlays the weapons ranges of the two ships as a pattern of concentric circles on the main display. After the Cardassians get off one volley, Data says that the *Phoenix* has moved out of the weapons range of the Cardassian warship. But the next shot of the screen shows the *Phoenix* still inside the circles of the Cardassian ship. This indicates that the *Phoenix has not* moved out of the Cardassians' weapons' range.

TRIVIA ANSWERS
1. Nebular Class, NCC 65420.
2. Every 5.5 minutes.

DEVIL'S DUE

Star Date: 99979.5

Responding to a distress call from an anthropological science team on Ventax II, the *Enterprise* finds a world in frenzy. One thousand years ago, the inhabitants made a "deal with the she-devil." In exchange for a millennium of peace, they agreed to give themselves and their planet. The thousand years have ended, and the populace believes "Ardra" will soon appear to claim her inheritance. In their hysteria, people from the planet have attacked the Federation science station. The *Enterprise* manages to rescue the head scientist, but the rest are taken hostage.

Picard beams down to the planet to talk with the prime minister. While there, Ardra appears and performs several "supernatural" tricks. She claims she is taking possession of the planet. Picard challenges her and demands to see the contract. In the process, he manages to get the hostages released and orders Data to review the contract and the planet's laws in detail. Back on the *Enterprise*, Picard discusses options with the senior officers. Afterward, Ardra appears on the bridge, claiming that she also owns the *Enterprise*, since it was in orbit around the planet when she took possession. Data, returning to the bridge from the planet, confirms her interpretation of the contract. Under orders from Picard, Data finds an obscure precedent in the planet's laws that allows the captain to call for arbitration. Unfortunately, Ardra presents a convincing case, proving her claims according to the planet's legal system.

Meanwhile, La Forge and the head scientist locate Ardra's power source. A Security team from the *Enterprise* boards Ardra's ship and takes control of her systems. Picard now performs the same tricks as Ardra and exposes her as a fraud. She withdraws her claim as Ventaxian guards escort her away.

Trivia Questions

1. Who made first contact with Ventax II?

2. Where was Ardra's ship?

GREAT LINES

"The advocate will refrain from making her opponent disappear."—Data, as arbiter, to Ardra after she makes Picard disappear during the trial.

PLOT OVERSIGHTS

• During a meeting with the senior staff in the observation lounge, Data claims that the people of Ventax II consider it bad luck to speak Ardra's name. However, the prime minister does it quite frequently.

• When Ardra shows up on the bridge of the *Enterprise*, Picard has her beamed back to the planet. Immediately afterward, he orders an ensign to put up the shields until further notice. The ensign turns around. It is Ardra again. A few moments later, she leaves of her own accord. Evidently she flustered Picard enough that he never repeated the order, and everyone on the bridge forgot he said anything about putting up the shields in the first place. At this point in the show, the source of Ardra's powers is a mystery, but the end of the show makes clear that she is using standard transporter technology. That means the crew never raised the shields, because if they did, Ardra could not have beamed into Picard's bedroom later in the show!

• During the trial, Ardra demands that Picard explain her abilities. He claims he can't. Granted, he doesn't know exactly where her power source is during this scene. However, earlier in the episode, he gave a good guess about her methods during a discussion with his senior staff. Instead of repeating that explanation, Picard simply replies that he can't explain Ardra's abilities. (I can tell you what happened. Ardra fried his brain when she showed up in his bedroom wearing *that* outfit! Describing *that* outfit would offend the sensibil-

ities of some readers. You'll have to watch the episode for yourself!)

EQUIPMENT ODDITIES

• When Data flies Picard back to the *Enterprise*, Data makes a complete loop around the ship for some reason. The first shot shows the shuttle approaching the back side of the *Enterprise*. Then there's a beautiful reflection of the port warp nacelle (engine) sweeping across the window of the shuttle as Picard and Data talk. At this point, the shuttle is aligned for docking in any of the shuttle bays. As the scene continues, Picard and Data talk about the possibility of third-party arbitration of Ardra's claim on the *Enterprise*. Afterward, a shot shows the backs of Picard and Data, with the *Enterprise* showing directly in front of them. At this point the shuttle once again sweeps around the port warp engine and lines up with the shuttle bays. The only way to resolve these images is to say the Data flew around the *Enterprise* once before docking. Did Data not have enough flying time logged to maintain his pilot's license? Is that why he took Picard for the extra lap?

• Is La Forge running multimodal reflection sorting of complex subspace signals on one of his workstations on the planet? If he is, that would explain why the graphic on one of the screens is exactly the same as the one on Data's screen during "The Best of Both Worlds," Part 2.

• After Picard performs Ardra's tricks, he explains that a team from the *Enterprise* took control of Ardra's ship. Picard then touches his communicator and thanks Riker for his help. Picard explains that the team had monitored him on his communicator. In other words, the communicator was already on. Does that mean that Picard shut it off when he tapped it?

CONTINUITY AND PRODUCTION PROBLEMS

• After Ardra leaves the *Enterprise*, Picard calls Data to his ready room. Before Data enters, Picard takes a drink of tea. When the shot reverses, the level of tea is back to the presip setting.

TRIVIA ANSWERS

1. The Klingons, seventy years ago.
2. It was 34 degrees north, 62 degrees east, and at a height of 210 kilometers, placing it above the western magnetic pole.

TREK SILLINESS:
THE TOP TEN ODDITIES OF
STAR TREK: THE NEXT GENERATION

1. *Earth-centric attitudes.* Do you ever wonder why most of the alien races on the show look basically the same as humans? They all have one head, two arms, two legs, etc. And how did Earth manage to become the central location for the Federation? According to "The Best of Both Worlds," it is in sector 001. Along the same line, shouldn't the Federation be a little more aware of the attitudes behind the names it gives? Why is the Bandi's space-port called "Farpoint" Station? Far from what? (On the same line, why is the Bajoran station called *"Deep Space 9"*?)

2. *The lack of "to boldly go where no one has gone before."* There's a definite deficit when it comes to exploring the far-flung reaches of the galaxy and discovering new and interesting life forms in the series. True, the *Enterprise* does a lot of mapping missions, but somehow I thought "boldly going" would be a little more exciting than this.

3. *Main bridge, design.* Granted, the curved railing on the main bridge makes a beautiful design statement, but it's very impractical. First of all, it puts a barrier between the chief of Security and the captain. Many times, attackers have beamed directly to the bridge to capture Picard. What does Worf do? He jogs down the ramp a little way and then jumps over the railing. Second, it puts a barrier between the top three officers and the science stations at the back of the bridge. To get a report from someone at these stations, the officers must look under the railing, walk around the railing, or have the person get up and walk to the edge of the railing.

4. *Main bridge, location.* The most important location on the *Enterprise* is—in essence—a hood ornament! Once the ship loses its defensive shields, the bridge is fully exposed to attack. It even has a bubble window for the enemy to shoot out.

5. *The relative loss of separation.* "Encounter at Farpoint" demonstrated a wonderful feature of the *Enterprise*: It can separate into a saucer section and star drive. Purportedly, this means that if the *Enterprise* is heading into danger, it can leave the saucer section behind to house the crew's families while the star drive goes in with guns blazing. The only problem here is that the ship has separated only *three* times! And one of those was done to give the Borg two targets to shoot at instead of one—not to keep non-

crew members at a safe distance.

6. *The relative lack of video communication.* Only twice has the show dabbled with any type of video connection with an away team—once with La Forge's visual acuity transmitter in "Heart of Glory" and once with a head-mounted videocamera in "Identity Crisis." The rest of the time, however, Picard is blind to the activities of the away team and must rely only on audio for the status of the mission.

7. *The "don't give Picard a straight answer" syndrome.* This problem has subsided in later shows, but in the early seasons, Picard would ask a direct question and his senior staff would sidestep it or respond with, "I think you better get down here and see for yourself." The worst example of this occurs during "Skin of Evil." Just after Armus rises from his oil slick, Picard calls down to the away team and says, "What is it, number one? What are you seeing?" Riker responds, "Trouble."

8. *Data's contractions.* Is it really believable that Data—this android with a positronic brain capable of sixty trillion calculations per second and an ultimate storage capacity of eight hundred quadrillion bits—cannot use contractions? Is it really that hard to set up a little file that says, "Whenever you are about to say 'I am' replace that with 'I'm' "? (As a programmer, I can tell you definitively that the answer is "NO!")

9. *Troi's outfit.* Why does Troi get to wear the skin-tight bunny suit? No one else in the entire series has worn this type of uniform. More to the point, why would Troi want to wear the bunny suit? Does she feel it will make her patients more comfortable? She is a trained professional counselor. How would you react to a psychologist dressed like this?

10. *Worf's marksmanship.* For the chief of Security and the tactical officer of the flagship of the Federation, Worf needs help. Guinan outshoots him on the phaser range in "Redemption." Worf's shots land off-target in "The High Ground" and "Power Play," and he completely misses a Ferengi less than twenty feet away in "Rascals." On top of all this, it takes him forever to decide to shoot the Borg who are kidnapping Picard in "The Best of Both Worlds."

CLUES

As the *Enterprise* flies toward an M Class planet to investigate, a space distortion appears. Moments later, Data turns in his chair to find the rest of the bridge crew stunned into unconsciousness. When Data revives them, he explains that they passed through an unstable worm hole. He claims it caused the crew to black out for thirty seconds. Because of the unstable nature of the worm hole, the *Enterprise* continues on its way. Several discrepancies soon show up to challenge Data's version of events. However, when confronted by Picard, Data refuses to answer any questions. Seeking to solve the mystery, Picard takes the *Enterprise* back to the location of the M Class planet. For the second time, the Paxans attack the ship. They claim they must destroy the *Enterprise*, since the plan failed. Data now explains what really happened.

The Paxans are isolationists. Normally, whenever a ship approaches, they stun the crew and tow away the ship. When the crew wakes up, they assume they passed through a worm hole and count their blessings. Using this method, the Paxans conceal their identity. Unfortunately, the stun field didn't affect Data, and—while Data defended the ship against them—he awakened the crew. Faced with fighting a superior foe, Picard negotiated a compromise. The crew destroyed all knowledge of the Paxans and allowed the Paxans to stun them again, erasing their short-term memory. Since the stun field wouldn't work on Data, Picard ordered him never to reveal the Paxans' existence. After Data finishes recounting the events of the first encounter, Picard asks for another chance. He dubs the first time a "dry run" to shake out the flaws. The Paxans agree. As the show ends, Data helps Picard to his feet. Data claims the *Enterprise* has just passed through an unstable worm hole....

Trivia Questions

1. When was "Gloria from Cleveland" (Guinan) supposed to meet "Dixon Hill" (Picard)?

2. What compound did Data release into the air flow system to revive the crew?

PLOT OVERSIGHTS

• The first time the episode shows the crew awakening, Data reports scattered injuries throughout the ship. A scene in sick bay shows Dr. Crusher mending the torn elbow ligaments of O'Brien. Crusher asks how the accident occurred. O'Brien replies that he was hanging a plant for Keiko, his wife, when the *Enterprise* passed through the worm hole.

In all, the Paxans stunned the crew three times. Data revived them the first time while the Paxans attacked. The second and third times, the crew woke up without any knowledge of the first time. In other words, when O'Brien says he was hanging a plant, he means he was hanging a plant the *first* time the Paxans stunned the crew. When the Paxans stunned the crew the second time, O'Brien knew they were going to stun him. Obviously O'Brien wanted to be doing the same thing he was doing before the first Paxan encounter so he wouldn't be bothered by the discrepancy. But why would he get up on a chair knowing that when he was stunned he would tumble to the floor? If he wanted to duplicate his position before the first stun, why not stand on the chair, drop the plant, get off the chair, lie down on the floor, and let them stun him?

• To prove that the crew lay unconscious for more than thirty seconds, Dr. Crusher finds the last person to use a transporter. After examining that person, she tells Picard that they were out for longer than thirty seconds, "a lot longer." Follow her reasoning. Dr. Crusher says human cells have developed rhythms based on a twenty-four-hour period, a daily cycle. She can measure the cellular change at a molecular level. Since the transporter trace contains information on the person's cells, Crusher can compare the reading from a person and the reading from

the person's transporter trace. She maintains that if they were unconscious for only thirty seconds, individuals' rhythms should be nearly the same as the last time they used the transporter.

This all sounds fine and good until you remember how long the crew was stunned. The rest of the show reveals a "missing day." In several places the dialogue suggests that they were out for twenty-four hours. If the crew was out for twenty-four hours, wouldn't the cellular rhythms have started over and therefore lined up with the transporter trace?

• When Data refuses a direct order from Picard, Picard threatens him with a court-martial. He asks Data if he realizes what that means. Data says that he does. Then Picard says, "Do you also realize that you would most likely be stripped down to your wires to find out what ... has gone wrong?"

Is this the same Picard who fought to establish that Data has rights as a sentient being in "The Measure of a Man"? Did Data lose those rights at some point prior to this episode? Or is Starfleet in the habit of dissecting any human it court-martials? To threaten Data with disassembly means either that he does not have the rights of a member of the Federation or that Starfleet has a policy of killing anyone it finds guilty in a court-marshal.

• At the end of the episode, Data narrates a flashback to the *first* encounter with the Paxans. During his narration, the episode shows Data waking everyone while the Paxans attempt to override the shields. At this point, no one can possibly know they are called the Paxans. The Paxans then penetrate the shields and take control of Troi. After she breaks Worf's wrist, Picard asks, "Who are you?" The Paxans, speaking through Troi, do not answer. They simply maintain that they must destroy the ship. The dialogue continues until Picard and the Paxans reach a compromise. Then Picard turns to Data and orders him never to reveal what has happened, to conceal his knowledge of the Paxans for as long as he exists. How did Picard know they were called the Paxans? The Paxans never mentioned their name.

CHANGED PREMISES

• One of the clues that led to the uncovering of the missing day concerned Worf's wrist. After the crew roused from the "worm hole" the first time, several scenes show Worf rubbing his wrist in the background. When he finally goes to see Dr. Crusher, she determines that his wrist was broken and mended during the missing day. Worf goes to Dr. Crusher because his wrist is *hurting*. Compare this with the bone-mending

scene in "Legacy." Dr. Crusher repairs broken ribs for Ishara Yar and then says, "I've fused the bone tissue along both fractures. The muscle around the area will be weak for a day or two, but you shouldn't feel any pain." Afterward, Ishara shows no sign of discomfort for the rest of the show.

• In this episode Picard claims he has never known Data to tell a lie. He must have forgotten about the incidents during "The Schizoid Man" when Dr. Ira Graves took over Data's body.

CONTINUITY AND PRODUCTION PROBLEMS

• The computer that drives the holodeck apparently doesn't know that dead people don't move their eyes. When Picard and Guinan play in the holodeck at the very start of the show, a holodeck character gets machine-gunned down. Picard and Guinan belly-crawl over to him. When Picard turns the man's head to face them, his eyes jerkily follow.

TRIVIA ANSWERS

1. Two o'clock.
2. ADTH, five parts per million.

★ FIRST CONTACT

Star Date: unknown

Prior to the beginning of this episode, Riker beams down to Malcoria III. He visits a group of Federation observers. The Malcorians are on the verge of warp drive capability. According to Federation policy, the time has come for "first contact." Unfortunately, Riker gets caught in a riot and is seriously injured. At the hospital, an examination exposes his physiological differences. Meanwhile, Picard and Troi beam down and present themselves to the chief scientist in charge of the warp drive experiments. They bring her back to the ship. When Picard informs the scientist that Federation observers have inhabited the planet for several years, she warns Picard not to disclose this information. Her people would think the observers were an invasion force.

The chief scientist introduces Picard to the head of state. He also tours the ship. The relationship seems to progress well until a Security report reveals Riker's existence at the hospital. As the chief scientist feared, the head of state and the chief of Security react badly to the news.

Trivia Questions

1. How many hours are in the Malcorian day?

2. Who is the Malcorian with whom Riker is intimate in this episode?

The chief of Security insists on interrogating Riker, even in his weakened condition. During the interrogation, the Security chief places Riker's phaser in Riker's hand and fires it at himself. He hopes to force the head of state to reject the Federation overtures. Meanwhile, the chief scientist convinces the head of state of the physical danger to Riker. The head of state tells Picard where Riker is. Dr. Crusher beams Riker and the Security chief to sick bay and cares for both of them. The head of state asks Picard to leave their planet alone for a few more years while he prepares his people for knowledge of other races.

PLOT OVER-SIGHTS

• The Malcorians are on the verge of warp drive. Early in the episode, the head scientist explains the warp experiment to the head of state. She talks of a spacecraft that will engage the warp drive and go to a neighboring star system. For the Malcorians to understand that the experiment was a success, they have to be able to monitor spacecraft in orbit around Malcoria III. This ability seems consistent with their level of technology. After all, the technologically inferior humans of the twentieth century routinely monitor satellites that orbit Earth. So why can't the Malcorians detect the *massive* Galaxy Class starship *Enterprise*? The *Enterprise* doesn't have a cloaking device. Does it have some sort of radar-evading stealth technology?

• The head of state needs a more observant receptionist. When the chief scientist introduces Picard to the head of state, they walk into his office. Actually, the scene features the calm voice of a receptionist—over an intercom—announcing that the chief scientist has someone for the head of state to meet. The receptionist's voice is amazingly dull considering the striking physical differences between Picard and the Malcorians. Evidently he was doing his nails and didn't bother to look up.

• While the head of state visits the *Enterprise*, Picard offers him a drink and proposes a toast. After the toast, the head of state says of the drink, "We have something very much like this on Malcoria III." Now, what are the chances that this man would use the same designation for his planet that Starfleet does, especially since the episode purports that the Malcorians believe they are the center of the universe? Would a culture that believes itself the center of the universe call its planet by the name of its sun and the planet count to that sun? Can you imagine Earthlings calling their planet "Sun III"?

CHANGED PREMISES

• This episode purports that the Federation waits until the inhabitants achieve warp drive before making contact. This idea makes a lot of sense. It seems absolutely reasonable. Of course, it flies in the face of many other episodes. Take "Justice," for instance. The *Enterprise* needs some rest and relaxation. They storm up to the next convenient planet, beam down, and start hugging the populace.

CONTINUITY AND PRODUCTION PROBLEMS

• The matte painting of a city in "Angel One" serves yet again in this episode. This makes three times: It was the main city on "Angel One"; it was also Starbase 515 in "Samaritan Snare"; and in this episode, "First Contact," the same cityscape serves as a medical facility in the capital city of Malcoria III.

TRIVIA ANSWERS
1. Twenty-nine.
2. Lanel.

GALAXY'S CHILD

Star Date: 44614.6

As the show opens, Picard invites La Forge to welcome Dr. Leah Brahms on board the *Enterprise*. Starfleet has sent her to study La Forge's engine modifications. La Forge became acquainted with Brahms when the computer created a holographic representation of her during "Booby Trap." He knows that he and the real Leah Brahms will be good friends. However, when Brahms beams aboard, the tension begins immediately. A possessive Brahms accuses La Forge of fouling up her engine designs. La Forge tries to smooth things over but isn't successful.

Meanwhile, Data notes an unusual energy reading in a nearby planetary system. The *Enterprise* investigates and finds a previously unknown life form. The life form lives in space, extracting energy directly from the stars. The creature probes the *Enterprise* and then attacks it. Picard orders only a low-intensity phaser burst, but the creature dies moments later. Picard, appalled at what they've done, heads for his ready room. Data begins sensing new energy readings from the creature. The crew determines that a baby exists within the creature. They release the baby by using the phasers as scalpels.

When the *Enterprise* tries to leave, the baby attaches itself to the *Enterprise* and begins drawing energy. Picard allows the baby to suckle while they adopt the same heading as the mother took. In Engineering, La Forge and Brahms work together to produce more energy and stabilize the ship. When the *Enterprise* reaches the baby's home, several of the adult creatures swim out to meet the *Enterprise*. Just in time, La Forge and Brahms develop a method to get the baby to release the *Enterprise*, and the ship flies to safety.

Trivia Questions

1. What phaser setting does Dr. Crusher use for the Cesarean section?

2. What program file contains La Forge's simulation of Brahms?

GREAT LINES

"Was it good for you?"—Brahms to La Forge after she discovers his holodeck re-creation of her, convinced that La Forge has been using her as a holodeck plaything.

PLOT OVERSIGHTS

• Early in the episode, as La Forge tries to score points with Brahms, he suggests they start with the dilithium chamber. She agrees, and La Forge takes the chamber off-line. This occurs at about the same time that Data detects the strange energy reading and the *Enterprise* alters course to intercept. A graphic just prior to these scenes shows the *Enterprise* traveling at warp. Doesn't shutting down the dilithium chamber mean the *Enterprise* loses warp drive capability? Yet La Forge never informs the bridge of his action; he just does it.

CHANGED PREMISES

• Great confusion surrounds this matter/antimatter ratio thing. When Brahms comes on board, she claims the matter/antimatter ratio has been changed. She says that the mixture isn't as rich as Starfleet specs call for. Isn't there only one matter/antimatter ratio? Wesley and Mordock, while taking the Starfleet exam in "Coming of Age," said the ratio is 1 to 1 and that the testing stations confirm this. Yet, in "Where No One Has Gone Before," Picard says Kozinski is coming on board to test "different intermix formulas." And the chief engineer in "Skin of Evil" talks about setting the ratio of matter and antimatter to 25 to 1.

By the way, the authors of the *Star Trek: The Next Generation Technical Manual* once again make a valiant attempt to explain away these discrepancies by saying that the inter-mix ratios change depending on the warp factor. At warp 8 and above, they maintain the ratio is 1 to 1, but it is different at lower speeds. However, that's not what Wesley and Mordock say when they finish the question about matter/antimatter ratios in "Coming of Age." The exact dialogue is:

"Once I realized it was a trick question, there was only one answer," the superintelligent Wesley Crusher comments.

The equally intelligent Mordock retorts, "Yes, there is only one ratio with matter/antimatter ... 1 to 1."

Sounds pretty conclusive, doesn't it? And then there's the method by which the warp drive generates its power in the first place. The energy needed for warp drive comes from the mutual annihilation of matter and antimatter as they mix in the dilithium chamber. When an electron and a positron (an antimatter electron) meet, an explosion occurs, destroying both entities. If two electrons and one positron meet, wouldn't that leave one electron with nothing to do? So if the ratio is anything *but* 1 to 1, what does the extra matter do once the antimatter is used up—hang around, hoping to score with a few stray gamma waves?

TRIVIA ANSWERS
1. Three percent, narrow beam.
2. File 9140.

NIGHT TERRORS

Star Dates: 44831.2-44842.1

The *Enterprise* locates the USS *Brattain*, missing for twenty-nine days. An away team beams over and finds everyone dead except a Betazoid and he is in a catatonic stupor. Troi tries to communicate with him telepathically, but his babbling makes no sense. Dr. Crusher examines the bodies and concludes that no external forces caused the deaths. Apparently the crew went mad and killed themselves. After a few days of investigation, the crew of the *Enterprise* begins to experience a gradual mental deterioration. Dr. Crusher advises Picard to leave the area immediately.

When the *Enterprise* attempts to leave, none of the propulsion systems responds. Data discovers that they are caught in a rift in space. It absorbs the energy they produce and keeps them from moving. Only a massive explosion can free them from the rift. Unfortunately, the *Enterprise* isn't carrying anything that could provide the necessary detonation. As Dr. Crusher performs more brain scans on the crew of the *Brattain*, she discovers that each had a

Trivia Questions

1. How many people died on the *Brattain*?

2. What is the catalog number for hydrogen, and how is it stored?

unique chemical imbalance—an imbalance caused only by a lack of dreaming. When she checks the crew of the *Enterprise*, she finds the same imbalance in everyone except Troi. While Troi can dream, she experiences only a recurring nightmare. When the comatose Betazoid speaks the same words as she hears in her dream, Troi finally understands what's happening to them. An alien ship is also caught in the rift, sending out a telepathic distress call. Unfortunately, their efforts are robbing the crew of the ability to dream.

Data and Troi work together on a plan. From Troi's nightmares, they conclude that the aliens need hydrogen to create an explosion and disrupt the rift. Troi enters a dream state, while Data releases the hydrogen. Seconds later, the hydrogen detonates, and both ships fly to safety.

PLOT OVERSIGHTS

• When the crew looks for a way to create a massive explosion and escape the rift, no one mentions setting the *Brattain* to self-destruct. Wouldn't an uncontrolled overload of a warp drive system cause a pretty good bang?

EQUIPMENT ODDITIES

• Evidently even the door for sick bay is disturbed by the carnage on the *Brattain*. While Picard and Crusher discuss the situation at the beginning of the show, they walk into sick bay. The door behind them closes very gradually, almost like it doesn't want to disturb their conversation.

• When looking for a message to send the aliens, Data scans through the available elements on the *Enterprise*. One shot shows the elements zipping by, from bottom to top. When Troi spots hydrogen, she tells Data to stop and go back. The next shot shows the elements scrolling slower, but they are still scrolling from bottom to top. This is *very bad* user-interface design. It would confuse the daylights out of the crew. True, information on a display screen can be configured to move in the same direction whether the user is going forward or backward through that information. But it would be very unnerving for the user, since the visual movement of the information doesn't correspond to the direction of the scan.

TRIVIA ANSWERS

1. Thirty-four.
2. It is 34-4077; the hydrogen is stored in the form of deuterium.

IDENTITY CRISIS

Star Dates: 44664.5-44668.1

For this episode, Lieutenant Commander Susanna Leitjen joins the *Enterprise*. She and La Forge served together aboard the USS *Victory*. While on the *Victory*, Leitjen and La Forge—along with others, including Hickman and Mendez—investigated the disappearance of a colony on a planet called Tarchannen III. Now, five years later, Hickman and Mendez have disappeared also. A short time later, something begins to happen to Leitjen. During a visit to the surface of Tarchannen III, she becomes violent. Only La Forge's restraint and quick action get her back to the *Enterprise* safely. Leitjen becomes preoccupied with returning to the planet, but La Forge—and Picard's standing order—deter her.

While working with La Forge in Engineering, Leitjen collapses. La Forge finds puffy blue veins on the back of her neck. Additionally, her three middle fingers on each hand weld together. La Forge delivers Leitjen to sick bay and returns to his search for an answer. While using the holodeck to view a recording of the original investigation, La Forge transforms also. Because of the change, he becomes invisible both to human eyes and to the sensors of the *Enterprise*. Soon he manages to get down to the planet. At the same time, Dr. Crusher discovers the parasitic cause of the change in Leitjen. Crusher operates and removes the infestation. Leitjen begins to return to normal and joins an away team that goes to the planet's surface and rescues La Forge.

Trivia Questions

1. What is the registry of the USS *Victory*?

2. What is the name of the shuttle from the USS *Aries*?

PLOT OVERSIGHTS

• When Leitjen begins to change into an alien, only the presence of La Forge saves her. But after she is delivered to sick bay, both Picard and Dr. Crusher allow La Forge to return to work alone—even though they know that the change can strike suddenly. Given the mysterious nature of the malady, wouldn't Picard assign Data to watch over La Forge? Data, on his own, does make a halfhearted attempt at offering his assistance to La Forge. La Forge gives him a feeble excuse. Data accepts this and leaves.

In a similar vein, La Forge convinces Picard and Crusher to let him work alone by suggesting that they program the computer to monitor his movements. Presumably someone does this. However, after La Forge changes into the alien, Dr. Crusher tries to locate him, and the computer says that La Forge is not on the *Enterprise*. (He really is, but the sensors can't find him.) If the computer was programmed to monitor La Forge's movements, wouldn't it sound an alarm as soon as La Forge disappeared? Of course, if Picard had assigned Data to La Forge—or the computer had sounded an alarm when La Forge disappeared—it would have been a short show.

• Evidently, the show was running a little short on time anyway. In one scene, Data takes twenty seconds to do a task that a human could do in about ten. He is converting a flashlight to emit ultraviolet light so they can locate La Forge on the planet's surface. Two things to remember: First, earlier in the show, Data states that he is "strongly motivated" to help La Forge. Second, Data is an android and, in other episodes, has worked so fast that his hands became blurred. If Data is so strongly motivated to help and he can work that fast, why is he moving like his batteries are nearly drained? To his credit, Data does make up for it later. He tells Riker that a task will take approximately two minutes, and finishes it in only fifty seconds! This is the same guy who can instantaneously calculate to the second how long it will take to arrive at a distant destination.

• At the end of the show, an away team beams down to rescue La Forge. Leitjen tells them to turn off their flashlights because the light will scare the newly formed aliens. Riker asks about Data's ultraviolet flashlight, but Leitjen assures him that the ultraviolet light is "beyond [the aliens'] visual spectrum." That's a fancy way of saying that they can't see it. Yet when Data illuminates them with his flashlight, La Forge and the other two aliens immediately turn and run away!

EQUIPMENT ODDITIES

• At one point during his investigation, La Forge examines a visual log from the original team that visited the planet five years earlier. He spots an odd shadow on the wall of a building and asks the computer to re-create the scene on the holodeck. At this point a small digression is needed.

In a few moments, the computer tells La Forge, "There is no object in the program that could generate the shadow." This is important. From the computer's viewpoint: There is a light source, there is a shadow on the wall of a building, and *there is nothing between*. To the computer, the odd shadow is merely a dark spot on the wall. We now join our regularly scheduled broadcast.

Soon after entering the holodeck, La Forge asks the computer to remove all the human characters from the scene. They and their shadows disappear. The fully outlined odd shadow remains. This is an amazing feat for the computer, since a human shadow overlapped most of the odd shadow. It is almost impossible to separate shadows from each other unless you know the shapes that caused the shadows in the first place. And, as just stated, the computer doesn't know what caused the odd shadow. (Maybe—and it is a *big* maybe—the computer could sense a slight density difference among the shadows from light bouncing off the back wall.)

La Forge then walks over to the shadow and leans in front of it. True to form, the shadow appears on La Forge's face! Remember that La Forge is on the holodeck. Everything he experiences is simulated by the computer. Why would the computer create a shadow on La Forge's face if it didn't believe anything existed between the light source and the wall?

• After discovering the cause of the change in Leitjen, Crusher immediately takes her into surgery. In preparation, a medical ensign rolls in a machine that was used in an earlier episode, "Shades of Gray." The machine looks like an arch on wheels. It has long metal rods that penetrate the arch and converge inside it. In "Shades of Gray," it directly stimulated Riker's brain. Once his head was slipped inside the arch, the rods penetrated his skull and the machine became operational. However, in "Shades of Gray," Riker's bed had a formed headrest. The top of the bed was shaped to conform to the head and shoulders of the patient. This allows the machine to fit snugly to either side of Riker's head. In "Identity Crisis," on the other hand, the bed Leitjen is on is shaped like a regular square bed. In other words, it is impossible for the machine to get close enough to Leitjen's head for it to stick the rods in her brain!

• One final equipment oddity. This is really grungy nitpicking. When the team goes to rescue La Forge, Data takes an ultraviolet flashlight. The flashlight allows the team to see the alien forms of La Forge, Hickman, and Mendez. Without the flashlight, the aliens are invisible. After the team finds La Forge, Leitjen hugs him. Data and his flashlight are behind Leitjen. A camera angle shows Leitjen's back and La Forge's illuminated face—because Data is behind Leitjen, and the ultraviolet light coming from Data's flashlight is shining on La Forge's face. Then the shot changes and shows La Forge's back and Leitjen's face. They also seem to be illuminated by Data's flashlight. Seconds later, the scene returns to the original shot. If the light from Data's flashlight is the only reason La Forge is visible, the ultraviolet light must be traveling around corners to shine on La Forge's face and back at the same time. (I suppose Data could be standing off to the side, but then only half of La Forge's face would be illuminated.)

CONTINUITY AND PRODUCTION PROBLEMS

• Just before beginning to change, La Forge works on the holodeck. During this scene, one camera angle shows a medium close-up of his face. Since the light strikes his visor at an angle, it also shows La Forge's eyes, including his black pupils. But in the series, La Forge is blind. Every time he takes his visor off, his eyes are totally covered with a white film. Of course, LeVar Burton—the actor who plays Geordi La Forge—needed to see when they shot the scene. So the makeup people didn't cover his eyes with the eyeball covers he wears when the script calls for him to remove his visor. The visor is usually enough to keep the viewer from seeing Burton's noncovered eyes. This time it wasn't.

TRIVIA ANSWERS

1. NCC 9754.
2. *Cousteau.*

THE NTH DEGREE

Star Dates: 44704.2-44705.3

The *Enterprise* arrives at the Argus Array, a deep-space telescope that has ceased functioning. Data detects an alien probe nearby, and Picard tells La Forge to take a closer look. After picking Lieutenant Reginald Barclay (see "Hollow Pursuits") to accompany him, La Forge flies a shuttle out to examine it at short range. Suddenly the probe emits a burst of energy, overloading the shuttle computer and knocking Barclay unconscious. The *Enterprise* beams La Forge and Barclay to sick bay, but Crusher finds nothing wrong with them and they return to Engineering. At the same time, the probe begins moving toward the *Enterprise*. All attempts to outrun it or destroy it with phasers fail, and the *Enterprise* is too close to the probe to use photon torpedoes.

Suddenly the *Enterprise* falls out of warp. Barclay reroutes warp power to the shields and tells Picard to fire photon torpedoes. Picard orders Worf to fire and destroy the probe. This and other incidents demonstrate a fundamental change in Barclay. When Dr. Crusher examines him lat-

er, she finds an extraordinary increase in his mental capabilities.

A few days later—as the fusion reactors of the array become unstable—Barclay grows impatient with the interface to the control computer. He goes to the holodeck and "hot-wires" himself into the computer, thereby fixing the array. Barclay then creates a new type of space travel and plunges the *Enterprise* into the center of the galaxy, thirty thousand light years away. An image appears and looks the crew over. The beings who made the probe are explorers of a different type. Instead of traveling out to other realms, these beings send out probes that give instructions on how to come to them. The beings return Barclay to normal, and the *Enterprise* spends a few days in an exchange of knowledge with the beings before returning to Federation space.

Trivia Questions

1. What is Barclay's IQ?

2. Which computer core does Barclay initially connect to?

GREAT LINES

"This isn't fantasy, it's theater."—Troi to Barclay, encouraging him when he wonders if trading his holodeck fantasies for acting has really improved his situation. (This is a very

interesting line, considering that it is spoken by an actress—performing in a television series about the twenty-fourth century—to an actor just after he performed a scene from a play written in the nineteenth century.)

PLOT OVERSIGHTS

• This is the first and last time a shuttle is used to gather information in the series. In all other cases, the *very* large and *very* sophisticated sensor arrays on the *Enterprise* have *always* proved sufficient. Of course, if La Forge and Barclay don't get in a shuttle and fly out to the probe, Barclay can't get flashed.

EQUIPMENT ODDITIES

• Normally—when La Forge transfers engineering control to the bridge—he walks off the turbolift, presses a button on the Engineering station, and the station lights up. At the beginning of this episode, La Forge walks on and the station lights up *before* he reaches it or says anything.

• Shuttle Craft 5 has changed again. In the episode "Times Squared," Shuttle Craft "05" was named *El-Baz*.

In the episode "The Ensigns of Command," it became the *Onizuka*. In "Transfigurations" Shuttle Craft 5 returned to the name *El-Baz*. Now, in "The Nth Degree," the shuttle craft gets a complete make-over. In all previous episodes, it was a two-passenger, angular-looking, subcompact craft. In "The Nth Degree" it becomes a sleek, rounded-edged, multiple-passenger unit.

CONTINUITY AND PRODUCTION PROBLEMS

• This is a very minor thing. Just before Troi visits Barclay in Ten-Forward, he takes a drink from his glass. The level of liquid is clearly at the black band near the top of the glass. Troi and Barclay discuss his newly found confidence, and Troi leaves. The next shot shows the level of liquid in Barclay's glass well below the black band, but Barclay never took any additional sips from the glass during their conversation.

TRIVIA ANSWERS
1. Between 1,200 and 1,450.
2. The starboard computer core.

QPID

Star Date: 44741.9

The *Enterprise* hosts an archaeological conference at which Picard will give the keynote address. When he returns to his quarters for the night, he finds Vash (see "Captain's Holiday") already there. In the morning, Dr. Crusher takes Vash on a tour of the ship. Vash becomes increasingly irritated to learn that Picard has never mentioned her to any of the crew. Meanwhile, Q appears in Picard's ready room. Q wants to repay Picard for his kindness during their last encounter (see "Déjà Q"). Picard refuses any gift and asks Q to leave the ship. The tension continues to build between Picard and Vash. She feels that he is embarrassed by her presence. At the same time, Picard discovers that Vash really came to dig in the off-limits ruins of the planet below.

Q seizes on the spat and taunts Picard over his love for Vash. Q then leaves, intent on proving that Picard's emotion for this woman will destroy him. As Picard begins his keynote address, Q suddenly transports the senior officers of the *Enterprise* to a re-created Sherwood Forest—with Picard as Robin Hood. Q explains that Maid Marion (Vash) lies captive in Nottingham Castle. She will be killed tomorrow. Picard views this conflict as personal, orders his staff to stay put, and heads for the castle alone. After a thwarted escape attempt, Picard and Vash face the executioner. The rest of the senior staff intervene just in time, and Q transports them back to the ship. Only Vash remains missing. Moments later, Vash appears. She has joined forces with Q. Intrigued by Vash, Q has promised to take her anywhere in the universe. After Picard secures Q's promise for her safety, Vash and Q disappear.

Trivia Questions

1. How long ago were the ruins on Tagus III sealed from outsiders?

2. How many archaeological digs on Tagus III produced findings of major importance?

GREAT LINES

"Sir, I protest. I am not a merry man."—Worf to Picard, angry over Q's selection of a fantasy and Q dressing him in a bright red outfit.

RUMINATIONS

Someone had the movie The Princess Bride *in mind when he or she wrote this episode. In the swordplay scene at the end of "Qpid," the head bad guy says he is the best swordsman in all Nottingham. After* fighting with Picard for a while, Picard replies, "There's something you should know. I am not from Nottingham." This sounds remarkably similar to the first sword fight in The Princess Bride, when the Spaniard says, "I am not left-handed."

PLOT OVERSIGHTS

• At one point Worf charges forward and attacks a man on horseback. I have never understood why people don't just stab the horse. I guess it's the same reason cowboys don't shoot the Indians' horses.

• When Q barges into Vash's room and discovers a rescue note to Riker, Q calls for the guards. Dutifully, the guards rush in, grab Vash, and march her out of the room. Just where are they taking her? They are already in Vash's cell. Have they decided to transfer her to another prison cell just for dramatic effect?

EQUIPMENT ODDITIES

• When Q returns the crew to the Enterprise, they immediately notice that Vash is missing. Picard taps his communicator and asks the computer to locate Vash. The computer replies that Vash is not on board the Enterprise, which brings up this question: How does the computer locate people?

In "The Naked Now," La Forge removes his communicator and wanders around the ship. Security finally locates him by physically searching the ship. In "Remember Me," Worf asks the computer to locate Dr. Crusher's friend. When the computer cannot find the man, Crusher tells Worf, "Lieutenant, Dr. Quaice is very old and rather frail. If he fell somewhere ... if his communicator were damaged ..." Worf nods understandingly and orders a physical deck-by-deck search. These two episodes seem to purport that the computer uses communicators to locate people. But Vash doesn't have a communicator. So how does the computer know Vash isn't on board?

CONTINUITY AND PRODUCTION PROBLEMS

• Picard's Robin Hood hat seems to slide around on his head. In the process of ordering Riker to stay put, Picard's hat goes from resting close to his eyebrows to pushed back on his forehead to back to his eyebrows.

TRIVIA ANSWERS
1. A century ago.
2. Seventy-four.

THE DRUMHEAD

Star Date: 44769.2

Admiral Norah Satie joins the *Enterprise* to investigate possible sabotage. A few days earlier, an explosion ripped the face off the dilithium chamber. Just prior to that event, a Starfleet report stated that the Romulans had received detailed schematics of the *Enterprise*'s dilithium chamber. Starfleet suspects that the same person who stole the plans blew up the chamber. Worf uncovers the guilt of a visiting Klingon exobiologist. Although the man confesses to stealing the plans, he denies any involvement in the explosion. Satie expands the investigation to those who associated with the Klingon.

She finds a young man named Simon Tarses. He claims his paternal grandfather was Vulcan, but in fact the grandfather was Romulan. On the basis of this one lie, Satie begins a deep, probing inquiry into Tarses' past. Picard expresses his concern over this course of action. By this time, the levels of radiation in the dilithium chamber have subsided. After six hours of study, Data and La Forge determine that the explosion was an accident. However, Satie continues the probing. When Picard attempts to block her efforts, Satie calls Picard to testify. Using half-truths and innuendos, she paints Picard as a Romulan collaborator. Starfleet finally recognizes what she is doing and stops the hearings.

Trivia Questions

1. State the time, to the millisecond, when the face plate on the dilithium chamber exploded.

2. Satie accuses Picard of violating the Prime Directive nine times. Name three episodes that contain a Prime Directive violation.

GREAT LINES

"Just because there was no sabotage doesn't mean there isn't a conspiracy"—Satie, on hearing that the dilithium chamber explosion was an accident.

PLOT OVERSIGHTS

• Does exobiology sound like a believable occupation for a Klingon? (It certainly seems like a "warrior line of work" to me! I bet it offers *a lot* of chances for glory.)

TRIVIA ANSWERS

1. It was 03:00:59.959.
2. "Justice," "Pen Pals," and "Who Watches the Watchers."

HALF A LIFE

Star Date: 44805.3-44812.6

For this episode, Lwaxana Troi, Deanna Troi's mother, visits the *Enterprise*. A scientist named Timicin also comes aboard. He soon falls for Lwaxana's charms. Over the past forty years, Timicin has worked to find a way to revive his planet's dying sun. To this end, he has written a control program for photon torpedoes. Hopefully these torpedoes, when fired into a dying sun, can reinvigorate it. The Federation agreed to assist with a test. After a three-year search, they located a star with the same characteristics as Timicin's dying sun. The *Enterprise* will ferry Timicin to the star, conduct the test, and bring him home.

At first the test seems to go well, but then the star destabilizes and explodes. When Lwaxana tries to encourage Timicin that he will eventually succeed, Timicin reveals that he must return home and die. On Timicin's planet, when a person reaches sixty, they celebrate a ceremony called "The Resolution." At this ceremony, the sixty-year-old commits suicide in the presence of friends and family. The custom shocks Lwaxana. She argues with Timicin over the value of it, trying to convince him that his planet needs his work. When Timicin begins to understand what went wrong with the experiment, he agrees with Lwaxana. Timicin asks for asylum on the *Enterprise*. He wants to finish his work but is unprepared for an outpouring of criticism and rejection from his planet. He finally recants and tells Lwaxana good-bye. Just before he leaves, however, Lwaxana asks to be present at the ceremony, and they beam down together.

Trivia Questions

1. What button does Lwaxana ask about on Worf's tactical station?

2. At what temperature should the test star stabilize?

GREAT LINES

"And it is Worf, madam, not woof."— Worf to Lwaxana, correcting her pronunciation of his name.

PLOT OVERSIGHTS

• When Timicin first beams aboard, Picard immediately sticks out his hand to greet him. This action confuses Timicin, and then he comments that he has heard humans shake hands to greet each other. Picard's action is troublesome. For a man as well versed in diplomacy as Picard, it seems unsophisticated. Timicin comes from an isolationist planet.

Why make him feel immediately uncomfortable by forcing him to participate in a human ritual? Prior to this episode, Picard initiates a handshake only one other time. In "Final Mission," when Picard meets the captain of the mining shuttle, the shuttle captain grasps Picard's shoulder. Picard correctly interprets this as a greeting and mimics the behavior. Picard then holds up his hand for the shuttle captain to shake. This exchange makes sense. The other party has initiated a physical greeting; Picard responds in the same way and only then initiates his own physical greeting. For Picard immediately to jam his hand toward Timicin makes Picard seem less refined.

• After Lwaxana finds out that Timicin will soon kill himself, she tries to beam down to the planet. Troi comes to the transporter and has a heart-to-heart talk with her mom. During this talk, Lwaxana communicates telepathically with Troi while physically weeping. Interestingly, Lwaxana's telepathic voice speaks with the same sobbing and gasping for air as her physical voice. The sound of her inhaling comes through clearly in her telepathic voice. Does this make sense?

CHANGED PREMISES

• At one point during "Ménage à Troi," Riker and Troi look for a quiet, romantic spot to relax on Betazed. Of course, Lwaxana comes bustling up, interrupting them. She spreads out a picnic, and Riker and Troi sit down. Lwaxana then offers Riker an Oskoid leaf. He acts like he's never had one before. Riker offers it to Troi, as if she'd never had one before. Yet in "Half a Life," Lwaxana orders Oskoid from the food replicator. When Timicin asks what it is, Lwaxana says it is a Betazed delicacy. If Oskoid leaves are a Betazed delicacy, why do Riker and Troi act like they'd never eaten them before, in "Ménage à Troi"? Troi grew up on Betazed, and Riker was stationed there for several years.

EQUIPMENT ODDITIES

• When Lwaxana and Troi have their heart-to-heart talk in the transporter room, O'Brien steps out to give them some privacy. Before he leaves, however, he presses a few buttons and locks the transporter. A closeup confirms this as a red rectangle flashes with the word "LOCKED" inside. At the end of the Trois' conversation, a long shot shows them embracing. The long shot also clearly shows the controls on the transporter station. The "LOCKED" rectangle is no longer flashing. Evidently the bulb burned out?

• When Timicin and Lwaxana transport to the planet we have—once again—the "joined hands that are outside the confinement beam but somehow still manage to transport OK" error mentioned in the Equipment Oddities section of "Sarek."

CONTINUITY AND PRODUCTION PROBLEMS

• Just before Timicin asks for asylum, he rechecks the sensor logs from the test with Data and La Forge. Seated at a workstation, Timicin us es his right hand to enter instructions. As each shot changes, so does the positioning of his hand—sometimes he uses his thumb to press the buttons, sometimes his fingers, and at other times his hand simply rests on the side of the screen.

• After Timicin asks for asylum and begins experiencing rejection from his planet, Lwaxana and Troi have a talk. The scene opens with a shot of Lwaxana reclined against a mirror. The mirror's reflection shows Troi seated in a chair. Lwaxana then stands up straight and walks toward Troi. A metal pole appears in the mirror and follows Lwaxana until the mirror disappears from view. A few moments later, both the camera and Lwaxana reverse the movement, retracing their steps. This time the pole doesn't appear. The pole doesn't appear because there are no metal poles in Lwaxana's quarters. The person holding the boom mike for the scene let it droop a little too low, and the camera caught its reflection in the mirror!

TRIVIA ANSWERS
1. The torpedo launch initiator.
2. The temperature of 220 million degrees Kelvin.

THE HOST

Star Dates: 44821.3-44829.4

The *Enterprise* ferries Ambassador Odan to negotiate a peace between two moon colonies. On the way, a romance sparks between Odan and Dr. Crusher. When the *Enterprise* arrives at the planetary system, Odan requests that a shuttle take him to the planet's surface. He claims to have an aversion to transporters. On the way down, a ship attacks the shuttle and damages it. Riker manages to pilot it back to the *Enterprise*, but Odan is seriously injured. Dr. Crusher becomes puzzled by Odan's medical readouts. She tells Odan that a parasite inhabits his body. Odan shocks her by admitting that the parasite is really himself. His race, the Trill, have existed as humanoid host and parasite for millennia.

Dr. Crusher removes the parasite and puts it in stasis. The host body dies. The *Enterprise* immediately contacts the Trill to send another host, but it will take forty hours to reach the *Enterprise*. Odan will die in two. Riker volunteers to host Odan for the negotiations. When Dr. Crusher implants Odan in Riker, Riker becomes

Trivia Questions

1. What is Picard studying on his display screen just before the original Odan meets with him in his ready room?

2. What does Crusher order from the food dispenser in her quarters?

Odan. Dr. Crusher must deal with loving Odan in Riker's body. Eventually she accepts the combination. Odan completes the negotiations, but Riker's body rejects the parasite. Crusher must remove Odan from Riker for Riker to survive. Just in time, the new Trill host arrives. Unfortunately, the host is a female. After Crusher implants Odan, Odan maintains his/her/its love for Crusher. Crusher assures Odan that she loves him/her/it but can't keep up with the changes.

PLOT OVERSIGHTS

• Before Dr. Crusher discovers Odan's true form, she visits the ship's beauty parlor. Troi strolls in and takes the seat beside her. Troi then looks over. A surprised expression comes over Troi's face, and she greets Crusher. Should Troi be surprised to see Crusher? When Troi walks into the room Crusher is slouched down in a chair, with her back to Troi. However, shouldn't Troi's empathic sense tell her that Crusher is in the chair? Wouldn't there be something like an emotional fingerprint?

• After Crusher implants Odan in

Riker, she asks why he didn't tell her. Odan replies that it never occurred to him to mention it. Yet, when Odan needs to give a reason for not using the transporter, he doesn't admit it would kill him. Instead, he comments that he feels uncomfortable using the transporter, just as others probably do. He also says that he would rather keep his atoms intact. In other words, Odan covers for that fact that he is a parasite in a humanoid host. The transporter won't kill the host. It is only dangerous to Odan, and Odan responds to that threat by selecting an avenue that will conceal his true nature. If Odan made an active decision to disguise his true nature with regard to the transporter, he probably made an active decision to disguise his true nature with regard to Crusher. He was lying when he said that it didn't occur to him to tell Crusher about his true form.

• Actually, it's amazing that Crusher deals with Odan's "parasiteness" so well. In "Symbiosis," when one group of humanoids suppresses another through drug addiction, Dr. Crusher vehemently argues for Picard to take action. In "Conspiracy," when crayfishlike aliens almost seize control of Starfleet by taking over human bodies, she fights fiercely to defeat them. In "The Best of Both Worlds," Part 2, when the Borg take over Picard, she uses microsurgery to remove all the implants. In "Identity Crisis" she finds and defeats a parasite that threatens to destroy La Forge's consciousness. Yet, when Odan finally discloses the true nature of his existence, Dr. Crusher takes it all in stride.

In essence, Odan exists by stealing a body from a humanoid host. When Odan takes over Riker, it appears that the consciousness of Riker gets put on hold. Only what Odan desires becomes important. From all indications, the humanoid host's consciousness ceases to function after implantation. So here are the Trill, composed of two races—one humanoid and the other lobsteroid. For thousands for years, the lobsteroids have exploited the humanoids, breeding the humanoids so that the lobsteroids could enjoy the benefits of things such as opposable thumbs. Obviously the lobsteroids don't have the gumption to get off their backsides and evolve into a higher form. Instead, they steal the benefits from someone else. (I would think that this arrangement would incense Crusher in the same way as the arrangement in "Symbiosis." Evidently not.)

• There is a minor tension point in the plot near the end, when Dr. Crusher removes Odan from Riker. Odan can survive in stasis for only a few hours, and the host is still nine hours away. To avert Odan's demise, the *Enterprise* rushes to meet the Trill ship at warp 9. What's the rush? Why not just implant Odan into another person on the *Enterprise*? Crusher could look around the ship, find a good-looking, well-muscled young man, and plant Odan in him. Or, better yet, maybe she could put Odan in Picard. At one point in "The Naked Now," Crusher was very interested in an interlude with him. Better yet, why not just implant Odan in herself? Then everyone would be happy.

CHANGED PREMISES

• Near the beginning of the episode, Picard pages Odan. When the page finds Odan, he and Crusher are embracing in his quarters. As soon as Crusher hears the page, she immediately covers her mouth, as if Picard can hear her if she speaks. Compare this to Picard's page of Troi at the beginning of "The Price." After Picard pages, Troi makes an offhand comment, sighs, taps her communicator, and finally responds as if Picard *can't* hear her *until* she taps her badge.

TRIVIA ANSWERS

1. Tyken's Rift. (The graphic on his screen is the same one Data used to illustrate a Tyken's Rift in "Night Terrors.")
2. Lemon tea.

THE MIND'S EYE

Star Dates: 44885.5-44896.9

As La Forge flies a shuttle to a conference, the *Enterprise* takes a Klingon ambassador to investigate charges that the Federation is aiding a rebellion on a Klingon colony. Suddenly a Romulan ship uncloaks in front of La Forge's shuttle. The Romulans overcome the shuttle's shields and beam La Forge aboard. After sending a replacement to the conference, they brainwash La Forge, using his direct neural interface. The interface was necessary to implement La Forge's visor, but it allows the Romulans to force La Forge to view whatever they wish.

Shortly after the *Enterprise* arrives at the Klingon colony, La Forge rejoins the ship. The Klingon commander of the colony insists that the Federation is supplying weapons to the rebels. He produces a Federation phaser rifle to prove his point. Data and La Forge analyze the weapon and discover that the Romulans manufactured it. Just as tensions begin to ease, La Forge transports a shipment of weapons to the planet's surface and then removes all record of the transfer. As Picard initiates an investiga-

tion, Klingon warships begin uncloaking around the *Enterprise*. The Klingon ambassador suggests that the Klingon commander board the *Enterprise* to view the ongoing search for the person who transported the weapons. The Klingon ambassador, a Romulan sympathizer, then orders La Forge to kill the commander. Meanwhile, Data traces down a pattern of strange energy blips. The Klingon ambassador is using these energy blips to control La Forge. Data deduces that La Forge transported the weapons and alerts the crew in time to stop La Forge from killing the commander. Data also exposes the Klingon ambassador.

Trivia Questions

1. How long has O'Brien served with La Forge on the *Enterprise*?

2. When did La Forge transport the weapons to the planet's surface?

GREAT LINES

"Motives, who cares for motives?"— The Klingon ambassador to Worf, after congratulating him for killing Duras (see "Reunion").

PLOT OVERSIGHTS

• When the show opens, La Forge flies through space in a shuttle. The stars move slowly, so he must be traveling at subwarp speeds. La

Forge asks the computer how long until he reaches his destination. The computer replies three hours. (I know I have beaten this dead horse, but this is another great example.) For the sake of argument, let's say that La Forge is halfway to the planet when he asks his question. Let's say that it takes six hours to get to the planet from where he started. How long would it take for the *Enterprise* to fly over at warp 7 and drop him off? Thirty-three seconds. (If you don't believe me, see the calculations in "Samaritan Snare.")

• The computer cheats. When La Forge plays a game with the computer, it tells him he will have twenty seconds to answer each question. When the computer asks the first question and La Forge replies that it is easy, the computer gives him an additional requirement. However, the computer begins the time he has to answer from the end of the question, not the end of the additional requirement.

CONTINUITY AND PRODUCTION PROBLEMS

• La Forge's shuttle is named *Onizuka*. Avid fans of this *Nitpicker's Guide* will recall that that is one of the names used for the ever-changing Shuttle Craft 5. (For more information, see Equipment Oddities in "Times Squared," "The Ensigns of Command," "Transfigurations," and "The Nth Degree.")

• The "Angel One" matte painting is back *again*! At least this time, the creators used the night version and disguised it a little. They changed the tops of some of the buildings and modified the building in the foreground, to the left. Aside from these minor changes, it is the matte painting used to show a night cityscape for "Angel One." This makes four episodes for this series of matte paintings: "Angel One," "Samaritan Snare," "First Contact," and "The Mind's Eye."

TRIVIA ANSWERS
1. Almost four years.
2. At 11:23 hours.

IN THEORY

As the show begins, Lieutenant Jenna D'Sora assists Data with reprogramming a photon torpedo. The torpedo will illuminate a "dark matter" nebula so the *Enterprise* can scan it more thoroughly. When the torpedo detonates, the scans show an M Class planet in the nebula. Picard sets course to investigate. As Jenna and Data continue to work together, Jenna finds herself attracted to Data. After she initiates a kiss, Data asks for advice from several of his friends. He considers their comments, researches romantic love, and decides to pursue the relationship.

Meanwhile, the *Enterprise* begins experiencing troubling oddities. Picard finds the items normally on his desk, on the floor beneath the desk. Yet Worf cannot detect an intruder. The computer registers explosive decompression in the observation lounge. When the crew regains access, all the furniture is shoved to one side. While searching for reported damage to deck 37, an ensign dies—her body half swallowed by the flooring. Data reprograms the

Trivia Questions

1. How high did the pile of O'Brien's socks get before Keiko picked them up?

2. What was Data thinking about when he kissed Jenna?

sensors and locates the problem. The unusually high density of dark matter in the nebula is causing pockets of subspace distortions. When one of these impacts the *Enterprise*, a piece of the ship momentarily disappears as it phases into subspace. Since the sensors can detect the distortions at close range only, Picard pilots a shuttle through the nebula, relaying course changes back to the *Enterprise*. This allows the *Enterprise* enough time to avoid the distortions. The plan works fine until a distortion disables the shuttle. After Picard beams back, Riker makes a "run for it," and the *Enterprise* breaks free. Later that evening, Jenna calls off the relationship with Data because he has no feelings for her.

GREAT LINES

"Then I will delete the appropriate program."—Data to Jenna when she informs Data they are no longer a couple.

PLOT OVERSIGHTS

• Whenever this episode shows a graphic of the distortions, it depicts them as static chunks moving through space. Yet, on the *Enterprise*, the distortions seem to appear and disappear randomly. If the chunks move through space retaining the same shape, their paths through the *Enterprise* should define a line. When a distortion hits the hull, there should be a decompression of the closest room. As distortion continues through the ship, the internal sensors should be able to track it until it exits. This isn't what happens on the *Enterprise*. The distortions phase in and out. Therefore the chunks must phase in and out. But if the chunks phase in and out, this would completely nullify the value of putting a shuttle craft out in front of the *Enterprise*. A distortion could disappear as the shuttle passed through it and then reappear before the *Enterprise* arrived at that spot.

• To escape the nebula, the *Enterprise* must make course changes to avoid the subspace distortions. Since the sensors can detect the distortions at close range only, Picard boards a shuttle and flies out ahead of the *Enterprise*. Hopefully he can detect the distortions and relay the course corrections to the *Enterprise* in time. To further this end, crew members directly link the navigational controls of the ship to the shuttle. If they can directly link the navigational controls, can't they link the sensors also? Why not put an unmanned shuttle out in front? The *Enterprise* could display the shuttle's sensors on the main viewscreen and make course corrections for itself and the shuttle at the same time. In that way,

if something happened to the shuttle, no lives would be lost. Instead, Picard places his life at risk. He doesn't usually display this much bravado.

CHANGED PREMISES

• When Data looks for advice on pursuing a relationship with Jenna, he consults Guinan. She tells him that she never advises people on their first love. Yet in "The Dauphin," Guinan not only helped Wesley with an introduction to the girl/beast/pillar of light, she was also actively involved when the relationship was in progress.

• As Data tries to please Jenna, he offers to organize her closets for her. He comments, "I have found that by grouping apparel, first by function, then by color—from light to dark—one can more easily find the desired choice." Considering that Data, of his own choice, has never worn anything but a uniform on this series, this is a very funny statement. (Data did wear something besides a uniform in "The Most Toys" and "Brothers," but in both cases the clothing was forced on him.) Even for his last romantic dinner with Jenna he wears his uniform. Since Data has only one type and color of clothing in his closet, what did he mean when he claimed that he had discovered the best way to group apparel? Has Data started his own business, "Closets by Data"? Or does he just volunteer his services to the crew? (I suppose, since the guy doesn't sleep, he has to occupy his time somehow.)

EQUIPMENT ODDITIES

• When the computer reports atmospheric decompression in the observation lounge, Worf claims that the sensors do not register a hull breach. Yet after life support is restored and the bridge crew enters the lounge, all the furniture is pushed against a window. Also, later in the show, Data states that the distortions are causing the problems on the ship. Evidently a distortion passed through the observation lounge window, venting the atmosphere into space and causing the furniture to pile up. Sure sounds like a hull breach, doesn't it?

CONTINUITY AND PRODUCTION PROBLEMS

• After Jenna brings Data a gift, she guides him in the appropriate response to her gift. Data puts the gift in an alcove. When Jenna grimaces, Data decides to choose a "more central location." As he picks up the gift, the shot shows the back of Jenna. She lowers her hands. In the next shot, Jenna's arms are immediately crossed as Data carries the gift to a table.

TRIVIA ANSWERS

1. Half a meter.
2. Reconfiguring the warp field parameters, analyzing the works of Charles Dickens, calculating the maximum pressure he should apply to her lips, considering a new food supplement for his cat, and more.

REDEMPTION

Star Dates: 44995.3–44998.3

The *Enterprise* travels to the Klingon home world so Picard can complete his responsibilities as arbiter of succession for leadership of the Klingon Empire (see "Reunion"). On the way to the Klingon home world, Picard urges Worf to challenge his discommendation and restore his family name (see "Sins of the Father"). Suddenly Gowron's ship greets them. Gowron beams aboard and tells Picard that the sisters of Duras—the other challenger for the leadership position, killed by Worf in "Reunion"—are readying a challenge to Gowron's leadership. Gowron wants Picard's pledge of support. Picard replies that he will deal with any challenge according to Klingon law. As Gowron leaves, Worf escorts him to the transporter. Worf discloses the truth about his discommendation. The dishonor of the High Council shocks Gowron, but Duras's family is still too powerful to expose the lie.

Just before Picard installs Gowron as leader, Duras's sisters present Duras's illegitimate son to challenge Gowron. When Picard refuses the boy's challenge, civil war brews. Worf offers Gowron the support of his brother Kurn and three other squadron commanders in exchange for Gowron returning Worf's family honor. At first Gowron refuses, but after Worf and Kurn repel an attack from forces loyal to Duras, he agrees.

After his installation as leader by Picard, Gowron asks for Federation assistance in smashing the rebellion. Picard refuses. Worf, torn between his duty to Starfleet and assisting Gowron, resigns from Starfleet. In the final moments of the show, Duras's sisters receive word that the *Enterprise* has left. They and their Romulan co-conspirators revel in the news, including a Romulan who looks surprisingly like Tasha Yar. (See "Skin of Evil" and "Yesterday's *Enterprise*.")

Trivia Questions

1. At what level does Worf practice on the phaser range?

2. What starbase has the records on the Khitomer Massacre?

GREAT LINES

"Do you hear the cry of the warrior calling you to battle, calling you to glory?"—Gowron, trying to convince Worf to help him.

PLOT OVERSIGHTS

• As Worf prepares to leave the *Enterprise*, he packs his belongings in a large chest. Picard comes to his quarters for a chat. During the conversation, Picard says he will make sure Worf's belongings get transferred to the Klingon ship. Just before Picard escorts Worf to the transporter, Worf closes the lid on the chest and they walk out. However, while they were talking, a pan of the room showed Worf's curved fighting weapon still hanging on the wall. In "Reunion," Worf explained to his son that the weapon had been in his family for ten generations. There is no way Worf would leave that behind. Was he hoping that Picard would remember to pack it also?

CHANGED PREMISES

• Near the beginning of the show, Worf and Guinan practice together on the phaser range. Guinan tells Worf she had a bet with Picard that she could make Worf laugh before he made the rank of lieutenant commander. (Data and La Forge are lieutenant commanders. They have two solid dots and one with a black center.) "Not a good bet today," he replies. The conversation seems to proceed as if Guinan has never made Worf laugh. In the opening scene of "Yesterday's *Enterprise*," however, Guinan did make Worf laugh. Was there an alternate reality that was caused in that episode by the older *Enterprise* coming through the time fissure and then returning so that Worf never laughed in Ten-Forward?

• When Gowron first tells Picard of the Duras sisters' challenge, Picard asks for details. Gowron has none, stating that women cannot serve on the High Council. That must be a new rule, because Gowron offered K'Ehleyr a seat on the High Council in "Reunion" and she was *definitely* a woman.

• The Great Hall of the Klingon home world has grown considerably between this episode and "Sins of the Father."

EQUIPMENT ODDITIES

• When the family of Duras attacks Gowron, Gowron is aboard his ship, conferring with Worf. Two Klingon warships attack, pummeling Gowron's ship. Picard observes the battle from the *Enterprise* as Data narrates. At one point, Data says "[Gowron's ship] has lost her port shield. It is unlikely that they will withstand another hit in that quarter." The shot changes to the main viewer of the *Enterprise*. As Data continues narrating, the graphics show Gowron's ship taking not one, not two, not three, but *four* more phaser hits on the port side, and in each of those hits the blast disperses as if the port shield still functions!

TRIVIA ANSWERS

1. Fourteen.
2. Starbase 24.

CONUNDRUM TOTE BOARD

1. Given Riker's insistence in "Encounter at Farpoint" that Picard remain on the ship for his own safety, the number of dangerous planets visited by the captain: twenty-two

2. Given Crusher's assertion in "The Battle" that humanity no longer suffers from the common cold (and presumably other viral-type illnesses), the number of respiratory viruses that show up in the series: two

3. Given Data's inability to use contractions, the number of times he does: several

4. Given Troi's ability to sense the emotional states of others, the number of times she can't sense deception in humans: two

5. Given Picard's statements in "Elementary, My Dear Data" that holodeck matter cannot leave the holodeck, the number of times it does: four

6. Given the fact that the *Enterprise* can fly at warp and most shuttles fly at impulse, the number of times crew members take multiple-hour trips when the *Enterprise* could take them to their destination in seconds: five

7. Given Gene Roddenberry's assertion that zippers would be obsolete in the twenty-third century, the number of times female crew members grope for zippers: two

8. Given that the *Enterprise* is filled with Starfleet's best and brightest crew members, the number of times Wesley comes up with the needed solution: seven

9. Given the kindness the crew shows toward other races in the twenty-fourth century, the number of times they resort to bashing twentieth-century humans: five

10. Given the close proximity of the turbolift near Picard's ready room, the number of times the crew use it: very few

REFERENCES:

1. Deneb IV in "Encounter at Farpoint," Ligon II in " Code of Honor," Rubicun III in "Justice," Mordan IV in "Too Short a Season," Aldea in "When the Bough Breaks," Minos in "Arsenal of Freedom," Vagra II in "Skin of Evil," Iconia in "Contagion," Delta Rana IV in "The Survivors," Mintaka III in "Who Watches the Watchers," the first Gatherer outpost in "The Vengeance Factor," Angosia III in "The Hunted," Rutia IV in "The High Ground," the Klingon home world in "Sins of the Father," Ventax II in "Devil's Due," Malcoria III in "First Contact," the Klingon colony in "The Mind's Eye," the Klingon home world again in "Redemption" and "Redemption II," a Bajoran refugee camp in "Ensign Ro," Moab IV in "The Masterpiece Society," Devidia II in "Time's Arrow" and "Time's Arrow II," a war-torn planet in "Man of the People," and Seltrice III in "Chain of Command," Part 1.

2. A virus ravages the crew in "Angel One" and Admiral Kennelly suffers from one in "Ensign Ro." (A note of explanation: Since the "common cold" does not come from one but hundreds of different viruses, successful elimination of the common cold would involve a broad-based cure for viral-type infections. At the very least, running a person through the transporter and its biofilters should eliminate the viruses, shouldn't it?)

3. Data says "I'm fine" at the end of "Datalore," and "It's me!" at the end of "We'll Always Have Paris." (Just to name a few.)

4. Rasmussen's deception eludes her in "A Matter of Time," as do Timothy's lies in "Hero Worship."

5. Wesley walks out of the holodeck and he's still wet in "Encounter at Farpoint." A snowball flies out and hits Picard in "Angel One." Lipstick remains on Picard's face during "The Big Good-bye." Data carries out a piece of paper in "Elementary, My Dear Data."

6. Troi travels back to the *Enterprise* in "Skin of Evil." Picard comes from Starbase 718 in "The Neutral Zone." Picard and Wesley go to Starbase 515 in "Samaritan Snare." Picard and Wesley fly off to meet with miners in "Final Mission." La Forge travels to Risa in "The Mind's Eye."

7. Crusher in "The Naked Now" and Troi in "The Price."

8. He changes the tractor beam to a repulser beam in "The Naked Now." He points out the similarity of wave forms in "The Battle." He fixes the holodeck in "The Big Good-bye." He figures out they could use a neutrino pulse to

contact La Forge in "The Enemy." He makes the crucial connection to the Elway Theorem in "The High Ground." He recognizes Riker's signal in "Ménage à Troi." He notes the game's additive nature in "The Game."

9. "Encounter at Farpoint" claims humans were a dangerous, savage child race when they wore World War II uniforms. In "Code of Honor," Picard states that Ligonian customs are the "same kind of pompous strutting charades that endangered our own species a few centuries ago. Riker compares us to the Ferengi in "The Last Outpost." In "Haven," Crusher says that the Tarellians had reached Earth's late-twentieth-century level of knowledge and then concludes, "That's all you need if you're a damn fool." And finally, Riker, in "The Neutral Zone," comments on the recently thawed humans by saying, "From what I've seen of our guests, there's not much to redeem them. It makes one wonder how our species survived. ..."

10. You didn't actually expect me to list them, did you?

Fifth

Season

REDEMPTION II

Star Dates: 45020.4-45025.4

With the Klingon Empire engaged in civil war, Picard presents a plan to Starfleet. Because of Picard's previous dealings with the family of Duras (see "Sins of the Father" and "Reunion"), he surmises that the Romulans are assisting the family of Duras in their attempt to overthrow Gowron, the rightful ruler of the Klingon Empire. To prevent Romulan intervention, Picard proposes that the Federation send a fleet of ships to the Klingon/Romulan border. These ships will blockade the border, using active tachyon beams. The ships should be able to detect any cloaked Romulan ship that crosses the beams while attempting to resupply the family of Duras.

The Federation approves of Picard's plan and musters up twenty-three ships from around the sector. Both Riker and Data take command of their own ships. Soon after they establish the blockade, the Romulans detect it. The Romulan commander decides to rattle Picard. She brings her ship to his location and introduces herself as "Commander Sela," the daughter of Tasha Yar. Later she relates some of the events of "Yesterday's *Enterprise*." She also tells Picard to remove the Starfleet ships or the Romulans will attack.

Picard contacts Gowron and asks him to launch an assault on the family of Duras. He hopes they will contact the Romulans for assistance and force the Romulans to run the blockade. The plan works, but the Romulans nullify the blockade by flooding the area with tachyon emissions. As the other Starfleet ships fall back, Data devises a method to locate the approaching Romulan ships. He then fires very-low-intensity photon torpedoes at them, exposing the ships. The Romulans abandon the mission, Gowron defeats the family of Duras, and Worf asks for permission to return to duty (he resigned at the end of "Redemption").

Trivia Questions

1. How long has Data served in Starfleet?

2. Give the first names of three of the men who serve under Captain Data in this episode.

GREAT LINES

"I understand your concerns ... request denied."—Data refusing his first officer's request to resign because Data is an android.

PLOT OVERSIGHTS

• At one point, men loyal to Duras attack Worf in a bar. They knock him unconscious and drag him out. Yet, earlier in the show, Worf's brother claimed that the bar was filled both with men loyal to Duras and those loyal to Gowron. Why doesn't anyone come to Worf's aid?

• The Romulan commander Sela gives Picard an accurate recounting of the facts of "Yesterday's *Enterprise*." Specifically, she knows that her mother came from twenty-two years in the future. Sela also says that when Yar tried to escape, Sela cried out and exposed her. Sela's father killed Yar for that attempt. Sela then proudly proclaims her commitment to the Romulan Empire. If the Romulans knew that Yar came from twenty-two years in the future, it is inconceivable that they would kill her. Yar was a tactical officer with in-depth knowledge of weapons systems. The Romulans had unlimited time to torture her until she cooperated (they proved their skills in "The Mind's Eye"). It makes no sense for them to throw away a resource like that just because she tried to escape.

• After the sisters of Duras fail to convince Worf to join their cause, Sela appears on a viewscreen and gives them new orders. Worf calmly looks at the screen before they lead him away. Is Worf still groggy from the beating in the bar? The viewscreen before him shows the face of a woman he called a friend—a woman he thought died years ago. His reaction should be similar to Picard's when Picard first sees Sela: shock and amazement.

• After the Romulans flood the border with tachyon emissions, the blockade field loses it effectiveness. Picard orders the ships to fall back, but Data realizes that the Romulan ships might be detectable for a short time. He gets to work immediately, disobeying a direct order from Picard. Data proves successful in his attempt and single-handedly turns back the Romulan supply ships. However—aside from the fact that everything in Data's programming supports his full compliance with orders from a superior officer—Data's disobedience is totally unnecessary. In the time that Data spends arguing with his first officer about Picard's orders, Data could simply say, "Data to Captain Picard. There may be another way to detect the Romulans. Stand by." Data's disobedience is simply a plot contrivance to add tension.

• Worf's resignation from Starfleet constituted a major component of the cliff-hanger nature of the finale for the fourth season ("Redemption"). One of the last scenes showed Worf walking to the transporter lined by fellow Starfleet officers, with everyone trying to keep a "stiff upper lip" at his departure. The creators made this *big* deal about Worf resigning. Then, just before this episode concludes, Worf turns to Picard and says, "Request permission to return to duty, sir." Picard says okay, and they leave together! That's it? That's all? A person can resign from Starfleet and all they have to do is say, "Oops, I've changed my mind," and everything's fine?

CHANGED PREMISES

• At the end of "Redemption," Picard chats with Worf before Worf leaves the ship. Picard says he understands that Worf will serve as weapons officer on Gowron's ship. Worf agrees. Yet this episode opens with Worf serving under his brother Kurn on Kurn's ship. Did Worf get a demotion?

EQUIPMENT ODDITIES

• Picard's entire plan for exposing Romulan involvement in the Klingon civil war hinges on the successful detection of cloaked Romulan supply ships. The successful detection of the supply ships rests solely on the viability of the blockade using active tachyon beams. At the beginning of the show, Picard explains how the blockade functions. He says, "Each ship will send out an active tachyon beam to the other blockading ships. In theory, any cloaked vessel that attempts to pass between our ships must cross that beam and be detected." Later in the show, when the main computers on both the *Enterprise* and Sela's ship show the blockade, the graphics substantiate Picard's explanation. Both the Starfleet and Romulan screens show lines connecting the Starfleet ships.

If the Starfleet ships are really using beams, they've got problems. No gap between the beams of the blockade can exceed the width of a Romulan ship. If it did, the Romulans could detect the gap and fly through it. To get that type of density in the blockade, however, the Starfleet ships would have to be clustered very closely together. And if the ships are clustered that closely together, then the Romulans could simply fly around the blockade. This is, after all, three-dimensional space!

Picard and the main computers on both the *Enterprise* and Sela's ship must be confused. The Starfleet ships *must* be sending out *waves* of tachyon emissions. This would fill in the gaps. It would also explain how O'Brien can tell Picard, "The detection net is picking up activity from the Romulans ... fifteen cloaked ships spreading out along the border." O'Brien says this before the Romulans cross into Klingon space. If the blockade could only detect a cloaked ship when it crossed a beam, how does O'Brien know that there are fifteen cloaked ships getting ready to cross?

• When Sela speaks with Picard, she asks why twenty-three Starfleet ships lie on the Romulan border. If there are *twenty-three* ships in the blockade, why do only *seventeen* show up on the viewscreens both on the *Enterprise* and Sela's ship?

• To speed the detection of the Romulans, Picard asks Gowron to stage an attack. The interchange shows Gowron seated in a massive chair, wearing his leader robe. The chair and the background look exactly like those seen in the Great Hall of the Klingon home world earlier in the episode. Yet when the transmission concludes, the last shot shows a picture of Gowron's ship! Evidently Gowron really liked that chair, so he had an exact duplicate made for his ship.

TRIVIA ANSWERS
1. Twenty-six years.
2. Christopher, Terry, and Keith.

DARMOK

The *Enterprise* arrives at a planet in the uninhabited El-Adrel system to meet with a ship from a race known as the "Children of Tama." During previous peaceful encounters, no communication was possible. One captain described their speech as incomprehensible. Picard finds that description accurate. While the Tamarian captain Dathon seems to want to communicate, his speech consists of reciting proper names and places. When Picard tries to answer, Dathon looks puzzled. The Tamarian captain then pulls out two knives and says, "Darmok and Jalad at Tenagra." He and Picard dematerialize as the Tamarians transport them to the planet. Riker reacts immediately to retrieve Picard, but the Tamarians put up a particle-scattering field that blocks the transporter.

Meanwhile, on the planet, Dathon tries to give Picard a knife. Picard refuses, believing the Tamarian wants to fight him. The next morning, an animal-like roar catches Picard's attention. When Dathon offers the knife again, Picard understands. They will fight the beast together. In the process, Picard realizes the Tamarians communicate by metaphor, by citing examples from their mythology and history. When the battle begins, Riker tries to beam Picard up but fails. Unfortunately, this also immobilizes Picard while the beast attacks the Tamarian captain. That night, Dathon dies. In the morning, the beast returns. Riker, having run out of options, attacks the Tamarian ship, disabling the scattering field. After O'Brien beams Picard aboard, the Tamarians attack the *Enterprise*, pushing it to the edge of destruction. At the last moment, Picard uses the few phrases he knows to appease the Tamarian first officer, satisfying him that his captain's sacrifice was worthwhile.

Trivia Questions

1. When did the *Enterprise* arrive at the planet? (Answer using a star date with one number following the decimal point.)

2. How many nonhumanoid races has Data met in his time with Starfleet?

GREAT LINES

"He who was my companion through adventure and hardship is gone forever."—Picard, ending his story as the Tamarian captain dies.

PLOT OVERSIGHTS

• In one scene, Data and Troi deduce that the Tamarians speak in metaphor when they cross-reference the proper names "Darmok" and "Tenagra" to a mythological account from one of the planets nearby. After they give this information to Riker, Troi claims that communication is hopeless, since all they know is that Darmok was a hunter and Tenagra an island.

If they know that Darmok is a mythological hunter, doesn't it seem likely that they would have access to some of the stories about him? Out of those stories, they might find something they could use. Also, since they know what planet Darmok came from, can't they try some of the other mythological accounts from that planet? Perhaps the Tamarians are familiar with those stories also.

CONTINUITY AND PRODUCTION PROBLEMS

• The last scene of the episode is shot from outside Picard's ready room window. We can see the ship's hull as we look back into the ship through the window. Picard faces us as he looks into space. Since the *Enterprise* is flying at warp, we can also see—on the outside surface of the glass—a reflection of streaking stars. The stars streak *toward* Picard.

The only way the stars could be streaking toward Picard is if the *Enterprise* was flying backward! *Reflection images are only flipped left to right.* They are not flipped front to back. From the position of the shot—on the back side of the ship and outside the hull—the stars would still be traveling away from Picard as he gazes out the window. Therefore, the stars should be traveling *away from* Picard in the reflection.

TRIVIA ANSWERS

1. It was 45047.2. (This is the star date Picard gives on the way to the planet. It is also the star date shown on the recording of their first encounter with the Tamarians. Since they were already at the planet when this communication took place, the *Enterprise* must have arrived at the planet at 45047.2.)
2. A total of 1,754.

★
ENSIGN RO

Star Dates: 45078.3-45077.8

*T*he *Enterprise* responds to an attack on a Federation colony. The ship that speeds away transmits a message in which the Bajoran claim responsibility for the attack. Decades ago, the Cardassians (see "The Wounded") conquered the Bajoran home world and chased them off. Since then, they have roamed the planets, living in refugee camps.

After delivering the survivors of the Federation colony to Lya Station Alpha, Picard confers with an Admiral Kennelly. Kennelly believes a Bajoran named Orta led the attack. He wants Picard to find Orta and convince him to return with his terrorists to a refugee camp. The admiral offers Federation assistance in resolving the Bajoran problem. He also assigns Ensign Ro Laren to the *Enterprise* crew for the mission. Ensign Ro, a Bajoran, served on the USS *Wellington* before her court-martial and subsequent imprisonment. The admiral was convinced she could be valuable, so he arranged her release from the stockade.

Under Ro's guidance, Picard eventually locates Orta, but the terrorist claims he had nothing to do with the attack on the outpost. That disclosure confuses Ro, and under the urging of Guinan, she confesses her real mission to Picard. The admiral instructed her to offer Orta weapons and ships if Orta would return to the camps. Picard, Ro, and Orta concoct a plan to uncover the truth. The *Enterprise* escorts an unmanned Bajoran transport back to a refugee camp. En route, Cardassian warships move in. When Picard consults with Starfleet, Kennelly orders Picard to withdraw and let the Cardassians destroy the ship. Picard then realizes the truth: Since the Bajoran ships do not have warp drive, the Cardassians must have attacked the colony. They then played on Kennelly's emotions, hoping the Federation could find Orta. When the Federation did, the Cardassians intended to eliminate him.

Trivia Questions

1. What is Picard's aunt's cure for the common cold?

2. How many people died on the away team mission that lead to Ro's court-martial?

GREAT LINES

"Sounds like someone I'd like to know."—Guinan, responding to La Forge's claim that Ro doesn't belong in a Starfleet uniform.

RUMINATIONS

*A*t one point, Picard, Data, Worf, and Ro visit a Bajoran refugee camp. Ro kneels down, takes off her outer coat, and puts it around a small child. In this scene, the creators make a special and successful effort with camera angles and custom-tailored uniform pieces to create Gene Roddenberry's vision of clothing fasteners that work seamlessly—far surpassing our antiquated twentieth-century zippers. (While this is absolutely "correct," I wouldn't be doing my job if I didn't point out that it is also in conflict with a scene in "The Naked Now" where Dr. Crusher unzips her uniform, and the opening scene in "The Price" when Troi reaches behind her back to get to her zipper.)

PLOT OVERSIGHTS

• When Riker signals Picard of the attack on the Federation colony, Data reports the *Enterprise* is twenty-six minutes away. Yet apparently the *Enterprise* makes no effort to chase the ship down. In "The Wounded," the *Enterprise* demonstrated its ability to do long-range scanning. The *Enterprise* showed its speed in "The Best of Both Worlds." Why not zip over to the colony, beam down a few medical teams, and then give chase?

• When Picard sees Orta's ships he realizes Orta couldn't have attacked the Federation colony. He tells the admiral that Orta's ships don't have warp capability and therefore cannot reach any other star systems. So why are the Cardassians so worried about Orta? The star system he inhabits is outside Cardassian territory. Without warp drive capability, it would take his terrorists *forever* to get to a Cardassian planet and attack it.

Think of it this way: Suppose that Palestinians had a terrorist camp on a planet in the Alpha Centauri system—which is the nearest star system to our own sun—and they could only travel at less than the speed of light. Would that bother the government of Israel? Of course not! It would take the Palestinians four and a half years to get here and another four and a half years to get back!

CHANGED PREMISES

• Near the beginning of the show, Picard offers the admiral his aunt's cure for the common cold. Evidently Picard believes the admiral has a cold. The admiral replies that he doesn't have a cold, he has a Cardassian virus. Picard must have forgotten that people no longer suffer from the common cold in the twenty-fourth century. His chief medical officer, Dr. Beverly Crusher, said so in "The Battle."

• When the Cardassians show up to incinerate the Bajoran ship, the captain is missing that cute little helmet the Cardassian captain wore in "The Wounded." Is he rebelling against the current Cardassian fashion trend known as the "Goofy Look"?

CONTINUITY AND PRODUCTION PROBLEMS

• The graphics at the beginning of this episode—showing the *Enterprise* arriving at Lya Station Alpha—

serve yet again. It is the same sequence used when the *Enterprise* docked at Starbase 133 in "Remember Me" as well as when the *Enterprise* docked at Starbase 74 in "11001001." Of course, it may just *look* like the same station. If it just *looks* the same as the other stations, all three stations orbit the same-colored planets, and all three planets have exactly the same-colored moons, and all three moons were in exactly the same orbital position when the *Enterprise* approached. (As I said in "Remember Me," wouldn't it have made more sense just to call them all Starbase 74?)

TRIVIA ANSWERS

1. Hot ginger tea with honey.
2. Eight.

SILICON AVATAR

Star Dates: 45122.3-45129.2

While the *Enterprise* attends to another mission, an away team of Riker, Crusher, and Data visit a new Federation colony. While they are reviewing building sites, a deep rumble fills the air. Riker looks up to see a crystal entity (see "Datalore") dropping from the sky. Data suggests the nearby caves as the best possible cover. The colonists make a run for it. On the *Enterprise*, Worf alerts Picard to an atmospheric disturbance on the planet, and the *Enterprise* races back to investigate. When they arrive, they find the planet stripped clean of life. Thankfully, the away team and all but two of the colonists survive.

A zenologist named Dr. Kila Marr joins the *Enterprise*. She is Starfleet's foremost authority on the crystal entity. Her son died when the crystal entity attacked Data's home world.

After Data discovers a way to track the entity, the *Enterprise* sets course to intercept it. Before they can reach the entity, however, it attacks and destroys a transport ship. In spite of this, Picard remains adamant that they will attempt to communicate with

Trivia Questions

1. What weaponry does the transport ship have to fend off the attack of the crystal entity?

2. What was Dr. Marr's son's worst subject?

the entity first before firing on it. Data and Dr. Marr begin sending a stream of graviton pulses. When the entity responds, they increase the frequency. The crystal entity then sends back some of its own pulses. When it becomes clear communication is possible, Dr. Marr locks the graviton stream into a continuous mode, climbing to ever higher frequencies. Picard orders her to stop but she refuses, hoping to avenge her son's death. Eventually, she succeeds: The crystal entity shatters from the vibrations.

GREAT MOMENTS

When the crystal entity attacks the colony, the effects are wonderful. The crystal entity fires a beam of energy that strafes across the ground. As it passes, everything in its path dissolves, leaving only the dirt.

PLOT OVERSIGHTS

• When Dr. Marr locks the graviton stream into a continuous mode, both Data and La Forge claim they can't stop her program. Why not just cut the power to the graviton emitters?

CHANGED PREMISES

• When Dr. Marr comes on board, Riker escorts her to a turbolift. When they reach it, Riker touches a control panel on the exterior doors and they wait for the turbolift to arrive. I believe this is the first time this happens in this series. For four years, no one has had to wait for a turbolift to arrive, and now, all of a sudden, they do. (There is one exception to this: During one scene in "Yesterday's *Enterprise*," Data walks to a turbolift and stands. When Yar finishes wandering around on the bridge she joins Data, and the doors pop open. But that was in a completely different time line, on the *warship Enterprise*. I always assume that they had to wait because they were conserving energy for battle, kind of like car-pooling.)

• In this episode, the *Enterprise* must use a pulsed graviton beam to investigate the *possibility* of communication with the crystal entity. Yet in "Datalore," Yar opened a communications channel, and Lore simply spoke to the entity and it responded.

EQUIPMENT ODDITIES

• Soon after Dr. Marr arrives, she and an away team go to the planet and study the effects of the devastation. Dr. Marr wanders around in the cave, using a tricorder to read the composition of the rocks. All appears normal until the very last shot of her using the tricorder. Then, for some reason, Dr. Marr begins taking readings holding the tricorder *upside down*! She continues using it this way until she puts it away. Maybe she has some strange form of dyslexia that kicks in occasionally.

• When Data discovers how to track the crystal entity, he and Dr. Marr are working with La Forge in Engineering. That's on deck 36. Dr. Marr and Data then head for the bridge. The shot shows them walking down a hall and into a turbolift. Once in the turbolift, Dr. Marr asks for the bridge, and the turbolift begins moving. But a door for the turbolift indicates that they boarded the lift on deck 12. What were they doing on deck 12? (I suppose they could have taken a little side trip, but nothing in the episode indicates what they did on this side trip.)

• Continuing on with this turbolift trip, when Dr. Marr and Data reach their destination, the doors pop open and they walk out. The shot shows a section of hallway through the open doors of the turbolift. Didn't Dr. Marr say "bridge"? None of the turbolift entrances on the bridge has a section of hallway like the one pictured. Later in the show, another conversation between Marr and Data occurs in a turbolift. When they exit after *that* conversation, the wall section looks suspiciously similar, but in that case there were going to deck 17.

CONTINUITY AND PRODUCTION PROBLEMS

• The mind meld with Sarek is getting to Picard (see "Sarek"). He's transmogrifying into that Vulcan look ... the one with one eyebrow raised. Moments after the crystal entity appears, Picard sits down in his chair. A close-up shows *the look* when he says, "Remarkable."

1. Low-level particle phasers.
2. Cellular biology.

★
DISASTER

Star Date: 45156.1

As the episode begins, the *Enterprise* rests in space while the crew relaxes. In Ten-Forward, Riker, Data, Worf, O'Brien, and Keiko discuss the name of O'Brien and Keiko's soon-to-be-born child. O'Brien leaves for the bridge. In a cargo bay, Dr. Crusher pesters La Forge to join the cast of her next musical extravaganza. As O'Brien arrives on the bridge, Troi introduces Picard to the three winners of the primary-school science fair. Picard has agreed to give them a tour of the ship, and the group departs in a turbolift. Suddenly two quantum filaments slam into the ship, knocking out many of the ship's systems, including the main computer. The episode continues as the main characters deal with the crisis.

The turbolift breaks Picard's ankle as the emergency brakes jar it to a stop. Together, he and the children climb out of the damaged turbolift and up the emergency ladder. Eventually they reach a door and crawl out onto that deck. In Ten-Forward, Riker and Data head for Engineering to reestablish control of the ship. Worf stays behind to care for the in-

Trivia Questions

1. What are the last names of the children Picard takes on the tour? (List from oldest to youngest.)

2. Where is Data's ventral access panel located?

jured. In the process, Keiko goes into labor, and Worf helps deliver her baby.

On the bridge, Troi, being the senior officer on the deck, assumes command. O'Brien and Ro (see "Ensign Ro") manage to restore power to some of the terminals. Ro finds a containment field problem in the warp engines. If not repaired, the *Enterprise* will explode in just a few hours. Troi orders them to channel energy to the terminals in Engineering, hopeful that someone will see the problem and fix it. On the way to Engineering, Data must use his body to interrupt an electrical arc that blocks the path. Since the arc short-circuits Data's body functions, Riker continues on, carrying Data's head with him. Once they reach Engineering, Riker and Data fix the containment field.

GREAT LINES

"A remarkable experience, commander."—Data, commenting to Riker after half a million amps pass through Data's body.

PLOT OVERSIGHTS

• After Ro finds the weakening of the antimatter containment field, she informs Troi. O'Brien then jumps in and adds more information. He concludes by saying, "If it falls to 15 percent, the field will collapse and we'll have a containment breach." Troi then asks what a containment breach is. At the beginning of "Contagion," the *Yamato* explodes when matter and antimatter mix uncontrollably. Troi is on the bridge at the time. One hour later, in the observation lounge, La Forge explains in great detail about the magnetic seals dropping and the catastrophic consequences of unregulated combination of matter and antimatter. Troi is also at that meeting. Why doesn't Troi know what will happen if the antimatter containment field goes down? How did she get a rank of lieutenant commander without learning about warp engines? No one expects her to be able to field-strip a warp coil, but antimatter containment seems pretty basic.

• When Picard and the children finally find a turbolift door they can open, Picard's waist is level with the deck floor. Picard heaves the top half of his body onto the floor and then yanks and pulls himself the rest of the way. I burst out laughing the second time I watched this episode. My wife gave me one of those looks, because it's supposed to be a dramatic moment in the episode. I offer the following explanation: Why is Picard going through all these gymnastics? The ladder goes all the way up the turbolift shaft, with the doors for each

deck to the right. His left ankle is the one that's broken. Why not just hop up a few more rungs with his right foot and then *step* off when his right foot is level with the floor?

CHANGED PREMISES

• After the quantum filaments hit the ship, Crusher and La Forge are trapped in a cargo bay. While La Forge tries to open the door manually, Crusher places her hand against a wall. She then tells La Forge the wall is hot, and La Forge says, "Where?" *Where?* La Forge can examine things *thermally*. He said so in "Encounter at Farpoint." That means he should be able to look at the wall and see the heat.

EQUIPMENT ODDITIES

• Trapped in a cargo bay, Crusher and La Forge decide to jettison some dangerous chemicals. La Forge opens the cargo bay door and depressurizes the room. To repressurize the room, La Forge must do two things—press a button on a panel near him to close the door, and stumble all the way across the room to get to another panel to pump the oxygen in. He gets the door closed but doesn't make it to the other panel. Crusher makes a supreme effort and manages to get to the far panel, slapping a handful of buttons. Thankfully, one of them is the correct one. A close-up shows the button La Forge pushes to close the cargo bay door. To the left of the button is a large panel labeled "Environmental Support." Doesn't this sound like a control area that could be used to get the oxygen back into a room? What could "Environmental Support" mean if it doesn't mean getting oxygen back into the room? Is this the panel you touch to make a contribution to Greenpeace?

• At the very end of the show, Picard returns to his ready room. Just as he makes a move for the door, it begins to close. Then the door stops, waits for him to go through, and finally finishes closing. Looks like the door got *a little* impatient.

CONTINUITY AND PRODUCTION PROBLEMS

• When the first quantum filament hits the ship, a long shot shows Ten-Forward tossed about. In the background, pieces fly off the three-dimensional chess set as a crew member puts her hand up to steady it. The next shot shows a close-up of the chess set, featuring the area that included the crew member's hand, except the hand is gone.

• As Picard discusses their predicament with the children, he decides to make them his crew. To this end, he drafts the eldest child, a girl, as his "first officer." Picard removes two of his pips (yes, that's what those dots on his collar are called) and attaches them to her collar. However, in the close-ups leading to this exchange, two holes are clearly visible on the girl's collar. The holes are not present when Troi introduces the children to Picard on the bridge. They simply appear in the close-ups of the girl as she agrees to join Picard's crew. Coincidentally, the holes are located precisely where Picard places the pips. Either the creators did the long shot first and then the close-ups, or they had to do multiple takes on the close-ups. In either case, the pips were placed on her collar and removed at least once.

TRIVIA ANSWERS
1. Flores, Graas, and Supra.
2. Two centimeters below his right ear.

THE GAME

When Riker vacations on Risa, a pleasure girl introduces him to a game. Riker brings it back to the *Enterprise*, replicating as many as needed. At the same time, Wesley Crusher rejoins the *Enterprise* during a short vacation from Starfleet Academy. He meets a young female ensign named Robin Lefler, from Engineering, and the two quickly become good friends. As the game spreads through the senior staff, Dr. Crusher calls Data to sick bay to help her program a tricorder. As soon as Data starts working, Dr. Crusher shuts him off and severs some of the connections between his brain and his body. This leaves Data in a comalike state.

Everyone who plays the game tries to encourage others to play the game also. Their high-pressure tactics raise suspicions in Wesley and Robin. They connect the game to a brain simulator and find that the game is psychologically addictive and modifies the centers for higher reasoning. Wesley gives this information to Picard, unaware of Picard's addiction to the game. Wesley then realizes

that the only person on board who wouldn't be affected is Data. He goes to sick bay and discovers Data's problem.

By this time, almost everyone on the *Enterprise* plays the game. An alien ship approaches, carrying the pleasure girl Riker met on Risa. She leads an invasion plan, and everyone under the influence of the game follows her commands. Picard gives orders to force everyone to play the game, including Wesley. Wesley evades them for a while, but eventually Riker and Worf catch him. Just as they hold him down and start the game, Data bursts onto the bridge, holding a palm beacon. The beacon flashes a series of optical bursts that free the crew from the aliens' influence. After Wesley repaired the damage to Data, he led the crew on the chase to give Data enough time to program the optical bursts.

Trivia Questions

1. How many lessons are in Data's course on dancing?

2. What initials did Picard carve in the prize elm tree at Starfleet Academy?

GREAT LINES

""Your neutrinos are drifting."—Robin to Wesley when he continues to shake her hand.

PLOT OVERSIGHTS

• When Riker wants to introduce the game to Troi, he seeks her out in Ten-Forward. He finds her enjoying a bowl of chocolate ice cream dripping with chocolate fudge and sprinkled with chocolate chips. She proceeds to describe for him the ritual of eating chocolate. Isn't it a little late in the series for new expositional material between Troi and Riker? Riker acts like he's never seen Troi eat a bowl of chocolate ice cream before. Yet she is doing it in Ten-Forward. Obviously this isn't a ritual she observes only in private. This the *fifth* season for the series, and Troi and Riker supposedly knew and dated each other before either joined the *Enterprise*. How could he never have seen this before?

• Near the beginning of the show, Picard tells Riker that Wesley will arrive by shuttle. When Wesley does arrive, he beams in from a science vessel, the same kind as in "Night Terrors."

• When Robin tells Wesley he needs to calibrate the sensors manually, he balks. He then tells Robin that the computer must do it. Of course, she proves him wrong by marching over and demonstrating. Has Starfleet Academy ruined Wesley? This is the same guy who turned a tractor beam into a repulser beam in his head when everyone said it was impossible in "The Naked Now." This is also the guy who helped the engineers reroute power when an alien entity took over the ship in "Lonely Among Us." He did both of these things when merely a child,

and now that he's in Starfleet Academy he doesn't know how to calibrate a sensor manually?

• Does it strike anyone else as odd that Picard will play the game but Wesley won't? (See Changed Premises below.)

• When Picard gives orders to cause everyone to play the game, Crusher and Worf come looking for Wesley. They find Wesley and Robin on Wesley's bed, simulating the game-playing using mock-ups. Crusher and Worf leave, satisfied. After this great success at deception, however, Wesley never puts the mock-up on again. Wouldn't it make more sense for him and Robin to continue to wear the game and fake the pleasure?

CHANGED PREMISES

• Until Riker and Worf force Wesley to play the game, everyone in the episode seems to play their first game voluntarily. This would seem to indicate that Picard first played the game voluntarily. Yet during "Captain's Holiday," Picard gives the distinct impression that he doesn't like games.

EQUIPMENT ODDITIES

• During the scene when Robin shows Wesley how to calibrate the sensors manually, one shot shows the control panel by looking over Robin's shoulder. The other shows a close-up. In the close-up, the panel begins flashing, "Manual Calibration Verified." A beeping sound accompanies the flashing. Then the scene cuts back to the shot over Robin's shoulder. The control panel is still visible and the sound still beeps, but the message isn't flashing on the control panel anymore. Also, in the two shots the panels are distinctly different colors.

• When Wesley and Robin check on Data, Wesley scans him, and Robin displays the result on one of the large screens. She then asks for a magnification of factor 4. A portion of the screen enlarges, and a legend on the screen indicates a magnification of factor 4. However the portion of the screen that eventually occupies the whole screen occupied only one ninth of the screen before magnification. Doesn't that mean that the magnification is actually factor 9?

• While Wesley prepares to elude the crew, he tells Robin that he programmed a site-to-site transport program. After he uses it, several lines of dialogue claim that Wesley used a site-to-site transport program. This all makes sense because it would allow Wesley to beam from anywhere to anywhere on the ship (just as when Data wanted to do a site-to-site transport and beam from the bridge to a planet in "Brothers"). In the actual beaming, however, Wesley beams from a hallway to the transporter pad in Transporter Room 3! That's not site-to-site, that's normal transport. In fact, because Wesley uses normal transport, La Forge can locate him, telling Picard that Wesley ended up on deck 6 (I sense some plot trickery here).

TRIVIA ANSWERS
1. Seventeen.
2. "AF."

UNIFICATION I

Star Dates: 45233.1-45290.6

Fleet Admiral Brackett summons Picard to Starbase 234 to discuss an urgent matter. Three weeks ago, Ambassador Spock disappeared. In the original *Star Trek* series, Spock served as Captain Kirk's first officer. He went on to become one of the Federation's most celebrated ambassadors, advising Federation leaders for generations. Two days ago, a long-range scan detected Spock on Romulus, the Romulan Empire's home world. Picard must find out if Spock has defected and, if he hasn't, why Spock is on Romulus. The *Enterprise* flies to Vulcan so Picard can meet with Sarek, Spock's father. Sarek tells Picard of Spock's friendship with a Romulan named Pardek. Sarek believes Spock went to Romulus to meet with Pardek.

Meanwhile, Starfleet also asks the *Enterprise* to decipher a pile of space wreckage. The wreckage came from boxes marked "medical supplies" aboard a crashed Ferengi transport ship. La Forge determines that the wreckage was a navigational array from a Vulcan ship called the *T'Pau*, which is supposed to be docked in a junkyard around Qualor II. Before going to Qualor II to investigating further, however, the *Enterprise* beams Picard and Data to a Klingon ship. The Klingons, using their cloaking device, will deliver Picard and Data to Romulus in an attempt to find Spock. When the *Enterprise* arrives at Qualor II, they find the *T'Pau* missing. They also catch a warship stealing from the junkyard. In the battle that follows, the *Enterprise* destroys the warship. Shortly after Picard and Data arrive on Romulus, Pardek's followers, posing as security personnel, "arrest" Picard and Data. They take Picard and Data to a cave, where they meet Pardek and Spock.

Trivia Questions

1. What is the difference in measurement between Picard's left and right eyes?

2. Where was the *T'Pau* supposed to be docked in orbit around Qualor II?

GREAT LINES

"He probably figures that we don't get to see a lot of handsome women out this way and someone like you might get a little more cooperation from me.... He's probably right."— The quartermaster of the junkyard ogling Troi after she intervenes to help Riker get information on the *T'Pau*.

PLOT OVERSIGHTS

• *Star Trek: The Next Generation* uses the metric system (centimeters, meters, kilometers, etc.) for measuring speed and distance. For instance, when the quartermaster of the junkyard gives directions to the location of the *T'Pau*, he says, "Helmsman, lay in a heading 141 by 208, ahead slow 200 kph." The designation "kph" stands for "kilometers per hour." However, when the quartermaster makes small talk with Troi he tells her about a "fourteen-foot Caldorian eel." Fourteen-*foot*? (I would have thought that feet, as a measurement, would be long dead in the twenty-fourth century. I suppose the quartermaster could be referring to an eel with fourteen feet, as opposed to an eel fourteen feet in length.)

EQUIPMENT ODDITIES

• After Picard and Data arrive on Romulus, a proconsul of the Romulan Senate calls Pardek in and shows him a picture of Picard. The proconsul displays Picard's picture on a workscreen that looks suspiciously similar to the ones used on the *Enterprise*. True, it has a few fins added here and there, but the basic design is the same. What are the chances that these enemies—the Federation and the Romulans—would develop a workscreen with the same shape and design? Federation and Romulan hand weapons differ greatly in shape and design. Also, the workstations on Sela's Romulan ship in the episode "Redemption II" didn't look anything like the one on the proconsul's desk.

CONTINUITY AND PRODUCTION PROBLEMS

• Picard seems to have a little difficulty making the Vulcan hand sign when saying good-bye to Sarek. Watch his little finger. It wiggles back forth when he forms the sign.

TRIVIA ANSWERS

1. Picard's right eye is .004 higher than his left (Don't ask me what the unit of measurement is; they never say. I would imagine it is centimeters.)
2. Section 18, Gamma 12.

UNIFICATION II

Star Date: 45245.8

In this continuation of "Unification I," Picard asks why Spock came to Romulus. Spock replies that Pardek has told of a growing "underground" movement on Romulus, a movement that desires "reunification." Generations ago, Vulcans and Romulans diverged from a single ancestor race. Those in the reunification movement want the Romulans to put aside their warlike ways and merge with the Vulcan race. Spock came because Pardek claimed a new proconsul in the Romulan Senate has joined the reunification movement. Pardek told Spock he believed the time was right for the initial overtures to peace. Spock came alone because he refused to risk anyone else's life on the venture.

Meanwhile, at Qualor II, the *Enterprise* continues its investigation of the stolen Vulcan ship, the *T'Pau*. After some "persuasion" from Riker, a fat Ferengi trader admits he took the *T'Pau* to Galorndon Core, a planet near Romulan territory. Riker takes the *Enterprise* to Galorndon Core to investigate further.

On Romulus, Spock and Picard

Trivia Questions

1. How many parts are in the Romulan information network cypher key?

2. How did Data manage to transmit a message from the Klingon ship to the *Enterprise* without the Romulans detecting it?

soon realize that Pardek wanted Spock to come for a purpose other than peace. Before they can escape, however, Sela arrests them. (See "Redemption" and "Redemption II.") Sela then reveals her entire plan. The Romulans have stolen three Vulcan ships. Using a holographic representation of Spock, Sela will broadcast a message claiming the Vulcan ships carry a joint peace delegation. In fact, the ships will carry an invasion force. Sela plans her own "reunification" effort—a reunification accomplished by Romulus conquering Vulcan. When Sela leaves to dispatch the Vulcan ships, Spock, Picard, and Data change the peace message into a warning, and the *Enterprise* stops the Vulcan ships. Picard and Data then escape, while Spock remains behind to encourage the true participants in the underground movement for reunification.

GREAT LINES

"Perhaps you would be happier in another job."—Data to his Romulan captor Sela, a high-ranking security officer, after she says how much she

enjoys writing and how little she gets to do it.

PLOT OVERSIGHTS

• In the previous episode, "Unification I," the quartermaster of the junkyard at Qualor II said, "In all the time that the Zakdorn have operated this depot, nothing has ever been lost ... never!" In "Peak Performance," the Zakdorn are described as the greatest strategists in the Federation.

The junkyard at Qualor II serves as a depot for all types of Federation ships, including ships with weaponry. For security reasons, doesn't it seem likely that the junkyard would be in an out-of-the-way and easily defensible location? Doesn't this make strategic sense?

Yet in this episode, we find that Qualor II has a bar reminiscent of the one in *Star Wars*—a place that serves as a crossroads for every sort of riffraff, including arms traders!

• In the episode "The Defector," a Romulan defector tells Data, "I know a host of Romulan cyberneticists that would love to be this close to you." Data replies that he doesn't find that concept appealing, and the Romulan agrees. It's easy to understand why the Romulans would want to capture Data. By examining and dismantling him, they might be able to build an entire army of powerful, absolutely loyal soldiers. Yet in this episode, "Unification II," Sela makes no effort to turn Data over to the cyberneticists even though she recognizes he is an android and she has a score to settle with him. (Data thwarted her plans in "Redemption II.")

• To create a diversion, Data programs holographic representations of Riker and two ensigns. "Riker" commands Sela and her guards to drop their weapons. The ruse doesn't work, but it does distract the Romulans long enough for Spock and Picard to disarm them. Afterward, Picard comments to Data that Data didn't get Riker's hair quite right. It's a cute moment, but not believable. Data is an android. His memories are precise and accurate, and he has served with Riker for over four seasons. (That may or may not be four years to you and me.)

• After Spock sends the warning about the Vulcan ships, a Romulan warship decloaks beside them and destroys them. La Forge comments that there were more than two thousand Romulan troops on the ships. Troi adds that they destroyed their own invasion force. Doesn't an invasion force of two thousand troops seem a little small to conquer an entire planet?

CONTINUITY AND PRODUCTION PROBLEMS

• The first time Riker visits the bar on Qualor II, he talks with a musician at a keyboard—a woman with four hands. The musician causes two continuity errors. In the first, she tries to convince Riker to giver her some money for her information about the stolen Vulcan ship. The shot over Riker's shoulder shows her placing her upper right hand down on the keyboard. In the very next shot, her hand is up again.

The second continuity error comes when the musician and Riker play a duet. Just before an overhead shot showing their hands, the musician plays the upper keyboard with both her upper and lower left hands. In the overhead shot, she plays the upper keyboard with her lower right and upper left hands.

• Galorndon Core seems to have changed color. When the *Enterprise* visits Galorndon Core in "The Enemy," every shot of the *Enterprise* in orbit around the planet shows a predominantly blue planet. In "Unification II," the planet is mostly yellow, gradually fading to blue at the very bottom. This is a case where the creators could have reused this expensive-to-produce footage and yet didn't.

• As Spock, Picard, and Data escape from Sela's office, the camera pans over her desk. The desk contains a reflective crystal pyramid.

When the camera sweeps past it, the face of a twentieth-century man—complete with glasses and chewing gum—shows up clearly on its mirrorlike finish! (I must confess that I did not find this jewel. In one of her editorial memos to me, Jeanne Cavelos added this postscript: "A friend of mine, Laurie Shanahan, asked that you make sure to include the reflection in the pedestal from 'Unification.'" Of course, that sent me scrambling for my tapes.)

TRIVIA ANSWERS

1. Forty-three.
2. He "piggybacked" it on a Romulan subspace carrier wave.

A MATTER OF TIME

As the *Enterprise* warps to assist with a crisis on Penthara IV, a small craft appears. Just after the *Enterprise* stops to investigate, the pilot of the craft beams directly to the bridge and introduces himself as Rasmussen, a historian from nearly three hundred years in the future. He claims to have come back in time to study Picard and the *Enterprise*. Although skeptical, Picard brings Rasmussen's craft into a shuttle bay and allows Rasmussen to accompany them. When the *Enterprise* arrives at Penthara IV, the crew find a planet suddenly cooled by the massive increase of dust in its atmosphere. The dust—created when an asteroid struck an unpopulated continent several days ago—is blocking the sunlight.

After the *Enterprise* saves the planet, Rasmussen says good-bye and heads for his ship. In the shuttle bay, Picard and several other bridge officers stop him from leaving. Picard believes Rasmussen stole a number of items from the ship, and he wants them back. Rasmussen agrees to allow Data to accompany him into the

> **Trivia Questions**
>
> 1. What is the distance from the door of Picard's ready room to the opposite wall?
>
> 2. How many anomalies did Data find in La Forge's computer simulations?

time machine on the condition that Data never reveals what he sees. Once inside, Rasmussen grabs a stolen phaser and points it at Data. He explains that he is really a frustrated inventor from the twenty-second century. Of course, the time machine isn't Rasmussen's creation. When a historian from the future brought it back to the twenty-second century to study that era, Rasmussen met him and commandeered the craft. Rasmussen plans to return to his own time and "invent" the items he stole from the *Enterprise*. Rasmussen then discovers that the phaser won't fire. The *Enterprise*'s computer has deactivated all the items Rasmussen stole. Data escorts Rasmussen out of the time machine, and Worf takes him to a detention cell. An autotimer returns the time machine to the twenty-second century without the scheming inventor.

GREAT LINES

"I assume your handprint will open the door, whether you are conscious or not."—Data making a veiled threat to encourage Rasmussen to open

the door of the time machine.

PLOT OVERSIGHTS

• When Rasmussen first appears on the bridge, he says that he's traveled "nearly three hundred years" into the past to meet them. He also says that he comes from the "late twenty-sixth-century." These two statements should tell Picard that Rasmussen is a fake. In "The Neutral Zone," Data gives the current year as A.D. 2364. If a television season is approximately one year, "A Matter of Time" occurs around three and one half years later (since "The Neutral Zone" is the last show of the first season). That puts "A Matter of Time" in the latter part of the twenty-fourth century. If Rasmussen has traveled back "nearly three hundred years," he came from the twenty-seventh, not the twenty-sixth, century. (For our purposes here, however, I will continue to refer to Rasmussen's temporal home as the twenty-sixth century since that's what he claimed. By the way, I didn't find this one. My copy editor, William Drennan, flagged it on the manuscript after it was in production.)

• Shortly after Rasmussen arrives, the bridge crew meets with him in the observation lounge. In Troi's presence, Rasmussen rehearses his lie that he is a twenty-sixth-century historian. Later, when Picard questions Troi, she says only that she feels Rasmussen is hiding something. Why can't Troi sense Rasmussen's deception? In the episode titled "The Battle," Troi sensed "considerable deception" from the Ferengi captain.

Troi should be able to sense Rasmussen's deception, but if she did, there would be no show! Then again, why can't La Forge sense Rasmussen's deception? In the episode "Up the Long Ladder," La Forge immediately spotted the deception from the prime minister of the colony of clones. In that show, La Forge claimed that his visor allowed him to see the physiological changes that accompany lying. He said it didn't always work on other races, but when it came to humans, he had them "pegged." Rasmussen is human.

• After taking Data inside the time machine, Rasmussen reveals his true purpose in coming to the *Enterprise*. He tells Data he intends to take the items he stole from the *Enterprise* back to the twenty-second century and "invent" them one at a time. Aside from the fact that one of the items Rasmussen stole was a Klingon dagger (don't they have knives in the twenty-second century?), Rasmussen's plan simply will not work. Consider the development of electronics over the past forty years. Suppose an inventor from 1950 appears in our time and steals a notebook computer. He gleefully returns to 1950—certain that fame and fortune await him when he "invents" this wonderful contraption and markets it to the public. Because the computer employs a graphical user interface, the "inventor" quickly learns to operate it. Next, he disassembles the computer and confronts his first problem. The computer uses "integrated circuits," known as ICs. These ICs look like flat rectangular boxes with small wires coming out of them. The inventor's electronic knowledge revolves around the vacuum tube. He doesn't know how ICs work! To him, they are magic *but* ... for the sake of argument, let's say that he figures out how they work. Now the inventor confronts an even worse problem. He has no way to *manufacture* ICs. An invention won't make you any substantial money unless you can mass-produce it. The infrastructure of manufacturing technology that allowed the creation of the notebook computer doesn't exist in 1950! The inventor has nothing more than an interesting artifact.

• At one point, Picard must decide on a course of action to save the planet. If he does nothing, tens of thousands could die. If he goes on a recommendation from La Forge, the *Enterprise* might accidentally burn off the planet's atmosphere, and all twenty million inhabitants will die. Although Picard isn't convinced that Rasmussen is from the future, he cannot overlook the fact that Rasmussen might know the outcome of this decision. Picard grills Rasmussen intensely, but Rasmussen refuses to offer any advice. The would-be "historian" claims that by offering advice, he might inadvertently alter his past: Picard might not try La Forge's recommendation, and one of the people who survive might go on to become the next Adolf Hitler. Picard brushes aside Rasmussen's argument, stating that "every first-year philosophy student has been asked that question since the earliest worm holes were discovered, but this is not a class in temporal logic."

However, at the end of the show, when Rasmussen begs to return to his own time in the twenty-second century, Picard won't let him. In fact, Picard asks Rasmussen a very peculiar question as the fake historian continues pleading. Picard says, "Now, what possible incentive could anyone offer me to allow that?" Try these on, Picard. Maybe Rasmussen is the great-great-great-great-great-grandfather of Riker. Maybe he helped Cochrane, the inventor of warp drive, with a few conceptual ideas in the early stages of development. Maybe he inspired a whole generation of leaders with his "fictitious tales" of life in the future. No one can know the impact of a single life, yet Picard—with all his supposed knowledge of temporal logic—rips Rasmussen from the past by refusing to allow him to return. Wouldn't the better course be to let Data accompany Rasmussen back in time, kick him out the door in the twenty-second century, return to the *Enterprise*, and then dispatch the time machine back to the twenty-seventh century? If Rasmussen can figure out how the time machine works, surely Data could also.

EQUIPMENT ODDITIES

• During a conversation with Picard, Rasmussen continues to act out the part of a historian by measuring the width of the captain's ready room. He backs up against the door and methodically paces off the distance to the window. So how did the door know not to open? Rasmussen backs right up to it and it remains closed.

• After arriving at his quarters, Rasmussen walks over to a built-in vanity to wash his hands. He pushes on the top left side of the vanity, and a box slides back into the wall, revealing the sink. However, in "The Hunted," Danar opens the vanity by pressing a button on the *right* side of the sink.

• The first time crew members of the *Enterprise* try to help the planet, they use phasers to drill holes in the mantle. They hope to release underground pockets of carbon dioxide. The carbon dioxide will trap the heat of the sun and raise the planet's temperature. La Forge comments that it shouldn't take more than twenty drill sites. During the drilling, Worf tells Picard, "Target fourteen complete, sir." This means there are at least fourteen drill sites. Later, the sections of the mantle around the drill sites collapse, causing earthquakes and volcanic eruptions. On one of the workstations, Riker shows Picard a graphic of all the drill sites. There are only *eight* drill sites in the picture. What happened to the other ones?

• After Data enters the time machine, Rasmussen points a phaser at him. While explaining his true purpose in coming to the *Enterprise*, Rasmussen carefully keeps the phaser trained on Data. Yet Rasmussen grips it at the very tip of the handle, far from the firing button. This would be like holding a pistol by the end of the handle and expecting a foe just a few feet away to be intimidated.

TRIVIA ANSWERS

1. Seven meters.
2. Two hundred nine.

NEW GROUND

Star Date: 45376.3

Helena Rozhenko, Worf's human mother, drops in for an unexpected visit. She brings Alexander, Worf's son, with her. Worf sent Alexander to live with his adoptive human parents after K'Ehleyr, Alexander's mother, died in the episode "Reunion." Helena explains that she believes Alexander would be better off with Worf. After she leaves, Alexander's problems become evident. He steals a dinosaur model and lies to cover the theft. After talking sternly with Alexander about the importance of honor, Worf believes the problem is solved.

Meanwhile, the *Enterprise* assists with an important experiment. In the experiment, an array of twenty-three field coils on a planet's surface generate a "soliton wave." The wave pushes a test ship into warp without the need for warp engines. The *Enterprise* follows the test ship, monitoring its telemetry. All seems to go well until the wave destabilizes and destroys the test ship. A shock wave hits and damages the *Enterprise*. While the crew works to repair the damage, Alexander's schoolteacher calls Worf

Trivia Questions

1. What is Worf's last name?

2. When was Alexander born?

in for a conference. Alexander is causing problems in class. Worf decides to send his son to a Klingon school and informs Alexander of his decision. When Worf returns to his duties, Alexander storms out.

With repairs complete, the *Enterprise* races to catch the soliton wave. Due to an increase in size and strength, the wave now threatens to destroy the planet selected for the experiment's destination. To prevent this, the *Enterprise* flies through the wave so it can fire photon torpedoes back into the wave and dissipate it. The trip through the soliton wave damages the shields and forces the evacuation of the rear sections of the *Enterprise*. After discovering that Alexander is trapped in one of those sections, Worf and Riker rescue him just in time for Picard to fire the photon torpedoes and disperse the wave.

PLOT OVERSIGHTS

• Alexander's schoolteacher seems to have marital problems. When Worf refers to her, he calls her "Miss Kyle," but when Troi refers to her, Troi calls her "Mrs. Kyle."

306

• Early in the show, La Forge raves about the soliton wave as a great improvement. He says that the soliton wave will allow ships to travel at warp speeds without bulky warp drives. Later, the head scientist of the project explains that a group of warp coils on a planet will generate the wave, which will push the test ship to the destination where another group of coils will dissipate the wave. How is this an improvement? What happens if you want to change course in the middle of the trip? How do you reach a destination "where no one has gone before"? On second thought, the better question is, How do you *stop* once you reach the place where no one has gone before?

In addition, the soliton wave emits a great deal of subspace interference. To monitor the test ship's telemetry, the *Enterprise* must stay within twenty kilometers. In other words, without further improvement, any ship traveling in a soliton wave won't be able to communicate with any ship more than twenty kilometers away!

CHANGED PREMISES

• At the beginning of the soliton wave test, Riker asks La Forge for the power efficiency of the soliton wave. La Forge reports that it is 98 percent. He adds, "There's less than a 2 percent energy loss between the wave and the ship." Data responds incredulously, "That is 450 percent more efficient than our own warp drive." However, in the episode "Allegiance," when Picard asks La Forge about their engine efficiency status,

La Forge claims they are operating at 93 percent. Picard asks him to bounce it to 95 percent and—before the end of the show—La Forge accomplishes this. Are the characters in these two episodes referring to different things when they talk about efficiency ratings? If each episode refers to the same thing, how do you get a 450 percent increase out of going from 95 percent to 98 percent?

• In the episode "The Nth Degree," an alien probe pursues the *Enterprise*. Phasers are ineffective, and Riker claims they can't fire photon torpedoes because the probe is too close. Lieutenant Barclay comes to the rescue by transferring warp power to the shield grid. The *Enterprise* drops out of warp, fires the photon torpedoes, and destroys the probe. Yet in this episode "New Ground," Picard listens stoically as Data counts down the distance between the *Enterprise* and the wave. Data reports that the wave has closed to one kilometer. Then Data says the wave is about to overtake them. Seconds later, Picard finally fires the photon torpedoes. Miraculously the ship survives, even though much of the aft shield grid was damaged when the *Enterprise* passed through the wave *and* the *Enterprise* is still traveling at warp, so they couldn't have transferred warp power to the shields!

CONTINUITY AND PRODUCTION PROBLEMS

• Several shots near the beginning of the episode show the *Enterprise* in orbit around the planet that serves as the origin point for the soliton wave experiment. It's the same footage used for Galorndon Core in the episode "The Enemy." (I understand the need to conserve costs by reusing these expense-to-produce sequences of the ship orbiting planets. I find it odd, however, that they aren't reused when they could be very legitimately. When revisiting Galorndon Core in "Unification II," the *Enterprise* flies around a completely different colored planet!)

• When La Forge recommends flying through the soliton wave to get in front of it, Picard asks why they can't fly around it. Data responds that the wave has increased in size and there isn't time to fly around it. Yet when a space scene shows the *Enterprise* chasing the soliton wave, the wave looks very flat. It sure looks like the *Enterprise* could just fly over it!

TRIVIA ANSWERS
1. Rozhenko. (True, that is the last name of Worf's *human* parents, not his Klingon parents, but this episode calls Worf's son "Alexander Rozhenko." If Worf's son has the last name of Worf's adoptive human parents, then probably Worf does, too.)
2. Star date 43205.

HERO WORSHIP

Star Date: 45397.3

Responding to a request from Starbase 514, the *Enterprise* investigates the disappearance of the research vessel *Vico*. The last contact with the *Vico* came during its survey of a "black cluster," a region densely populated with collapsed "protostars" and subject to high gravitation forces. When the *Enterprise* locates the *Vico* outside the cluster, it finds a ship literally torn apart. Everyone aboard is dead, except a boy named "Timothy." Although in shock from the loss of both parents, Timothy describes an attack on the *Vico* by an alien ship. When Timothy forms an attachment to Data, Troi suggests Data spend time with him. She thinks Data can help Timothy through this traumatic experience.

After studying the sensor information on the *Vico*, Picard takes the *Enterprise* into the black cluster to solve this mystery. The crew realizes the *Vico* couldn't have been attacked inside the cluster because the high gravitational forces in the cluster render all sensors and weapons systems useless. Timothy finally admits he lied about the attack. The boy believes he caused the destruction of the *Vico* by accidentally leaning on a computer console. Troi assures Timothy that he didn't destroy the *Vico*. The devastation simply occurred at the same time as Timothy touched the panel. At that moment, a gravitational wave hits the *Enterprise*. When Timothy says that's how the destruction started, Picard tries to take the *Enterprise* out of the black cluster, but the next impact temporarily knocks out the engines. Picard orders more power to the shields. Timothy mumbles that the crew of the *Vico* did the same thing. Data quickly runs an analysis and discovers that increasing power to the shields simply increases the strength of the gravitation wave. Picard drops the shields moments before a "killer" wave would have decimated the ship. As soon as the shields go down, the wave dissipates and the *Enterprise* flies to safety.

CHANGED PREMISES

• When Timothy asks Data about his lack of emotions, Data replies, "My positronic brain is not capable

Trivia Questions

1. What percentage of the *Vico*'s computer records are lost?

2. What color does Timothy run out of while painting?

of generating those conditions." Yet Dr. Noonian Soong, Data's creator, must have thought it was, because he created a set of emotional subroutines for Data in "Brothers." And Lore, Data's brother, proved a positronic brain is capable of generating those conditions in "Datalore." *And* Dr. Graves showed emotions when he transferred his essence into Data during "The Schizoid Man." *And* Q made Data's positronic brain experience laughter at the end of "Déjà Q," after which Data comments that it was a wonderful feeling.

EQUIPMENT ODDITIES

• The *Vico* must have a humongous computer core. (I hesitate to use such a highly technical and scientifically precise term such as "humongous," but I believe it's justified in this case.) While discussing the destruction of the *Vico* with La Forge, Picard punches up a side view of the *Vico* on a monitor. He indicates the midpoint of the saucer section with his finger and comments, "The boy was here." La Forge agrees, adding that Timothy was in the hallway outside the computer core. La Forge then points to the lower portion of the drive section to show Picard where the second away team found the body of Timothy's mother. He tells Picard she was *in* the computer core. Does the computer core on a research vessel stretch from the saucer section all the way through the yoke and all the way down to the bottom of the drive section? (As I said, that's one humongous computer core!)

• To test the effectiveness of the phasers inside the black cluster, Picard orders Worf to fire them at maximum yield. Picard gives a firing direction of "zero zero one mark zero four five" (001.045). According to the episode "Datalore," the first number is in degrees—from 0 to 360—in a horizontal circle. The second number is also in degrees, but this time with a vertical circle. So the heading Picard gives should be directly in front of the ship and raised at an angle of 45 degrees. The following shot of the ship shows the phasers firing twice. The first time the phasers fire they shoot directly ahead, a heading that would be described as something like "zero zero one mark zero zero one." The second time, the phasers finally approximate the right heading. Does Worf need a practice shot to figure out how to fire the phasers in the right direction?

CONTINUITY AND PRODUCTION PROBLEMS

• At one point in the show, Data and La Forge review the computer logs of the *Vico*. They view the scrambled files on a large display screen in Engineering. One shot clearly shows the reflection of La Forge's visor on the terminal. The funny thing is that the reflection of La Forge is not in sync with La Forge! La Forge looks up, down, and to the side, and his reflection lags far behind him and sometimes doesn't make the movements at all!

• Under Troi's encouragement, Data visits Timothy in his quarters. (Of course, Timothy is alone in the room, but that's normal Starfleet procedure for a boy who's just lost his parents. See the episode "The Bonding" for another example of this.) Data finds Timothy working with some architectural building blocks, trying to construct an ancient temple. When Timothy fails, Data rapidly builds it for him before leaving. In one of the last shots of the scene, Timothy admires the completed building. A close in-spection of the building reveals that the top piece of flooring is off-center and the very top section of construction seems to be leaning a little. Wouldn't Data be a little more precise than that?

TRIVIA ANSWERS
1. Nearly 83 percent.
2. Red ocher.

VIOLATIONS

Star Dates: 45929.3-45935.8

The *Enterprise* transports three Ulians to their next destination. The Ulians are telepathic historians, creating a "living" history by probing and recording the memories of a planet's inhabitants. During a dinner with the bridge crew, Tarman, the leader of the Ulians, boasts of his ability and belittles another member of the Ulian team, Jev. Jev also happens to be Tarman's son. When Jev leaves abruptly, Troi follows. While riding a turbolift to their respective quarters, Troi cheers him up.

Later, as Troi prepares for bed, a memory flashes through her mind. The memory builds in intensity until she collapses in a coma. When Dr. Crusher examines Troi in the morning, the physician can find nothing wrong with her. Since Jev was the last person to see Troi well, Riker questions him. Shortly afterward, Riker, too, falls into a coma. Dr. Crusher then suggests that she test the Ulians during a memory probe, and she also becomes comatose. Trying to establish a link between the Ulians and the comas, Data and La Forge examine the medical records from

Trivia Questions

1. What is the precise wording of the search parameters La Forge supplies to the computer for his investigation of Irisine syndrome on Melina II?

2. When did the unexplained comas in the Epsilon Nel System occur?

the planets previously visited by the historians.

When Troi awakes, she can't remember what happened to her. Jev, wanting to prove the Ulians' innocence, suggests that he probe Troi's memory. During the probe, Troi testifies that Tarman mentally raped her. The *Enterprise* heads for the Ulian home planet. Meanwhile, Data and La Forge's research finds several cases of comas during Ulian visits. However, Tarman was not present in every case. When Jev goes to say good-bye to Troi, he is once again overcome by her beauty. He tries to rape her mentally a second time, but she begins fighting him. Data bursts in with a team from Security, having determined that Jev was the only Ulian present for all the cases of comas.

GREAT MOMENTS

*T*his episode contains one of the best food replicator effects in the entire Star Trek: The Next Generation television series. After talking with Jev in the turbolift, Troi prepares for bed. She changes into a nightgown and begins brushing out her *hair. When Jev evokes the first memory in her mind, Troi decides to get some hot chocolate to calm her nerves. As she walks in front of the food replicator, the reflections of her nightgown play across its surface. Troi then orders the hot chocolate. The drink materializes; she picks it up and walks away. The entire sequence with the food replicator uses only one shot—no edits. It is beautiful.*

Normally, the special-effects engineers use a "frozen" shot of the inside of the replicator to "white out" the food that is already sitting in the replicator when the actor orders it. They then dissolve out that whited-out shot, and the food appears (see Equipment Oddities for "Future Imperfect"). In this case, however, a reflection of Troi's nightgown dances across the inside of the replicator as she passes—the inside of the replicator is definitely not a frozen shot. The only discrepancy I can find in the entire effect is that the chocolate immediately starts jiggling just after it materializes and before Troi touches it.

EQUIPMENT ODDITIES

• After Jev leaves the dinner because of his father's remarks, Troi follows. She catches up with him outside a turbolift. They board together, and Troi decides to cheer him up by telling Jev about her domineering mother. The turbolift arrives at Troi's deck, and she leaves. In the final seconds of the scene, the turbolift doors close as Jev watches her go. In shooting this scene, the director decided to do it without any edits. From the time Troi joins Jev outside the turbolift, until she departs and the turbolift doors close, the director used one continuous shot. (When I saw this episode for the first time, I started getting excited as this scene unfolded. I kept waiting for the end of the turbolift ride because I thought I knew what the director intended. I was sure the director chose a continuous shot to pull a little sleight of hand with the deck numbers on the turbolift doors; it turns out I was wrong.)

Careful examination of the turbolift doors when Jev and Troi get on the turbolift reveals that first two numbers on the signage are "03." When the doors close on Jev at the end of the scene, the turbolift door signage once again begins with "03." The door signage isn't correct at *either* end of this trip! The first two numbers on a turbolift door stand for the deck number. Many, many episodes support this including "The Dauphin," "Times Squared," and "Transfigurations." When La Forge and Data go to the dinner, La Forge asks the turbolift to take them to deck 2. Therefore, the dinner with the captain is on deck 2. When Troi and Jev board the turbolift, she asks for deck 8. The signage on the turbolift doors should have read "02" at the beginning of the scene and "08" at the end. (This is what I thought the director had in mind when I watched the scene the first time.)

• Toward the end of the show, Data and La Forge search medical records for comas on the planets visited by the Ulians. At one point, La

Forge finds two cases of "Irisine syndrome" during the Ulians visits Melina II. A close-up of his computer screen shows the title "MELINA II PLANETARY MEDICAL DATA BASE." Data—looking at La Forge's screen—immediately comments on La Forge's success by saying, "Two cases of Irisine syndrome on Jarada III at exactly the time Tarman and his group were there." *Jarada III?* The last comment La Forge made concerned Melina II, and his computer screen showed he was still working with the Melina II medical data base.

TRIVIA ANSWERS

1. Search parameters: instances of unexplained comas or medical cases diagnosed as Irisine syndrome during periods when Ulian telepathic historians were present on the planet.

2. Star dates 45321 and 45323.

THE MASTERPIECE SOCIETY

Star Date: 45470.1

The *Enterprise* tracks a stellar core fragment as it passes through the Moab system. As the fragment drifts by the planets in the system, science teams will monitor the disruptions it causes. A problem arises when Data discovers a colony on Moab IV. At first the colony refuses to communicate with the *Enterprise*, but after Picard explains the danger from the intense gravitational forces of the fragment, the leader of the colony responds. His name is "Aaron Conor." When Riker, La Forge, and Troi beam down to discuss the crisis, Conor explains his hesitancy to speak with the *Enterprise*. The colony is a genetically engineered society. Each person, each animal, each plant, even each microbe performs a function vital to the balance of the society. Interactions with outsiders can only upset that balance. However, due to the circumstances, Conor has no choice.

By working with the head scientist of the colony—a woman named "Hannah Bates"—La Forge increases the power of the tractor beam and alters the course of the stellar frag-

Trivia Questions

1. How many generations have lived in the genetically engineered society?

2. What range of frequencies does La Forge's visor receive?

ment. In addition, engineering teams from the *Enterprise* install new shield generators to supplement the colony's own defensive shields. The combination works, and the fragment passes by without destroying the colony. Unfortunately, the colonists' interaction with the crew of the *Enterprise* causes many to ask Picard for asylum. They wish to leave the biosphere and explore the universe. Conor tries his best to dissuade them, but they are adamant. Finally Conor agrees to let them go, even though he understands the terrible cost to the colony. As the show ends, Picard ponders that the *Enterprise* might have been a greater threat to the colony than even the stellar fragment.

GREAT LINES

"Who gave them the right to decide whether or not I should be here, whether or not I might have something to contribute?"—La Forge to Hannah Bates after she agrees that La Forge wouldn't exist in her society. He would have been terminated during pregnancy because of his blindness.

PLOT OVERSIGHTS

• After encountering a problem in the tractor beam research, La Forge comments to Hannah Bates, "I haven't had any sleep in so long my eyelids feel like I have lead weights attached to them." This implies that La Forge is struggling to keep his eyes open. Isn't this a rather odd statement for *La Forge* to make? Normally, people try to keep their eyes open when they are tired because they can't *see* with their eyes closed. La Forge's visor pumps the information directly into his brain through little attachments near his temples. It doesn't matter whether his eyes are open or closed!

EQUIPMENT ODDITIES

• After successfully diverting the stellar fragment, Picard reports the good news to Conor at the colony. Conor then asks to talk with Bates, who is still on the *Enterprise*, and congratulates her for her work. She communicates with him using one of the screens in the center island in Engineering. A control panel lies at the base of the screen. However, a close-up of the same screen in the episode "Hollow Pursuits" shows *two* control panels in that location.

• At the end of the show, Picard and Troi ride a turbolift from deck 1 to Transporter Room 3. Since the episode "The Game" established that Transporter Room 3 is on deck 6, Picard and Troi ride the turbolift from deck 1 to deck 6. It takes more than forty-two seconds to make this trip, even after factoring a "halt" instruction from Troi. However, in the episode "Violations," it takes only eighteen seconds for Troi and Jev to go from deck 2 to deck 8. That means it takes more than twenty-four seconds longer for Picard and Troi to travel *five* decks than it takes for Troi and Jev to travel *six*! Do the turbolifts have a "conversational sensor" that helps them calculate how long the trip should take based on the content of the dialogue between or among the persons in the lift? (I admit that it's tacky to point this out. No one could be expected to go to the expense of rewriting dialogue just to make sure every trip in a turbolift approximates the correct length of time.)

CONTINUITY AND PRODUCTION PROBLEMS

• The creators spelled the name of the actor who played Aaron Conor wrong when this episode first aired. When Paramount first uplinked this episode, the credits listed "John Synder." All subsequent reruns list the actor correctly as "John Snyder."

• In one scene, Troi and Conor discuss the colony. The scene begins with a boy playing "Prelude in C Minor" by Chopin. The prelude serves as background music for Troi and Conor's walk, conversation, and subsequent kiss. The boy must be playing the extended-play dance version of the prelude. (It certainly differs from the one I learned. I know. The creators had to stretch it to make it last the length of the scene.)

TRIVIA ANSWERS

1. Eight.
2. One to one hundred thousand terrawatts.

TRIATHLON TRIVIA ON OTHER CHARACTERS

(So named because—like the athletic event—no one should be able do this.)

MATCH THE CHARACTER TO THE DESCRIPTION
TO THE EPISODE

CHARACTER	DESCRIPTION	EPISODE
1. Alcar, Ambassador Vas	A. Data's pen pal	a. "Code of Honor"
2. Ardra	B. Extraordinary telepath	b. "Half a Life"
3. Armus	C. Put Riker on trial for murder	c. "Imaginary Friend"
4. Bok, DaiMon	D. Propulsion design engineer	d. "True Q"
5. Brahms, Dr. Leah	E. Posed as a she-devil	e. "The Price"
6. Conor, Aaron	F. Was really a Douwd	f. "The Wounded"
7. D'Sora, Lieutenant Jenna	G. Captain of the USS *Essex*	g. "Conundrum"
8. Danar, Rogo	H. Fought Yar for Lutan	h. "The Offspring"
9. Dathon, Captain	I. Lived in a bad novel	i. "Violations"
10. Elbrun, Tam	J. Leader of the Bandi	j. "Tin Man"
11. Fajo, Kivas	K. Crusher's Trill Lover	k. "The Battle"
12. Faralon, Dr.	L. Experimented with time	l. "The Masterpiece Society"
13. Gowron	M. Empathic metamorph	m. "The Emissary"
14. Graves, Dr. Ira	N. Data's "grandpa"	n. "A Matter of Perspective"
15. Jarok, Admiral	O. Riker's androgynous friend	o. "Peak Performance"
16. Jelico, Captain Edward	P. Killed by Riker	p. "Brothers"
17. Jev	Q. Wesley's beast/girlfriend	q. "Power Play"
18. K'Ehleyr, Ambassador	R. Wanted to date Data	r. "The Drumhead"
19. K'Mpec	S. Enhanced soldier	s. "Redemption II"
20. Kamala	T. Beat Data at Strategema	t. "The Royale"
21. Kolrami, Sirna	U. Spock's Romulan friend	u. "Silicon Avatar"
22. Krag	V. Put Picard on trial	v. "The Outrageous Okona"
23. Kurn, Commander	W. Isabella was her friend	w. "The Most Toys"
24. Lal	X. Used Troi for psychic waste	x. "The Quality of Life"
25. MacDuff, Commander	Y. Mated with Worf	y. "The Perfect Mate"
26. Maddox, Bruce	Z. The cast-off desires of titans	z. "Redemption"

CHARACTER	DESCRIPTION	EPISODE
27. Madred, Gul	AA. Kidnapped Data	aa. "Chain of Command," Part 1
28. Manheim, Dr. Paul	BB. Mentally raped Troi	bb. "Sins of the Father"
29. Marr, Dr. Kila	CC. He and Picard fought together	cc. "In Theory"
30. Maxwell, Captain Ben	DD. Searched for the Tox Uthat	dd. "Skin of Evil"
31. Nagilum	EE. Was really Q	ee. "Chain of Command," Part 2
32. Odan, Ambassador	FF. Created Data	ff. "Unification I"
33. Okona	GG. Became leader after K'Mpec	gg. "Pen Pals"
34. Pardek	HH. Worf's brother	hh. "The Outcast"
35. Ral, Devinoni	II. Wanted to destroy the Lysians	ii. "The Survivors"
36. Richie, Colonel Steven	JJ. A Romulan traitor	jj. "The Vengeance Factor"
37. Rogers, Amanda	KK. Data's child	kk. "The Dauphin"
38. Salia	LL. Tortured Picard	ll. "The Host"
39. Sarjenka	MM. Invented the exocomps	mm. "Where Silence Has Lease"
40. Satie, Admiral Norah	NN. Used a thoughtmaker device	nn. "Evolution"
41. Sela, Commander	OO. Died from poison	oo. "The Schizoid Man"
42. Shumar, Captain Bryce	PP. Genetically engineered leader	pp. "The Hunted"
43. Soong, Dr. Noonian	QQ. Wanted to disassemble Data	qq. "Booby Trap"
44. Soren	RR. Captain of the USS *Cairo*	rr. "Devil's Due"
45. Stubbs, Dr. Paul	SS. Committed suicide at sixty	ss. "Reunion"
46. Sutter, Clara	TT. Killer of nanites	tt "Darmok"
47. Timicin	UU. Yar's daughter	uu. "Man of the People"
48. Uxbridge, Kevin	VV. Troi's empathic lover	vv. "The Measure of a Man"
49. Vash	WW. Loved a cargo of canaries	ww. "We'll Always Have Paris"
50. Yareena	XX. Engulfed the *Enterprise*	xx. "The Defector"
51. Yuta	YY. Attacked the Cardassians	yy. "Captain's Holiday"
52. Zorn, Groppler	ZZ. Felt Data caused son's death	zz. "Encounter at Farpoint"

SCORING
(BASED ON NUMBER OF CORRECT ANSWERS)

0	Normal
1–5	Trekkier
6–10	Trekkiest
11 and up	Most extremely Trekked

CHARACTER ANSWER KEY

1. X uu	10. B j	19. OO ss	28. L ww	37. EE d	46. W c
2. E rr	11. AA w	20. M y	29. ZZ u	38. Q kk	47. SS b
3. Z dd	12. MM x	21. T o	30. YY f	39. A gg	48. F ii
4. NN k	13. GG z	22. C n	31. XX mm	40. V r	49. DD yy
5. D qq	14. N oo	23. HH bb	32. K ll	41. UU s	50. H a
6. PP l	15. JJ xx	24. KK h	33. WW v	42. G q	51. P jj
7. R cc	16. RR aa	25. ll g	34. U ff	43. FF p	52. J zz
8. S pp	17. BB i	26. QQ vv	35. VV e	44. O hh	
9. CC tt	18. Y m	27. LL ee	36. I t	45. TT nn	

CONUNDRUM

Star Date: 45999.2

Trivia Questions

1. What does holodeck program 47C contain?

2. How many phaser banks does the *Enterprise* have?

While investigating some sporadic subspace transmissions, the *Enterprise* encounters a small craft. A probe from the craft overpowers the *Enterprise*'s shields, and a yellow beam sweeps through the ship. Afterward, no one on board can remember who they are, but they do remember how to perform certain tasks. The probe also knocks out major portions of the computer memory. With some work, La Forge accesses a partial crew roster, including Captain Picard, Commander MacDuff, Commander Riker, and others. La Forge and Data then discover records that provide some historical background and their current mission. According to the records, the Federation is at war with a genocidal race called the Lysian Alliance. Lately the Lysians have begun using a new weapon that allows them to capture Federation ships easily. The weapon disrupts both computer and human memory. To end the war quickly, Starfleet has ordered an all-out assault on the Lysians. The *Enterprise*'s mission calls for it to fly to the Lysian central command and destroy it.

As the *Enterprise* enters Lysian territory, a warship attacks, but the *Enterprise* easily obliterates it. This troubles Picard. How could the Federation be threatened by such an inferior foe? Several hours later, when the *Enterprise* arrives at the Lysian central command, Data reports no defensive systems of any consequence. Picard refuses to fire on the center. Commander MacDuff tries to take control of the ship, but Riker and Worf stop him. In later discussions with the Lysians, Picard learns that MacDuff is actually part of a race—called "Sartaaran"—who have been battling the Lysians for decades. MacDuff hoped to use the superior firepower of the *Enterprise* to win the war finally.

PLOT OVERSIGHTS

• At the very beginning of the show, Troi beats Data at a game of chess. *Troi* beats Data? *Troi?* To lend credence to this unbelievable juxtaposition, the creators have Troi say, "Chess isn't just a game of plays and gambits, it's a game of intuition." *Chess* is a game of intuition? Ever try playing "intuitively" with a chess computer program? It will slaughter you in no time flat. Considering that Data is about a bijillion times more powerful than present-day desktop computers and that present-day chess programs are really tough, is it even remotely believable that Troi could beat Data at this game? There is no way Data would not have seen the checkmate coming. Then again, maybe Troi made Data play on a "below novice" setting.

• After the first encounter with the Lysians, Picard tells MacDuff his doubts about their mission. The fact that the Federation greatly outmatches the Lysians troubles Picard. Then, at the end of the show, Picard seems to indicate that the Lysians and the Sartaaran have approximately the same level of weapons technology. If the Sartaaran are at that level, how could MacDuff so easily overcome the shields of the *Enterprise*? That act implied that the Sartaaran were far more advanced than the Federation. In addition, the rest of the episode gives us several hints that the Sartaaran are very powerful: MacDuff *selectively* erases the memory of every crew member on the ship; he blocks files in the main computer and rewrites the mission logs to his specifications; he even tampers with Data, precisely shutting down certain sections. At the end of the show, Riker expresses it best when he says, "With all the power that MacDuff had to alter our brain chemistry [and] manipulate the computers, it's hard to believe he needed the *Enterprise*." Very well said,

Will.

EQUIPMENT ODDITIES

• As Data and La Forge try to access files in the main computer, the camera pans across the center island in Engineering. The shot temporarily provides a view of the same workstation screen mentioned in Equipment Oddities for "The Masterpiece Society." The control panels are on the move again. Now it looks like someone took the control panel that was at the base of the screen and moved it under the built-in panel to the right of the screen! Are these things like remote controls you can stick anywhere you want? Come to think of it, that would be great! Everybody knows how much guys like remotes.

CONTINUITY AND PRODUCTION PROBLEMS

• At one point Picard calls MacDuff to the ready room and expresses his concern over the mission. After MacDuff leaves, Picard walks over and looks out his window. A reverse-angle shot shows the outside of the ship and Picard gazing into space. Unfortunately, the reflection of the stars is missing from the window. In the episodes "Best of Both Worlds," Part 2 and "Darmok," the ready room window reflected whatever Picard was looking at.

TRIVIA ANSWERS

1. The Cliffs of Heaven on Sumico IV.
2. Ten.

POWER PLAY

Star Dates: 45571.2-45572.1

Responding to a weak distress call, the *Enterprise* drops into orbit around a reportedly uninhabited moon. The call comes from the USS *Essex*, a ship that disappeared more than two centuries ago. Picard decides to investigate when Troi senses life. Since the intense magnetic storms that rage on the moon rule out using the transporter, Riker, Data, and Troi take a shuttle to the surface. Unfortunately, the shuttle loses power as it flies through the atmosphere. Shortly afterward, it crashes. With Picard's permission, O'Brien risks a trip in the transporter and manages to get to the surface with a pattern enhancer. This device allows the *Enterprise* to beam the away team back, but not before small points of light enter Data, Troi, and O'Brien.

After returning to the bridge, Data, Troi, and O'Brien try to commandeer the *Enterprise*. They fail and are forced to settle for taking hostages in Ten-Forward. During the standoff, Picard swaps himself for the hostages in need of medical attention. Troi then introduces herself as Bryce Shumar,

Trivia Questions

1. What did O'Brien name his daughter?

2. What was the designation of the *Essex*?

captain of the *Essex*. She claims that she and two other bridge officers became disembodied spirits two hundred years ago when their ship crashed on the moon. Troi demands that the *Enterprise* take them to the south pole of the moon and retrieve their remains. She claims this will allow them to rest. Eventually Picard complies and takes Troi, Data, and O'Brien to a cargo bay so O'Brien can beam their remains to the ship. Unexpectedly, O'Brien beams up a group of spirit "prisoners." Troi explains that they are really convicted felons, separated from their bodies and left to drift in the electrical storms on the moon. At this point the bridge crew releases a field of energy similar to the one on the moon, trapping all of the spirits. Picard threatens to release the cargo bay hatch—and blow everyone out into space—if the spirits do not release Troi, Data, and O'Brien. Faced with no other choice, they comply and the entire colony of felons is beamed back to the moon.

GREAT MOMENTS

*W*hen Data, Troi, and O'Brien try to take over the Enterprise, the bridge crew responds exactly as they should. In other episodes, such as "The Hunted" and "Brothers," bridge security and protection of the command chain always seemed wimpy. But in this episode, they aren't. As soon as Riker recognizes Data's attempt to commandeer the ship, Riker kills all the power to the workstations on the bridge with a few simple words. When the felons head for Engineering, Riker restores everything, and the remaining bridge crew starts to work. Moments later, they stop Data, Troi, and O'Brien from getting to Engineering. This seems exactly right. This is, after all, the flagship of the Federation. Shouldn't it have this type of very efficient methodology for dealing with attempts to commandeer the Enterprise?

GREAT LINES

"Yeah, pretty sure that's broken."— Riker, nodding to his arm after the crash-landing in the shuttle (doing his John Wayne impersonation).

PLOT OVERSIGHTS

• During one rescue attempt, La Forge and Ro climb into an access tube and situate themselves directly above Ten-Forward. While they settle in, they discuss their strategy. Once they are in place, La Forge hits his communicator and begins whispering to the bridge. Why is La Forge whispering? He talks at medium volume the entire time they set up the equipment. If he was worried that the conspirators in Ten-Forward would hear him, wouldn't he whisper the entire time he was in the access tube?

• At the end of the show, the spirits release Troi, Data, and O'Brien because Picard threatens to detonate the cargo bay hatch. Picard claims this will kill all the spirits when everything in the cargo bay is blown into space. In other words, the spirits need an oxygen environment to live? Troi says that the prisoners were brought to this moon and separated from their bodies. Since all the mechanisms for metabolizing oxygen are found in the physical body, does it seem likely that these spirits require oxygen for survival?

EQUIPMENT ODDITIES

• During the shuttle craft trip down to the planet, Troi sits in the back bench seat. The bench seat butts up against a wall. After the crash, Riker blows an escape hatch from the *back* end of the shuttle, and they climb out. Evidently Starfleet designers put the escape hatch behind a wall that is blocked by a bench seat. Does this seems like a reasonable location for an escape hatch?

• Just after Troi, Data, and O'Brien leave the bridge, Worf traps them in a turbolift. O'Brien helps them escape by accessing the main computer. How does he access the computer? He uses the panel on the *inside* of the turbolift to the left of the door! As the great Yogi Berra said, "It's déjà vu all over again." As I explain in the review of "Brothers," during the first four and one half seasons of *Star Trek: The Next Generation*—filled with scenes of the crew entering and exiting turbolifts—there has never been a control panel on the inside of a turbolift to the left of the doors. However, since O'Brien needed computer access while in a turbolift, someone decided that for this one scene, for this one show, the turbolifts would get a new panel to the *left* of the doors!

• Shortly after Troi, Data, and O'Brien take hostages in Ten-Forward, Picard tries to negotiate with Troi, Data, and O'Brien. He begins by saying, "Ten-Forward, this is Captain Picard." After listening to Picard for a few minutes, Troi tells Data and O'Brien what the captain is trying to accomplish. She talks as if Picard cannot hear them. Then Data tries to pick a fight with Worf. Afterward, Picard tries to open a dialogue again by saying, "Please respond, Ten-Forward. Are there any members of my crew who require medical assistance?" This time Troi talks, and evidently Picard can hear her. What's the difference? What indication does Troi give the computer that some of her statements are meant for her fellow conspirators and others are meant for Picard?

TRIVIA ANSWERS
1. Molly.
2. NCC 173.

ETHICS

Star Date: 45587.3

While investigating a chemical leak, Worf is injured by a falling container. It crushes seven vertebrae at the base of his spine and leaves him paralyzed from the waist down. A neural specialist named "Toby Russell" from Starfleet joins the *Enterprise* to assist Dr. Crusher. Russell brings an experimental device she believes might help Worf recover. It can scan the DNA of an organ and create an entirely new replacement. Russell suggests using the machine to create a new spinal cord for Worf. When Crusher realizes that the machine has never been used on a humanoid before, she balks. Crusher wants to work with conventional therapy rather than try an experimental cure. If they tried the machine and it failed, Worf would die.

A short time after learning of his paralysis, Worf calls for Riker. In accordance with Klingon tradition, he asks Riker to help him commit suicide. Although shocked by Worf's request, Riker takes time to consider it. Meanwhile, Crusher attempts to persuade Worf to use a standard method of recovery, but Worf refuses when

he hears that the method can restore only a portion of his mobility. Against Crusher's wishes, Russell then steps in and offers her machine to Worf. Picard also votes for the experimental surgery. Picard understands that Worf will kill himself unless he can regain the use of his legs. Eventually, Riker refuses to help Worf kill himself, correctly pointing out that Klingon tradition dictates that the "honor" of bringing the injured a ceremonial knife belongs to the eldest son. Worf calls for his son, but instead of committing suicide, he chooses the dangerous operation and a chance for full recovery. Unfortunately, Worf dies at the end of the operation. Later, however, he comes back to life.

Trivia Questions

1. The crisis with the transport ship *Denver* delayed the *Enterprise*'s survey of which sector?

2. When did Dr. Russell begin manually scanning Worf's ganglia?

RUMINATIONS

*J**ust before Worf goes into surgery, he asks Troi to care for his son if he should die. Troi seems stunned by the request but claims she is honored and agrees. At this point, the medical ensign comes in to prep Worf for the operation, and Troi leaves. Although the episode doesn't tell us where Troi goes, I have* a pretty good idea. Troi immediately walks into Crusher's office, grabs the chief medical officer of the Enterprise by the neck, hoists her to her feet, yanks her to within inches of her own face, and says with gritted teeth, "Worf had better come through this operation alive because if he doesn't I'm going to be stuck with that Marclosian wind-devil that he calls his son." Troi then finishes her explanation by shaking Crusher silly and shouting, "Do you understand?" At least ... that's a scene I'd like to see.

PLOT OVERSIGHTS

• During his first visit with Worf, Riker makes small talk by commenting that Worf looks pretty good tor someone who's been eating sick bay food for three days. How can institutional food still have a stigma in the twenty-fourth century? Everything is replicated. Do the food terminals in sick bay not work as well as those on the rest of the ship? Or, have the programmers of the replicators decided to keep the stigma alive by making the food terminals in sick bay not function quite as well as the others?

• When Worf dies at the end of the operation, Dr. Crusher goes to some extreme measures to try to revive him. She even uses a drug that under normal circumstances would kill him. Yet even after being taken completely off life support and giving flatline readouts on all the medical displays, Worf manages to come back to life! Dr. Crusher makes a comment that Worf must have a "backup for his synaptic functions." Even if Worf had a backup for his synaptic functions, wouldn't the lethal drug Crusher administered have killed that, too? Also, why didn't the medical displays show the activity of his synaptic backup? And why didn't Worf's backup show up on a medical scan? Dr. Crusher described the rest of Worf's physiology in great detail at the beginning of the show.

CONTINUITY AND PRODUCTION PROBLEMS

• When the barrel falls on Worf, it ends up near his foot. Another barrel follows it down, and when it hits the floor, the top pops off. Yet in the next shot, La Forge runs up and pushes a barrel away from Worf's *side*. Also, the second barrel suddenly has its top back on.

TRIVIA ANSWERS

1. Sector 37628.
2. At 10:14 hours. (The ensign who assists in Worf's operation says, "Cerebral cortex placed on life support at 08:31 hours. Three hours, twenty-six minutes remaining until onset of primary brain dysfunction." When Dr. Russell begins scanning the ganglia manually, the ensign says, "One hour, forty-three minutes until primary brain dysfunction." Using simple addition, 08:31 plus 3:26 means primary brain dysfunction will occur at 11:57. Taking that time and subtracting 1:43 yields 10:14 hours.)

THE OUTCAST

The *Enterprise* responds to a call for help from an androgynous race called the J'naii. (If the terminology used by the episode is physiologically correct, a member of the race would be both structurally and functionally male and female.) The J'naii have asked for assistance in locating one of their shuttles. It mysteriously disappeared, and the J'naii have been unable to find it. Once the *Enterprise* nears the last known location of the shuttle, Data launches a probe. The probe also disappears. After further research, the crew and the J'naii conclude that a section of "null space" swallowed both the J'naii shuttle and the probe. Null space absorbs electromagnetic energy from anything that enters it. It also bends energy around its surface, making it naturally cloaked.

Riker and a J'naii named "Soren" map the null space in an *Enterprise* shuttle using phasers. They calculate the edge of the void by noting where the phaser beam stops. Soren is injured when the shuttle clips the edge of the null space and loses an engine, but he/she recovers quickly.

Trivia Questions

1. What is the name of the shuttle used by Riker and Soren?

2. When was the Federation founded?

Afterward, Soren tells Riker that he/she finds him attractive. He/she explains that occasionally J'naii have tendencies toward maleness or femaleness. Soren tends toward female. The J'naii culture looks on these tendencies as deviant behavior and routinely uses "psychotectic" treatments to cure the individuals who manifest them.

After Riker and Soren rescue the J'naii trapped in the null space, Soren is arrested for manifesting gender. Riker tries to save Soren by claiming full responsibility, but Soren refuses to live in hiding any longer. He/she is lead away for treatment. That evening, Riker and Worf try to rescue Soren, but he/she refuses to go with them. Soren no longer has any feminine tendencies. He/she apologizes for what he/she did and leaves.

PLOT OVERSIGHTS

• When Riker and Soren discuss mating, Soren says both persons in a J'naii couple inseminate a fibrous husk, which then serves as an incubator. The dialogue seems to indicate that the mixing of these seminal fluids replaces the function of the sperm and the egg in gender-separate races. (I do not wish to be indelicate, but it is necessary to examine the line of reasoning that the dialogue evokes and follow it through to its probable conclusion.) My question is: What sort of genitalia would Soren have?

If Soren can inseminate a husk, she probably has an "inseminator." This makes sense, actually. Human androgynous children usually have external male genitalia. The presence of the "Y" chromosome ensures this—even though their multiple "X" chromosomes may create *internal* female genitalia as well. Has Riker thought this through? He acts like he is ready to spend the rest of his life with Soren. Yet I never pictured him as a person willing to marry a small-breasted boy.

• Isn't Picard responsible for the actions of his crew? After Soren's arrest, Riker discusses his options with Picard. Picard tells him that interfering will be a violation of the Prime Directive. Near the end of the meeting, Picard lightly warns Riker not to do anything to jeopardize his career. Riker and Worf then go to the planet, beat up two J'naii, and try to hustle Soren back to the *Enterprise.*

Clearly, Picard knew Riker would try to rescue Soren. Clearly, Picard knew that was a violation of Starfleet code, but he quietly lets Riker proceed. Picard makes no effort to stop him and offers no rebuke after the attempt fails. On the other hand, Picard *severely* reprimands Worf in the episode "Reunion" when Worf—acting *within* the bounds of Klingon culture—departs from the *Enterprise* and kills Duras. Doesn't this seem backward?

CONTINUITY AND PRODUCTION PROBLEMS

• Pointing out this next problem easily qualifies for the cheapest shot in the book. When Riker and Soren have lunch, they discuss gender over bowls of split-pea soup. From one camera angle, Soren lifts a spoonful to her mouth. Soup drips to her bowl. When the camera angle changes, the spoon suddenly quits dripping! (It's a dirty job, but someone's got to do it.)

TRIVIA ANSWERS

1. *Magellan.* (Look closely near the front of the shuttle when Riker and Soren walk around the outside of it.)
2. In 2161.

CAUSE AND EFFECT

Star Date: 45852.1, 45852.1, 45852.1, 45852.1

When the bridge crew cannot regain control of a badly damaged *Enterprise*, Picard gives the order to abandon ship. Seconds later, the *Enterprise* explodes.

As the *Enterprise* maps the Typhon Expanse, a feeling of déjà vu haunts Dr. Crusher. That night, she hears voices in her quarters. The next morning, a time-space distortion appears near the ship. The *Enterprise* tries to back away, but all of the main power systems fail. A spaceship emerges from the distortion, on a collision course with the *Enterprise*. Riker suggests decompressing the main shuttle bay to move the *Enterprise* out of the way, but Picard decides to try the tractor beam instead.

The tractor beam helps some, but not enough. The other ship impacts the *Enterprise*'s starboard warp drive engine, causing massive damage. When the bridge crew cannot regain control, Picard gives the order to abandon ship. Seconds later, the *Enterprise* explodes.

The *Enterprise* is caught in a fragment of time, started by the massive explosion near the time-space dis-

> **Trivia Questions**
>
> 1. What card did Riker need to complete his straight in the poker game?
>
> 2. How many couples were engaged in romantic encounters in the echoes from previous loops?

tortion. Each time through the "temporal causality" loop, the crew's feelings of déjà vu grow stronger. During one of the loops, Crusher manages to record the voices in her quarters. Data analyzes the recording and overhears Picard giving the order to abandon ship. From this, the crew realizes they are in a loop and must avoid the next explosion to break free. La Forge and Data devise a way to send a one-word message into the next loop. This time, just before the ship explodes, Data transmits the word "three." At the end of the next loop, Data suddenly realizes "three" could stand for the insignia rank of Riker. (Riker has three pips on his collar.) Data immediately takes Riker's suggestion to decompress the main shuttle bay. The *Enterprise* moves away from the other ship, the time-space distortion disappears, and the loop ceases.

GREAT MOMENTS

*T*he special-effects people did a great job on the explosion of the Enterprise. *Normally, when a ship explodes, the devastation instantly* engulfs the ship. It looks like footage of the explosion is superimposed on the footage of the model. Models are, after all, very expensive to build. It doesn't pay to blow them up! In this episode, however, the special-effects technicians went to the extra step of building a slightly cruder model of the Enterprise so they could blow it up. They expertly matched the positions of the finished model and the crude model during the explosion scene, and the overall effect works very well.

PLOT OVERSIGHTS

• Each time through the loop, the crew forgets what happened in the previous loop. To explain this, La Forge says they are stuck in a specific fragment of time. Then he adds, "Every time the loop begins again, everything resets itself and starts all over." This "resetting" includes the ship's chronometers. The obvious explanation for this is that the explosion of the Enterprise knocks it backward in time. The crew can't remember the events of the loop because they haven't happened yet. However, at the end of the show, Worf checks with the nearest starbase and discovers that the Enterprise has been stuck in the loop for more than seventeen days. If that's true, the crew hasn't been repeating the same fragment of time. If they were repeating the same fragment of time, the ship's chronometer would line up with the starbase's chronometer, since—in essence—the entire universe would get reset at the beginning of each loop. Instead, the

crew of the Enterprise must have been repeating the same actions, and somehow everything on the ship—including the crew's memories and the ship's chronometers—got reset at the beginning of each loop. This is quite a feat, considering the loop doesn't restart until after the explosion. That means that something or someone has to put the entire ship back together and bring everyone back to life!

• The episode never adequately explains where the other ship came from. At the end of the show—just after Picard learns that they have been in the loop for seventeen days—the crew discovers that the other ship is an eighty-year-old Starfleet vessel called the USS Bozeman. When Picard asks the captain of the Bozeman if he realizes what has happened, the captain of the Bozeman claims that his sensors detected a temporal distortion. Then the Enterprise appeared and they nearly collided. In response, Picard explains that the Enterprise has been caught in temporal causality loop. Picard suggests that the same thing has happened to the Bozeman.

Does Picard mean to imply that the Bozeman has been caught in a loop for eighty years? If so, how did the Bozeman get started with its loop? According to La Forge, the Enterprise began its loop when the ship exploded. The captain of the Bozeman made no mention of any explosion before seeing the Enterprise. He simply said the time-space distortion appeared and was followed by the Enterprise.

The *Bozeman could have* jumped forward in time eighty years when it entered the time-space distortion. It *could have* then exited the distortion and collided with the *Enterprise.* That would explain the lack of explosion for the *Bozeman.* It would also explain how the *Bozeman* ended up in an area of space described by Picard as "unexplored," since time-space distortions can fling a ship across space as well as time. If *that's* true, however, Picard should be treating the *Bozeman* the same way he treated the *Enterprise*-C in "Yesterday's *Enterprise.*" Just after the *Enterprise*-C came through the temporal rift, Picard realized that disclosing information to the crew of the *Enterprise*-C could fundamentally alter history if the *Enterprise*-C ever returned to its own time. He stringently warned Riker against revealing anything to the crew of the *Enterprise*-C. In "Cause and Effect," Picard's behavior is quite the opposite. He immedi-

ately invites the captain aboard for a conference. (Personally, I think the creators should have tied up these loose ends. They had the time to do it. After all, they showed mostly the same sequence of events *four* times in this episode.)

CONTINUITY AND PRODUCTION PROBLEMS

• The previews for this episode show a display that differs from the one shown in the actual episode. At one point in the show, Data runs a level 2 diagnostic on the warp subsystems. This display shows a series of medium-size 3's. The preview for the episode uses a clip of this scene, but in the preview the display shows *large* 3's.

TRIVIA ANSWERS

1. A nine. (Data dealt Riker an eight, a ten, a jack, and a seven.)
2. Five.

THE FIRST DUTY

The *Enterprise* travels to Earth so Picard can give the commencement address at Starfleet Academy. As part of the commencement exercises, Nova Squadron—a precision flying team that includes Wesley Crusher—will provide a demonstration of its championship skills. While en route to Earth, Picard receives a message from Admiral Brand. Nova Squadron has had an accident, destroying all five of the ships. One pilot, a cadet named "Joshua Albert," died. The others sustained injuries.

During the inquiry that follows, several disturbing discrepancies surface. The group's navigator, Cadet Hajar, has only a feeble explanation why Nova Squadron strayed two thousand kilometers from its flight plan. The leader of the group, Cadet Locarno, suddenly reveals that Cadet Albert had become sloppy in his flight skills. Locarno claims the accident was Albert's fault. The following day, Wesley narrates the fragmentary evidence from his badly damaged flight recorder. He confirms Locarno's version of the mishap. Admiral Brand's assistant then displays a visual recording from a navigational satellite. It contradicts Wesley's testimony.

Back on the *Enterprise*, Data and La Forge investigate the evidence. They find an oddity in Wesley's flight recorder. Just prior to the accident, Wesley opened a maintenance coolant valve. Picard suddenly understands what happened. Nova Squadron was trying to perform the Kolvoord Maneuver, a spectacular and dangerous stunt banned over a hundred years ago. Picard gives Wesley an ultimatum: Tell the truth, or Picard will bring his suspicions to the Board of Inquiry. The next day, Wesley confesses. Locarno is expelled, the others have their credits for their current year revoked, and an official reprimand is placed on their permanent records.

PLOT OVERSIGHTS

• This episode answers an interesting question: How old is Picard? When talking with the gardener, Picard claims to have graduated in "the Class of '27." Using this piece of in-

Trivia Questions

1. What navigational satellite file proves the cadets are lying?

2. What is Cadet Hajar's first name?

formation and a few others from previous episodes, we can finally answer this burning question. The episode "Encounter at Farpoint," Part 2 establishes that Data graduated in the Class of '78. In "Redemption II," Data states that he has had twenty-six years of experience in Starfleet. For the moment, suppose that Data believes his experience with Starfleet began with his entrance into Starfleet Academy. In "Datalore," Data tells Lore that he spent four years at the academy. That means twenty-two years have elapsed since Data's graduation. Since Data graduated with the Class of '78 and twenty-two years have elapsed, this season of Star Trek: The Next Generation must be happening somewhere around the year '00. (I haven't included the first two digits because that would be mere speculation.) Now if Picard graduated in the Class of '27, seventy-three years have elapsed since his graduation. If Picard was twenty at the time, he must be over ninety years old!!! (This all makes a very small amount of sense until you remember that Data quoted the year in the episode "The Neutral Zone" as A.D. 2364.) Evidently something is wrong in one of these figures.

• Why is Picard so upset over Wesley's omissions in his testimony? Trying to get Wesley to crack, Picard pontificates about the "first duty" of a Starfleet officer: TRUTH! But wait: Isn't this the same Picard who flings aside his oath to the Prime Directive whenever he judges it inconvenient? When Starfleet officers swear to uphold the Prime Directive, does the ceremony include an exception for when a Starfleet officer would rather not? The point is this: If Picard can cast off an oath to a foundational principle such as the Prime Directive when situations become difficult, shouldn't he allow Wesley the same latitude with this "first duty" of Starfleet officers? After all, Wesley's confession could have gotten the entire flight team kicked out of the academy, and it almost did. Wouldn't that consequence provide enough reason to "bend the truth" a little? (I trust you can hear the satiric edge in these words.)

• Starfleet Academy banned the Kolvoord Maneuver a hundred years ago due to a training accident. Yet Locarno convinces Nova Squadron to try it. What was he trying to accomplish? Did he think Starfleet wouldn't reprimand him if the maneuver was successful? A banned maneuver is a banned maneuver. Starfleet doesn't base its punishments on the outcome. Or does it? But Locarno's actions are believable. College seniors can do strange things.

EQUIPMENT ODDITIES

• The graphics of the ships in formation and the visuals from Wesley's flight recorder show Wesley on the left wing of a starting formation and Albert on Wesley's starboard quarter. But in testimony, Wesley claims he was on the right wing and Albert was on his port quarter.

• The dormitory doors at Starfleet Academy have regular door handles and hinges, yet every time someone opens one, the door gives a little "erp erp" sound. If the doors are human-powered, doesn't it seem like a waste of energy to have them "erping" every time they are opened?

CONTINUITY AND PRODUCTION PROBLEMS

• In one scene, Picard has a long talk with the Starfleet Academy groundskeeper about Nova Squadron. Each close-up of Picard's face shows his breath escaping as if cooled by the morning air. However, the groundskeeper's breath doesn't show in his close-ups. Evidently some time elapsed between shooting Picard's footage and shooting the groundskeeper's footage. Either that or the groundskeeper is part lizard (i.e., he's cold-blooded).

TRIVIA ANSWERS

1. Saturn Navcon File 6-379.
2. Jean. (Locarno refers to it when trying to convince Wesley not to tell the truth.)

COST OF LIVING

Star Date: 45733.6

As the show opens, the *Enterprise* destroys a stray asteroid that threatens to collide with a planet. Before the *Enterprise* can leave the area, however, the "metal parasites" that inhabited the asteroid enter the ship. Meanwhile, in Troi's office, Worf and his son, Alexander, argue over domestic duties. Troi pacifies the situation by suggesting that they draw up a contract clearly defining each person's responsibility. After Worf and Alexander leave, Troi learns that her mother, Lwaxana, has just beamed aboard. Later, in Ten-Forward, Lwaxana shocks Troi by revealing that she has chosen the *Enterprise* as the location for her wedding to a man she has never met. At this point, Worf and Alexander appear, still arguing over the contents of the contract. Lwaxana finds the whole idea of a contract ghastly but takes an immediate liking to Alexander.

The next day, when Alexander should be meeting with Troi, Lwaxana whisks him off to the holodeck. She treats him to a mud bath at the Parralex Colony, a society of free-thinkers. Troi resents her mother's intrusion. She feels Lwaxana is undermining her efforts to teach Alexander some responsibility. Meanwhile, random problems erupt as the metal parasites eat the ship's "nitrium," a metal used in virtually every subsystem. At the same time, Lwaxana's husband-to-be joins the ship. He is a dour-looking aristocrat named "Campio." Protocol Minister "Erko" accompanies him. Almost immediately, friction develops between Lwaxana and Erko. Eventually the crew rids the *Enterprise* of the metal parasites, and the wedding proceeds. When Lwaxana shows up naked—in typical Betazoid style—Erko quickly hustles Campio out of the room, pronouncing the whole thing scandalous.

GREAT LINES

"Nothing would please me more than to give away Mrs. Troi."--Picard agreeing to hold the wedding on the *Enterprise* and act as "father of the bride."

PLOT OVERSIGHTS
• Does it strike anyone odd that

Troi—a person who has never had children and can't even get along with her own mother—is providing parenting advice for Worf?

• During Lwaxana and Alexander's first mud bath, a dancer entertains them. She writhes about nude, except for three strategically placed decorations. Are the creators of this episode purporting that this is acceptable entertainment for a young boy?

• When Lwaxana and Alexander prepare to leave for their second mud bath, Campio insists that she stay with him. Protocol Minister Erko has pronounced it time to discuss the prenuptial arrangements. Lwaxana continues to leave, and Campio turns to Troi for help. "Counselor Troi, have you no influence?" Campio asks. Troi responds with, "Ha!" *Ha?* Lwaxana has told Troi that this man is royalty, and Troi responds to a direct question with "Ha!"? Obviously the situation is frustrating for Troi, but common respect would dictate an answer other than "Ha!"

• After La Forge and Data discover the metal parasites, Data claims the sensors cannot detect the metal parasites. He also suggests a strategy to slow them down, but La Forge comments, "The problem is finding them." Why don't they scan the ship for nitrium, wait a few seconds, and scan the ship again? Wouldn't the parasites be wherever nitrium is disappearing?

• The crew rids the *Enterprise* of the metal parasites by flying to an asteroid field rich in nitrium and coaxing them to leave the ship. Just be-

fore the *Enterprise* makes a mad dash to this field, Campio and Erco board the ship. After Data successfully cleans the *Enterprise* of the bugs, the wedding proceeds. There is no mention that Campio departed and rejoined the ship later. Did Picard drag Campio and Erco all the way to the asteroid field with them? During the trip, life support became tenuous, and people started passing out. In addition, the structural integrity of the dilithium chamber decayed, and the entire ship almost exploded. Picard knew the danger involved with the parasites before the trip began, and he allowed a person of royalty to stay aboard anyway?

CONTINUITY AND PRODUCTION PROBLEMS

• As the *Enterprise* prepares to fly back to the asteroid field, Picard and Data board a turbolift for the main bridge. During this entire scene in the turbolift—shot from multiple camera angles—Picard has only *three* pips on his collar. That gives him the rank of commander! Thankfully, as soon as Picard walks off the turbolift, he's back to four pips on his collar and the rank of captain.

TRIVIA ANSWERS

1. Starboard. (The reflections of the stars streak from right to left in Lwaxana's mirror. That means the stars are actually streaking from left to right in her window, which puts the front of the ship to the left of the window and her quarters on the starboard side of the ship.)
2. Twenty-eight percent.

THE PERFECT MATE

Star Dates: 45761.3-45766.1

The *Enterprise* hosts a peace conference and trade negotiations between the planets Krios and Valt Minor. After beaming Kriosian Ambassador Briam and his cargo aboard, Picard sets course for the conference location. On the way, the *Enterprise* rescues two Ferengi from an exploding shuttle. A short time later, one of the Ferengi sneaks into Cargo Bay 1 and begins examining Briam's property—a large golden egg-shaped object supported by energy beams. When a team from Security arrives and startles the Ferengi, he accidentally breaks one of the supporting energy beams. The egg-shaped object floats to the ground, its outside dissolves, and a beautiful woman emerges. Her name is "Kamala." She is a gift for Chancellor Alrik of Valt Minor. Centuries ago, two brothers' mutual desire for the same beautiful woman began the war between the planets. Kamala hopes to end it. She is an "empathic metamorph," a woman capable of sensing the emotional needs of men and becoming whatever they desire. The moment she bonds with

> **Trivia Questions**
>
> 1. Where did Picard send the Ferengi after they injured Ambassador Briam?
>
> 2. When was Kamala separated from her parents?

Alrik, she will imprint his ideal of the perfect mate on herself, to serve him the rest of his life.

The Ferengi view Kamala as valuable property. They try to bribe Briam and acquire Kamala. When Briam refuses the offer, a scuffle ensues and Briam is injured. Under Kamala's urging, Picard assumes the role of representative for the Kriosians. She tutors him in the ceremonies involved and briefs him on the trade negotiations. During their time together, Kamala grows to love the person she becomes when she is with Picard. Just before the ceremony with Alrik, Kamala imprints Picard's ideal of the perfect mate on herself. Her heightened sense of duty leads her to marry Alrik anyway, however, while Picard looks on.

PLOT OVERSIGHTS

• At the beginning of the episode, Briam asks Picard to declare Cargo Bay 1 off-limits. The ambassador indicates that the cargo is very precious and irreplaceable. Picard agrees to do this. Yet after the Ferengi come on board, one of them simply waltzes into the cargo bay, apparently without resistance. Why didn't Picard station a guard outside the cargo bay or at least lock the door? True, Worf detects the intrusion of the Ferengi, but by the time the team from Security gets there, the Ferengi has dragged over several barrels to use as a platform. In other words, he had plenty of time to damage the cargo if he had wanted to.

EQUIPMENT ODDITIES

• Under Kamala's instruction, Picard learns to play a set of Kriosian xylophones. The four instruments are supposedly arranged according to tradition. Kriosian musicians must have odd wiring in their brains. When Picard plays the lower-right-hand xylophone, the notes get lower as he moves to the right. However when Picard plays one of the center xylophones, the notes get *higher* as he moves to the right. In other words, to play a scale on the center xylophone, the musician must move from left to right, but to play a scale on a lower xylophone, the musician moves from right to left. This would be very confusing.

CONTINUITY AND PRODUCTION PROBLEMS

• At their first meeting, Picard and Alrik have an extended conversation in the observation lounge. The scene uses two camera angles, one featuring Picard and the other, Alrik. In the shot showing Picard, the stars in the observation window drift slowly from right to left. Yet in the shot showing Alrik, the stars remain still.

• During the last scene of the show, Picard says good-bye to Ambassador Briam. Briam then beams off the *Enterprise* to return to Krios. The scene then cuts to footage of the *Enterprise* and a smaller ship flying off in different directions. The footage comes from the end of "Suddenly Human," and the ship is Talarian, not Kriosian.

TRIVIA ANSWERS
1. Starbase 117.
2. At age four.

IMAGINARY FRIEND

Star Date: 45852.1

When the *Enterprise* enters an unusual nebula formed around a neutron star, one of the energy-based aliens who inhabit the nebula enters the ship to investigate its energy sources. The alien eventually finds Clara Sutter, a lonely girl with only an imaginary friend named Isabella for companionship. The alien transforms herself into Isabella and, with Clara, explores life on the *Enterprise*. After a few days, Isabella becomes convinced that humans are unnecessarily cruel to their children and deserve to die. A short while later, more aliens arrive and begin feeding on the *Enterprise*'s shields. They intend to destroy the ship and absorb its energy.

Picard meets with Isabella and explains that the rules humans make for their children are solely for the children's safety. In this way, humans protect their children from harm. Isabella accepts this explanation and leaves, as do the other aliens.

RUMINATIONS

On the good side, this episode does carry the message that it is the responsibility of adults to provide a framework of boundaries for the protection of children. Unfortunately, the creators also purport that the future will see the continuing disintegration of the nuclear family (father, mother, children). La Forge gives a little speech about his disjointed childhood, bouncing from place to place, sometimes with his father, sometimes with his mother, and passes off this dysfunction as one "great adventure." In the same vein, Clara's father moves quickly from starship to starship, dragging Clara along. Since the creators make no mention of Clara's mother, presumably she is on another assignment somewhere else in the galaxy while her daughter struggles with her fractured existence.

CONTINUITY AND PRODUCTION PROBLEMS

• At the beginning of the show, as Troi interviews Clara about her imaginary friend, Clara states that Isabella has pierced ears. When Isabella materializes, her appearance exactly matches Clara's description, except that the actress who plays Isabella

Trivia Questions

1. What is the name of the nebula?

2. Name the occupations of La Forge's parents.

doesn't have pierced ears, or the holes have been covered with make-up.

1. FGC-47.
2. His father was an exozoologist; his mother, a command officer.

I BORG

While mapping a star system for possible colonization, the *Enterprise* intercepts an unknown transmission. When they investigate, the crew finds a badly damaged Borg scout ship (see "Q Who" and "The Best of Both Worlds," Part 1 and Part 2) on the surface of a moon. Only one of the five occupants is still alive, but just barely. Dr. Crusher immediately begins resuscitation efforts. After consideration, Picard allows her to beam the Borg into a detention cell on the *Enterprise* so she can continue her ministrations. Once they are on the ship, Crusher discovers that several of the Borg's biochips were damaged in the crash. Picard seizes the opportunity and orders La Forge to replicate new chips, complete with a computer virus to destroy the Borg collective when this Borg returns to it.

Gathering information on the biochips from the Borg gives La Forge a chance to discuss their different ways of life—the Borg's homogeny and the humans' individuality. In the process, La Forge becomes friends with "Hugh"—his name for the Borg—and Hugh, for the first time, achieves individuality. When Picard discovers Hugh's individuality, he scraps the mission, unwilling to use a sentient being as an instrument of destruction. Picard offers Hugh asylum, but Hugh refuses, knowing that the Borg would seek him out and destroy the *Enterprise*. Instead, Hugh returns to the crash site and waits for another Borg ship to arrive and reassimilate him into the collective.

Trivia Questions

1. What is Hugh's designation?

2. What is the mass of the Borg ship that comes for Hugh?

PLOT OVER-SIGHTS

• When recruiting an individual to write the "invasive" program that will destroy the Borg, Picard chooses La Forge. Doesn't this seem like an odd choice? Who is the resident computer programming expert? Isn't it Data? Of course, if Data wrote the program, he would be the one to do the research with the Borg, and he wouldn't get all mushy and name the Borg "Hugh." (I imagine the next encounter with the Borg will go something like, "We are Hugh. Resistance is futile.")

• The invasive program that will destroy the Borg turns out to be a picture. Supposedly it isn't possible to analyze the picture fully, so when Hugh attempts it he won't be able to, and his subconscious will continue to work on it. Then when Hugh is re-assimilated, the rest of the Borg will start working on it, and they won't be able to analyze the picture fully either, and finally they will all fall down because they are thinking so hard about this picture. *This will not work!* In the old days of personal computers (way back in the 1970s and early 1980s), most had BASIC built in. BASIC is an easy-to-learn programming language. Kids who knew a few lines of BASIC would get their yucks by going to a store with personal computers and typing at the ">" prompt:

```
>1 PRINT "I AM GOING CRAZY"
>2 GOTO 1
>RUN
```

In a flash, the computer screen would fill with "I AM GOING CRAZY," madly flickering as new lines scrolled onto the bottom and old lines popped off the top. Left alone, the computer would senselessly putter at this litany until a power failure or until its chips decayed. The computers of the twentieth century can't recognize when they are caught in an unproductive loop. That's why the creators chose this type of problem to confound the Borg. Evidently they believe that computers will never be able to recognize an unproductive loop. However, since the Borg are fully integrated with computers, they *must* have this ability. There are too many mathe-

matical conundrums with no final solutions. For instance, if one of the Borg tried to find the square root of two—a number for which there is no final solution because the digits after the decimal point appear to stretch on forever—will the entire Borg consciousness crash? Of course not! If the Borg have the ability to recognize this sort of unproductive loop and say "We've calculated this to one million decimal places. We think that's good enough," then they can recognize when they can't fully analyze a picture. (As my fellow nitpicker Darrin Hull said, "In other words, the *Enterprise* could have destroyed the Borg by simply showing them an M. C. Escher print?")

• After deciding to abandon the invasive program, Picard takes heart in the fact of Hugh's newfound independence. Picard wonders if this might be the most invasive program of all, the Borg encountering a moment when they feel Hugh's desire for self-identity. Haven't the Borg felt this concept of self-identity from many of the species they have assimilated? Isn't Picard a paragon of self-identity? Didn't he struggle to maintain his distinctiveness when the Borg assimilated him? If it didn't bother the Borg to experience Picard's desire for autonomy, does it seem likely that their reaction to Hugh will be any different?

• Just before beaming Hugh back to the surface to await the arrival of the Borg ship, Picard tells La Forge that the *Enterprise* will hang close to the sun to obscure their presence from the Borg's sensors. Why is he telling La Forge this in front of Hugh? The episode clearly states that as soon as the Borg hook Hugh back into their consciousness, they will know everything he knows. What good will it do to hide by the sun if your enemy knows you're there?

CHANGED PREMISES

• All of a sudden, at the start of this episode, Dr. Crusher becomes very benevolent with her Borg patient. She champions his cause. She balks at sending Hugh back with the invasion program. She asks for clarification on the term "total system failure," trying to make the point that they are contemplating destroying an entire race. Isn't this the same person who was drilling large phaser holes in the chests of the Borg during "The Best of Both Worlds," Part 2? Isn't she the same one who suggested using the Nanites to invade the Borg ship and destroy them? What's the difference between using Nanites and using a computer virus?

• Just before bringing the Borg on board the *Enterprise*, Picard instructs La Forge to isolate him from all subspace signals. Yet in "The Best of Both Worlds," Part 2, the crew couldn't do that to Picard, because Picard would die if they cut him off from the Borg collective consciousness.

The episode clearly established that the Borg consciousness was made up of a series of interactive signals that traveled in subspace. So why didn't Hugh die when they isolated him from the signals?

• In the original Borg episode, "Q Who," Q transports the *Enterprise* seven thousand light-years with a snap of his fingers. In this new location, the crew finds a world with great rips in the surface. "It is as though some great force just scooped all the machine elements off the face of the planet," Worf comments. A short time later, the Borg appear. Q identifies the Borg as the ultimate users, seeking only new technologies to improve themselves. Q says they are interested only in the technology on the *Enterprise*. They view it as something they can consume. Then in "The Best of Both Worlds," Part 1, the activities of the Borg change a little. Now they also assimilate people. They desire to add the human distinctiveness to themselves, so they convert Picard into a Borg. By the time "I Borg" comes along, assimilation is the main activity of the Borg.

TRIVIA ANSWERS
1. Third of five.
2. It is 2.5 million metric tons.

THE NEXT PHASE

Star Date: unknown

When La Forge and Ro Laren disappear while beaming back from assisting a badly damaged Romulan ship, Picard concludes that they are dead. In reality, the Romulans were conducting experiments with a new type of cloaking device that not only makes matter invisible but also puts it "out of phase" with normal matter. A surge in the damaged system during transport caught La Forge and Ro and made them cloaked. They discover this when they reappear on the *Enterprise*—but no one can see or hear them and they can walk through walls and doors.

When Data traces the transporter malfunction back to the damaged ship, the Romulans become concerned that Data will learn of their cloaking experiments. They decide to sabotage the emergency energy link between the *Enterprise* and their ship. In time, a distortion wave will build up in the *Enterprise*'s warp drive. When the *Enterprise* enters warp, it will explode. La Forge and Ro learn of the plan but are powerless to inform Picard. At the same time, their movements through the *Enterprise* create "chroniton field distortions." As Data decontaminates the affected area, La Forge discovers that the cleansing energy partially returns him to normal. He and Ro create increasingly larger distortions until the cleansing energy momentarily makes them visible. Data finally realizes what has happened and increases the level of cleansing energy until La Forge and Ro are completely decloaked—just in time for La Forge to alert the crew to the threat in the warp drive.

Trivia Questions

1. What was displayed on Crusher's tabletop terminal when she was filling out La Forge and Ro's death certificates?

2. In how many different cultures did Data research funerary customs?

GREAT MOMENTS

T he special-effects people worked overtime on this episode, with wondrous results. My favorite happens in Engineering. La Forge tries to make Data aware of his presence by walking through the center island in Engineering and creating more chroniton field distortions. Each time, the top of the work area shows La Forge's reflection before and during his pass through the table. The effect is quite lovely.

GREAT LINES

"But ... my uniform ... my visor ... are you saying I'm some blind ghost with clothes?"—La Forge, incredulously responding to Ro's assertion that they are dead.

PLOT OVERSIGHTS

• Some plot oversights are unavoidable. In this episode, La Forge and Ro supposedly get phased so they can pass through normal matter such as doors, tables, and walls. Interestingly, the floors seem to be perfectly solid, however! Of course, there would be no show—or at least a much more expensive show—if the floors weren't solid. On the other hand, several gaffes concerning La Forge and Ro's ability to pass through normal matter were avoidable. La Forge sits on a transporter pad. Ro touches her navigator's chair and terminal on the bridge. La Forge and Ro sit on benches in a shuttle as it travels to the Romulan ship. One of the Romulans—also phased in the accident—sits in a chair. Later, on the *Enterprise*, when the phased Romulan shoots Ro in the leg, she falls down, and a plant in front of her jiggles. Finally, La Forge and Ro dive behind a couch, and a cluster of balloons dance from the air disturbance. If La Forge and Ro can really pass through normal matter, why did these events happen?

• Of course, the plot can't survive some of the other problems of being truly out of phase with normal matter. At the end of the show, La Forge comments that he hasn't eaten in two days. That makes sense: He couldn't pick up any food. Along the same line, how can his lungs absorb normal oxygen? Would he and Ro suffocate shortly after being phased? And even if they didn't, how can they hear the conversations of the other crew members? Hearing comes from the impact of waves of air on the eardrum. Wouldn't the normal air molecules pass right through their eardrums, leaving them deaf?

TRIVIA ANSWERS

1. Her personal appointment calendar.
2. More than five thousand.

★ THE INNER LIGHT

Star Date: 45999.1

As the *Enterprise* approaches, a probe of unknown origin emits an energy stream toward the ship. Picard immediately reacts, collapsing unconscious to the floor. When he opens his eyes, a concerned woman stands over him. No longer on the *Enterprise*, Picard inhabits a home with adobelike walls. Trying to find out how he arrived in this place, Picard spends the rest of the afternoon and early evening walking through the community and the hills beyond. As night comes, he returns to the house and learns that it is his house and the woman is his wife. Meanwhile, on the *Enterprise*, the crew works to terminate the link between the probe and Picard. Unfortunately, when they try to interrupt the energy beam, Picard goes into a seizure. Data quickly restores the beam to keep Picard from dying.

In Picard's mind, the drama continues. As the years pass, he accepts this alternate reality. He and his wife start a family and have two beautiful children. Picard researches to discover the cause of the drought that threatens all life on his adopted planet. He eventually concludes that their sun will soon explode, destroying all life on the planet. When Picard tries to take his findings to the authorities, they tell him that they already know and are taking steps to preserve some memory of their existence and their culture. As his life draws to a close, Picard's children cajole him into witnessing the launch of a missile. His friends then reveal that the missile carries a probe that will seek out a person to be a teacher. The probe will teach that person about the lives of the people on the doomed planet. Hopefully, the newly trained teacher will relate the information to others. Of course, Picard is the person the probe found. At this point, Picard wakes up on the *Enterprise* and begins the struggle to reacquaint himself with his real life.

Trivia Questions

1. What is Picard's occupation in his alternate life?

2. How do the communities in Picard's alternate life communicate with each other?

GREAT MOMENTS

As always, Patrick Stewart does a masterful job in his portrayal of Jean-Luc Picard. This episode especially highlights his acting abilities as he plays through a wide range of emotions, from shock to anger to *love to enlightenment.*

PLOT OVERSIGHTS

• The creators of this episode expect us to believe that a society at the technological level of midtwentieth–century Earth can manufacture a device that can create an alternate reality *within* an unknown alien mind. Look at what this probe accomplishes. It scans the *Enterprise* and overpowers the ship's shields. It finds Picard and attaches an energy beam to him. This energy beam creates an alternate reality so complete that—by Picard's own words—it is as real as his life on the *Enterprise*. Every time he reaches out to touch on object, the device must respond by transmitting to his brain all the normal feedback from the muscles in that arm as well as analyze what Picard is reaching for *and* when Picard finally touches it *and* what the nerve endings would transmit back to his brain if he actually touched such an object!!! Does this sound like a project undertaken by a community who

have just begun to launch missiles? In the late 1950s, if the nations of Earth discovered that the Sun would soon explode, is it even conceivable that those nations would decide to preserve their heritage by setting out to build such a device? (I'm a pretty good programmer, but it boggles the mind even to consider the prospect—aside from the fact that the probe may encounter a wholly alien brain configuration that wouldn't be compatible.)

CONTINUITY AND PRODUCTION PROBLEMS

• As part of his alternate reality, Picard plays a flute. In one of the close-ups—just before Picard tells his *faux* wife that they should start their *faux* family—he quits blowing on the flute, but the flute music continues. Must be like a bagpipe flute?

TRIVIA ANSWERS

1. He is an iron weaver.
2. Using voice transit conductors.

TIME'S ARROW

Star Dates: 45959.1-45985.3

The *Enterprise* is recalled to Earth after construction uncovers a cave containing several artifacts from the late nineteenth century, including what appears to be Data's nonfunctioning head. In addition, the researchers find that the site was exposed to an energy source never in use on Earth. Data confirms that the artifact is his head and concludes that—at some time in the future—he will travel back in time to the nineteenth century, when he will die. At the same time, La Forge locates in the cave a cellular fossil that came from a planet called Devidia II. When the *Enterprise* arrives at Devidia II, Data finds a small temporal distortion on the surface. An away team investigates, but it sees nothing because the beings in the place exist slightly ahead of them in time. Data uses a device contained in his brain to modify a subspace field and synchronize himself to the beings. Moments later, he is caught in a temporal rift and swept back to nineteenth-century Earth.

Once there, Data quickly acclimates himself to the new surroundings. He wins money in a poker game, rents a hotel room, and begins constructing a machine. After seeing an announcement for a literary reception in Guinan's honor, Data goes to meet her. Unfortunately, she has not come from the future to find him. Instead, she is exploring the galaxy and has stopped by Earth to listen to its inhabitants for a while. Data explains his situation, which she readily accepts as the truth—as does an eavesdropping Samuel Clemens ("Mark Twain").

Back in the twenty-fourth century, La Forge constructs a larger subspace field on the surface so that an entire away team can synchronize to the beings. Just before activating it, Picard beams down. Guinan has told him that it is imperative for him to go on this away mission. After synchronizing in time with the beings, the away team discovers that they are visiting nineteenth-century Earth, capturing the life energy of humans, and returning to ingest it. As the episode ends, Picard and the others follow a pair of the beings back to the nineteenth century to learn more.

Trivia Questions

1. When was the .45-caliber double-action cavalry pistol invented by Colt Firearms?

2. What is the date on the newspaper Data finds shortly after arriving in the nineteenth century?

PLOT OVERSIGHTS

• As the *Enterprise* warps toward Devidia II, La Forge tells Guinan about finding Data's head in a cave on Earth. Guinan replies, "That's why the *Enterprise* is being sent back to Earth." Something's wrong here, because the *Enterprise* has already been sent back to Earth by this time in the episode. It is on its way to another planet when she makes this comment.

CHANGED PREMISES

• When Guinan asks Picard if he is going on the away team mission, he replies that it is standard Starfleet policy for him not to go on away team missions. Starfleet policy must have changed in the past five seasons. In the very first episode, "Encounter at Farpoint," Picard derides his newly arrived first officer, Will Riker, over Riker's policy of refusing to allow his former captain to go on away team missions. The entire conversation centers on the fact that it is Riker who has made a unilateral decision that captains should not go on away teams.

(This conversation was necessary for the premiere because the creators wanted to make a transition from the Kirk-knows-this-is-the-most-dangerous-planet-in-the-universe-so-he-takes-the-entire-senior-staff-with-him-when-he-beams-down syndrome so prevalent in the original *Star Trek*.)

CONTINUITY AND PRODUCTION PROBLEMS

• The person on the sound effects knob got a little echo-happy during this episode. Just after arriving at Devidia II, an away team beams down to an underground cavern. Data stays on the *Enterprise* to monitor their progress. Of course, when the away team talks, the sound effects include echoes, to simulate the cavern. At one point, however, the shot changes to Data on the *Enterprise*, and the echoes continue on his voice!

TRIVIA ANSWERS

1. In 1873.
2. August 13, 1893.

THE CREATOR IS ALWAYS RIGHT

As noted in Continuity and Production Problems for "We'll Always Have Paris," the Eiffel Tower moves around during Picard's enjoyment of a holodeck re-creation of Paris. Now, this might lead some of the harsher critics of *Star Trek: The Next Generation* to rant and rave about the lack of production and continuity control in the series. Since I am a diehard Trekker, however, I choose to see it another way. Maybe it was done that way on purpose. *Maybe* the creators of the episode *wanted* the Eiffel Tower to move around in the different shots! *Maybe* the creators knew that all the merchants of Paris got together in the twenty-fourth century and decided to construct a giant platform for the noted landmark. In that way engineers could move the tower from place to place and—at some point during the course of a week—every major store in Paris could enjoy a spectacular view of this great tourist attraction. Now, that sounds *plausible*, doesn't it? What seemed like an obvious error turned out to be exactly what the creators of *The Next Generation* intended.

"The Creator Is Always Right" refutes what you might think are blatant errors in *Star Trek: The Next Generation* by constructing "plausible" explanations. Just for the fun of it, I've posed the results in the form of questions. To help you get the right answer, I've listed the episode that had the original "mistake." The review of that episode will mention the error I'm explaining. Before looking up the answer, turn to the review of the episode and try to guess the mistake involved.

MULTIPLE CHOICE

1. Why did Zelbob Geeb of Icthni III resign in disgrace from the Nightpluck Institute of Technology? (Hint: "Encounter at Farpoint.")

   A. While finalizing the documentation for his section of code in the Universal Translator, Version 11.5.58, junior engineer Geeb accidentally switched the variables for the directional indicators "left" and "right" in the primitives baseline matrix.

   B. As the department manager for customer support, he campaigned vigorously against the complexity of the user interface for the retunable phaser. The elegance of Geeb's argument so impressed Starfleet that they did away with frequency tuning in phasers altogether. Shortly after the incident with the Borg (see "The Best of Both Worlds"), Geeb went to work for *MacGalaxy* as a software reviewer.

   C. His status as a spy became known after a coworker discovered his phone book open to the espionage recruitment section of the Yellow Pages. Geeb had circled an advertisement that read, "Attention, Engineers! Need

Xtra $$$. Romulans pay BIG. CALL NOW! 1-800-U2CAN-BASPY." (By the twenty-fourth century, I'm sure we'll have more than seven digits in our phone numbers.)

2. What contribution did Mervi von Anglebottom make to the computer work-stations of the twenty-fourth century? (Hint: "The Naked Now.")

A. He designed a system for inputting computer commands that utilizes a lim-ited set of buttons. The genius of the enhancement lies in its double ben-efit. Not only does it increase the modality of the user interface, which makes the programmers happier, it also allows the user to look busier, since several key strokes are required to implement the simplest of tasks.

B. He lobbied the workstations designers until they included a gluteus max-imus sensor on all touch-sensitive surfaces.

C. He produced the first pizza box capable of traveling faster than the speed of light. This invention let engineers enjoy hot and fresh Chicago-style pizza even though they were working at Mars Station—dramatically im-proving the productivity of late-night sessions.

3. What led to the dismissal of Oops Gavelnod, arbiter of the Galactic Court for Race Name Conflict Resolution? (Hint: "Heart of Glory" and "Haven.")

A. She refused to decide which race would receive rights to a given name based on the race's population. Maps Galore—the major funder of the Galactic Court for Race Name Conflict Resolution—had decreed that the smaller race should always prevail. This ensured the largest possible mar-ket when a larger race had to reprint all its maps after it lost the rights to use its name.

B. She reawarded the race name "Tarellian" to the Tarellian A petitioners in exchange for a significant stake in Spheroid Furnishings, their house-wares manufacturing company.

C. She showed up in court one too many times wearing a full-length leather robe, swinging a Ferengi phaser whip, and shouting, "Down, petitioners! On your knees before your arbiter! When your hearts are sufficiently bowed, you may crawl forward and kiss the glove!"

4. What contribution did Prissy de la Snoot make to Starfleet uniforms? (Hint: "Contagion.")

A. Knowing that men like to grab their clothing from time to time, she split the familiar jumpsuit into two sections. This allowed the male Starfleet of-ficers to adopt the "smartly snap" by clutching the bottom of their shirt and pulling quickly downward.

B. She finally achieved true equality between the genders by creating an outfit for certain male ensigns that features the same submicron skirts previously reserved for female ensigns. Both sexes now agree on the uniform's impracticality.

C. She perfected a rapid-drying fabric capable of quickly dispelling that most unsightly of all *haute couture faux pas* (high-fashion blunders): perspiration.

5. During "Brothers," Data commandeers the *Enterprise* and flies it to the home of his creator, Dr. Noonian Soong. How does this episode end?

A. Data returns control of the ship to Picard, and the *Enterprise* just barely manages to get to Starbase 416 in time to save the boy's life.

B. Data returns control of the ship, but Picard reassigns him to Commander Bruce Maddox (see "The Measure of a Man"). Maddox dismantles Data and deactivates the homing device so it can never be used again. Unfortunately, reassembling Data becomes a problem.

C. Data cannot return control of the ship. The sick boy dies, and Data's raging guilt drives him into a fantasy world in which he constantly imagines that he returned control of the ship to Picard, the boy lived, and the *Enterprise* went on to even greater exploits.

ANSWERS

1.A. Geeb's unintentional mistake had severe consequences. After the release of the software, every new race encountered by the Universal Translator had the information for "left" and "right" backward. When humans would say "left," the newly encountered race would hear "right." Both races thought the other one had it wrong. As these newly encountered races entered the Federation, they had to remember constantly that when humans said "left," they really meant "right." In addition—because of the nature of Geeb's error—when the new races spoke among themselves, everything was fine. Eventually the new entrants outnumber the older, established members of the Federation. Once they did, they convened the Congress on Handedness and forced the Federation to change to a revised format—"left" would now be called "right," and "right," "left."

The decision threw Starfleet into a panic. After all, the new Galaxy Class starships were almost ready for delivery. As always, the programming teams rose to the task—albeit somewhat disgruntled with the last-minute change. Then came the bombshell: One month after the commissioning of the *Enterprise*, the Nightpluck Institute of Technology released a statement detailing the bug and promising an immediate update to correct the problems it caused. It also assured the public that it had taken a sizable chunk of flesh from Mr. Zelbob Geeb before kicking him out the door.

Unfortunately, Zelbob Geeb never recovered from his simple mistake. He was last seen boarding a freighter bound for the Cosmard System. The inhabitants of the planet in this system differ from other humanoid races in one important respect: They have only a single appendage.

Of course, this explains why the computer, in the episode "Encounter at Farpoint," tells Riker to turn right and he turns left. At this point—just after the commissioning of the Enterprise—everyone still operated on the revised format because no one knew about Zelbob Geeb's bug in the Universal Translator. By the next show, the revision of system software had arrived, and humans no longer had to remember that when the computer said "right" it really meant "left." By the way, it's also quite possible that the glitches in the holodeck's assignment of left-handedness and right-handedness during "Ship in a Bottle" can be a holdover from this problem as well.

2. B. Owing to the unique construction of his posterior, Lieutenant Commander Mervi von Anglebottom found the workstation chairs very uncomfortable. As chief engineer aboard the USS *Stardust*, he made a habit of sitting on the data entry area instead. He solved the problem of craning his neck to see the displays by rigging a mirror on the back of the subsequently unused chair. All went well until one day when he shifted his weight and shunted power from the shields into the warp coils.

The crew was able to escape in shuttle crafts, but the resulting explosion decimated the appropriately named ship. An investigation followed. Thanks to *Ensign* Anglebottom's efforts, individuals can now sit on the data entry area of a workstation without fear of repercussion.

Anglebottom's sensor is the reason Riker can sit down on the data entry area of a bridge workstation with such confidence during "The Naked Now." He knows the sensor will protect the ship from harm.

3. B. The Galactic Court for Race Name Conflict Resolution (or GalCouRaNaConRes, for short) ensures that only one race will have the right to use a given name at any time. Whenever it's discovered that more than one race uses the same name, both races must bring a case before a GalCouRaNaConRes arbiter. As part of her regular caseload, arbiter Oops Gavelnod reviewed the lawyers' arguments in the case of *Tarellians* v. *Tarellians*. The Tarellians (hereafter known as Tarellians A) were a dying race, infected by their own biogenetically engineered virus (featured in "Haven"). The other Tarellians (hereafter known as Tarellians B) were a warlike race, vibrant and strong (featured in "Suddenly Human"). After

considering all the arguments, arbiter Gavelnod ruled in favor of the Tarellian A race. Tarellian B begrudgingly adopted the name "Talarian."

Two years later, the Altsians destroyed the last known Tarellian vessel. Immediately the Talarians refiled for the name "Tarellian." Thinking that no Tarellians still existed, arbiter Oops Gavelnod approved the Talarian request. The Talarians became Tarellians once again.

The final chapter in this story began when the *Enterprise* came in contact with a Tarellian A vessel during the episode "Haven." After Dr. Wyatt Miller healed the last survivors, these Tarellians repetitioned to get their name back from the Tarellians who had become Talarians but recently changed back to Tarellians. As in the first case, Oops Gavelnod ruled in favor of the Tarellian A race. Suspicion later arose, however, when an audit discovered that arbiter Gavelnod had recently acquired a significant share of ownership in Spheroid Furnishings, a housewares manufacturing company owned by Miller and the Tarellians. Although Gavelnod was dismissed from GalCouRaNaConRes for possible conflict of interest, her decision stood.

All this name-changing wreaks havoc in the mind of a starship captain. That's why Picard, in the episode "Heart of Glory," calls the Talarian vessel a Tarellian *vessel. And if you must have evidence of Wyatt Miller's success at healing the Tarellians, just look at the spheroid chair on the Tarellian ship in "Haven." This same chair shows up in Worf's quarters during "Peak Performance" and "Reunion." Obviously the Tarellians now have a thriving furniture business and hefty contracts to outfit Starfleet vessels.*

4. C. Being a Proboscian, Ms. de la Snoot found the odoriferous fumes caused by the sweat of male officers particularly offensive. Although Ms. de la Snoot had every right to file charges of nasal harassment against these individuals, she found a more creative way to solve the problem. Ms. de la Snoot invented a temperature- and humidity-sensitive fabric that actually sucks up any water or water vapors escaping from the body, preventing the bacterial growth that leads to excessive body odor.

This wondrous fabric makes it possible for La Forge to sprint to a turbolift, work up a sweat, and still appear at the bridge completely dry in "Contagion."

5. C. In reality, the last few minutes of "Brothers" come from the insane visualizations of Data's mind. Since the access code Data speaks to the computer is different from the one the computer hears, Data couldn't return control of the ship. Since Data could not return control of the ship, the boy dies, and the *Enterprise* remains in orbit around this planet for the rest of the show's life.

Actually, this works out quite well for the creators of Star Trek: The Next Generation. *At any point in the future, they can have an episode where the crew finally figures out how to get command functions returned. That show will explain that all the intervening shows simply occurred in Data's mind. This gives the creators the ability to kill off characters at will and bring them back at a later date. Obviously, this episode was written by a person in management during contract negotiations. (In fact, one of the executive producers, Rick Berman, wrote the episode!)*

Sixth
Season

TIME'S ARROW, PART II

Star Date: 46001.3

After following a pair of alien predators back to nineteenth-century Earth, Picard and his away team steal the aliens' time-travel device. It is a walking cane tipped with an ivory serpent's head. The away team also finds Data. Together, they retreat and plan their next move. With Guinan's help, the away team gains access to the cave that contained the artifacts discovered at the beginning of "Time's Arrow." They determine that the cave itself focuses the energy from the walking stick.

At this point, Samuel Clemens interrupts, intent on capturing the whole group and turning them over to the police. Suddenly the aliens reappear and try to take back the walking cane. Data stops them, but the cane activates and blasts open the portal to the twenty-fourth century. The force of the impact decapitates Data, hurling his body through the portal while his damaged head remains behind. Seeing the open portal, the male alien abandons his wounded companion and leaps through. Picard orders his away team to follow, while he stays behind to care for the injured Guinan.

Seizing the opportunity, Clemens jumps through the portal as well, just as it closes. As Guinan rests, Picard questions the female alien and learns that if the *Enterprise* uses photon torpedoes to destroy the aliens' origination point on Devidia II—as he suspects they will—nineteenth-century Earth itself will also be destroyed. Picard sends this message back to twenty-fourth–century Earth by using a metal file to tap a code into Data's head.

On the *Enterprise*, La Forge reattaches the five-hundred-year-old head found in "Time's Arrow" to Data's body. Data immediately processes Picard's message and informs the crew of the danger to nineteenth-century Earth. They modify the photons to prevent any cascading destruction of Earth. Clemens then uses the cane to return to the nineteenth century so Picard can return to the twenty-fourth. Afterward, the *Enterprise* destroys the aliens' origination point.

PLOT OVERSIGHTS

• Shortly after Picard and the away team arrive in the nineteenth century, they establish a base of operations in a boardinghouse. One of the lighthearted bits of the episode has Picard trying to squirm his way out of paying the rent. However, the second time this bit occurs, Data has rejoined the group. Doesn't Data have money from his winnings in poker? He changes outfits between this episode and the last. Did he blow all his money on the machine he built and then resort to stealing "new duds"? Also, at the end of the show, Picard asks Clemens to settle up the bill at the boardinghouse but never mentions the clothing the away team wore. Since the away team didn't have any money—as indicated by their not paying the rent—don't they also have an obligation to pay for the clothing they stole?

• Toward the end of the episode, Troi takes Clemens to visit La Forge as La Forge works on reconnecting Data's head. After entering the room, Clemens spies his watch on a table and immediately grabs the watch. If you recall from "Time's Arrow," the watch was among several items—including a pair of spectacles, a gun, and Data's head—found in the cave below San Francisco. Neither the gun nor the spectacles are on the table with Clemens's watch. Doesn't it seem likely that a watch from the nineteenth century would be on its way to a museum instead of lying on a table in La Forge's lab?

• While struggling to reattach Data's head to his body, La Forge finds a metal file at the base of the opening in the back of the android's head. Removing this metal file apparently

fixes the problem of activating Data's head because, moments later, Data comes to life. The episode seems to indicate that Picard left the file in Data's head five hundred years before when he tapped in his message. If that's true, then the file was in the head when Data examined it in "Time's Arrow." If fact, that episode showed Data looking into the very opening that supposedly contained the file. Doesn't it seem likely that Data would try to reactivate the head and access its storage? Doesn't it seem likely that Data would find the file? If the file is all that is keeping the head from functioning, isn't it reasonable to believe that Data could have activated the head? (I realize that La Forge had the added benefit of attaching the head to an android body, but the episode "Disaster" proves that Data's head can function perfectly well without his body.)

• Before departing for the nineteenth century, Samuel Clemens states that he wants to go back because he has more books to write. Later, while preparing to fire the torpedoes to destroy the aliens' origination point, Riker expresses concern that Picard should have gotten back already if Clemens had returned to the nineteenth century. Worf then laments, "We have no way of knowing if Mr. Clemens was successful." They have no way of knowing if Clemens was successful? Can't they check their historical data base to see if Mark Twain (Clemens's pen name) wrote any books after August 1893 (the time frame for this adventure)?

• At the very end of the show,

Clemens instructs the medics who carry Guinan off in a stretcher. One question: Do the doctors of nineteenth-century Earth really have the medical knowledge to help a woman whose physiology is so different that she lives at least five hundred years?

CHANGED PREMISES

• Phasers reacquire the ability to be tuned to different frequencies in this episode. Originally, phasers had this capability, as demonstrated in "Arsenal of Freedom" when Data tunes his phaser to the specific frequency needed to override a force field that traps Riker. Then phasers lost the capability in "The Best of Both Worlds." Apparently the encounter with the Borg convinced Starfleet that this was an important feature and was worth the headaches it caused users (see Equipment Oddities for "The Best of Both Worlds").

EQUIPMENT ODDITIES

• Picard sends a message to Data by tapping on the back of his head with a metal file. After Data comes to life, he says, "Torpedoes ... phasing ... alien" and then tells La Forge that he is processing a binary message from Picard. A *binary* message? Binary uses only two numbers, "0" and "1." It is ideally suited to computers

because it relates well to electricity—OFF equal "0," ON equals "1." Let's suppose that Picard sent only the three words: "torpedoes," "phasing," and "alien." (I realize that these three words don't make much sense by themselves, and Picard must have sent additional clarifying words for Data to get the gist of the message, but for the sake of argument, let's say he didn't.) There are twenty-one characters in these three words. Adding two spaces to separate the words brings the grand total to twenty-three.

If Picard uses standard ASCII codes to represent these characters, each character would contain eight binary digits (also called "bits"). That means Picard would have to tap a series of 184 1's and 0's to relate the message. Just for the record, the string of 1's and 0's would be as follows:

```
0111010001101111011001001
1000001100101011001000110
1110110010101110011001000000
0111000011010000110000101
1100110110100101101110011000
1110010000001100001011011
0011010010110010101101110
```

TRIVIA ANSWERS

1. Number 314.
2. Frequency .047.

REALM OF FEAR

Star Dates: 46091.1-46093.6

The *Enterprise* warps to the last known location of the USS *Yosemite*: a high-energy plasma stream. An away team—which includes Lieutenant Barclay of "Hollow Pursuits" and "The Nth Degree"—finds a deserted and damaged ship. After collecting fragments of a smashed container, they return to the *Enterprise*. As Barclay beams back, he sees a wormlike object swimming in the matter stream of the transporter. Just as he materializes, the object races toward him and bites his arm. The experience disturbs Barclay. Later his arm lights up with a blue glow and pulses with pain.

After studying the evidence, La Forge and Data determine that the crew of the *Yosemite* beamed plasma into the smashed container to study it. Unknown to them, the plasma contained quasi-matter/energy life forms. When the crew of the *Yosemite* began scanning the container, the life forms reacted and exploded the container. This action exposed the crew to high-energy plasma and wiped out all computer functions. Evidently—as Barclay beamed back—some of the

Trivia Questions

1. What technological breakthrough stopped the illness "transporter psychosis"?

2. What temperature does Barclay request the first time he orders water?

life forms mixed with his pattern and are causing the pain in his arm. La Forge and O'Brien decide to cleanse Barclay's system by using a modified transporter. During the process, Barclay observes more of the wormlike objects. In a sudden inspiration he grabs one just as O'Brien rematerializes him. Moments later, Barclay appears with a crew member from the *Yosemite*. Barclay sends a team from Security into the transporter to rescue the rest of the crew members and then explains. The crew members of the *Yosemite* were also trying to cleanse themselves of the life forms. Unfortunately, their patterns got caught in the plasma stream and they couldn't get out.

PLOT OVERSIGHTS

• This episode gives the very first "from the inside" view of experiencing a transport, so it's very difficult to find fault with the events. In spite of that, doesn't it seem as if Barclay is staying conscious for a *long* time through this process of molecular *deconstruction*?

• The away team finds a Lieutenant Kelly—dead and covered with second- and third-degree burns—on the USS *Yosemite*. Crusher states that he didn't die from the burns. The odd thing about this episode is that it never says what Lieutenant Kelly *did* die from.

• The away team also determines that the blast that disabled the *Yosemite* originated in the transport chamber. Later in the episode, however, La Forge and Data discover that the disabling explosion occurred when the crew of the *Yosemite* began running tests on the plasma. Presumably, then, the crew of the *Yosemite* ran their plasma tests with the container still on the transporter pad. Don't they have a lab for this type of activity? This is, after all, a science vessel.

• After seeing the first worm in the transporter and turning up nothing in the transporter diagnosis, Barclay begins to wonder if he is coming down with "transporter psychosis." He decides to go back into the transporter after discovering that he was the only one of the away team who experienced an "ionic energy fluctuation" during transport. He wakes up O'Brien and asks O'Brien to transport him to and from the *Yosemite*. He also points out the ionic energy fluctuation and asks O'Brien to reproduce it during transport. In the transporter matter stream, Barclay sees the worm again, convincing himself that he is sane. When he exits the transporter, he wakes up the senior staff and tries to convince them of what he saw. At first the staff seems skeptical, but eventually they take his word for it. Wait a minute: If

O'Brien can reproduce the ionic energy fluctuation on command so a person in the transporter matter stream can see the worms, why not just send someone else in and confirm Barclay's observations?

• So the crew members of the *Yosemite* got caught in the transporter and turned into worms, but when they came out they were people again?!? To corrupt a Picardian phrase from the episode "Power Play," if the worms in the transporter are members of Starfleet, aren't they behaving rather badly? (One did—after all—bite Barclay's arm.)

CHANGED PREMISES

• Main Engineering gets a rework in this episode. For the past five seasons, the doors adjacent to the center island in Main Engineering have led to turbolifts. In "Déjà Q," Crusher used the one on the right side of the island (when facing the dilithium chamber) to rush to relieve Q's backache. Yet in this episode, Barclay opens this same door and the turbolift is gone! Now it's some kind of auxiliary engine room.

• Transporter Chief O'Brien must have done something terrible between the episode "Power Play" and this one. At some point he got busted back down to ensign! He takes a "direct order" from Barclay. The action puzzled me because I thought both Barclay and O'Brien were lieutenants. On closer inspection, however, O'Brien is wearing only one pip, and a black-centered one at that! Isn't this the rank of the lowliest of lowly ensigns, or has Starfleet come up with a new type of designation?

EQUIPMENT ODDITIES

• After discovering the life forms in Barclay's arm, Crusher gives him an armband monitoring device. She says it will tell her if "there is the slightest sign" of the life forms increasing in his system. Later, in Engineering, Barclay collapses as a blue glow erupts from both arms and his neck. Oddly enough, the monitoring device attached to his arm doesn't seem to inform Crusher of this development.

CONTINUITY AND PRODUCTION PROBLEMS

• The graphics of a binary star system and the *Enterprise* from the episode "Evolution" serve this episode as well. (Actually, this isn't really a problem. I suppose there are many binary star systems that have a red giant and a smaller white star. Just thought I'd point it out.)

TRIVIA ANSWERS

1. Multiplex-pattern buffers.
2. Ten degrees Celsius.

MAN OF THE PEOPLE

Star Dates: 48071.8-48075.1

The *Enterprise* comes to the aid of the freighter *Dorian*, under attack by one faction in a nearby planet's civil war. By request from the *Dorian*'s captain, the *Enterprise* beams aboard a peace negotiator, Ambassador Vas Alcar, and his "mother." They are traveling to the planet to seek a resolution to the civil crisis. Shortly afterward, Alcar's mother dies, and Alcar asks Troi to join him in a funeral meditation.

In the days that follow, Troi deteriorates both physically and mentally, becoming a domineering, jealous, lewd, aging wench (I could add a few more adjectives to the list, but I think you get the idea). As Alcar prepares to beam down to the war-torn planet, Troi tries to attack him with a knife because he won't take her with him. Picard intervenes, and Crusher takes Troi to sick bay. When an examination turns up similarities in the brains of Troi and Alcar's dead mother, Crusher does an autopsy and finds that the woman was only thirty. Picard beams down to the planet and demands some answers from Alcar. The ambassador reveals that

Trivia Questions

1. Whose counseling session did Troi cancel?

2. When did Troi die, and what did she die from?

he uses individuals as receptacles for his negative emotions. This allows him to stay focused on the peace negotiations he conducts. When one of his receptacles dies, he simply chooses another. Picard finds Alcar's behavior appalling, but Alcar refuses to release Troi. After Picard returns to the *Enterprise*, Crusher suggests killing Troi. When Alcar breaks his connection with Troi, Crusher can then revive her. The plan works, and just as Alcar attempts to establish a receptacle link with a female in his party, Picard beams her to safety. Left without a receptacle and faced with the backwash of emotion coming from Troi, Alcar instantly ages and dies while Troi returns to normal.

PLOT OVERSIGHTS

• When Crusher proposes to kill Troi so Alcar will break his link, Riker reacts immediately. Crusher responds that she will be able to revive Troi as long as thirty minutes do not elapse before resuscitation. Why thirty minutes? In "The Neutral Zone," Crusher revived humans who had been frozen for hundreds of years. Are the preservation techniques of the twentieth century better that the preservation techniques of the twenty-fourth century?

EQUIPMENT ODDITIES

• At one point, a seductive Troi slinks into Ten-Forward, looking for Alcar. After making a scene, Troi gets escorted out by Riker. They immediately board a turbolift, and the doors close. The doors read "08 Turbolift." The first two numbers are supposed to be the deck numbers, but Ten-Forward is on deck 10, not deck 8.

• At the end of the show, Picard predicts that Alcar will attempt to find another receptacle as soon as Troi dies. To protect Alcar's intended victim, he contacts Transporter Room 2 and tells them to lock on to the female in Alcar's quarters. But when he wants to beam her out he says, "Picard to Transporter Room 3. Ener-

gize!" How does the transporter chief in Transporter Room 3 know what to do? Picard gave the instructions of whom to beam out to the person in Transporter Room 2.

CONTINUITY AND PRODUCTION PROBLEMS

• After Alcar admits that he is using Troi as a psychic waste receptacle, Picard tries to take him back to the *Enterprise* forcibly. Unfortunately, two guards on the planet intervene and disarm Worf, forcing Picard to leave without Alcar. Evidently the guards shop at the local Talarian uniform shop for their outfits, because they are identical to the ones the Talarians use in "Suddenly Human."

TRIVIA ANSWERS

1 Ensign Janeway.
2. Death occurred at 14:30 from respiratory and renal failure.

Star Date: 48125.3

Responding to a distress call from the USS *Jenolan*, the *Enterprise* finds it crashed on the surface of a Dyson's sphere—a ball two hundred million kilometers in diameter that surrounds a small star. When an away team to the *Jenolan* finds a jury-rigged transporter still functioning, they are shocked to discover a seventy-five-year-old pattern in the pattern buffer. Since it seems to be viable, La Forge activates the transporter, and an injured Captain Montgomery Scott ("Scotty" from the original *Star Trek* television series) materializes. They return to the *Enterprise* so Crusher can doctor his wounds. Picard then asks La Forge to accompany Scotty back to the crashed ship and extract its records. Meanwhile, Data locates an opening in the sphere. When the *Enterprise* arrives at the opening, Worf opens a communication channel. Immediately the huge bay door opens and tractor beams lock on to the *Enterprise*, sweeping it inside. Unfortunately, the sphere's star is unstable, and the solar flares erupting from its surface will even-

tually destroy the ship. On the *Jenolan*, La Forge discovers that the *Enterprise* is missing. He and Scotty get the *Jenolan* flying and trace the *Enterprise* to the opening. They trick the bay doors into opening and then use the *Jenolan* and its shields to keep the doors open. Seizing the opportunity, the *Enterprise* makes a dash for the doors. When the *Jenolan*'s engines fail, Picard transports Scotty and La Forge back to the *Enterprise*, blows up the *Jenolan*, and flies the *Enterprise* through to safety. In appreciation for his help, Picard loans Scotty one of the *Enterprise* shuttles so he can explore the Federation on his own.

Trivia Questions

1. What scan does Data use to locate the *Jenolan*?

2. What is the name of the shuttle Picard loans to Scotty?

GREAT LINES

"Oh, laddie, you've got a lot to learn if you want people to think of you as a miracle worker."—Scotty, shocked to find that La Forge told Picard that he'd have a report done in an hour when, in fact, it will take an hour to compile the report.

PLOT OVERSIGHTS

• When the *Enterprise* first discovers the Dyson's sphere, Data states it is 200 million kilometers in diameter. Upon hearing this, Riker responds, "That's nearly as large as the Earth's orbit around the Sun." The Earth's orbit around the Sun averages almost 186 million miles in diameter, or 297.6 million kilometers. (I leave it for you to decide if a difference of 97.6 million kilometers qualifies as "nearly.")

• When Scotty shows up in Ten-Forward, he disdains the taste of synthahol scotch. Data immediately responds that Guinan keeps a store of true alcoholic beverages and proceeds around the bar to fetch some. Can anyone just help themselves to Guinan's provisions, or is this privilege reserved for senior staff officers who've subbed for her in the past (as Data did in the beginning of "Disaster")?

EQUIPMENT ODDITIES

Near the end of the show, the *Jenolan* holds open the sphere's bay door with its shields. Unfortunately, its engines have failed, and it can't move out of the way to let the *Enterprise* escape the sphere. Picard quickly solves problem by transporting La Forge and Scotty onto the *Enterprise* and then destroying the *Jenolan*. One problem: Aren't the *Jenolan*'s shields up when the transporter beams them aboard? Don't the shields inhibit transporter activity?

• The shuttle that Picard loans to Scotty is the same type used by Riker in "The Outcast." However, in that episode, Riker had to punch a button near the back hatch to get it to close. In "Relics," Scotty simply walks in. Is the button punch just habitual in the same way the badge tap is not really necessary for the communicators?

CONTINUITY AND PRODUCTION PROBLEMS

• When Scotty rematerializes after seventy-five years in the transporter of the *Jenolan*, his arm is in a sling. Later, Crusher states that he has a hairline fracture of the humerus—the long bone of the upper arm. Surprisingly, Scotty seems to feel no pain as La Forge—escorting him to sick bay—bumps the arm several times and gives it a good thump right where the injury is! Also—even though Crusher says "it will ache for a couple of days"—Scotty sits down in his quarters by using this same arm to support his weight fully as he descends into the chair.

• Evidently Troi liked the look of the new hairdos she experimented with while acting as a psychic waste receptacle for Ambassador Alcar in the previous episode, "Man of the People." The only scene she appears in comes at the very end of "Relics," and she is wearing her hair pulled back in a loose ponytail with her bangs on her forehead. (It's difficult to be objective about this "look." Five years is a long time to see someone's hair fixed in a certain general way. I suppose she was due for for a change.)

TRIVIA ANSWERS

1. FWD Navigational Scan 302.
2. *Goddard.*

SCHISMS

Star Dates: 48159.2-48191.2

As the *Enterprise* maps the dense globular cluster called the Amagosa Diaspora, several crew members report vague and disturbing flashbacks to Troi. She gathers a few of them together—including Riker, La Forge, and Worf—to discuss their remembrances. Piece by piece, they reconstruct a room with an examination/torture table and strange clicking sounds emanating from the darkness.

At the same time, an area of subspace instability appears in Cargo Bay 4. Apparently the instability is being controlled from a region deep within subspace. La Forge proposes that his own experiments might have caused both problems. To speed up the mapping of the Amagosa Diaspora, he modified the sensor array to utilize warp energy. Some of his modifications dipped deep into subspace. Evidently those signals caught someone's attention. Because the subspace instability threatens the ship, the crew devises a method to close the hole by firing a graviton pulse. To be successful, however, La Forge must know where the aliens

are in subspace. Riker volunteers to wear a homing device. Since the aliens have taken him to their laboratory several times, he hopes they will again.

That night, the aliens take Riker once again. The homing device works, and La Forge begins firing the graviton pulse. At the last possible moment, Riker jumps from the examination table, grabs the other crew member whom the aliens had kidnapped, and dives through the disappearing subspace hole to safety on the *Enterprise*.

PLOT OVERSIGHTS

• When Riker first goes to Crusher complaining of tiredness, she finds nothing physically wrong other than muscle tension. She then wonders out loud that his problems might come from REM sleep deprivation (dreamlessness). But in "Night Terrors," Crusher said that this condition causes a unique chemical imbalance in the brain, and she is able to verify that crew members have this imbalance. If she really suspects dream deprivation, why not just check for the chemical imbalance?

Trivia Questions

1. When does Picard give Crusher her first taste of his Aunt Adelle's hot toddy?

2. How many classifications of tables does the computer have?

• After the discovery of his abduction, Data states that he is missing ninety minutes, seventeen seconds of time. Later he tells Picard that he was absent from the *Enterprise* during the hours 12:54 till 14:26. One of these numbers is wrong, because even if Data disappeared at 12:54:59, he would have reappeared at 14:25:16, not 14:26:00.

• In the last captain's log of the episode, Picard reports that all crew members are "safe and accounted for." He must have an interesting definition of the word "safe" because, moments later, Riker states that one of the abductees—although "accounted for"—is dead!

EQUIPMENT ODDITIES

• While trying to reconstruct their abductions, Troi takes a group to the holodeck. Since everyone in the group remembers a table of some kind, Troi asks the computer to create a conference table. La Forge responds that the table is too high and orders the computer to lower it. The computer instantly responds. Worf says the table should be tilted. Instead of tilting the conference table, however, the computer replaces it with an entirely different table! Then Riker says the table should be metal, and the computer replaces the angled wooden table with a metal examination table. At no time does anyone ask for a different table *design*, simply *modifications* to the current design, but the computer takes it upon itself to start from scratch

every time. Does this seem right?

• Everyone in the holodeck agrees that the aliens' examination/torture table was tilted. However, when the episode finally shows the aliens' lair, the tables are flat.

CONTINUITY AND PRODUCTION PROBLEMS

• After La Forge makes his modifications to the sensor array, the computer reports a massive explosion in Cargo Bay 4. The next shot shows the emergency team "rushing" to the scene. Actually, they are sauntering ... well ... more like strolling.

• When a crew member reappears after an abduction, Worf reports his quarters as being on "deck 9, section 17." However, when Crusher needs a plasma infusion unit to minister to the stricken crew member, she tells her medical technician to bring the unit to "deck 9, section 19."

• Just before Riker makes his desperate dash through the closing subspace hole, he grabs up a fellow crew member. This action pops his phaser loose from its holster, and it falls to the floor. The amazing thing is that once Riker returns to the *Enterprise*, the phaser is back! Yet at no time does Riker stop to pick it up. How did he get his phaser back? (Maybe he's wearing one of those new yo-yo phasers?)

TRIVIA ANSWERS

1. During the episode "Cause and Effect."
2. It has 5,047.

★
TRUE Q

Star Dates: 48192.3-48193.8

After being selected from a pool of applicants, an orphan named Amanda Rogers joins the *Enterprise* as an intern. Although human in appearance and physiology, Amanda soon exhibits superhuman powers. With a wave of her hand, she prevents a container from falling on Riker. She contains an explosion in the engine room and saves the ship from destruction. During a subsequent meeting of the senior staff, Q appears to explain the mystery. Amanda's parents were actually members of the Q Continuum. They took on human form almost two decades ago—even to the point of having a child. Since they refused to return to the Continuum and they wouldn't refrain from using their powers, the Q Continuum terminated them. Now Q has come to determine if Amanda is fully Q or some mixture of Q and human. In the end, Q determines that Amanda is fully Q and offers her the same choice the Continuum offered her parents: Return to the Continuum, or pose as a human but abstain from any more superhuman displays. Amanda initially chooses the latter, but when a crisis erupts, she is compelled to help. Reluctantly, she admits that she is Q and leaves with Q for the Continuum.

Trivia Questions

1. Where are Amanda's quarters?

2. How many puppies appear in Amanda's quarters?

PLOT OVERSIGHTS

• In one of the first scenes of the episode, Crusher tells Picard that Amanda has done honors work in "neurobiology, plasma dynamics, and ecoregeneration." Yet later in the show, Crusher gives Amanda the task of testing several tricorders and explains their function to Amanda. Shouldn't someone who's done honors work in neurobiology already know how to use a tricorder?

• Q gives Amanda only two choices at the end of the episode: Return to the Continuum, or refrain from using her powers. Isn't there another choice? Earlier in the episode, Amanda claimed that she just wanted to become a normal human again. Isn't that the third choice? In "Déjà Q," the Continuum turned Q into a human, stripped him of his powers, and dumped him on the *Enterprise*. Why couldn't they do the same to Amanda, if that's what she really wants?

CHANGED PREMISES

• Until this episode, the first contact between humans and the Q Continuum supposedly came during "Encounter at Farpoint." During "Hide and Q," both Q and Picard make several references to this "first" encounter. At one point Q says, "At Farpoint, we saw you as savages only. We discovered instead that you are unusual creatures ... in your own limited ways." This episode definitely gives the impression that until Farpoint, the Q Continuum knew little and cared less for humanity. However, "True Q" purports that two members of the Q Continuum had been on Earth, took on human form, and even conceived a child at least a decade before "Encounter at Farpoint"!

• The transformation of the former turbolift on the right side of the island in Main Engineering proceeds in this episode (see Changed Premises in "Realm of Fear" for its beginnings). While giving Amanda a tour, La Forge points to the door and identifies it as an entrance to a Jefferies tube.

EQUIPMENT ODDITIES

• When Amanda begins testing tricorders near the start of the show, she holds the first one pointing away from her body. The rest she holds pointing toward her body. Shouldn't the first one be held the same way? Isn't Amanda taking readings from her own body for the tricorder tests?

TRIVIA ANSWERS

1. Deck 7, section 4.
2. Ten. (The interesting thing here is that Amanda talks to Riker about wishing she had her "zoo"—a term she later explains as her three dogs. She also states that she would like to have a dozen. Yet, when the dogs appear, there are not three or twelve but *ten*.)

RASCALS

Star Dates: 4б235.7-4б23б.3

As Picard, Guinan, Ro, and Keiko return to the *Enterprise*, an energy field envelops their shuttle. Riker orders an emergency transport to pull the occupants out of the disintegrating shuttle. When they appear on the transporter pads, however, all four have reverted to preteenagers. Crusher begins studying the effect as Riker takes command and the *Enterprise* warps to answer a distress call from a science team on Ligo VII. Soon after arriving, two Klingon ships decloak and stage a surprise attack. After they knock out the *Enterprise*'s shields, the Ferengi who commandeered the Klingon ships begin transporting to the *Enterprise*. When two Ferengi appear on the bridge, Riker shuts down all command functions, effectively freezing the Ferengi out of the main computer. After the Ferengi secure the *Enterprise*, they transport all the adults on the ship to the surface so they can assist the science team in a forced-labor mining operation. Only Riker remains. The Ferengi captain needs him to return control of the main computer.

Meanwhile, Picard, Guinan, Ro, and Keiko—left aboard the *Enterprise* because of their childlike appearance—plan to regain control of the ship. Picard throws a tantrum and demands to see his "father." When the Ferengi finally take him to see Riker, Picard secretly relays a message: Return command control to the computer terminal in schoolroom 8. When Riker accomplishes this, Picard and the other "kids" use the transporter to trap the Ferengi in a force field and take back the ship. As the show concludes, Crusher and O'Brien use the transporter to return Picard, Guinan, Ro, and Keiko to normal.

PLOT OVER-SIGHTS

• As discussed in "Reunion," use of star dates makes it very convenient to obscure the length of time of a given period. Keiko bore her child during the episode "Disaster." That episode occurred at star date 45156.1. "Rascals" takes place during star dates 46235.7–46236.3. The question then is: How much time elapsed between these star dates? According to the evidence sited in "Reunion," about *one* year. In

Trivia Questions

1. What is the name of the shuttle that is destroyed at the beginning of the episode?

2. How many people are in the science team on Ligo VII?

other words, Keiko's child has grown to the time when it can put together a sentence such as, "I want Mommy!" in the same amount of time it takes backwater twentieth-century humans to begin gurgling "Dada" and "Mama." Now, that's evolutionary progress for you!

• Once again, the creators invoke the "just switch the DNA with the transporter so everything will be okey doke" plot trickery to fix the problem of changing the crew back to adults. At least the creators are consistent. This is basically the same tack they used to resolve a crisis in "Unnatural Selection." In that episode, Dr. Pulaski's DNA was altered, and she aged rapidly. Then the crew used the transporter to change her DNA back, and—ba-bing! bang!! boom!!!—everything was fine. Pulaski was, once again, her youthful self. As pointed out in Plot Oversights for that episode, evidently the creators believe that if you change a person's DNA, you immediately reverse all signs of aging, including bad hairdos!

Actually, "Rascals" seems to indicate that the transporter uses a person's DNA to guide the reconstitution process. On the other hand, shows such as "Encounter at Farpoint," and "Realm of Fear" seem to indicate that the transporter converts matter into energy, molecule by molecule, squirts it through subspace, and reverses the process at the other end. If the transporter can reconstruct a person by DNA, *everyone can live forever*. Simply put a few skin cells in stasis when you are twenty. On your eightieth birthday, step into the transporter, use the twenty-year-old DNA, and return to the body of a youngster with all your memories and judgment intact (which is exactly the type of transformation shown in both "Unnatural Selection" and "Rascal").

• When asked by the Ferengi captain how many people are on board the *Enterprise*, Riker replies, "One thousand fourteen" (1,014). Is this a magical number for the *Enterprise*? During the episode "Remember Me," Data claims there are 1,014 people on the *Enterprise* at that point. What are the chances—given transfers, promotions, sabbaticals, childbirth, etc.—that there would be exactly the same number aboard the *Enterprise* during both these shows?

EQUIPMENT ODDITIES

• Worf needs to get back to the phaser practice range. When two Ferengi materialize on the bridge, Worf fires a shot ... and misses! The Ferengi can't be more than twenty feet away, and the chief of Security for the flagship of the Federation misses? (As I said in Equipment Oddities for "Q Who," no wonder Klingons prefer using knives!)

• When Picard first attempts to access the main computer from a school terminal, the top of the screen reads "CLASSROOM 7." Yet when Picard meets with Riker, he asks Riker to turn on the computer in "schoolroom 8." (I suppose that the terminal in schoolroom 8 could be named "Classroom 7," but doesn't that seem needlessly complex?)

CONTINUITY AND PRODUCTION PROBLEMS

• Much of the footage showing two Klingon ships attacking the *Enterprise* initially aired as part of "Yesterday's *Enterprise*." Also, the initial decloaking of the Klingon ships looks very, very similar to a scene from the end of "The Defector"—minus one Klingon ship and two Romulan—along with other minor differences.

• Just after Riker shuts down all command functions, a shot of Data and his Ferengi captor shows the corner of Data's ops display. The display is *still* lit. In "Powerplay," when Riker transferred command function to Engineering, *all* displays went dead. Later, another shot shows that the ops display has finally gotten with the program and shut off also. It was probably just having a bad day and didn't feel like responding immediately.

• Toward the end of the show, Riker restores command functions at one of the workstations at the back of the main bridge. Accordingly, the workstation lights up with the standard displays. Riker then begins stalling for time by using humongous words to explain the computer to a hapless and thoroughly confused Ferengi. However, when Picard bursts onto the bridge with his phaser flailing, Riker's terminal is suddenly off again. What happened?

TRIVIA ANSWERS

1. *Fermi.*
2. One hundred three.

A FISTFUL OF DATAS

Star Dates: 48271.5-48278.3

As La Forge tries to hook Data up to the main computer, Worf joins his son, Alexander, and Troi on the holodeck for an "Ancient" West adventure in the town of Deadwood. Unfortunately during the interface experiment, a surge in Data's positronic brain causes a portion of Data's programming to overwrite a key piece of software in the main computer. At the same time, some files from the main computer get written into Data. As a result, Data begins speaking with an Ancient West accent and the holodeck adventurers are trapped inside a holodeck whose built-in safeguards have suddenly been suspended.

Worf becomes suspicious of the holodeck safeguards after a villain who looks just like Data tries to injure him. When the computer refuses to freeze the holodeck program, Worf makes a run for it. A gunshot wound to his left arm convinces Worf that something is very wrong. As Worf confers with Troi, every villain in the adventure takes on Data's appearance and abilities. Knowing he can't outshoot the villains, Worf fashions a personal force field from an old telegraph and his communicator. During the final confrontation, Worf activates the force field and calmly waits for the head villain to empty his six-shooter. Then the force field collapses, leaving Worf vulnerable. At the same time, one of the head villain's men tosses the head villain another loaded gun. The head villain catches the gun and spins toward Worf, but Worf draws and shoots the weapon from the villain's hand—telling him to take his men and leave Deadwood forever. Moments later, a progressive memory purge—started by La Forge to clean up both the main computer and Data—returns everything to normal as the *Enterprise* flies off into the sunset.

Trivia Questions

1. Which feline supplement does Data offer Spot?

2. How many parts does Brent Spiner play in this episode?

GREAT LINES

"I'm beginning to see the appeal of this program."—Worf, after he finally gets to beat up a few of the bad guys in his son's Ancient West holodeck program.

RUMINATIONS

*T*his episode opens with Picard in his quarters, practicing his flute.

A pan shot starts at his written music and ends with Picard. Astonishingly, the written music is actually the part supposedly played by Picard!!

PLOT OVERSIGHTS

• In the opening scene of this episode, Data and La Forge visit Picard in his quarters. They ask permission to take the computer in Engineering off line. La Forge says they are working on a new interface so Data could act as an emergency backup in the event of a shipwide systems failure. Data adds, "In theory, my neural network should be able to sustain key systems until primary control is restored." In theory? Hasn't the crew already done this? Wasn't it a direct link between Data and the engineering systems that prevented the destruction of the *Enterprise* during the episode "Disaster"?

• In the first saloon scene, the bad guy Worf's supposed to arrest rises slowly to his feet. Worf seizes the opportunity and knocks him out with one blow. Immediately, Alexander stops the program and complains that the arrest was too easy. He then restarts the sequence, with a higher difficulty level. The odd thing here is that the second time through, the arrestee gets up from his chair with the same slothfulness he showed before, only this time Worf lets him back out of range.

• After La Forge discovers that problem in the main computer's subroutine C47 (Does "C47" sound familiar? In "Conundrum" Crusher mentions holodeck program "47C." A co-

incidence? I wonder), he tells Picard it will take a couple of hours to fix it. Isn't this problem similar to that faced by the main computer in "Contagion"? In that episode, La Forge simply shut everything off and reloaded all the programs from the protected archives. Why not do the same thing here? Answer: The creators needed to stall the resolution of the computer crisis for two *television* hours so Worf could be in the shoot-out on Deadwood's main street.

EQUIPMENT ODDITIES

• To make his personal force field, Worf tears apart his communicator. Let me say that again: Worf tears his *communicator* apart. Why not just tap it and call for help? La Forge said only secondary systems were affected by Data's overwrite. Communications is a primary system. Shouldn't it still be functioning? Granted, the voice commands in the holodeck may be messed up, but doesn't the communicator transmit like a radio or wireless telephone? Does the holodeck put up some sort of jamming field that prevents communication outside the holodeck? If so, what would be the purpose of such a field?

• Worf certainly has improved his marksmanship skill since the previous episode. Here he quick-draws a Colt .45-caliber and shoots it out of the head villain's hand! Yet in "Rascals," Worf fires a phaser—an eminently more accurate weapon—and *misses a Ferengi from not more than twenty feet away.*

CONTINUITY AND PRODUCTION PROBLEMS

• At one point, when Worf tries to arrest the head villain's son, a Mexican bad guy whips a shotgun into position. In the background, the creators dubbed in the sound of a rifle cocking. Wait a minute: The Mexican is holding a sawed-off double-barreled shotgun. It doesn't make a cocking sound like the rifle Troi carries.

TRIVIA ANSWERS

1. Number 127.
2. Six: Data, four bad guys, and a floozy.

THE QUALITY OF LIFE

Star Dates: 46307.2-46317.8

The *Enterprise* arrives at a space station orbiting Tyrus VII to evaluate a new, experimental method for mining. The station uses a plasma fountain to lift material from the surface of the planet. Unfortunately, when La Forge beams over to meet with Dr. Faralon, the station's creator, La Forge finds the mining experiment fraught with technical problems.

Trivia Questions

1. The original plans for the plasma fountain called for what level of performance?

2. When did the exocomp burn out its control circuitry?

As the crew of the *Enterprise* tries to assist with the mining experiment, Data beams over to work with Faralon. All goes well until one of Faralon's robotic tools, called an "exocomp," refuses to do a seemingly routine task. Moments later, an explosion rocks the space station. Had the exocomp obeyed its orders, it would have been destroyed. Data interprets this action as self-preservation and, through this and some additional evidence, concludes that the exocomps are alive.

As work proceeds on the space station, Faralon gives Picard a tour. Suddenly the plasma fountain loses internal confinement and begins flooding the station with radiation. Just before the radiation overrides transporter function, everyone beams off except Picard and La Forge. On the *Enterprise*, Faralon suggests sending the exocomps on a suicide mission to rescue Picard and La Forge, but Data balks and locks out the transporters. Only when Riker agrees to give the exocomps the right to choose to go on the mission does Data restore the controls. The exocomps accept the challenge and—once beamed to the station—absorb enough energy to reestablish transporter function. Once Picard is safely returned, Data explains that just as Picard once defended his own right to choose (see "The Measure of a Man"), so he had to defend the exocomps' right to choose.

RUMINATIONS

The years aboard the Enterprise *seem to have tempered Crusher's cockiness over the definition of life. During this episode, Data asks her to define life, and Crusher sputters around for a while before finally coming up with an answer (sort of). During the first season of* Star

Trek: The Next Generation *she was a lot surer of herself. When posed with a similar question in "Home Soil," she immediately answered that organic life must have the ability to assimilate, respire, reproduce, grow and develop, move, secrete, and excrete.*

PLOT OVERSIGHTS

• Prior to a meeting concerning the exocomp, Picard makes a log stating that he has called a meeting of the senior staff. In the meeting, however, both Riker and Worf are missing.

• The exocomps have the ability to replicate the tool attachment they need for a specific job. Normally, the exocomp dematerializes this attachment as soon as it completes the job. Very conveniently, toward the end of the show an exocomp forgets to dematerialize the attachment. This forgetfulness allows Data to see the tool and come to the conclusion needed to move the plot along—namely, that the exocomps are alive.

• When the bridge crew quickly runs through the options for rescuing Picard, Faralon claims that they don't have time to send a shuttle to the space station. Yet mere seconds before, Riker tells everyone they have twenty-two minutes! Twenty-two minutes isn't enough time to fly a shuttle next door to an orbiting space station? It's amazing the dance the creators go through to keep the tension up on this show. In the episode "Coming of Age," a young man comman-

deers a shuttle and tries to "run away from home." It takes all of one minute for Yar to claim that he's out of transporter range. Now think about this: If it only takes a minute for a shuttle to fly out of transporter range, and the *Enterprise* has been beaming people on and off the space station continuously for the first forty-five minutes of "The Quality of Life," isn't it reasonable to assume that a shuttle craft could reach the space station in less than a minute? Of course, if the *Enterprise* sent a shuttle, the exocomps wouldn't be in danger, and Data couldn't save them, and so on, and so on, and so on.

CONTINUITY AND PRODUCTION PROBLEMS

• When La Forge first meets with Faralon on the space station, they hold a conversation over a work console. A clear plastic bubble sits on the console between them. In the shot featuring Faralon's face and La Forge's back, the decorative lines on the bubble are straight. Yet in the opposite shot of La Forge's face and Faralon's back, the lines are bent.

• At one point, La Forge gives a five-second countdown. The only problem is that it lasts *ten* seconds!!!

TRIVIA ANSWERS

1. The plasma fountain was originally designed to lift five hundred kilograms per minute.
2. At 11:50 hours.

CHAIN OF COMMAND, PART 1

Star Dates: 46357-9-46358.2

After arriving on the USS *Cairo*, an admiral beams aboard the *Enterprise* and relieves Picard of duty. In Picard's place she installs the *Cairo*'s captain, Edward Jelico. The admiral explains that Starfleet believes the Cardassians will soon attempt to steal one of the disputed star systems that line the border of Federation space. The Federation has called for an emergency meeting between itself and the Cardassians. Having negotiated the current armistice, Jelico will lead the meeting. In addition, Jelico has battle experience with the Cardassians. Hence, his assignment to captain the *Enterprise*. No one really expects the meeting to stop the Cardassian invasion.

As the crew struggles to adjust to their new domineering captain, Picard, Crusher, and Worf train on the holodeck. Starfleet also believes the Cardassians are experimenting with a new "metagenic" weapon. Metagenics are genetically engineered viruses that, when released into a planet's atmosphere, seek out and destroy all forms of DNA. In one month the viruses themselves die, leaving the planet's infrastructure ready for occupation. Intelligence reports now indicate that Cardassians on the planet Seltrice III are testing a "theta band" subspace carrier wave delivery system for metagenics. Because Picard studied theta band emissions while captaining the *Stargazer*, the admiral wanted him to head a seek-and-destroy mission. Shortly after arriving on Seltrice III, the commandos discover that the lab doesn't exist. Recognizing the trap, the team tries to retreat, but Picard is captured. As the episode ends, a Cardassian gloats over his prize, proclaiming that breaking Picard will be his greatest challenge.

Trivia Questions

1. What setting does Worf use to evaporate the stones covering the lava tube?

2. What is Picard's serial number?

RUMINATIONS

While rearranging the Enterprise *to suit his own taste, Jelico tells Troi that he prefers a certain formality on the bridge. He then requests that she wear a standard uniform. After seeing Troi function in a standard blue uniform, I suddenly realized the injustice the creators have done to her character for the past* five seasons. In a standard uniform, Troi becomes a serious professional woman of the same standing as Crusher. I know that I have used certain less than complimentary phrases in this book when referring to Troi—phrases such as "babe-counselor." My justification for using them has always been that the creators crafted her part, not I. The creators chose the outfit, the dialogue, the reactions of the male officers, the love scenes, etc. Yet when I see Troi functioning in this show, I realize that her character could have been just as effective—probably more so—had the creators opted for something other than the obvious. Certainly Troi's physical beauty is not diminished by clothing it in a standard uniform. Indeed, I find it enhanced—for there remains room for subtlety.

PLOT OVERSIGHTS

• I'll reserve my comments on the admiral's selection of Picard for this mission until the Plot Oversights of "Chain of Command," Part 2.

• As the commandos navigate through a maze of caves on Seltrice III, a cave-in buries Crusher. Unbelievably, she's okay even though she was buried under a huge pile of rocks. Maybe the rocks were the Seltrice III equivalent of pumice?

CHANGED PREMISES

• The episode "Allegiance" featured a race called Mizarians, a hooded race of passive bureaucrats who continually bow to conquerors. The episode gave the impression that Mizarians cared little for adventure.

Against this backdrop, it is humorous to note that during the backwater bar scene—where Picard searches out transportation to Seltrice III—the creators placed a Mizarian in the background as "alien filler." Obviously this particular Mizarian doesn't fall into the mold of his planet!

EQUIPMENT ODDITIES

• Shortly after taking over the Enterprise, Jelico tells Riker to change the functions of the Science I and Science II workstations in the aft portion of the bridge. They are supposed to be "dedicated to damage control and weapons status from now on." (Emphasis mine.) Yet when reporting that the theta band emissions from Seltrice III have stopped, Riker stands with Jelico in front of Science I and it still says "Science I" at the top and Riker is still using it for planetary scanning, not weapons status, as Jelico ordered.

CONTINUITY AND PRODUCTION PROBLEMS

• Picard chooses a rather unusual location to search out covert transportation to Seltrice III. The place he chooses is, in fact, the genetically engineered and supposedly completely-sealed-from-all-external-influences colony on Moab IV!!! You may recall that in the episode "The Masterpiece Society," the Enterprise rescued the colony from certain destruction by a stellar fragment, but not without cost. Exposure to life outside their bubble caused many of the colonists to leave Moab IV. This greatly distressed the colony leader because every person had been genetically bred to fulfill specific roles. At the end of the show, Picard despaired that the arrival and influence of the *Enterprise* might have been the greatest threat of all to the colony. Obviously, a guilt-ridden Picard knew conditions at the colony had seriously deteriorated, because he travels there to find a Ferengi smuggler. Perhaps Picard hoped to improve the situation a little by contributing some of his hard-earned Starfleet monetary tokens to the Moab IV economy. (Okay, I'm joking. Actually, the creators chose to reuse the matte painting of the colony on Moab IV as an establishing shot just before the bar scene!)

TRIVIA ANSWERS

1. Setting 16.
2. SP-937-215.

CHAIN OF COMMAND, PART 2

Star Date: 46360.8

After capturing Picard during a failed commando raid, the Cardassians hand him over to Gul Madred, their expert in extracting information. To begin with, Madred injects Picard with truth drugs. He wants to know the Federation's defense plans for Minos Corva—the location of the Cardassians' planned incursion into Federation territory. Picard responds to the drugs, but Madred cannot uncover the defense plans because Picard doesn't know them. Refusing to give up, Madred turns to torture. The Cardassians implant a pain-inducing device in Picard. Madred then methodically sets about breaking Picard, asking only that Picard admit there are five lights above Madred's desk when in fact there are only four.

Meanwhile, on the *Enterprise*, meetings continue between the Cardassians and Edward Jelico. The Cardassians flaunt their recording of a drugged Picard confessing to his attack on Seltrice III. They try to pressure Jelico into admitting that Picard was acting under Starfleet orders. Jelico refuses, and then refuses to negotiate for Picard's release.

As Picard's torture continues, the crew of the *Enterprise* correctly deduces that Minos Corva is the location of the planned Cardassian invasion by examining the hull of a Cardassian ship. Jelico immediately takes the *Enterprise* there. He believes the Cardassian attack fleet is waiting inside a nearby sensor-damping nebula. Needing the best pilot on the *Enterprise*, Jelico asks Riker to fly a shuttle into the blinding nebula and place antimatter mines beside the Cardassian ships. After Riker completes his task, Jelico forces the surrender of the Cardassians and the safe return of Picard. As the show concludes, Picard returns to his post as captain of the *Enterprise*.

Trivia Questions

1. What is Edward Jelico's favorite hour?

2. What scan does La Forge use on the Cardassian ship?

RUMINATIONS

I find Gul Madred's question of the lights very intriguing, not because I enjoy watching torture, but because of the numbers and symbolism involved. Most of the shots of Madred standing behind his desk show him in the middle of the lights—putting two on either side of him. In other *words, Madred is demanding that Picard admit that the two lights to his right and the two lights to his left add up to five. Does this sound familiar? In George Orwell's frightening vision of the future,* 1984, *the torturers demand that their victims recite and believe the equation "2+2=5." I don't know if the creators of this episode had Orwell in mind when they gave Madred his question, but the parallels are interesting.*

GREAT LINES

"THERE ... ARE ... FOUR ... LIGHTS!!!"—Picard, refusing to bow to Madred's demands for the last time before returning to the *Enterprise.*

PLOT OVERSIGHTS

• As the show opens, Madred questions a drugged Picard. Madred asks Picard the names and ranks of those who accompanied him on the raid. Picard responds with "Chief Medical Officer Beverly Crusher and Lieutenant Worf." Isn't "chief medical officer" more of a title than a rank? Crusher's rank is commander, in the same way that Riker's rank is commander and his title is first officer (pick, pick, pick, pick, pick, pick).

• Both Part 1 and Part 2 of "Chain of Command" purport that the Cardassians were able to lure Picard into their trap simply by using theta band emissions as the bait. Of course, this begs the question "Is Picard really the only person in Starfleet who knows about these kinds of subspace waves?" What happened to the rest of the crew on the *Stargazer?* "Chain of Command," Part 1, indicated that

Picard and his Stargazer *crew* studied theta band emissions. What happened to the rest of the crew?

Data seems to address this question during Part 2 when he says that Picard is "one of only three Starfleet captains with extensive experience in theta band devices. The other two are no longer in Starfleet." Of course, this comment begs another question: "Is this the type of mission that Starfleet feels must be lead by a captain?" Isn't this really just a commando raid to seek out and destroy a Cardassian lab? Does it seem reasonable to send the captain of the flagship of the Federation on a grenade-throwing mission? (I realize that Starfleet sent Picard to Romulus to investigate Spock's disappearance in "Unification," but that mission involved one of the most honored humanoids in the Federation. Sending Picard on this mission is like getting Norman Schwarzkopf to do a Delta Force job.) In addition, if it is not reasonable for Starfleet to send Picard on this mission, it is even less reasonable that the Cardassians would expect that they could capture Picard simply by transmitting a bunch of theta waves.

TRIVIA ANSWERS

1. It is 1400 hours. (That's when he wants readiness reports from each department head in Part 1, and wants La Forge's interpretations of Crusher's tricorder reading, and needs a shuttle outfitted for the nebula in Part 2.)

2. Quantum resonance scan 047.

SHIP IN A BOTTLE

Star date: 48929.1

As Lieutenant Barclay searches for an error in a Sherlock Holmes holodeck adventure, Dr. Moriarty appears (see "Elementary, Dear Data"). Greatly disturbed, Moriarty demands to know why Picard has not kept his four-year-old promise to find a way to free Moriarty from the holodeck. A short time later, Picard, Data, and Barclay meet with Moriarty on holodeck 3 and explain that Starfleet scientists still have not figured out how to make a holodeck retain its cohesion once it leaves the holodeck grid. Moriarty decides to take matters into his own hands and promptly walks off the holodeck. The confused trio follows, not realizing that Moriarty has tricked them. In fact, they are still on the holodeck—programmed by Moriarty to simulate the Enterprise.

Eventually Moriarty reaches the goal of his ruse and tricks Picard into giving him the codes to take command of the Enterprise. He then demands that Riker find a way to bring him out of the holodeck. At about the same time, Picard, Data, and Barclay realize that they are still on the holodeck and decide to play a ruse of their own. From inside Moriarty's holodeck simulation of the Enterprise, they program another simulation of the Enterprise. A short time later, a simulated Riker acquiesces to Moriarty's demands, beams him off the holodeck, and allows him to leave in a shuttle. In exchange, Moriarty returns control of the Enterprise and frees Picard, Data, and Barclay. Picard stores the simulation Moriarty is still experiencing in active memory and lets it continue. In that way, Moriarty will live out his life believing that he actually escaped the confines of the holodeck.

Trivia Questions

1. What does Picard ask Worf to launch toward the colliding planets?

2. In what shuttle does Moriarty leave?

CHANGED PREMISES

• In case there was any doubt about the disposition of holodeck matter, this episode absolutely confirms that it cannot exist outside the holodeck. The dialogue again and again pounds this point home. For instance, Picard says, "Although objects appear solid on the holodeck, in the real world they have no substance." To prove it, he picks up a book and tosses it through the holodeck entrance. The book immediately vaporizes (much quicker, by the way, than the villains did in "The Big Good-bye"). True, this scene occurs within Moriarty's simulation of the *Enterprise*, but Picard acts like the book behaved exactly as he expected.

And if holodeck matter cannot exist outside the holodeck, the following anomalies exist. Wesley, drenched in holodeck water, walks off the holodeck and remains wet in "Encounter at Farpoint." Picard, kissed by a 1940s holodeck woman in "The Big Good-bye," leaves the holodeck with her lipstick intact on his cheek. During "Angel One," a snowball flies out of the holodeck and hits Picard. And finally, Data carries a piece of holodeck-created paper to a meeting of the senior staff in "Elementary, Dear Data."

EQUIPMENT ODDITIES

• In the opening scene of the episode, Data and La Forge enjoy a holodeck Holmsian adventure. At one point, La Forge tells the computer to "freeze program." While the charac-

ter quits moving, the clock keeps ticking and the fire keeps burning. Shouldn't these freeze also?

• The secondary theme of the show concerns two colliding planets, which are gas giants. In one scene, Data and La Forge discuss the upcoming phenomenon with two individuals from the engineering crew. La Forge walks over to the far end of the center island in Engineering and punches a few buttons. Then all four of them stare at the tabletop like something's happening. The scene then cuts to a close-up of what they are supposedly looking at—an animated sequence showing a simulation of the planets colliding. Unfortunately, the special effects people didn't include the animation in the next shot. When the scene cuts back to La Forge and the others, they are still staring at the static graphic normally seen on the tabletop.

TRIVIA ANSWERS

1. Four class 8 probes.
2. *Sakarov*.

AQUIEL

Star date: 46461.3

As the episode begins, the *Enterprise* arrives at a communications relay station near the Klingon border. When the station does not respond to repeated hails, an away team beams over to investigate. They find the station deserted by both of its Starfleet officers. They also find blood traces from station officer Lieutenant Aquiel Unari, Unari's pet dog, and someone's charred cellular remains. In addition, the station's shuttle craft is missing. Crusher takes the remains back to the *Enterprise* for further study.

Picard contacts the area Klingon governor and asks him to investigate as well. A short time later, the governor shows up, intent on proving they had nothing to do with the disappearances of the station's personnel. He parades Lieutenant Unari into the observation lounge, stating that they found her in the station's shuttle on the Klingon side of the border. Picard asks Unari for an explanation. She says that the other station officer attacked her. She managed to break free and head for the weapons lockers but she can't remember anything after that. A short time later, Crusher discovers that the remains actually come from a coalescent being, one that absorbs its victims before assuming their shape. Evidently the being had already absorbed the station officer who attacked Unari and it was trying to absorb her. Unsure if the being succeeded, the crew puts Unari under close observation. They don't realize that once Unari escaped from the station, the being attacked and absorbed her dog. When the dog turns into a blob and tries to attack La Forge, however, he kills it and frees Unari from suspicion.

Trivia Questions

1. Lieutenant Unari accepted com traffic for which station?

2. How long was Unari missing?

PLOT OVERSIGHTS

• After La Forge rifles through all of Unari's personal logs, he tries to access the logs for the other station officer and cannot. He reports his progress to Riker, who responds, "Well, maybe [the other station officer] didn't make the official logs. Unari could have been responsible for them." La Forge says he doesn't think so because Unari was the junior officer. But earlier in the episode, La Forge asks for the *station* logs;

Unari's voice makes them, *and* they deal strictly with station business, not personal matters. Wouldn't station logs and "official" logs be close to the same thing?

• In one of her personal logs, Unari yearns for a glass of real muskin seed punch, the kind her mother used to make. She doesn't think the replicator does a very good job on it. Later in the episode, La Forge brings her a glass of muskin seed punch in Ten-Forward and Unari acts like it is wonderful. Did La Forge get into Guinan's personal supply, or is Unari just trying to make him feel good?

• This coalescent being is either not very smart or it made a bad mistake. Crusher states that it probably has to change bodies every few days. The episode supports this by saying that the coalesced officer arrived at the relay station several days before the incident with Unari. Supposedly he attacked Unari because he needed the food. But the episode's dialogue indicates that the station assignment lasts for a year. What was the being going to do after it consumed Unari and her dog? The sta-

tion is out in the boondocks. If the being absorbed the officer before he arrived at the station—as the episode seems to indicate—why would he go somewhere with such a limited supply of nutrition?

• This coalescent being is also quite resilient. Crusher stated that the charred remains had been fried with a phaser on level 10 for thirty to forty seconds. Amazingly, it comes back to life!

CONTINUITY AND PRODUCTION PROBLEMS

• Someone got a little "boop"-happy in the sound effects department. During the last scene between La Forge and Unari, they sit close together in Ten-Forward. At one point, the "boop" sound effect for a companel page momentarily interrupts their conversation. Strangely, no one pages La Forge or Unari, and the scene proceeds as if nothing happened!

TRIVIA ANSWERS
1. Relay Station 194.
2. Forty-six hours.

FACE OF THE ENEMY

Star date: 46519.1

A kidnapped Troi wakes to find herself aboard a Romulan warbird, and surgically altered to look like a Romulan. She is now a major in Romulan intelligence, escorting cargo to the Kaleb sector. On the way there, a Romulan soldier named Nevek explains. The three boxes of cargo actually contain a high-ranking member of the Romulan government and his two aides—all in suspended animation. They wish to defect, and Nevek—part of the underground movement encouraged by Spock (see "Unification II")—is assisting them. The warbird will rendezvous with a freighter in the Kaleb sector. From there, Troi will accompany the men to Federation space.

At the same time, Picard receives a request from Spock to meet the freighter. Unfortunately, when the freighter rendezvouses with the Romulan warbird, Troi senses that the pilot of the freighter has no intention of delivering the "cargo." She tells this to Nevek, and he immediately destroys the freighter. Although shocked by the action, Troi tells the Romulans to cloak the warbird and wait for further instructions.

Trivia Questions

1. Where did the Romulans kidnap Troi?

2. During this episode, a Starfleet ensign who defected to Romulus twenty years earlier returns to the Federation. Where are his quarters on the Enterprise?

When the freighter misses its appointment with the *Enterprise*, Picard starts searching for the freighter. A short time later, the cloaked Romulans watch the *Enterprise* approach. The Romulans decide to attack, but Troi assumes command. She decloaks the warbird, and speaks with a stunned Picard, convincing him to lower the *Enterprise*'s shields. At this, Nevek immediately beams the defectors to the *Enterprise*, exposing his treason. The Romulans kill him and prepare to take Troi into custody, but the crew of the *Enterprise* beam her aboard and race off at warp 9.

PLOT OVERSIGHTS

• The Universal Translator serves a wonderful function for *Star Trek: The Next Generation*. It makes it possible to have the series! If the characters couldn't communicate with new life forms or if they had to keep learning new languages every week, it would make for a very boring series. For the sake of the show, everyone winks at this standard oversight and lets the Universal Translator perform with impossible perfection.

However, this episode pushes the "everybody can understand everybody" plot contrivance a bit too far. The Romulans have kidnapped Troi and thrown her into a Romulan warbird. Does Troi speak Romulan? Is it standard training for Starfleet cadets? Or do the Romulans—out of their deep desire to achieve harmony in the galaxy—conveniently speak some sort of Galactic Standard aboard their own vessels?

CHANGED PREMISES

• Romulans serving on warbirds seem to have acquired insignia on their collars since "Redemption II." Of course, the insignia on the collar make it possible for Troi to point to her collar in this episode and say, "THIS gives me the right!"

CONTINUITY AND PRODUCTION PROBLEMS

• Do all Romulan commanders (captains of warbirds) look alike, or just some of them? Commander Toreth in this episode looks just like an older version of Subcommander Taris from "Contagion." In fact, they are played by the same actress, Carolyn Seymour. Wouldn't it have made more sense just to name them both "Taris"? "Contagion" occurred during the second season; there was time for her to get a promotion.

TRIVIA ANSWERS

1. The Neuropsychology Seminar at Bacar VI.
2. Deck 12.

★

TAPESTRY

Star date: unknown

A s the episode begins, an away team beams up with a badly injured Picard. Seconds later, the captain dies because of complications with his artificial heart. When Picard awakes in a light-drenched room, the robed, godlike figure in the distance turns out to be Q. He tells Picard that they'll be spending eternity together. Before they begin, however, Q wonders if there is anything Picard regrets. He points out that if Picard had had a real heart instead of a cardiac replacement, he would still be alive (see "Samaritan Snare"). Picard admits that there are many things about his brash youth that he regrets. At this, Q sweeps him back in time to Starbase Earhart. Picard is now an ensign. It is two days before the ill-conceived fight he will pick with a trio of Norsicans—the fight that will result in a Norsican dagger piercing his heart. Q tells Picard that if he can avoid the fight he will keep his natural heart and survive his death thirty years into the future.

Using the wisdom and maturity gained over the years, Picard keeps the altercation from occurring. After congratulating Picard, Q returns him to the present. Unfortunately, once Picard made the choice to act more responsibly in his youth, his future changed. Assistant astrophysics officer Lieutenant Picard is a hard-working, steady, punctual person but definitely not command material. He will spend the rest of his life in safety—collecting data, analyzing them, and delivering reports to his superiors. Picard pleads for Q to give him a chance to put things back the way they were, even if it means he will die. Q agrees, and as the resulting fight ends, Picard chuckles at the dagger in his chest. At that moment Captain Picard comes back to life with his artificial heart functioning once again.

Trivia Questions

1. Who does Crusher assign to ward 3 for the ambulatory patients?

2. Who captains the Enterprise in Picard's altered future?

RUMINATIONS

D uring "Samaritan Snare," Picard recounts his fight with the Norsicans to Wesley Crusher. In that recounting, he mentions the he laughed when he saw the dagger sticking out of his chest. The laugh makes sense in this context—here is Picard, young and brash, feeling the warmth of the blood spreading through his chest cavity, giddy from the fight, and finding the blade quite humorous. "Tapestry" picks up the laugh and spins it in another direction. Picard looks at the dagger, knows that his life will remain as it was and he laughs. It is a delightful twist, adding new dimension to a few lines of dialogue written several years before.

PLOT OVERSIGHTS

• When the injured Picard arrives in sick bay, Crusher asks what happened. Riker responds that they were attacked outside the conference room by Lenarians. Moments later, she asks Worf what kind of weapon did the damage, and Worf tells her, "A compressed terrion beam." However, in talking with Q, Picard bemoans that had he been more mature in his youth he would not have "died from a *random* energy surge" thirty years later. An attack with a compressed terrion beam doesn't sound very random, does it?

CHANGED PREMISES

• As previously mentioned, Picard gives Wesley a fairly detailed narrative of his encounter with the Norsicans during "Samaritan Snare." There seem to be some discrepancies between that narrative and the events of this episode, however.

First, Picard tells Wesley that he and several young officers were on leave at Starbase Earhart. In "Tapestry," Picard tells Q that they came to Starbase Earhart right after graduation "to await our first deep space assignments."

Second, Picard tells Wesley that when the Norsicans came into the Bonstell Recreation Facility, the other Starfleet officers in the group "had the good sense to give these Norsicans a wide berth, to stand off." On the other hand, Picard says he "stood toe to toe with the worst of the three" and he insulted the Norsican. That's when the fight broke out. The account differs from the events in "Tapestry." In this episode, a Norsican picks a fight with one of Picard's buddies, and that officer stands up to the Norsican. He does not give the Norsican a "wide berth."

Third, in the "Samaritan Snare" account, Picard says he had one of the Norsicans down on the floor in a "devious joint lock" when another one pulled a weapon and stabbed him from behind. A "joint lock" usually refers to some type of wrestling hold and incapacitates an opponent. In "Tapestry" both of the reenacted fight scenes show Picard flipping a Norsican just before he gets stabbed. I don't believe a joint lock and a judo flip are the same thing.

Finally, Picard *has* matured since his first encounter with the Norsican trio. In that encounter—according to "Samaritan Snare"—Picard tells Wesley that he told the worst Norsican "what I thought of him, his pals, his planet, and I possibly made some passing reference to his questionable parentage." At the end of "Tapestry," while striving to restore his future, Picard dispenses with all these unimportant details and simply attacks the guy.

EQUIPMENT ODDITIES

• The panel is back on the inside of the turbolift! This infrequently appearing panel—last seen during "Power Play"—seems to come and go at the whim of the creators. You'll find it in the scene where Lieutenant. Picard boards a turbolift to report to La Forge. The panel is to the left of the turbolift doors. Oddly enough, it is not illuminated as it was during "Power Play." If fact, it is not illuminated at all. Maybe the lights burned out?

TRIVIA ANSWERS

1. Dr. Selar. (Just for your information, Selar is also mentioned in "Remember Me" and "Suspicions." She appeared in "Schizoid Man.")
2. Thomas Holloway.

BIRTHRIGHT, PART I

Star date: 46578.4

T he *Enterprise* docks at Station Deep Space 9 (DS9) to assist in the reconstruction of aqueducts on Bajor. Dr. Bashir—chief medical officer for DS9—comes aboard with an alien device he's been studying. After catching Bashir making unauthorized use of the computer in sick bay, Data suggests they take the device to Engineering and study it further. During the tests, a plasma shock erupts from the device and stuns Data. While unconscious, Data has a vision of his father. Subsequent tests show that Data's creator, Noonian Soong, built in a set of circuits to allow Data to dream. Evidently Soong planned to activate them once Data reached a certain level of cognitive ability. Although the plasma shock activated them prematurely, Data decides to spend part of every day exploring this new facet of his intelligence.

Meanwhile, an information broker approaches Worf on DS9. He claims that Worf's father is alive, that he was captured—not killed—by the Romulan attack on Khitomer decades ago. At first, Worf refuses to believe the broker's story. If a Klingon allows himself to be taken prisoner, he dishonors not only himself but his children and their children as well. After considering the matter, however, Worf decides he must know for sure. He finds the information broker and forces the broker to take him to the site of the Romulan prison camp. Worf sneaks into the camp that night and does find Klingons who were captured by the Romulans at Khitomer, but they tell him that his father died in battle with honor. Unfortunately, they also tell him that he can never leave the camp.

Trivia Questions

1. How long is Data unconscious during his first dream?

2. The Ferengi view the hammer as what?

PLOT OVERSIGHTS

• Dr. Bashir seems terribly casual about making unauthorized usage of sick bay's computer systems in this episode. He gives the excuse that it would have taken him hours to analyze the device using the computers on DS9. How long would it have taken to ask permission? Fifteen seconds? Also, is Dr. Crusher the only person who works in sick bay? True, she is on DS9 at this point in the episode, but where is the rest of the medical crew?

• When introducing himself to Worf,

the information broker says he's a "*man* with information." He's not a man, he's a Y'Ridian! Doesn't "man" refers to Earthlings, as in "hu-man"?

CHANGED PREMISES

• Interestingly, the snug body suit that Worf wears during this episode doesn't show any ridges down his back. "Ethics" established that Worf has a dinosaurlike ridge running down his spinal cord.

CONTINUITY AND PRODUCTION PROBLEMS

• The hot stock tip for the week: Invest heavily in any company that manufactures those flared-bottom untippable coffee mugs. According to the scene with La Forge and Worf in a DS9 eating establishment, they are still in use in the twenty-fourth century!

• When Data gets hit with the plasma shock the first time, a tricorder flies out of his hand. In the background, the sound effects personnel dubbed in the sound of it hitting the floor, bouncing a few times, and coming to rest. Then the scene cuts to another view of Data being electrocuted. Then the shot cuts back to Data and he falls down. To the left, the tricorder is bouncing across the floor. It should definitely be done bouncing by this time in the scene. Did La Forge kick it as he was running across to help Data?

• While "convincing" the informa-

tion broker to take him to see his father, Worf claims the broker has a ship capable of warp. Yet in the scene showing the craft going to the Romulan camp, the stars are not streaking. (I suppose you could say that they are about to arrive and have already dropped out of warp. Unfortunately in the scene that follows, the broker tells Worf to get some rest because it will be three *hours* before they reach their destination. Why would they go to impulse if they still had three hours to go?)

• Before attempting to re-create Data's vision, La Forge hooks him up to the computer in Engineering by attaching an optical fiber to Data's head. After the plasma shock hits Data for the second time, a close-up shows his face. The optical cable is missing, but the center island of Engineering is clearly visible in the background. The scene then cuts to Data's dream sequence. He rises from a chair in front of a set of turbolift doors and walks out to find Soong. If the close-up of Data's face was part of the dream sequence, the optical cable should be missing. However, if Data is still in Engineering, the cable should still be attached, since the dream sequence doesn't include any scenes from Engineering.

TRIVIA ANSWERS

1. Forty-seven seconds.
2. Sexual prowess.

BIRTHRIGHT, PART II

Star date: 46759.2

After breaking into a Romulan prison camp, Worf discovers that the Klingons—captured and brought there from Khitomer decades ago—do not want to leave. They want their families on the Klingon home world to believe that they died in battle with honor. Years ago, they decided voluntarily to stay in the prison camp and raise new families. To allow them to do so, the Romulan camp commander gave up his military career and remained at the camp. He even married one of the female Klingon warriors. Unfortunately, all these facts mean that Worf must remain as well. No one must know of the Klingons' dishonor.

Undeterred, Worf tries to escape and rendezvous with the ship that brought him to the camp (see "Birthright, Part I"), but the Romulans recapture him. Knowing Worf will try again, the senior Klingon prisoner assigns a young Klingon male to guard him. After discovering that the Klingon children in the camp know nothing of true Klingon ways, Worf begins to instruct them. Soon they grow restless with life in the camp, desiring to leave and assume the roles of true warriors. The camp commander realizes that if Worf continues, his peaceful camp will be torn apart. He tries to kill Worf, but the young people band together and stand with their newfound teacher in front of the executioners. The camp commander recants, giving Worf and the children permission to leave. Before they go, however, Worf orders the young people never to reveal the location or existence of the camp. In this way, the original families of the Klingon prisoners can retain their honor.

PLOT OVERSIGHTS

• One of the burning questions that this episode evokes is: Why is "Birthright" a two-parter? Nothing happens with Data during "Part II." It seems like Data's dreaming could have been expanded into one episode and Worf's prison experience compressed into another. Aside from the strained connecting theme of "fatherhood," these stories have little to do with each other.

• The dialogue of the episode seems to indicate that the Klingons have been at this camp for the past twenty-three years. Yet other dia-

> **Trivia Questions**
>
> 1. Who threw the sword into the ocean?
>
> 2. What data base does La Forge use to track the Y'Ridian's ship?

logue puts this camp at the edge of Romulan space. Does it make sense to put a prison camp at the edge of the territories you control?

• Supposedly, the "official" story for the sudden appearance of these Klingon youths will be that they are survivors of a crash in the system four years ago. Are the Klingons really this bad at tracking their ships? Won't they know that there wasn't a missing Klingon ship in that area? And how will they explain all the things that the Klingon children don't know about functioning in a Klingon culture? Worf gave them an introduction, but they must have huge gaps in their knowledge and understanding of Klingonhood.

CHANGED PREMISES

• When the senior Klingon prisoner questions Worf as to why he came, the prisoner points out that if Worf's father was alive, Worf would be dishonored. When Worf says he has no place in his heart for shame, the Klingon prisoner shoots back, "I can only hope that if my son came here he would be Klingon enough to kill me." Does this mean that killing a captured parent is the honorable Klingon thing to do? If so, the Klingon commander in "A Matter of Honor" acted dishonorably because he tells Riker that his father was captured by the Romulans and later returned to the Klingon home world. While the Klingon commander refuses to see his father, he never says anything about killing him.

CONTINUITY AND PRODUCTION PROBLEMS

• The Romulan camp commander in this episode sacrificed his career for the Klingons in his camp. His son made up for it, though. You may have noticed that Admiral Mendak of "Data's Day" bears a striking resemblance to the camp commander. Obviously he's a close relative. (Actually, both parts are played by Alan Scarfe.)

• The star date for this episode is a little odd. "Birthright, Part I" occurs at star date 46578.4. Yet Picard's first log in Part II—heard in the middle of the show—has a star date of 46759.2. Notice the jump of 180.8 units. Later, La Forge establishes that only one week has elapsed since Worf left with the Y'Ridian. Since 1,000 units is one television year, don't 180.8 units seem large for only one television week? (I'm wondering if Patrick Stewart or the script typists switched the third and fourth digits in the second star date.)

TRIVIA ANSWERS

1. Morath. (At least I assume it was Morath. Worf says it was Kahless's brother. Worf tells Alexander about the brothers during "New Ground.")
2. Deep Space 9 Traffic Control Database.

STARSHIP MINE

Star date: 46682.4

*T*he episode opens with the *Enterprise* docked at the Remlar Array. The array will cleanse the starship of the barion particles it has absorbed while traveling at warp over the past five years. However, since the removal beam is lethal to living tissue, the entire crew and their families must evacuate to Arkaria, the planet that administers the process. During a welcoming reception, Picard learns of Arkarian horses and decides to go for a ride. He reboards the *Enterprise* to get his saddle before the barion sweep begins.

Outside his quarters, Picard notices an open ODN junction box and a bundle of severed optical fibers. Moments later, a Remlar Array worker threatens him with a laser welder. After rendering the man unconscious, Picard races back to the transporter. Unfortunately, the autoshutdown sequence turns off main power before Picard can beam back to Arkaria and summon help. After learning that the workers are on board to steal trilithium resin—a highly toxic and volatile waste product produced by the warp drive—Picard executes a series of ambushes, staying just ahead of the thieves and the barion sweep. Eventually he and the head conspirator fight it out in Ten-Forward, the last place scheduled for barion removal. When Picard loses the fight, the head conspirator beams onto an escape vessel with the trilithium, not realizing that Picard has removed the stabilizer from the trilithium storage unit. Seconds later, the trilithium detonates and destroys the escape vessel. Picard then frantically pages the Arkarian base and they shut off the barion sweep just before it reaches him.

Trivia Questions

1. What authorization code does Picard use to disable command function?

2. Which race prefers a room temperature that matches their body temperature?

PLOT OVER-SIGHTS

• Picard beats up the first worker on deck 7 just outside his quarters. A few scenes later, he appears to drag the worker into sick bay. (The door indicates they are on deck 12, and the sick bay emblems can be seen on a wall.) Bear in mind that the turbolifts are not working at this point in the show because primary power is off. So Picard beats this guy up, then carries him down five decks on the access tube ladders just so he can inject him with a general anesthetic. Does this make

399

sense?

• Speaking of ship locations, Picard successfully stages his ambushes with the knowledge that the thieves *must* head for Ten-Forward, the last place scheduled for barion removal. Originally, the thieves plan to stay in Engineering with the trilithium, since a field diverter would protect them from the removal beam. After Picard destroys the diverter, they head for Ten-Forward. But these are the same people who installed a field diverter on the main bridge at the beginning of the episode. Why not go there and wait for the removal beam to pass, just as they planned to do in Engineering?

• While making small talk during the welcoming reception, Data says, "I have found that humans prefer a body temperature of 21 degrees Celsius." Twenty-one degrees Celsius is 69.8 degrees Fahrenheit. (As far as I know, only dead humans prefer that body temperature. I think Data was supposed to say, "prefer a *room* temperature of…")

• Also, while making small talk with Commander Hutchinson—the Starfleet officer assigned to Arkaria—Data says that there are five Tarellians serving on the *Enterprise*. If Data is referring to the same race featured in "Haven," Wyatt Miller has done an outstanding job. In that episode, the young doctor is touched with the sufferings of the last few infectious disease-ridden survivors of the Tarellian race, victims of their own genetically engineered doomsday weapon. Wyatt risks his life by beaming over to their ship. The episode

ends as the Tarellian ship flies off. Obviously, Miller not only found a cure, he also arranged to have five of the Tarellians posted to the *Enterprise*.

EQUIPMENT ODDITIES

• Evidently the creators have decided to keep the panel inside the turbolift to the left of the doors. It first showed up as an illuminated panel in "Power Play." Then it reappeared in "Tapestry," but it wasn't lit up. It's also in this episode and the next episode, "Lessons."

CONTINUITY AND PRODUCTION PROBLEMS

• The star date at the beginning of this episode answers a question from "Birthright, Part II." That episode has a star date of 46759.2, a jump of 180.8 units from "Birthright, Part I." Since Part II establishes that only a week has gone by, the jump seemed a little large. Evidently someone transposed the third and fourth digits in the star date for Part II because "Starship Mine" has a star date of 46682.4, which puts the events in this episode between the events in "Birthright, Part I" and "Birthright, Part II." Otherwise, Worf must have a twin brother who took over his job in "Starship Mine" while he was at the Romulan prison camp for most of "Birthright, Part II."

• Just after capturing Picard for the second time, a female worker calls the head conspirator and says, "I'm on deck 10. I have Mot." (At this point, the conspirators think Picard is Mot, the barber.) Oddly enough, if you watch the woman's lips she appears to say, "I'm on deck 2. I have Mot." Also, when the head conspirator joins up with them, she walks through a door with "02" on the left side, indicating that they are, in fact, on deck 2. Why would the creators redub the sound to say "deck 10"?

If they really are on deck 2, the barion sweep has already passed them. At this point in the show, the graphics showing the progression of the barion sweep through the *Enterprise* place the current position of the sweep in the front third of the saucer section moving toward Ten-Forward. Deck 2 sits directly under the main bridge (deck 1) in the center of the saucer section and extends only a short distance forward.

• At least we know what happened to the other Varon T disrupter. In the episode "The Most Toys," a collector named "Kivas Fajo" kidnaps Data and threatens him with an illegal weapon called a Varon T disrupter. Fajo says only five prototypes were manufactured and he has four of them. Evidently the head conspirator got the other one, because the weapon she holds at the end of the episode looks just like the one Fajo had.

TRIVIA ANSWERS
1. Gamma 6073.
2. The Sheliak.

⭐ LESSONS

Star Dates: 45693.1-45697.2

After visiting his ready room at 3:00 A.M. and finding all the major computer systems allocated to stellar cartography, Picard heads to their lab to find out why. Lieutenant Commander Nella Darrin, the newly arrived head of stellar cartography, explains that they are taking precise gravometeric readings. She hopes to use them to predict the configuration of an emerging star system. Picard finds the discussion fascinating. Later, Picard encounters Darrin again. This time she plays the piano for a Mozart trio. The discussion of music leads Darrin to visit Picard's quarters as he practices the flute that he received in "The Inner Light." Moments later, she cajoles him into a duet with her.

The relationship progresses until it meets the critical test. The Federation colony on Bersallis III requests evacuation. A massive fire storm threatens its existence. Darrin leads six teams to set up a series of thermal deflectors to protect the colony during evacuation. When Darrin informs Riker that the deflectors will need to be manually calibrated con-

tinuously, Picard orders the team to hold their positions until all the colonists can be transported up to the Enterprise. Afterward, the Enterprise attempts to retrieve the deflector teams but two are lost, including Darrin's. Thankfully, after the storm passes, the crew recovers Darrin and several others. Picard tells her that he could never place her in danger again. She replies that as long as she is stationed on the Enterprise, the possibility exists that it may happen again. Since neither wish to resign their commissions, Darrin puts in for a transfer and leaves the Enterprise.

Trivia Questions

1. Where did Darrin report for Enterprise duty?

2. What is the most acoustically perfect spot on the Enterprise?

GREAT MOMENTS

There is a very cute effect in this episode. During Darrin's performance with the trio, the camera shows us a close-up of someone actually playing the piece and then pans across the side of the piano and up to show us Darrin's face. At first it looks like one continuous cut. It isn't. Those clever creators spliced in the second shot of Darrin when the scene was blacked out by the side of the piano. It's done very well.

PLOT OVERSIGHTS

• Supposedly, the thermal deflection teams were the only things keeping the colony from incineration. Presumably they would be the last ones to be beamed up to the *Enterprise*. When visited by Picard in sick bay, Riker says they recovered all the colonists and retrieved all but two of the deflection teams. Each team had two people. That makes five individuals who are missing, four team members and Darrin. Yet when the *Enterprise* beams up survivors, six get off the transporter, and then Darrin materializes with a team member. That makes eight. Where did the other three come from?

• The episode ends with Darrin requesting a transfer because Picard doesn't want to put her in danger again and neither will resign their commissions in Starfleet. Certainly, Picard would be reluctant to resign. He's a command-level person. There aren't a lot of civilian corollaries to commanding a starship. On the other hand, Darrin is a scientist. Couldn't she resign her commission and continue her work on the *Enterprise*? Keiko O'Brien wasn't in Starfleet, and she held a high scientific position on the ship. And why are Picard and Darrin acting like resignation is such a big step? If they don't like civilian life, can't they just say "Oops, I've changed my mind" (just as Worf did

in "Redemption II")?

• One more point on Darrin's need to request a transfer. Many episodes reference the fact that only the best and brightest get posted to the *Enterprise*. Those shows indicate that Starfleet officers work hard to achieve this prodigious assignment. In other words, Darrin's arrival on the *Enterprise* was the culmination of discipline and diligence in her career. Yet shortly after she arrives, she is forced to resign. Why? Because Picard cannot bring himself to treat her as he would any other officer under his command. Picard feels compelled to constrain her activities to those he deems "safe." Darrin correctly recognizes that this constraint will hinder her opportunities for advancement and requests a transfer. Her only other option would be to bring Picard up on charges of sexual harassment! Picard routinely sends officers into danger. Officers for whom he cares deeply, officers like Riker. These missions provide the officers with opportunities to "get noticed." Darrin will no doubt receive a commendation on her record for her valor in leading the thermal deflection teams. Yet, Picard has made a decision to use his position of authority to deprive her of any further opportunities based on the fact that she is a woman and he is in love with her. Certainly sounds like sexual harassment, doesn't it?

TRIVIA ANSWERS
1. Starbase 218.
2. The fourth intersection of Jefferies
Tube 25.

THE CHASE

Star dates: 96731.5-96735.2

Picard's former archaeology instructor, Professor Galen, visits the *Enterprise* with an unexpected offer. He wants Picard to join him on an expedition. The professor claims that he is on the verge of a profound discovery but refuses to say any more. Picard reluctantly turns Galen down, citing his responsibilities on the *Enterprise*. While en route to the next assignment, however, the *Enterprise* receives a distress call from Galen. He is under attack by Y'Ridians. The *Enterprise* engages the Y'Ridians' ship and destroys it but not before Galen is fatally wounded.

With the information gathered from Galen's shuttle, Picard begins retracing the professor's steps. After uncovering the purpose of the expedition, Picard understands Galen's caution. The professor had discovered that certain fragments of DNA from many different worlds were compatible. These fragments, when joined, would form a four-and-one-half-billion-year-old computer program. Unfortunately, the Cardassians, Klingons, and Romulans have also learned of Galen's research.

Trivia Questions

1. How many buttons are on the Klingon captain's belt buckle?

2. What is the composition of Data's upper spinal column?

Eventually everyone meets on a planet containing the final missing strand of DNA. Picard runs the completed program on a tricorder and the group watches silently as the projection of a spokesperson comes to life. The spokesperson says that humanoid life evolved on her planet before all others. To preserve their legacy, her race seeded the primordial soup on many worlds with DNA that would eventually evolve into humanoid life. They left this programmed message so that someday it would testify to their existence.

GREAT LINES

That's all? If she were not dead, I would kill her.—The Klingon commander—referring to the projected spokesperson—having chased across many planets after the elusive prize of the DNA computer program only to find out that it was simply a message in a very old bottle. (I understand his sentiment.)

PLOT OVERSIGHTS

• After racing to Professor Galen's rescue, the *Enterprise* fires on the Y'Ridian attacker. Immediately, the

Y'Ridian vessel explodes. Riker chastises Worf, but Worf claims the phasers weren't set high enough to do that much damage. So why did the Y'Ridian ship blow up? The episode never says.

• This episode answers part of one of my top ten oddities of *Star Trek: The Next Generation*. Namely, why do most of the alien races look basically the same as humans? Supposedly, four and one half billion years ago, a humanoid race seeded a bunch of planets with a DNA code that would guide the evolution of the planet toward a humanoid life form. I'm confused. I thought DNA was similar to a blueprint—as an organism develops, cells grow and specialize based on the information they find in their DNA. According to this episode, however, our DNA is not only a blueprint but also, in the past, acted as a kind of mutation evaluator, encouraging mutations that led toward a final humanoid form while suppressing those that did not. How did it do this? Did it already know, in advance, the precise sequence of mutations required to create a humanoid form? If so, why did it take four and one half billion years to get through them? Or did our DNA only know the final result it wanted to achieve? Did it have to wait for a mutation and only then determine if the mutation was headed in the right direction? In this case, how did it know if the mutation was a "good" one? The only way this makes sense is if our DNA had a copy of humanoid DNA lying around. It could then compare the mutated DNA to the humanoid DNA and de-

termine if the mutation should be encouraged. But if our DNA had a copy of humanoid DNA so that it could guide the evolution toward a humanoid form, why not just forget about the four and one half billion years of evolution and jump to the final product?

EQUIPMENT ODDITIES

• Just before telling the professor that he can't go on the expedition, Picard listens as Galen outlines their itinerary. The professor illustrates their travel plans on a map of the galaxy. As he discusses their first stop, Galen's finger transverses a distance of one fifth the length of the galaxy. Since our galaxy is approximately 100,000 light-years in length, Galen plans to travel 20,000 light-years to reach his first stop! He originally told Picard they would be away for up to one year. His time estimates are off. In "Q Who," Data claimed it would take the *Enterprise* over two and one half years to travel 7,000 light-years at maximum warp. Using these figures means it will take Galen over seven years to reach his initial locale.

• When Picard and Crusher first decipher Galen's research, a display shows the computer identifying eighteen strands of DNA. Oddly enough, all the dialogue refers to *nineteen* strands of DNA. Also, when the Cardassians and Klingons add in their data, the display shows many more additional strands locking into the program. However, when Crusher plots the origination points for all the strands, her graphics show only twenty-two origination points! Did she not know where some of the strands came from?

CONTINUITY AND PRODUCTION PROBLEMS

• Picard must have changed quarters. In "Lessons," Picard and Darrin have dinner in Picard's quarters while the *Enterprise* travels at warp. The window in the scene shows the stars streaking toward the window. Since the *Enterprise* can only travel forward in warp, Picard's quarters must be in the front of the saucer section. However, in "The Chase," Picard sits in front of what looks like the same window while the *Enterprise* travels at impulse and the stars crawl by from right to left. That means his quarters are now on the starboard side of the saucer section. Maybe he couldn't bear the thought of living in the same quarters now that Darrin has left. (My wife suggested another possibility. She surmised that the *Enterprise* was traveling at "crab impulse"—moving sideways—thereby accounting for the horizontal shift of the stars.)

TRIVIA ANSWERS

1. Five.
2. A polyalloy.

★
FRAME OF MIND

Star date: 46778.1

Riker rehearses with Data for a play called *Frame of Mind*. In it, he portrays a patient buffeted by the personnel of a mental hospital. The next morning, Picard tells Riker that the government of Tilonus IV has collapsed. Reports from Tilonus IV suggest that the warring factions have turned to torture to get strategic information. Picard believes a Federation research team stationed on the planet is a prime target. He wants Riker to escort them back to the *Enterprise*. Riker decides to go alone posing as a Tilonian merchant. Since the *Enterprise* won't arrive at Tilonus IV for five days, Riker goes ahead with his performance of *Frame of Mind*. While receiving a standing ovation at the end of the play, he looks up and suddenly finds himself in ward 47 of the Tilonus Institute for Mental Disorders. A staff member claims he was admitted after stabbing a person to death. When Riker attacks the man for lying, the staff inject him with drugs.

At this point, Riker shudders awake from his dream. The next night, he performs *Frame of Mind* but images

Trivia Questions

1. How many sticks does the male patient hold when Riker first visits the common area of ward 47?

2. How many containers sit on the carts that line the entrance of the common area?

from the play and his real life start overlapping. One moment he's on the *Enterprise*, then he's in ward 47, then Worf and Data rescue him from ward 47 and take him back to the ship. Riker finally grabs a phaser and shoots himself to find out what's real. One reality after another shatters until he finally regains consciousness on Tilonus IV. He was kidnapped shortly after beaming down. His captors have been trying to extract information using a "neurosomatic" technique. Riker leaps from the table, signals the *Enterprise* for emergency transport, and is beamed to safety.

GREAT MOMENTS

The summary doesn't do this episode justice. This was a great episode. Not only did it have a nicely turned plot but it also featured a beautiful "shattering" visual effect. Every time Riker broke through a false reality, the pieces of that reality would fly outward, rotating as they went.

RUMINATIONS

Obviously, this episode was almost impossible to nitpick. All but the last few minutes of this episode came from Riker's mental meanderings. However, as you can see below, I did find some items to gripe about. Nonetheless, the episode has much to commend, including several subtle hints that its events weren't "real." Hopefully, they were planned. For instance, one of Data's first lines while in rehearsal is "You're becoming agitated again." Can Data use contractions if he's reciting for a play? Then there's the stars in Picard's ready room window. Anarchy reigns on Tilonus IV, endangering a Federation research team. Picard plans a rescue mission, but the Enterprise won't arrive at the planet for five days. Why? Because the stars indicate the ship is creeping along at impulse. Also, Crusher visits Riker in the mental institute and keeps calling him "Commander" instead of "Will." Finally, while rescuing Riker, Worf hits a staff member with a closed fist. Worf's normal punch uses the base of his opened palm.

PLOT OVERSIGHTS

• Riker's mental imaginings in the episode suggest that he went to Tilonus IV to recover a Federation research team. According to these scenes, he went undercover, posing as a Tilonian merchant. Additionally, when Riker wakes up on the table, he is wearing Tilonian clothing and is outfitted with a Tilonian knife and a disguised communicator. From this— and Picard's comments at the end of the show—we can assume that Riker did, in fact, go to Tilonus IV and that he went undercover even though much of the evidence to prove this comes from parts of the episode that clearly occur in Riker's mind. If Riker did go to Tilonus IV as a Tilonian merchant, his makeup is wrong when he wakes up on the table. He should be surgically altered to look like a Tilonian, just as he was altered to look like a Malcorian in "First Contact."

TRIVIA ANSWERS

1. Four.
2. Five.

SUSPICIONS

Star dates: 46830.1-46831.2

While attending a conference, Dr. Crusher meets a Ferengi scientist named Regar who claims to have invented a new kind of shielding. Back on the *Enterprise*, Crusher invites several prominent scientists to the ship, hoping to provide Regar a friendly forum to present his discovery. Four respond—a Vulcan and her human husband, a Klingon, and a T'Karian named Jobril. Regar opens the discussions by claiming that his "metaphasic" shield is already functional and capable of protecting a shuttle as it flies through the corona of a star. As expected, the other scientists balk at his claims. Regar then announces that the shield has been installed on an *Enterprise* shuttle and that he will fly it into a nearby star. The scientists agree to the test but recommend a less biased pilot. Jobril volunteers.

Jobril enters the star's corona safely. Moments later, however, he begins having difficulty breathing. He manages to return to the *Enterprise* but later dies in sick bay. A short time later, Regar also dies, apparently

from suicide. A suspicious Crusher believes someone sabotaged the metaphasic shield test to discredit Regar and then killed him so they could continue his research unhindered. When Crusher can find no evidence of her theory, she disobeys a direct order from Picard and performs an autopsy on Regar. The autopsy proves nothing. In desperation, Crusher flies the shuttle into the star's corona, demonstrating that the shield works. At this, Jobril emerges from the shuttle's storage—having resuscitated from his self-imposed suspended animation. In the fight that follows, Crusher evaporates Jobril with a phaser. She then returns the shuttle to the *Enterprise*.

Trivia Questions

1. Where did Regar die?

2. What the first name of Crusher's Oriental medical assistant?

PLOT OVERSIGHTS

• Originally, Jobril volunteers to pilot the shuttle because he is recognized as an impartial observer. Is an impartial observer really needed for this test? The shuttle will fly into a star. Surely the test needs to fulfill only two simple requirements: Did the shuttle survive the flight? Is the pilot still alive?

• After Crusher performs Regar's autopsy, Picard relieves her of duty, and Starfleet schedules a formal inquiry. After all, Crusher violated Picard's direct order on top of the fact that Regar's family had expressly forbidden the procedure. This is serious stuff. Then, when Crusher proves that Regar's shield works and by default that Regar was probably murdered, everything is okay-fine, she is reinstated, and she apparently doesn't even have to appear at an inquiry. How does this change the fact that she disobeyed orders or violated Ferengi death customs? At one point, Crusher herself says that the family was more concerned about rituals than finding the truth of how Regar died.

CHANGED PREMISES

• This episode states that Regar's big breakthrough in shielding will make it possible to travel into the corona of a star. The reactions of the scientists seem to indicate that this would be a major achievement. However, Kern's ship in "Redemption II" flew into the corona of a star and survived in spite of damaged shields. And the *Enterprise* hid in the corona of a star while a Borg ship retrieved Hugh in "I, Borg."

TRIVIA ANSWERS

1. Science lab 4.
2. Alyssa.

Star date: 46852.2

Seeking answers for a crisis of his faith, Worf makes a pilgrimage to Borath, a sacred planet predicted as the site of the return of Kahless, the greatest Klingon of all. After ten days of meditation without experiencing a vision, a discouraged Worf packs his bag. Only the prodding of an elder Klingon keeps him from leaving. During the next time of meditation, Kahless appears to Worf, not in a vision but in flesh and blood (purple blood, that is). Of course, Kahless's return causes a variety of reactions among the Klingons, from skepticism to joyful celebration.

In response to a request from the Klingon High Council, the *Enterprise* takes Kahless and his entourage to a rendezvous with Gowron, the council's current leader ("Redemption"). Gowron attempts to disprove Kahless's return by bringing a sacred knife stained with the real Kahless's blood, but the plan fails. Crusher's testing indicates an exact DNA match between the blood and the returned Kahless. However, when a still defiant Gowron challenges Kahless to a fight and wins, Worf un-

Trivia Questions

1. How many people walk off the turbolift with Riker at the beginning of the show?

2. How many medals does Gowron wear on the lapels of his coat?

covers the truth. Kahless is merely a clone of the real Kahless and was created by his disciples on Borath. Still, many Klingons are powerfully moved by this incarnation of the mighty warrior from the past. Worf proposes a solution. He suggests that Kahless be given the figurehead role of emperor. Gowron will still hold the power, but Kahless can be a much-needed spiritual leader of the Klingon Empire, restoring the true honor in its warriors.

PLOT OVER-
SIGHTS

• Shortly after Kahless boards the ship, Data asks Worf, "In the absence of empirical data, how will you determine if this is the real Kahless?" Worf replies that it is not an empirical matter but rather a matter of faith. In this context, Data replies, "As an android, I am unable to accept that which cannot be proven through rational means." That statement makes sense until the episode nears its end. Data speaks to Worf about his own crisis of the spirit. He says that shortly after activation, Starfleet officers told him he was merely a collection of computational circuits in a humanoid form. Data then says that he didn't want to be limited to that definition. He says he chose to believe that he was a person. He says he made a leap of faith. Does a "leap of faith" classify as a *rational means* to arrive at an acceptable conclusion?

• Does a Klingon century consist of only 66.67 years? While chiding Worf for waiting only ten days for a vision of Kahless, an elder Klingon says they have waited for fifteen centuries. Later, however, Gowron claims that Kahless has been dead for 1,000 years. The only way both these statements can be true is if a Klingon century lasts for 66.67 years.

CHANGED PREMISES

• At one point Data refers to the Starfleet officers who "first activated me." Yet in "Datalore," Data says that a sensing device activated him when the officers approached. (I realize this sort of vague recollection is normal for a human, but wouldn't Data be a little more precise?)

TRIVIA ANSWERS

1. Five.
2. Sixteen.

★
SECOND CHANCES

The *Enterprise* arrives at Nervala IV, a planet encased in a distortion field. Once every eight years, it passes close enough to its sun to dephase the distortion field and allow transport to the surface. The last time this occurred, Lieutenant William Riker—then stationed on the *Potemkin*—led an evacuation from the Starfleet research station on Nervala IV. He almost didn't make it out. Now that the distortion field has dephased again, Commander Riker will lead an away team to retrieve the data that the researchers hurriedly left behind eight years ago. The away team beams down, and Data's tricorder registers a humanoid in the station. It is Lieutenant Riker.

Back on the ship, La Forge discovers that when the *Potemkin* beamed Riker aboard, a second confinement beam reflected back to the surface and created an exact duplicate. Neither Riker knew of the other's existence. Interestingly, Lieutenant Riker is still very much in love with Troi. At the time of the *Potemkin*'s visit to Nervala IV, Riker hadn't made his career a priority to the ex-

Trivia Questions

1. What is the name of one stop the *Potemkin* made after rescuing the researchers on Nervala IV?

2. What are the first two numbers on the table Lieutenant Riker crawls under to tap into the command pathways?

clusion of all else. Suddenly Commander Riker must defend the decisions he's made over the past eight years, and Troi is faced with a man she deeply loved—a man who is still deeply in love with her. The Rikers eventually resolve their differences and, as Lieutenant Riker leaves for an assignment on the USS *Gandhi*, Troi leaves open the possibility of continuing their romance.

GREAT MOMENTS

This episode has several nice effects combining two versions of Riker. The creators have gotten quite good with these "doppelgänger" shows (other episodes include "Datalore," "Hollow Pursuits," "Brothers," and "Birthright, Part I"). Two of the scenes are particularly lovely. In one, Commander Riker walks completely around Lieutenant Riker. In the other, Commander Riker places a trombone on a table, and Lieutenant Riker walks over and picks it up.

RUMINATIONS

There are only so many ideas in the world. Early on while re-

searching this book, I kept a list of potential plot lines. I suppose every writer who's a fan of Star Trek dreams of writing an episode someday. I had also come up with the idea of a transporter accidentally creating a duplicate Riker. I thought it would make an interesting episode given Riker's violent reaction to being cloned in "Up the Long Ladder."

PLOT OVERSIGHTS

• Presumably, the distortion field on Nervala IV is so bad that shuttle craft cannot safely fly through it and land on the surface. That's why the away team must wait for openings in the field to retrieve the data from the research station. Bear in mind that even with the more advanced transporters of the *Enterprise*, the away team has only three opportunities. The first two last for twenty-six and thirty-six minutes, respectively. The episode also makes it clear that these openings in the distortion field occur only every eight years and that the *Potemkin's* transporters had even more difficulty with the field. So how did the research station get down there in the first place? Evidently no shuttles could carry building supplies down.

• A small side point concerning the previous plot oversight: I suppose Starfleet could beam down a large replicator that could manufacture all the building supplies on the surface. "Data's Day" showed us that the gift shops on the *Enterprise* simply consist of graphic representations of the items offered. Once an individual makes a selection, a replicator creates the item. Can a starship do this on a much larger scale? Perhaps we could take this one step further. Could a combination of transporters and replicators manufacture a complete research station on a planet's surface in just a few seconds?

• It's amazing the role that genetics plays in behavior. For instance, Lieutenant Riker just happened to grow a beard during the same time period as Commander Riker. (Riker didn't have a beard during the first season of *Star Trek, The Next Generation*. Then again, maybe a beard was his standard attire and he just wanted to make a good impression on Picard so he shaved it off and kept it off for the first year of their service together.) Also, as soon as Lieutenant Riker gets one of the new uniforms, he adopts the "clutching of the bottom of his shirt and pulling down" maneuver so common to Commander Riker.

EQUIPMENT ODDITIES

• This episode raises many intriguing possibilities, since it demonstrates that individuals can be duplicated with a transporter. See Equipment Oddities under "Lonely Among Us" for more details.

CONTINUITY AND PRODUCTION PROBLEMS

• Lieutenant Riker's doorbell doesn't seem to be working. Just before Troi enters his quarters for the first time, Riker's head snaps up like he hears it, but the sound isn't on the tape.

• When a metal bridge collapses under Lieutenant Riker, Commander Riker drags him up from the precipice. Then Lieutenant Riker slithers over Commander Riker, crawls on his hands and knees behind an abutment, stands up, and reaches out to pull Commander Riker to his feet. The only problem is that Lieutenant Riker's backside hasn't even made it completely behind the abutment before he stands up! (And even after he's standing, you can still see the stunt double's feet disappearing.) To accomplish this, Riker would have to be able to stand up and turn around while the bottom half of his body continues to crawl forward on his knees. Given this amazing physical feat of flexibility, I suppose we should rechristen him "William Thomas 'Gumby' Riker."

TRIVIA ANSWERS
1. Turkana IV (see "Legacy").
2. 05.

TIMESCAPE

Star date: 98999.2-98995.3

While returning to the Enterprise, Troi notices that fellow travelers Picard, Data, and La Forge momentarily freeze in time. Then Troi does the same while the others remain normal. Soon Data and La Forge discover that temporal distortions fill this area of space. Rendezvousing with the Enterprise, the group finds it trapped—along with a Romulan warbird—in a very slow-moving pocket of time. Picard, Troi, and Data beam over to the Enterprise and discover a warp core breach under way in Engineering. Later, on the Romulan ship, the group finds a nonfunctioning engine core and an alien from another space-time continuum. After questioning the alien, Picard pieces together events as they occurred. Normally, the aliens incubate their young in black holes. They misjudged the singularity of the Romulan engine core as an appropriate place to nest their children. This caused the engine core to fail. Responding to a distress call from the Romulan ship, the Enterprise attempted a power transfer to its core. This threatened the nest and creat-

ed the massive temporal distortions. To protect their young, the aliens attacked the Enterprise, causing a warp core breach.

By manipulating the temporal discharges from the nest, Picard and the others force time backward within the pocket that traps both ships. As time begins to move forward again, they disrupt the power transfer beam, thereby averting the warp core breach and the destruction of the Enterprise. Picard also evacuates the Romulans from their crippled ship and returns them to Romulan space.

Trivia Questions

1. What are the first three numbers on the compartment that houses the emergency transporters for the runabout?

2. Initially, how long does Data say it will take for the warp core breach explosion to destroy the ship?

GREAT LINES
I thought it was a topic you were interested in—A somewhat confused Data to Troi after she states that she refused to assist a scientist in gathering empirical data for his thesis on intraspecies mating rituals.

PLOT OVERSIGHTS
• At one point, before the group rendezvous with the Enterprise, Picard reaches out for a bowl of fruit. He immediately screams in pain and retracts his hand. It now sports fingernails one-half inch long. Troi rushes

in, takes a tricorder reading, and states that the metabolism of the cells in his hand is fifty times faster than normal. As she continues to take readings, it slows back down. Data then comes in and reports that Picard pushed his hand into a temporal distortion in which time is accelerated approximately fifty times normal speed. In other words, every second Picard had his hand in the distortion was equivalent to 50 seconds in normal time. So far so good, except that the time between Picard's scream and Troi's proclamation that his hand has returned to normal is no more than thirty seconds. That means Picard's hand was in accelerated time for thirty seconds, which is the equivalent of 1,500 normal seconds (30 times 50), or 25 minutes. Can Picard really grow fingernails one-half inch long in 25 minutes?

• Part of the tension of this episode comes from the fact that the viewer doesn't know if the Romulans attacked the *Enterprise*. To add to this tension, the creators show us pictures of Romulans with disrupters on the bridge and in sick bay. On the other hand, Worf and two security officers stand in transporter room 3 with phasers at the ready as three *unarmed* Romulans prepare to step off the transporter pad. Later the show reveals that the *Enterprise* was, in fact, evacuating the Romulans from a disabled ship. If that's true, why are there Romulans with disrupters on the bridge and in sick bay? Romulans are, after all, still the enemy, and even if you are on a mission of mercy you do not let an armed enemy board

your ship. And, most of all, you don't allow an *armed* enemy access to your main bridge!

CHANGED PREMISES

• Suddenly Lieutenant Commander Deanna "What's a Containment Breach?" Troi seems to have become an engineering expert on Romulan propulsion. She's come a long way in her understanding of technical matters since "Disaster." In that episode, Troi assumes command of the *Enterprise* when a quantum filament slams into the ship and she ends up as the highest-ranking officer on the bridge. During her command, Ro discovers a weakening of the antimatter containment field and O'Brien states, "If it falls to 15 percent, the field will collapse and we'll have a containment breach." Troi then asks what a containment breach is. The scene gives the impression that Troi is not exactly up to speed on how these "engine things" work. Yet, here she gives detailed technical advice as Data and La Forge look through the Romulan engine room. The creators gloss over this change of mind by having Picard talk about Troi's recent experience aboard a Romulan ship in "Face of the Enemy." Supposedly that experience is the source of her newfound knowledge. However, in that episode Troi was kidnapped and forced to pose as an intelligence officer not as a Romulan engineer. Why would the Romulans who kidnapped her give her detailed information on their warp propulsion systems when all they wanted was for her to escort three stowaways to freedom?

CONTINUITY AND PRODUCTION PROBLEMS

• After Data discovers the warp core breach, he summons Picard. Picard examines the frozen explosion for a few moments and then reaches up and doodles a drawing in the expanding particles. It's amazing how icons become lodged in the subconsciousness of an entire race, lying dormant until exposed by high levels of stress. As Picard awaits the explosion destined to destroy the ship he loves, he doodles a "happy face," that round, yellow, smiling caricature so popular several years ago. (I would have thought that the happy face would have long since been forgotten. I guess that's the amazing power of the human mind.)

TRIVIA ANSWERS

1. 855.
2. Nine hours, seventeen minutes.

★ DESCENT

Star date: 46982.1-46984.6

Responding to a distress call from an outpost, the crew of the *Enterprise* finds a large, odd-shaped spacecraft orbiting the planet. An away team finds only dead bodies at the outpost. They also find a group of Borg. When the Borg attack, Data strangles one of them to death, experiencing anger during the process and pleasure at its conclusion. At the same time, the *Enterprise* gives chase as the Borg ship breaks orbit, but suddenly it disappears. While La Forge tries to figure out how the Borg ship escaped, Data tries to recreate the emotional experience but fails.

A short time later, the Borg attack another colony. This time Picard puts the *Enterprise* in tight pursuit. Just as the Borg ship disappears, the *Enterprise* is sucked into an energy vortex. When the *Enterprise* emerges on the other side, the wounded Borg ship attacks and two Borg appear on the bridge. Worf kills one and wounds the other but not before their ship escapes. In the brig, the Borg taps a device on his arm and then goads Data into an intense discussion about Data's emotional

Trivia Questions

1. At the beginning of this episode, Stephen Hawking wins a round of poker with four sevens. What is the fifth card in his hand?

2. At what moment in time does the replay of Hugh freeze (Hugh appeared in "I Borg")?

experience. Data is unable to resist his craving for emotion and the Borg's promise that their leader will supply them. He helps the Borg escape in a shuttlecraft. The *Enterprise* pursues but finds only the abandoned shuttlecraft on a distant planet. Picard orders an extensive foot search of the planet. When Picard, La Forge, and Troi find a large building, the Borg surround them, and Lore appears as their leader. Unfortunately, so does Data, claiming, "The sons of Soong have joined together and together ... we will destroy the Federation."

PLOT OVERSIGHTS

• The Borg, again? For the season finale, again!? (See "The Best of Both Worlds.") Isn't it about time to invent another enemy? Why not have Lore build a bunch of androids with frenzied emotions? Wouldn't that have worked just as well? (True, some of the elements of this plot would have to be adjusted, but I get the distinct impression that the creators are trying to amortize their investment in the Borg costumes by using them in as many shows as possible.) Let's say that Lore could build one android per month and each of those androids could build another in the next month. In the two years since Lore last appeared he could have an army of 16,777,216. That would be a pretty bad enemy.

• In "I Borg," just after bringing Hugh back to the ship, Picard orders La Forge to put a subspace damping field around Hugh's cell. This prevents him from sending out a subspace homing signal. Yet in "Descent," Picard forgets to do this. Consequently he must have Data make sure that the captured Borg is not sending any subspace signals. Instead of doing this with the large sensor arrays of the *Enterprise*, Data performs the sweep with a tricorder. All these little events conspire to put Data in the same room with the Borg for an extended time and give the Borg time to talk him into betraying the Federation.

• During the intense conversation in the brig with the Borg captive about reexperiencing emotions, Data claims he would do anything for the experience, including kill his best friend, Lieutenant Commander Geordi La Forge. All this time, a security officer sits a few feet away, seemingly oblivious to everything. What is it with this guy? Isn't his job to guard the prisoner? Shouldn't he be interested in a conversation between the Borg and Starfleet officers? Wouldn't Picard like to know that Data is admitting he would kill La Forge to feel emotions again?

• One of the true oddities of the original *Star Trek* occurred whenever the *Enterprise* approached a plan-

et. I call it The Kirk-knows-this-is-the-most-dangerous-planet-in-the-universe-so-he-takes-the-entire-senior-staff-with-him-when-he-beams-down Syndrome. Unbelievably, this syndrome occurs in "Descent." After finding the abandoned shuttlecraft on the planet, Picard orders all available personnel down to the surface to conduct a search on foot for Data. He even includes himself in the search, leaving a skeleton crew captained by Dr. Crusher on the *Enterprise!* Ostensibly, this is because electromagnetic radiation is blocking their sensors, but Picard has already said he's going to use shuttles for low-level reconnaissance. Wouldn't it make more sense to fly the shuttles over the terrain and then beam a single away team to any locations of interest? Of course, if Picard did this, there would be no reason for him to go to the surface with Troi and La Forge and they couldn't get captured by the Borg and ....

• And speaking of shuttlecraft, they seemed completely to have missed this large building sitting on a hilltop. It takes Troi to find it—on foot. Then everyone goes inside to look around because La Forge's tricorder is blocked by the building's energy damping field. Has Troi lost her empathic awareness? In "Night Terrors," Data claims there is no known technology to block telepathic transmissions. Since Troi's empathic powers are a scaled-down version of telepathy, shouldn't she be able to sense the intense emotions coming from Lore, Data, and the Borg horde within?

CHANGED PREMISES

• When questioned by Picard about his purpose, the Borg captive states that he wants to destroy all inferior biological life. Picard responds, "But you are Borg. Your goal is not to destroy but to assimilate us into your collective." Picard seems to have forgotten that acquiring technology was the sole interest of the Borg in "Q Who." They obliterated everything else in their path. The Borg "assimilation-thing" came about only because the creators wanted the Borg to kidnap Picard and turn him into Locutus during "The Best of Both Worlds."

CONTINUITY AND PRODUCTION PROBLEMS

• Dr. Noonian Soong, Data's creator, must have been one of those "if you get it out, put it away"-type people. He certainly programmed it into Data. Just before the fight breaks out between the away team and the Borg at the beginning of the episode, Data removes a small wall panel with his right hand to override primary control on a door and open it. The door opens. The Borg on the other side fires at Riker, and the fight begins. When Data fires on the Borg, he still holds the panel. Several phaser shots and plasma bursts later, another Borg physically attacks Data. Data throws him against a wall, the same wall that had the small wall panel. The wall panel falls off. In other words, Data—in the middle of a ferocious battle— decides to rid himself of the wall panel by putting it back where he found it instead of throwing it down on the floor, as a human would. In some ways, he really is superior.

• After the first encounter with the Borg, Picard reviews the events in "I Borg." He's afraid Hugh, the Borg they nursed back to health, has caused a change in the Borg. Specifically, Picard replays the video record of the scene when La Forge named the Borg "Hugh." A clock—counting time down to one tenth of a second— runs at the bottom of the screen. The odd thing is that the replay is different from the original events. Several pieces of dialogue are missing. Does the computer automatically edit the raw footage it shoots for the official record? If it does, why does the computer play back the edited log with a timer running at the bottom of the screen? Doesn't that give the impression that this is unabridged footage?

• The graphics for the bumpy ride through the energy vortex come from "Times Squared."

TRIVIA ANSWERS
1. The jack of diamonds.
2. 07:19:04.4.

ATTENTION ALL NITPICKING TREKKERS!

Join the Nitpicker's Guild Today

Just send in a mistake that you've found in *Star Trek: The Next Generation*, one that isn't included in this book (you can also send in stuff on *Deep Space Nine* and even the original series). That entry will make you an official member of the Nitpicker's Guild!

Send your mistake to:

Phil Farrand, Chief Nitpicker
The Nitpicker's Guild
P.O. Box 6248
Springfield, MO 65801-6248

Note: All submissions become the property of Phil Farrand and will not be returned. Submissions may or may not be acknowledged. By submitting material, you grant permission for use of your submission and name in any future publication by the author. Should a given mistake be published in one of the mediums of Nitpicker's Guild, an effort will be made to credit the first person sending in that mistake. However, Phil Farrand makes no guarantee that such credit will be given.

INDEX

A

Academy marathon, 211
Acamarians, 106, 160
Acamar III, 160, 203
Aceton assimilators, 153, 154
Active tachyon beams, 279-281
Acts of Cumberland, 97
ADTH, 244
Age of Ascension, 113
Albert, Cadet Joshua, 332, 333
Alcar, Ambassador Vas, 317, 365, 366, 368
Aldea, 49, 203, 274
Aldeans, 49, 50, 71
Alexander, 224, 225, 306, 308, 335, 336, 376, 377, 398
Alien probe, 255
"Allegiance," 70, 107, 181-183, 382
Alliance, 221
Alrik, Chancellor, 337, 338
Altsians, 354
Alyssa, 411
Amagosa Diaspora, 369
Amazons, 203
Angel One, 42, 43, 203
"Angel One," 42-43, 46, 60, 83, 116, 122, 135, 171, 204, 246, 267, 274, 387
Anglebottom, Lieutenant Commander Mervi von, 351, 353
Angosia III, 274
Angosians, 164-166
Animal things, 27, 28, 71, 122
Ansata terrorists, 70, 167, 168
Antedians, 106, 126, 127
Antedi III, 126, 203
Anya, 99-101
Apgar, Dr., 70, 173, 174
Apgar, Mrs., 173, 174

"Aquiel," 388-389
Arbitration, 237
Ardra, 172, 237-239, 317
Argus Array, 255
Ariana, 29, 31
Arkaria, 399, 400
Armis IX, 42, 203
Armus, 61, 62, 70, 71, 241, 317
"Arsenal of Freedom, The," 33, 57-58, 104, 201, 202, 203, 210, 274, 361
ASCII, 361
Aster, Dr. Marla, 151, 152
Aster, Jeremy, 151, 152
Atlantis Project, 212
Attack pod, 57, 58

B

B. Dalton, 168
Bacar IV, 391
Bach, J. S., 154
Bajor, 395
Bajorans, 106, 240, 274, 285, 286
Bandi, 3-5, 106, 115, 203, 240, 317
Baratas III, 131, 203
Baratas System, 129
Barclay, Lieutenant Reginald, 171, 188, 189, 255, 256, 307, 362-364, 386
Barion particles, 399, 401
Barron, Dr., 149, 150
Barzan II, 157
Bashir, Dr., 395
BASIC, 342
Bates, Hannah, 315, 316
"Battle, The," 24-26, 43, 134, 145, 195, 215, 230, 273, 274, 286, 303, 317
Battle of Maxia, 24
Beata, Mistress, 42, 43, 171
Beetlelike creature, 66, 67
Bendii syndrome, 193
Benzites, 53, 95
Berra, Yogi, 323
Bersallis III, 402

"Best of Both Worlds, The," Part 1, 70, 119, 200-202, 209, 210, 240, 241, 286, 341, 343, 350, 361, 422
"Best of Both Worlds, The," Part 2, 70, 90, 209-211, 236, 238, 264, 321, 341, 343
Betazed, 126, 195, 203, 261
Betazoids, 13, 25, 29, 30, 106, 158, 186, 193, 195, 249, 335
B'Etor, 172
"Big Good-Bye, The," 32-34, 46, 83, 107, 126, 127, 171, 172, 274, 387
Binary, 361
Biofilters, 60, 134
Biomolecular physiologist, 122
"Birthright, Part 1," 395-396, 397, 400, 414
"Birthright, Part 2," 397-398, 400
Black cluster, 309, 310
Bok, DaiMon, 24, 25, 317
"Bonding, The," 151-152, 311
Bones, 4
"Booby Trap," 106, 153-155, 172, 189, 198, 204, 247, 318
Borath, 412
Borg, 70, 106, 117-119, 200, 201, 209-211, 212, 213, 240, 241, 341-343, 350, 361, 411, 420-422
Brackett, Fleet Admiral, 297
Brahms, Dr. Leah, 153, 155, 172, 247, 248, 317
Brand, Admiral, 332
Bre'el IV, 169, 203
Brekkians, 59, 60, 106, 136
Briam, Kriosian Ambassador, 337, 338
Brianon, Kareem, 89, 90
Bringloidi, 106, 123, 124

Brooks, Ensign, 231, 232
"Brothers," 71, 137, 214-216, 269, 296, 310, 317, 323, 352, 354, 414
Brussels, European Alliance, 159
Buzzard collectors, 120
Bynars, 44-46, 106

C

Calamarain, 71, 106, 169
Caldorian eel, 298
Campio, 335, 336
"Captain's Holiday," 106, 171, 172, 184-185, 203, 257, 295, 318
Captain's mess, 180
Cardassians, 71, 106, 235, 236, 285, 286, 318, 381, 384, 385, 405, 406
Cardiac replacement, 120, 392
Cathode-ray tubes, 93
"Cause and Effect," 71, 329-331, 370
Cesarean section, 247
"Chain of Command, Part 1," 71, 204, 274, 318, 381-383, 385
"Chain of Command, Part 2," 318, 384-385
Chalnoth, 106, 181
Channing, Dr., 20
Charnock's Comedy Cabaret, 86
"Chase, The," 405-407
Chess, 320-321
"Child, The," 75-77, 135, 203
Children of Tama, 106, 283
Chopin, Frédéric, 316
Chorgan, 160
Chroniton field distortions, 344, 345
Chrysallians, 106, 157
Class 8 probe, 387
Clavdia III, 101
Clemens, Samuel, 348, 359-361
Cliffs of Heaven on Sumico IV, The, 321
Clones, 123, 124

Closets by Data, 269
"Clues," 71, 106, 150, 227, 242-244
Coalition, 221, 222
"Code of Honor," 10-12, 22, 46, 83, 106, 136, 204, 274, 275, 317
Colt .45 caliber, 377
Colt Firearms, 348
"Coming of Age," 16, 53-54, 66, 83, 96, 106, 204, 222, 248, 380
Comnet Database 2442219, 67
Compressed terrion beam, 393
Conor, Aaron, 171, 315-317
"Conspiracy," 66-67, 70, 135, 160-161, 264
Constantinople, 89
Constellation Class NCC 2893, 26
"Contagion," 71, 80, 103-105, 107, 127, 189, 274, 292, 351, 354, 377, 391
"Conundrum," 106, 171, 317, 320-321, 377
Cosmic string, 231
"Cost of Living," 71, 137, 172, 335-336
Cousteau, 254
Crusher, Jack, 212, 213
Cryogenically frozen humans, 68
Crystal, 51-52
Crystal entity, 35, 36, 106, 288, 289

D

Daled IV, 99-101, 203
Damage tote board, 70-71
Danar, Rogo, 164-166, 305, 317
Dark matter, 268
"Darmok," 70, 107, 283-284, 318, 321
Darrin, Lieutenant Commander Nella, 171, 402-404, 407
Darwin Genetic Research Station, 92

"Datalore," 35-37, 60, 107, 178, 214, 274, 288, 289, 310, 333, 413, 414
"Data's Day," 172, 233-234, 398, 415
Dathon, Captain, 70, 283, 317
"Dauphin, The," 99-102, 135, 172, 203, 269, 313, 318
Davis, Ensign, 114
Deadwood, 376, 377
Deaging drug, 47, 48
Deep Space Nine, 41, 240, 395, 396, 398
"Defector, The," 162-163, 203, 215, 300, 318, 375
"Déjà Q," 71, 106, 169-170, 203, 257, 310, 363, 371
Delta Rana IV, 274
Deneb IV, 3, 4, 203, 274
Denver, 325
"Descent," 420-422
Desert moon, 229
"Destruction," 90
Deuterium, 250
Devidia II, 203, 274, 348, 349, 359
"Devil's Due," 172, 203, 237-239, 274, 318
Devinoni Ral, 137, 155, 157, 159, 171, 318
Dickens, Charles, 270
Dilithium chamber, 55, 56, 168, 189, 248, 259, 336, 363
Dilithium crystals, 114
DiMaggio, Joe, 32, 33
Dimensional shifting, 167, 168
Dirgo, Captain, 229, 230
"Disaster," 71, 291-293, 360, 368, 373, 377, 418
Discommendation, 179, 212, 224, 271
Disintegrator beam, 42-43
Distortion field, 414, 415
DNA, 92, 93, 123, 124, 325, 374, 381, 405, 406, 412
Doe, John, 107, 197, 198, 204

Doppelgänger shows, 414
Dorian, 365
Douwd, 106, 107, 147, 148, 317
Dreaming, 249
Drema IV, 114-116, 203
"Drumhead, The," 106, 225, 259, 317
D'Sora, Lieutenant Jenna, 171, 268-270, 317
Duras, 179, 224, 266, 271, 272, 279, 280, 328
Dynamic Adaptive Design (DAD), 58
Dynamic Relationships Test, 54
Dyson's sphere, 367, 368

E

Echo Papa 607, 57
Edo, 21, 22, 106
Eiffel Tower, 64-65, 350
El-Adrel system, 283
El-Baz, 112, 146, 199, 256
Elbrun, Tam, 186, 317
"Elementary, My Dear Data," 33, 34, 81-84, 273, 274, 386, 387
Elway Theorem, 275
"Emissary, The," 129-131, 172, 176, 203, 224, 225, 230, 317
Empathic metamorph, 317, 337
"Encounter at Farpoint, Part 1," 3-6, 56, 61, 70, 83, 107, 109, 115, 135, 136, 202, 204, 214, 240, 273, 274, 275, 292, 318, 348, 350, 353, 372, 374, 387
"Encounter at Farpoint, Part 2," 3-6, 11, 28, 46, 333
Endar, 217
"Enemy, The," 156, 203, 275, 301, 308
Energy cloud, 18-20
Energy field, 151, 373
Energy vortex, 110, 111, 219, 420
"Ensign Ro," 106, 274, 285-287, 291

"Ensigns of Command, The," 71, 101, 106, 144-146, 171, 199, 256, 267
Enterprise-C, 175, 176, 213, 331
Environmental Support, 292-293
Epithelial cells, 125
Epsilon Nel System, 312
Erko, Protocol Minister, 335, 336
Escher, M.C., 342
"Ethics," 325-326, 396
"Evolution," 71, 107, 141-143, 172, 318, 364
Exocomp, 318, 379, 380
Exozoologist, 340

F

"Face of the Enemy," 390-391, 418
Fajo, Kivas, 174, 191, 192, 317, 401
"Family," 171, 212-213
Faralon, Dr., 317, 379, 380
Farpoint Station, 3-6, 240
Fastest Crossed Legs in the Universe, 234
Felicium, 59, 60, 115
Ferengi, 13, 14, 24, 25, 55, 71, 106, 132, 133, 157, 158, 184, 195, 196, 203, 215, 241, 275, 297, 299, 337, 338, 373-375, 377, 383, 385, 411
Fermi, 375
FGC-47, 340
Ficus Sector, 123
"Final Mission," 229-230, 261, 274
"First Contact," 71, 106, 203, 245-246, 267, 274, 409
"First Duty," 332-334
"Fistful of Datas, A," 71, 172, 376-378
Floozy, 378
.45-caliber double-action cavalry pistol, 348
"Frame of Mind," 408-409
"Future Imperfect," 22, 225, 226-228, 313

FWD Navigational Scan, 302, 368

G

Galactic Court for Race Name Conflict Resolution, 351, 353, 354
"Galaxy's Child," 172, 247-248
Galen, Professor, 405, 406
Gallup poll, 150
Galorndon Core, 156, 203, 299, 301, 308
"Game, The," 171, 172, 275, 294-296, 316
Gamma Taori IV, 13, 203
Garbage ship, 229, 230
Garushta Disaster, 186
Gatherers, 106, 160, 204, 274
Gavelnod, Oops, 351, 353, 354
Geeb, Zelbob, 350, 352, 353
Genetically engineered society, 315, 382, 400
Genetic engineering, 92
Geometrical constructivism, 173
Gettysburg, 48
Globfly, 85
Gloria from Cleveland, 242
Goddard, 368
Gosheven, 71
Gowron, 224, 271, 272, 279-281, 317, 412, 413
Graves, Dr. Ira, 89-91, 244, 310, 317
Graviton pulses, 288, 289, 369
Great Bird of the Galaxy, 158
Greenpeace, 293
Grizzelli, 106, 144
Guiltless Pleasures, 159, 176
Guinan, 76, 97, 101, 102, 117, 119, 175, 177, 210, 241, 244, 269, 272, 285, 348, 349, 359, 361, 368, 373, 389

Gumby, 416
Guy thing, 144-145

H

Haftel, Admiral, 177, 178
Hajar, Cadet Jean, 332, 334
"Half a Life," 118, 137, 260-262, 317
Hathaway, 132, 133
Haven, 29, 30, 203
"Haven," 18, 29-31, 55, 61, 107, 203, 275, 351, 353, 354, 400
Hawking, Steven, 420
"Heart of Glory," 45, 55-56, 107, 131, 135, 136, 165, 241, 351, 354
Henshaw, Christie, 155, 172, 198
"Hero Worship," 274, 309-311
Hesterdel, Medical Trustee, 76, 77
Hickman, 251, 253
"Hide and Q," 27-28, 70, 71, 79, 118, 121-122, 172, 204, 372
"High Ground, The," 70, 167-168, 204, 241, 274, 275
Hill, Dixon, 32-34, 126, 127
Holloway, Thomas, 394
"Hollow Pursuits," 154, 172, 188-190, 202, 255, 316, 362, 414
Holmes, Sherlock, 81, 82, 84, 386
Holodeck, 32-34, 44-46, 63, 64, 81-84, 113, 114, 126, 127, 129, 130, 136, 153, 173, 174, 188, 189, 244, 247, 251-253, 255, 370, 376, 377, 386, 387
"Home Soil," 51-52, 380
Homm, Mr., 30, 127
"Host, The," 106, 158, 171, 263-265, 318
Hotel Brian, 359
Hotel Royale (Matthews), 108, 109

Hot toddy, Aunt Adelle's, 369
Hugh, 341-343, 411, 420-422
"Hunted, The," 96, 164-166, 204, 216, 274, 305, 318, 323
Husnak, 106, 147, 148
Hutchinson, Commander, 400
Hyperonic radiation, 144
Hyperspace Physics Test, 54
Hytritium, 191, 192

I

Ian, 75
"I Borg," 341-343, 411, 420-422
"Icarus Factor, The," 70, 96, 113, 135, 171, 196, 202
"Ichner" radiation, 75
Iconia, 103, 274
Iconians, 103, 106
Icthni III, 350
"Identity Crisis," 204, 225, 241, 251-254, 264
"Imaginary Friend," 317, 339-340
Imperial Klingon Information Net, 224
Inertia, 230
"Inner Light, The," 171, 172, 346-347, 402
Intermix formula, 16-17, 248
"In Theory," 171, 268-270, 318
Invidium, 188, 189
Ionic energy fluctuation, 363
Iralius IX, 153, 154, 203
Irish unification, 167
Irisine syndrome, 312, 314
Iron weaver, 347
Isabella, 317, 339
Iverson's disease, 47

J

Jalad, 283
James, William, 122

Jameson, Admiral Mark, 47, 48, 136
Jameson, Anne, 47
Janeway, Ensign, 366
Jarada, 32, 33, 106, 121
Jarada III, 203, 314
Jarok, Admiral, 162, 317
Jefferies tube, 164, 372, 404
Jelico, Captain Edward, 317, 381, 382, 384
Jeremy, 151, 152
Jev, 204, 312, 313, 316, 317
J'naii, 106, 327, 328
Jobril, 410, 411
Jol, Etana, 171
Jono, 106, 218
Josh, 37
Judge Adjutant General (JAG), 97, 98
"Justice," 21, 27, 64, 106, 115, 135, 171, 204, 246, 259, 274

K

Kahless, 398, 412, 413
Kaleb sector, 390
Kamala, 107, 172, 317, 337, 338
Kargan, Captain, 70
Karnas, 47, 48
Keel, Captain Walker, 66-67
K'Ehleyr, Ambassador, 129-131, 172, 176, 224, 225, 272, 306, 317
Kelly, Lieutenant, 362-363
Kennelly, Admiral, 274, 285, 286
Kern, 411
Khitomer, 179, 203, 395, 397
Khitomer Massacre, 179, 271
Kirk, Captain James, 27, 297
Klingon Empire, 129, 175, 176, 224, 271, 279
Klingon High Council, 179, 224, 271, 272, 412

Klingons, 14, 50, 55, 56, 67, 87, 95, 96, 99, 106, 108, 113, 119, 121, 129-131, 136, 152, 162, 165, 172, 175, 176, 179, 224, 239, 259, 266, 271, 272, 274, 279, 297, 325, 373, 375, 388, 395, 397, 398, 405, 406, 410, 412, 413

K'Mpec, 224, 317, 318

Kolrami, Sirna, 132, 317

Kolvoord Maneuver, 332, 333

Kozinski, 15, 16, 100, 248

Krag, 173, 317

Krieger waves, 173, 174

Krios, 203, 337, 338

Kriosians, 106

Kurn, Commander, 179, 180, 271, 280, 281, 317

L

Lal, 177, 178, 317

Lambda field generator, 173, 174

Lanel, 246

Laser drill, 51

"Last Outpost, The," 13-14, 25, 67, 70, 71, 106, 135, 195, 196, 204, 275

Lefler, Robin, 172, 294-296

"Legacy," 203, 221-223, 244, 416

Legarans, 106, 193, 194

Leitjen, Lieutenant Commander Susanna, 251-253

Lemon tea, 265

Lenarians, 393

"Lessons," 171, 400, 402-404, 407

Liator, 171

Lighten, Commander, 225

Ligo VII, 203, 373

Ligonians, 10-11, 107, 275

Ligon II, 10, 203, 274

Linear Models of Viral Propagation (Pulaski), 94

Locarno, Cadet, 332-334

Locutus, 200, 209, 210, 422

Lollipop, 57

London Kings, 34

"Lonely Among Us," 18, 47, 48, 71, 76, 204, 295, 415

Lore, 35, 36, 214, 216, 289, 310, 333, 420, 421

Lornack, 160

"Loss, The," 13-14, 25, 231-232

"Loud as a Whisper," 87-88, 135, 171, 204

Lunar V, 164, 203

Lutan, 10-11, 317

Lya Station Alpha, 285, 286

Lysian Alliance, 320

Lysians, 107, 318, 320, 321

M

MacDuff, Commander, 317, 320, 321

Macet, Captain Gul, 235

Maddox, Commander Bruce, 82, 97, 98, 178, 233, 317, 352

Madred, Gul, 318, 384, 385

Magellan, 328

Magnetic containment field, 44

Maid Marion, 257

Making of Star Trek, The (Whitfield), 158

Malcoria III, 203, 245, 246, 274

Malcorians, 71, 107, 245, 246, 409

Manheim, Dr. Paul, 63-65, 193

Manheim, Jenice, 63-65

"Manhunt," 30, 107, 126-128, 203

"Man of the People," 274, 318, 365-366, 368

Marouk, 160

Marr, Dr. Kila, 288, 289, 318

Marta, 171

Martinez, 150

"Masterpiece Society, The," 171, 203, 274, 315-316, 317, 321, 382

"Matter of Honor, A," 54, 70, 95-96, 130, 131, 135, 187, 398

"Matter of Perspective, A," 70, 173-174, 192, 204, 317

"Matter of Time, A," 203, 274, 302-305

Matthews, Todd, 109

Maxia Zeda star system, 26

Maxwell, Captain Ben, 235, 318

McCoy, Dr., 4

McKenzie, Ard'ian, 171

M Class planet, 21, 268

"Measure of a Man, The," 82, 97-98, 178, 215, 233, 243, 318, 352, 379

Medical scans, 60

Melina II, 203, 314

MELINA II PLANETARY MEDICAL DATA BASE, 314

"Ménage à Trois," 13, 25, 158, 195-196, 204, 261, 275

Mendak, Admiral, 398

Mendez, 251, 253

Mendon, Ensign, 95

Menthars, 153

Merculite rockets, 56

Metagenic weapon, 381

Metal parasites, 335, 336

Metaphasic shield, 410

Miller, Dr. Wyatt, 18, 29, 30, 354, 400

Mind meld, 193, 289

"Mind's Eye, The," 266-267, 274, 280

Mining shuttle, 229

Minos, 57, 203, 274

Minos Corva, 384

Mintaka III, 149, 203, 274

Mintakans, 107, 149, 150, 181, 218

Minuet, 44-46, 172, 226

Mizarians, 107, 382

Moab IV, 204, 274, 315, 382, 383

Molecular decay detonator, 225

Molly, 291, 322, 324, 373, 374

Morath, 398
Mordan IV, 47, 48, 204, 274
Mordock, 53, 54, 96, 248
Moriarty, Dr., 70, 81-84, 386, 387
"Most Toys, The," 71, 96, 115, 170, 174, 191-192, 269, 317, 401
Mot, 400, 401
Multi-modal reflection sorting, 211
Multiplex-pattern buffers, 364
Muranium alloy, 160
Muskin seed punch, 389

N

Nagilum, 78, 79, 318
"Naked Now, The," 7-9, 67, 135, 158, 171, 258, 264, 274, 286, 295, 351, 353
Nanites, 71, 107, 141, 142, 318, 343
NASA, 108
Navigational deflector, 200, 209
Nelvana III, 162, 204
Nervala IV, 414, 415
Neuropsychology Seminar at Bacar IV, 391
Neutral Zone, 42, 43, 55, 56, 68, 103, 118, 119, 162, 233
"Neutral Zone, The," 68-69, 76, 107, 118, 121, 274, 275, 303, 333, 365
Neutrino beacon, 156
Nevek, 390
"New Ground," 306-308, 398
New Providence Colony, 119
"Next Phase, The," 344-345
Nightpluck Institute of Technology, 352
"Night Terrors," 61, 249-250, 265, 295, 369, 421
1984 (Orwell), 385
Nitpicker's Guild Entrance Exam, 38-41
Nitpicker's Prime Directive, xiv, 27, 158

Nitrium, 335, 336
Norsicans, 107, 120, 121, 392, 393
Nottingham Castle, 257
Nova Squadron, 332, 333
"Nth Degree, The," 171, 255-256, 267, 307, 362
Null space, 327

O

O'Brien, Keiko, 234, 243, 268, 291, 292, 373, 374, 403
O'Brien, Molly, 291, 322, 324, 373, 374
O'Brien, Transporter Chief, 111, 129, 134, 174, 192, 201, 233, 234, 236, 242, 243, 261, 266, 268, 281, 283, 291, 322-324, 362, 363, 373, 418
Odan, Ambassador, 158, 171, 263-265, 318
O'Dell, Brenna, 171
Oden, 42, 43
Odet IX, 75, 76, 204
ODN junction box, 399
Offenhouse, Robert, 68, 69
"Offspring, The," 36, 64, 69, 90, 177-178, 317
Okona, 85, 86, 318
Omicron Theta star system, 35
Onarans, 107, 115, 136
"11001001," 25, 44-46, 76, 79, 105, 106, 111-112, 135, 172, 215, 220, 226, 287
Onizuka, 146, 199, 256, 267
Ornarans, 59, 60
Orta, 285, 286
Orwell, George, 385
"Outcast, The," 106, 318, 327-328, 368
"Outrageous Okona, The," 85-86, 88, 317
Ozone layer, 49, 50

P

Pacifica, 126

Pakled, 107, 120-122
Pardek, 297-299, 318
Parliament, 18, 204
Parralex Colony, 335
Passive lure stratagem, 155
Pattern enhancer, 322
Paxans, 71, 107, 242-244
"Peak Performance," 31, 106, 132-133, 300, 317, 354
"Pen Pals," 114-116, 203, 259, 318
Penthara IV, 204, 302
"Perfect Mate, The," 107, 172, 203, 317, 337-338
Phase, the, 126
Picard, Robert, 212, 213
Picard A, 110-112, 198
Picard B, 110-112, 198
Picard Maneuver, 25
Pike, 192
Planetary minerals surveys, 114
Plasma fountain, 379, 380
Plasma plague, 75, 76
Pluto, 50
Potemkin, 222, 414, 415
"Power Play," 71, 216, 241, 317, 322-324, 363, 375, 394, 400
Prelude in C Minor (Chopin), 316
"Price, The," 107, 137, 155, 157-159, 171, 265, 274, 286, 317
Prime Directive (Nitpicker's), xiv, 27, 158
Prime Directive (Starfleet), 21, 22, 47, 48, 59, 114-116, 259, 328, 333
Prime numbers, 182-183
Princess Bride, The, 257-258
Promellians, 107, 153-155
Psychic waste receptacle, 317, 365, 366, 368
Psychotectic treatments, 327

Q

Q, 3, 4, 27, 28, 70, 71, 109,

117-119, 169, 170, 210, 257, 258, 310, 318, 343, 371, 372, 392, 393

Q Continuum, 3, 27, 117, 169, 371, 372

"Qpid," 70, 171, 203, 257-258

Quaice, Dr. Dalen, 219, 220, 258

"Quality of Life, The," 203, 317, 379-380

Qualor II, 204, 297, 299, 300

Quantum filaments, 291-293, 418

Quantum phase inhibitor, 185

Questor Tapes, The, 109

Quinn, Admiral Gregory, 53, 54, 66, 67, 70

"Q Who," 70, 71, 107, 117-119, 200, 201, 209, 210, 341, 343, 374, 406, 422

R

Rana IV, 147, 148, 204

"Rascals," 204, 241, 373-375, 377

Rasmussen, 274, 302-305

"Realm of Fear," 362-364, 372, 374

"Redemption," 71, 225, 241, 271-272, 274, 279, 299, 317, 412

"Redemption II," 172, 274, 279-282, 298, 299, 317, 333, 391, 403, 411

Red ochre, 311

Regar, 410, 411

Relay Station 194, 389

"Relics," 367-368

Relva VII, 53, 204

"Remember Me," 219-220, 258, 287, 374, 394

Remlar Array, 399

Remmick, Lieutenant Commander Dexter, 53, 54, 66, 67

REM sleep deprivation, 369

Repeaters, The, 123-124

Replicative fading, 123-124

Resolution, The, 260

"Reunion," 31, 224-225, 266, 271, 272, 279, 306, 318, 328, 354, 373

Rex, 126

Rice, Captain Paul, 57

Ricellas System, 75

Richie, Colonel Steven, 108, 109, 318

Rifle, 378

Rigalian Ox, 91

"Rightful Heir," 412-413

Riker, Jean-Luc, 226, 228

Riker, Kyle, 113, 171

Risa, 172, 184, 204, 274, 294

Riva, 87, 88, 171

Ro, Ensign Laren, 106, 171, 285, 286, 291, 292, 323, 344, 345, 373, 418

Robin Hood, 257

Rock Banging 101, 98

Roddenberry, Gene, 109, 149, 158, 273, 286

Rogers, Amanda, 318, 371, 372

Romulans, 24, 42, 50, 68, 69, 71, 78, 96, 103, 107, 118, 121, 127, 132, 156, 162, 163, 175, 179, 186, 203, 224, 226, 227, 233, 259, 266, 271, 279-281, 297-300, 344, 345, 375, 390, 391, 395-398, 405, 417, 418

Romulus, 297-299

Rosa, Jeremiah, 217, 218

"Royale, The," 108-109, 172, 204, 317

Rozhenko, Helena, 306

Rubicun III, 23, 204, 274

Rubicun system, 21

Russell, Dr. Toby, 325, 326

Rutia IV, 167, 204, 274

S

Sakarov, 387

Salia, 70, 99-102, 172, 318

"Samaritan Snare," 106, 120-122, 246, 267, 274, 392, 393

Sarek, 193, 194, 297, 298

"Sarek," 106, 193-194, 261, 289

Sarjenka, 114-116, 318

Sartaaran, 107, 320, 321

Satie, Admiral Norah, 259, 318

Saturn Navcon File 6-379, 334

Saucer section, 56, 57, 240, 310, 407

Sawed-off double barreled shotgun, 378

"Schisms," 369-370

"Schizoid Man, The," 19, 89-91, 130-131, 194, 244, 310, 318, 394

Science Station Delta 05, 118

Scott, Captain Montgomery ("Scotty"), 367, 368

"Second Chances," 414-416

Sela, Commander, 71, 137, 279-281, 298-301, 318

Selar, Dr., 89, 131, 394

Selcundi Drema System, 114

Seltrice III, 204, 274, 381, 382, 384

"Shades of Gray," 134-135, 253

Shelby, Commander, 119, 200-202, 210, 211

Sheliak, 401

Sheliak Corporate, 144-146

Sherwood Forest, 257

"Ship in a Bottle," 70, 353, 386-387

Shumar, Captain Bryce, 318, 322

Shuttle Bay 2, 141, 142

Sigma III, 27, 204

"Silicon Avatar," 288-290, 317

Singer stone, 116

Singh, Lieutenant, 20

"Sins of the Father," 96, 179-180, 204, 224, 225, 271, 274, 279, 318

"Skin of Evil," 56, 61-62, 70,

71, 91, 134-136, 175, 204, 241, 248, 271, 274, 318

Snoot, Prissy de la, 351-352, 354

Solari V, 87, 88, 204

Soliton wave, 306-308

Soong, Dr. Noonian, 35, 89, 98, 137, 214, 310, 318, 352, 395, 396, 422

Soren, 318, 327, 328

Sousa, John Philip, 143

Sovak, 184, 185

Spock, Ambassador, 137, 193, 297, 299-301, 317, 385, 390

SS *Mariposa*, 123, 124

Starbase 24, 272

Starbase 73, 112

Starbase 74, 44, 45, 220, 287

Starbase 84, 56

Starbase 103, 58

Starbase 117, 338

Starbase 133, 219, 220, 287

Starbase 173, 97

Starbase 179, 95

Starbase 218, 404

Starbase 234, 297

Starbase 336, 131

Starbase 416, 214, 352

Starbase 514, 309

Starbase 515, 120-122, 246, 274

Starbase 718, 68, 274

Starbase Earhart, 392, 393

Starboard computer core, 256

Star drive, 57, 58, 240

Starfleet Academy, 53, 96, 98, 222, 294, 295, 332-334

Starfleet Prime Directive, 21, 22, 47, 48, 59, 114-116, 259, 328, 333

Stargazer, 24, 25, 230, 381, 385

"Stars and Stripes Forever," 143

"Starship Mine," 399-401

Star Trek, 4, 21, 149, 193, 297, 367, 421

Star Trek: The Next Generation Technical Manual, 20, 33, 83, 121, 133, 158, 168, 170, 178, 223, 248

Star Wars, 300

Static warp bubble, 219, 220

Station Salem 1, 156

Stellar cartography, 402

Stellar core fragment, 315

Stockholm syndrome, 218

Strategema, 132, 317

Strnad system, 21

Stubbs, Dr. Paul, 141-143, 318

Styris IV, 10, 204

Sub-micron matrix transfer technology, 177

"Suddenly Human," 86, 107, 150, 217-218, 338, 353, 366

Sumico IV, 321

Superconducting magnet (SCM) Model 3, 100

"Survivors, The," 106, 107, 147-148, 203, 225, 274, 318

"Suspicions," 394, 410-411

Sutter, Clara, 318, 339

"Symbiosis," 59-60, 106, 107, 115, 135, 136, 264

System J25, 119

T

T-9 energy converter, 13

Tagus III, 204, 257

Talarians, 55, 107, 136, 218, 338, 354, 366

Tamarians, 283, 284

Tanuga IV, 173, 174, 204

"Tapestry," 171, 392-394, 400

Tarchannen III, 204, 251

Tarellians, 29-31, 55, 56, 107, 136, 275, 351, 353-354, 400

Taris, Subcommander, 391

Tarman, 312, 314

Tarses, Simon, 259

Temporal causality loop, 329, 330

Tenagra, 283, 284

Ten-Forward, 76, 77, 97, 101, 102, 142, 158, 160, 177, 182, 197, 272, 291, 295, 322-324, 366, 368, 389, 399, 400

Terraforming, 51-52

Theiss, William, 21

Theiss Titillation Theory, 21, 64

Thermal deflection, 402, 403

Theta band subspace carrier wave, 381, 382, 385

Theta VIII, 108, 204

Third of Five, 343

Thompson, 143

Thought-making device, 24

Tilonus IV, 408, 409

Time distortion, 63-65

"Time's Arrow," 203, 274, 348-349

"Time's Arrow, Part 2," 274, 359-361

"Timescape," 417-419

"Times Squared," 110-112, 146, 198, 256, 267, 313, 422

Timicin, 260-262, 318

Timothy, 274, 309-311

Tin Man, 71, 186, 187

"Tin Man," 71, 186-187, 317

T'Karians, 410

Tkon Empire, 13, 67

Toaster, 98

Tomalak, 226

"Too Short a Season," 19, 47-48, 136, 204, 274

Toreth, Commander, 391

Tox Uthat, 184, 318

T'Pau, 297-299

T'Pei, 233

"Transfigurations," 107, 155, 197-199, 204, 256, 267, 313

Transporter, 19-20, 44, 45, 54, 60, 96, 101, 124, 134, 180, 196, 374

Transporter code 14, 184

Transporter psychosis, 362, 363
Traveler, 15
Trilithium resin, 399, 400
Trill, 107, 263, 264, 317
Troi, Lwaxana, 29, 30, 118, 126-127, 137, 193, 195, 196, 260-262, 335, 336
"True Q," 317, 371-372
Turkana IV, 204, 221, 222, 416
Twain, Mark, 348, 360
Two-dimensional beings, 231, 232
Tyken's Rift, 265
Typhon Expanse, 329
Tyrus VII, 204, 379

U

Ulians, 107, 203, 312-314
Unari, Lieutenant Aquiel, 388, 389
"Unification I," 203, 297-298, 300, 318
"Unification II," 137, 299-301, 308, 385, 390
Universal Translator, 51, 113, 141, 145, 155, 163, 350, 352, 390
"Unnatural Selection," 86, 92-94, 112, 122, 135, 215, 374
"Up the Long Ladder," 106, 123-125, 135, 171, 303, 415
USS *Aries*, 113, 202, 251
USS *Berlin*, 43
USS *Bozeman*, 330, 331
USS *Brattain*, 249, 250
USS *Cairo*, 318, 381
USS *Charleston*, 68
USS *Drake*, 57, 202
USS *Essex*, 317, 322
USS *Gandhi*, 414
USS *Hood*, 4
USS *Intrepid*, 180
USS *Jenolan*, 367, 368
USS *Lantree*, 92, 93
USS *Melbourne*, 202
USS *Phoenix*, 235, 236
USS *Repulse*, 75, 77

USS *Stardust*, 353
USS *Tripoli*, 35
USS *Tsiolkovsky*, 7-9
USS *Victory*, 81, 251
USS *Wellington*, 285
USS *Yamamoto*, 78-80, 103-105, 292
USS *Yosemite*, 362, 363
Uxbridge, Kevin, 147, 148, 318
Uxbridge, Rishon, 147

V

Vagra II, 61, 204, 274
Valt Minor, 337
Vandor IV, 63, 204
Varley, Captain Donald, 103-105
Varon T disrupter, 401
Varria, 71
Vash, 171, 184, 185, 257, 258, 318
Velara III, 51
"Vengeance Factor, The," 106, 160-161, 203, 274, 318
Ventax II, 204, 237, 238, 274
Ventral access panel, 291
Vico, 309, 310
"Violations," 106, 203, 312-314, 316, 317
Visual acuity transmitter, 55, 56, 241
Voice transit conductor, 347
Vorgons, 107, 184
Vulcans, 53, 54, 107, 130-131, 193, 194, 299, 300, 410

W

Walking cane, 359
Weapons Room, 111
Wedding day jitters, 233
"We'll Always Have Paris," 63-65, 172, 204, 274, 318, 350
Well-Tempered Clavier (Bach), 154
Whalen, 32-34
"When the Bough Breaks," 49-50, 71, 203, 274

"Where No Man Has Gone Before," 27, 100
"Where No One Has Gone Before," 15-17, 219, 248
"Where Silence Has Lease," 19, 78-80, 83-84, 104, 163, 215, 318
Whitfield, Stephen, 158
"Who Watches the Watchers," 91, 107, 149-150, 181, 204, 218, 259, 274
Williams, Ensign, 174
Worm hole, 106, 157, 158, 242-244
Wormlike object, 362, 363
"Wounded, The," 107, 235-236, 286, 317

Y

Yar, Ishara, 221-223, 244
Yareena, 10-11, 22, 136, 318
"Yesterday's *Enterprise*," 70, 136, 175-176, 198, 213, 271, 272, 279, 280, 289, 331, 375
Yoshimitsu computers, 125
Y'Ridians, 396, 398, 405, 406
Yuta, 160, 161, 318

Z

Zakdorn, 107, 132, 300
Zalkon, 197, 204
Zalkonians, 107
Zendi Sabu star system, 24
Zipper, 158, 273, 286
Zoldans, 53, 107
Zorn, Groppler, 318